AN
INTRODUCTION
TO
LANGUAGE

AN INTRODUCTION TO LANGUAGE

SECOND EDITION

Victoria Fromkin
University of California, Los Angeles

Robert Rodman
North Carolina State University, Raleigh

Holt, Rinehart and Winston
New York   Chicago   San Francisco   Atlanta   Dallas
Montreal   Toronto   London   Sydney

To our spice
lack and Joanne

Library of Congress Cataloging in Publication Data

Fromkin, Victoria.
  An introduction to language.

  Includes bibliographies and index.
  1. Language and languages. 2. Linguistics.
I. Rodman, Robert, joint author. II. Title.
P106.F75 1978   410   77-16616

ISBN 0-03-089947-8 (College Edition)

ISBN 0-03-049211-4 (International Edition)
International Edition is not for sale in the
United States of America, its dependencies
or Canada.

   0 1 2   059   9 8 7 6

Preface

A revolution in linguistics occurred in 1957 with the appearance of Chomsky's theory of transformational-generative grammar. Since that time many textbooks have appeared which deal with language from this point of view. Yet when we searched for an appropriate text to be used in an introductory course for both linguistics and non-linguistics students we were unable to find one. No existing text was broad enough in scope or rich enough in content. The first edition of this book was designed to fill that need. It was directed toward students of many disciplines because the interest in human language is not limited to linguists. As such it proved to be very successful. But since the first edition a number of developments have occurred which have enriched our understanding of the nature of language. We have attempted to reflect these changes in this second edition.

The second edition differs from the first in both organization and content. Instead of being combined, morphology and semantics are treated in two separate chapters (6 and 7), each more extensively than in the first edition; morphophonemic rules are covered in the morphology chapter and speech act theory is included in the semantics chapter, along with many other revisions and additions. A chapter on child language acquisition (9) has been added, and some chapters have been reordered. The chapter on animal "languages" now occurs earlier (3); it includes the most recent studies on teaching language to primates. The biological and evolutionary aspects of language and the brain are now discussed in the expanded chapter on language origin (2). A section on acoustic phonetics has been added to the phonetics chapter (4). The chapters on phonology and syntax (5 and 8) have been revised with greater emphasis on the processes and kinds of rules one can expect to find in the world's languages. Sections on language in a sexist society and language and obscenity have been included in the chapter on language and society (10). The Comparative Method is now discussed in the chapter on historical linguistics (11), and the sign languages of the deaf, especially AMESLAN (American Sign Language), are now discussed in the chapter on languages of the world (12) to show the universality of human language. The table of world languages in that chapter has been expanded and updated. Exercises to all chapters have been extensively revised and expanded. The references, too, are revised and some are now annotated.

Like the first edition, this edition aims to dispel a number of myths about language by dealing with questions such as these: What is language? What do you know when you know a language? What is the origin of language? Where do words come from? Is language unique to humans? Or can chimpanzees and gorillas learn language? How do children learn languages? Why are there many languages and how are they related? How and why do languages change? Are some languages or dialects superior to others? Is there any hope for a universal language? Some of these questions have been discussed for thousands of years. We believe this book is unique in that it treats both historical and current views of these issues. In addition, it aims to provide detailed information about the main components of language—phonetics and phonology, morphology, semantics, and syntax. In every section the universals which underlie the diversity of phenomena observed in human language are discussed.

We believe that language is a unique human ability. We also believe that it is among the most complex of all human cognitive achievements. We have tried neither to avoid the complexities nor to oversimplify the concepts. Nonetheless, we have been primarily concerned with basic ideas rather than a detailed exposition of the grammar of English or of any other language. The text assumes no previous knowledge on the part of the reader. Technical terms are explained and new concepts exemplified. "Formalisms" are presented to enlighten, not to overwhelm, the student.

A good introductory text stimulates further investigation by the reader. Therefore, we have included a short list of references at the end of each chapter; some of these are annotated.

For the purpose of further elaboration of the points made in each chapter, exercises are provided. These exercises, which range in difficulty from "easy" to "thought-provoking," are conceived to enhance the student's interest in and comprehension of the textual material.

• • •

In the writing of the first edition we were very grateful to the members of the UCLA faculty who had written and rewritten some of the exercises for introductory classes. We still are, and we are still particularly grateful to Jacquelyn Schachter of the University of Southern California for sharing with us her insightful views on the nature of meaning, and to Stephanie Jamison for valuable counseling on presenting historical linguistics.

The revisions for this second edition could not have been made without the many suggestions of myriad faculty members and teaching assistants who used this book and were kind enough to write us detailed criticisms. Our own colleagues were especially helpful. Those who had some input into the changes that were made are far too numerous to name. Nevertheless, we wish to express our thanks particularly to the following, who read the manuscript and made constructive suggestions: Donald C. Freeman, University of Massachusetts; Robert J. Geist; Philip J. Greenfeld, San Diego State University; Ian F. Hancock, University of Texas, Austin; Judith N. Levi, Northwestern University; Derry L. Malsch, University of Oregon; David Michaels, University of Connecticut; Don L. F. Nilsen, Arizona State University; Marc Okrand, University of California, Santa Barbara; John Oller, University of New Mexico; C. Eugene Scruggs, University of South Florida; Ann D. Zwicky, Ohio State University; Arnold Zwicky, Ohio State University.

Above all, we are grateful to the thousands of students who have listened to our lectures, questioned our concepts, completed our assignments, and in these ways helped us to rewrite this book.

V.F.

R.R.

Contents

5 PHONOLOGY: THE SOUND PATTERNS OF LANGUAGE 101

6 THE WONDER OF WORDS 138

7 WHAT DOES IT MEAN? 163

8 THE SENTENCE PATTERNS OF LANGUAGE 195

CHAPTER

What Is Language?

When we study human language, we are approaching what
some might call the "human essence," the distinctive
qualities of mind that are, so far as we know, unique to
man.
NOAM CHOMSKY, *Language and Mind*

Whatever else people may do when they come together—
whether they play, fight, make love, or make automobiles—they talk. We
live in a world of words. We talk to our friends, our associates, our wives
and husbands, our mothers and mothers-in-law; we talk to total strangers
and to our adversaries. We talk face to face and over the telephone. And
everyone responds to us with more talk. Television and radio further swell
this torrent of words. As a result, hardly a moment of our waking lives is
free from words. We talk even when there is no one to answer. We talk
to our pets. We sometimes talk to ourselves. And we are the only animals
that do this—that talk.

The possession of language, more than any other attribute, distinguishes humans from other animals. To understand our humanity one must
understand the language that makes us human. According to the philosophy expressed in the myths and religions of many peoples, it is language
which is the source of human life and power. To some people of Africa,
a newborn child is a *kuntu*, a "thing," not yet a *muntu*, a "person." Only
by the act of learning language does the child become a human being.[1]
Thus according to this tradition, we all become "human" because we all
know at least one language. But what is it that we know? What does it
mean to "know" a language?

Linguistic Knowledge

When you know a language, you can speak and be understood by others who know that language. This means you are able to produce sounds which signify certain meanings and to understand or interpret

[1] Diabate, Massa-Makan, "Oral Tradition and Mali Literature," in *The Republic of Mali*
(Mali Information Center).

1

the sounds produced by others. We are referring here to normal-hearing individuals. Deaf persons produce and understand signs just as hearing persons produce and understand spoken language.

How is it possible for you to do this and is there anything more that you know when you have acquired knowledge of a language? Much of your knowledge is unconscious knowledge; you are not even aware of what you know when you know English, or French, or Japanese as a native speaker of these languages. We hope to convince you in this book that your knowledge is profound, and also hope to show you what this linguistic knowledge includes.

For one thing, if you know a language, you know, without being aware of it, which sounds are part of the language and which are not. This knowledge is often revealed by the way speakers of one language pronounce words from another language. If you speak only English, for example, you may (and usually do) substitute an English sound for a non-English sound when pronouncing "foreign" words. How many of you pronounce the name *Bach* with a final *k* sound? This is not the German pronunciation. The sound represented by the letters *ch* in German is not an English sound. If you pronounce it as the Germans do, you are using a sound outside of the English sound system. Have you noticed that French people speaking English often pronounce words like *this* and *that* as if they were spelled *zis* and *zat*? This is because the English sound which begins these words is not part of the French sound system, and the French mispronunciation reveals their unconscious knowledge of this fact.

Knowledge of a language also includes knowing which sounds may start a word, end a word, and follow each other. The name of the former president of Ghana was *Nkrumah*. Ghanaians pronounced this name with an initial sound identical to the sound ending the English word *sing* (for most Americans). But most English speakers, including radio announcers, would start the word with a short vowel before the *n* sound, or insert a short vowel after the *n*. We would predict that you would do this also, and would probably similarly pronounce the name *Ngaio Marsh*, the mystery story writer. The reason for this is that in English no word may begin with the *ng* sound. As children, when we learn English, we learn or discover this fact about our language, just as Ghanaians learn that words may begin with the *ng* sound.

Knowledge of the sounds and sound patterns in one's language constitutes just part of our linguistic knowledge. The most important aspect of knowing a language is knowing that certain sounds or sound sequences signify or represent different concepts or "meanings." Knowing a language is therefore knowing the system which relates sounds and meanings. When you don't know a language, the sounds spoken to you in this foreign tongue mean nothing to you. You can't even figure out by any logical or rational process what the speaker's message is. This is because the relationship between speech sounds and the meanings they represent is, for the most part, an **arbitrary** relationship. You have to learn (when you are acquiring the language) that the sounds represented by the letters *house* (in the written form of the language) signify the concept ⌂ ; if you know French, this same concept is represented by *maison*; if you know Twi, it is represented by ɔdaŋ; if you know Russian, by *dom*; if you know Spanish, by *casa*.

Similarly, the concept is represented by *hand* in English, *main* in French, *nsa* in Twi, and *ruka* in Russian.

The following are words with definite meanings in some different languages. How many of them can you understand?

a. kyinii	d. asubuhi	g. wartawan
b. doakam	e. toowq	h. inaminatu
c. odun	f. bolna	i. yawwa

If you don't know the languages from which these words are taken, you undoubtedly don't know that they mean the following:

a. a large parasol (in a Ghanaian language, Twi)
b. living creature (in an American Indian language, Papago)
c. bridge (in Turkish)
d. morning (in Swahili)
e. is seeing (in a California Indian language, Luiseño)
f. to speak (in a Pakistani language, Urdu); ache (in Russian)
g. reporter (in Indonesian)
h. teacher (in a Venezuelan Indian language, Warao)
i. right on! (in a Nigerian language, Hausa)

These different words show that the sounds of words are only given meaning by the language in which they occur. The idea that something is called X because it looks like X or called Y because it sounds like Y was satirized by Mark Twain in his book *Eve's Diary*:

> The minute I set eyes on an animal I know what it is. I don't have to reflect a moment; the right name comes out instantly. . . . I seem to know just by the shape of the creature and the way it acts what animal it is. When the dodo came along he [Adam] thought it was a wildcat. . . . But I saved him. . . . I just spoke up in a quite natural way . . . and said "Well, I do declare if there isn't the dodo!"

There is some "sound symbolism" in language. That is, there are words whose pronunciation suggests the meaning. A small group of words in the vocabulary of most languages is "onomatopoeic"—the sounds of the words "imitate" the sounds of "nature." Even here, the sounds differ from one language to another, reflecting the particular sound system of the language. In English we say *cockadoodledoo* and in Russian they say *kukuriku* to represent the rooster's crow.

One also finds particular sound sequences which seem to relate to a particular concept. In English many of the words beginning with *gl* have to do with sight, such as *glare, glint, gleam, glitter, glossy, glaze, glance, glimmer, glimpse,* and *glisten*. Many rhyming word pairs begin with *h: hoity-toity, harum-scarum, hotsy-totsy, higgledy-piggledy*. But these are a very small part of any language, and *gl* may have nothing to do with "sight" words in another language.

When you know English you know these *gl* words, the onomatopoeic words, and all the words in the basic vocabulary of the language. You know their sounds and you know their meanings. It's extremely unlikely, of course, that there are any speakers of English who know the 450,000 words listed in *Webster's Third New International Dictionary*. But even if they did, and that was all they knew, they would not know English.

Imagine trying to learn a foreign language by buying a dictionary and memorizing words. No matter how many words you learned, you would not be able to form the simplest phrases or sentences in the language or understand what was said by a native speaker. No one speaks in isolated words. (Of course you could search in your traveler's dictionary for individual words to find out how to say something like "car—gas—where?" After many tries, a native might understand this question and then point in the direction of a gas station. If she answered you in a sentence, however, it is highly probable that you would be unable to understand her or even look up what she said in your dictionary, since you would not know where one word ended and another began.)

Your knowledge of a language enables you to combine words to form phrases, and phrases to form sentences. Unfortunately, you can't buy a dictionary with all the sentences in any language, since no dictionary can list all the *possible* sentences. This is because knowing a language means being able to produce new sentences never spoken before and to understand sentences never heard before. The linguist Noam Chomsky refers to this ability as part of the "creative aspect" of language use. This doesn't mean that every speaker of a language can create great literature, but it does mean that you, and all persons who know a language, can and often do "create" new sentences every time you speak and are able to understand new sentences "created" by others. This is because language use is not limited to stimulus-response behavior. We are "free" from the constraints of either internal or external events or states. If someone steps on our toes we will "automatically" respond with a scream or gasp or grunt. These sounds are really not part of language; they are involuntary reactions to stimuli. After we automatically cry out, however, we can say "That was some clumsy act, you big oaf" or "Thank you very much for stepping on my toe because I was afraid I had elephantiasis and now that I can feel it hurt I know it isn't so," or any one of an infinite number of sentences, since the particular sentence we produce is not controlled by any stimulus. Of course knowing a language also means knowing what sentences are appropriate in various situations; saying "Hamburger costs 98 cents a pound" after someone has just stepped on your toe during a discussion on the weather in Britain would hardly be an appropriate response, but it would be possible.

Consider, for example, the following sentence:

> Daniel Boone decided to become a pioneer because he dreamed of pigeon-toed giraffes and cross-eyed elephants dancing in pink skirts and green berets on the wind-swept plains of the Midwest.

You might not believe the sentence; you might question its logic; you might even understand it to mean different things; but you can understand the sentence, although it is very doubtful that you have heard or read it before now.

It is obvious, then, that when you know a language you can recognize and understand and produce new sentences. All of them do not have to be as "wild" as the Daniel Boone sentence. In fact if you go through this book counting the number of sentences you have ever seen or heard before, we predict the number would be very small. Next time you write an essay or an exam or a letter see how many of your sentences are new. It can't be that all possible sentences are stored in your brain and that when you speak you pull out a sentence which seems to fit the situation, or that when you hear a sentence you match it with some sentence already stored. How can one have in his or her memory a totally novel sentence never heard before?

In fact, it can be shown that simple memorization of all the possible sentences in a language is impossible *in principle*. If for every sentence in the language one can form a longer sentence, then there is no limit on the length of any sentence and no limit on the number of sentences. We can illustrate this by a well-known example in English. When you know the language, you know you can say:

> This is the house.
>
> *or*
>
> This is the house that Jack built.
>
> *or*
>
> This is the malt that lay in the house that Jack built.
>
> *or*
>
> This is the dog that chased the cat that killed the rat that ate the malt that lay in the house that Jack built.

And one needn't stop there. How long, then, is the longest sentence? One can also say:

> The old man came.
>
> *or*
>
> The old, old, old, old, old man came.

How many "old's" are too many? Seven? Twenty-three?

We will not deny that the longer these sentences become, the less likely one would be to hear or to say them. A sentence with 276 occurrences of "old" would be highly unlikely in either speech or writing, even to describe Methuselah. But such a sentence is *theoretically* possible. That is, if you know English, you have the knowledge to add any number of adjectives as modifiers to a noun, as in:

> The beautiful, rich, snobbish, stubborn, blond, blue-eyed princess married the hunchbacked, gnarled, lame, dirty old man.

To memorize and store an infinite set of sentences would require an infinite storage capacity. But the brain is finite, and even if it were not we could not store totally novel sentences.

But when you learn a language you must learn something, and that something must be finite. The vocabulary is finite (however large it may be), and that can be stored. If sentences in a language were formed by putting one word after another in any order, then one's knowledge of a language could be described simply by a list of words. That this is not the case can be seen by examining the following strings of words:

(1) a. John kissed the little old lady who owned the shaggy dog.
    b. Who owned the shaggy dog John kissed the little old lady.
    c. John is difficult to love.
    d. It is difficult to love John.
    e. John is anxious to go.
    f. It is anxious to go John.
    g. John who was a student flunked his exams.
    h. Exams his flunked student a was who John.

If you were asked to put a star or asterisk before the sentences that seemed "funny" or "no good" to you, which ones would you "star"?[2] Our "intuitive" knowledge about what "is" or "is not" a sentence in English convinces us to "star" sentences *b, f,* and *h*. Which ones did you "star"?

Would you agree with our judgments about the following sentences?

(2) a. What he did was climb a tree.
    b. *What he thought was want a sports car.
    c. Drink your beer and go home!
    d. *What are you drinking and go home?
    e. I expect them to arrive a week from next Thursday.
    f. *I expect a week from next Thursday to arrive them.
    g. Linus lost his security blanket.
    h. *Lost Linus security blanket his.

If you "starred" the same sentences we did, then it is clear that not all strings of words constitute sentences in a language, and our knowledge of the language determines which do and which do not. Therefore, in addition to knowing the words of the language you must know some "rules" to form the sentences and to make the judgments that you made about the examples in (1) and (2). These rules must be finite in length and finite in number so they can be stored in our finite brains. Yet they must permit us to form and understand an infinite set of new sentences as was discussed above. How this is possible will be discussed in Chapter 8. It is one of the most interesting properties of human language.

We can say then that a language consists of all the sounds, words, and possible sentences. And when you know a language you know the sounds, the words, and the rules for their combination.

What You Know and What You Do: Linguistic Competence and Performance

"What's one and one and one and one and one and one and one and one and one and one?"

"I don't know," said Alice. "I lost count."

"She can't do Addition," the Red Queen interrupted.
LEWIS CARROLL, *Through the Looking-Glass*

We have mentioned some aspects of a speaker's linguistic knowledge. We said, for example, that our linguistic ability permits us to form longer and longer sentences, illustrating this by showing how we can

---

[2] It has become customary in presenting linguistic examples to use the asterisk before any of them which speakers reject for one reason or another. We shall use this notation throughout the book.

keep piling up adjectives as modifiers of a noun. We pointed out that this is theoretically, if not practically, possible. That is, whether one limits the number of adjectives to three, five, or eighteen in speaking, one cannot limit the number of adjectives which one *could* add if one wanted to. This demonstrates that there is a difference between having the necessary knowledge to produce such sentences and the way we use this knowledge when we are performing linguistically. It is a difference between what one *knows*, which linguists refer to as one's linguistic **competence,** and how one *uses* this knowledge in actual behavior, which is called linguistic **performance.**

You have the competence to understand or produce an infinitely long sentence. But when you attempt to use that knowledge—when you perform linguistically—there are physiological and psychological reasons why you cut off the number of adjectives, adverbs, clauses, and so on. You may run out of breath; your audience may leave; you may lose track of what has been said if the sentence is too long; and of course you don't live forever.

In discussing what you know—your linguistic competence—we are not talking about your conscious knowledge. We learn the rules of the language without anyone teaching them to us and without being aware that we are learning such rules. That this knowledge is learned is clear from the fact that you use it to speak, to understand, and to make judgments about sentences.

The fact that linguistic competence and performance are not identical and that "knowing" something is not the same as "doing" something is not unique to language knowledge and behavior. The quote from *Through the Looking-Glass* at the beginning of this section illustrates this difference. Alice could count up the "ones" if they were written down on paper. She knew the rules of addition. She had the competence, but her performance was impeded by the limitations of her short-term memory.

Lewis Carroll was intrigued with the difference between competence and performance in linguistic matters as well, as is shown by the following excerpt from *Alice's Adventures in Wonderland*:

> "I quite agree with you," said the Duchess, "and the moral of that is—'Be what you seem to be'—or, if you'd like it put more simply—'Never imagine yourself not to be otherwise than what it might appear to others that what you were or might have been was not otherwise than what you had been would have appeared to them to be otherwise.' "
>
> "I think I should understand that better," Alice said very politely, "if I had it written down: but I'm afraid I can't quite follow it as you say it."
>
> "That's nothing to what I could say if I chose," the Duchess replied, in a pleased tone.

The Duchess and Alice were both correct. The Duchess had the knowledge to go on indefinitely, and Alice would have understood the sentence better, if not entirely, had it been written down.

To see why this is so, try the following. Combine sentence *a* with sentence *b* to form one sentence.

   a. The girl milked the cow.
   b. The cow was brown.

You might have come up with sentence *c, d,* or *e*.[3]

    c. The girl milked the cow and the cow was brown.
    d. The girl milked the cow that was brown.
    e. The cow the girl milked was brown.

Now add sentence *f*.

    f. The boy kissed the girl.

If you used the same "combining rule" as was used to form sentence *c*, you would get:

    g. The boy kissed the girl and the girl milked the cow and the cow was brown.

If you used the rule which formed sentence *d,* you would get:

    h. The boy kissed the girl who milked the cow that was brown.

And if you followed the pattern of sentence *e,* you would get:

    i. The cow the girl the boy kissed milked was brown.

Even when "written down," sentence *i* is not an easy one to understand. But knowing the rule—and you must know it if you could understand sentence *e*—you could work out the meaning and even produce such a "crazy" sentence. You have the competence to do so. Sometimes when we use this competence in forming and understanding sentences we get "performance-blocked."

Another example of the difference between competence and performance is illustrated in a quote from the nineteenth-century *Mathematical Gazette* (Vol. 12) attributed to a certain Mrs. La Touche:

> I do hate sums. There is no greater mistake than to call arithmetic an exact science. There are permutations and aberrations discernible to minds entirely noble like mine; subtle variations which it requires a mind like mine to perceive. For instance, if you add a sum from the bottom up, and then again from the top down, the result is always different.

In using our knowledge of the rules of arithmetic we can make mistakes, as did Mrs. La Touche.

In using our knowledge of language in speaking we also make mistakes —slips of the tongue, false starts, and so on. But this doesn't mean that we can't recognize errors—we have the knowledge to do so.

The word "spoonerism" was invented to describe a common type of error made famous by an eminent don of Oxford University. When the Reverend Spooner said "You have hissed my mystery lecture—you have tasted the whole worm" instead of "You have missed my history lecture— you have wasted the whole term," or when he mistakenly called a prominent member of the royal family "queer old dean" instead of "dear old queen," he was making performance errors. He knew what he wanted to say, but his tongue "slipped."

---

[3] There are, of course, other ways to combine these sentences; for example, *The girl milked the brown cow.* The particular "conjoining rules" illustrated are used to make a specific point.

Someone may say, "Well, like, man, I mean—uh—like, you know the —uh—girl like—er—is—you know—going," but that same person would probably not accept that as an "unstarred" sentence of English. His linguistic competence, his knowledge of the language, tells him it isn't proper. His performance could have been the result of a number of factors, mostly nonlinguistic in nature.

If someone is riding a bicycle and falls off, that does not mean she doesn't know how to ride the bicycle. Or if she gets tired in fifteen minutes and stops to rest, it doesn't mean she hasn't the knowledge to ride the bicycle continually for a month, or a year, or forever, if she lived that long. She might not be able to tell you the physical laws she is obeying to maintain her balance, but she knows how to ride the bike. Similarly, you may not be able to state the linguistic "laws" (rules) which account for your knowledge, but these rules make it possible for you to produce and understand an unlimited number of unfamiliar utterances.

A large part of this book will be concerned with discussing just these kinds of rules that you know without knowing that you do. We will be discussing the nature of such rules—the nature of linguistic competence.

What Is a Grammar?

I don't want to talk grammar. I want to talk like a lady.
G. B. SHAW, *Pygmalion*

When you learn a language you learn the sounds used in that language, the basic units of meaning, such as words, and the rules to combine these to form new sentences. The elements and rules constitute the **grammar** of a language. The grammar, then, is what we *know*; it represents our linguistic competence. To understand the nature of language we must understand the nature of this internalized, unconscious set of rules which is part of every grammar of every language.

Every human being who speaks a language knows the grammar. When linguists wish to describe a language they attempt to describe the grammar of the language which exists in the minds of its speakers. There may of course be some differences between the knowledge that one speaker has and that of another. But there must be shared knowledge because it is this grammar which makes it possible for speakers to talk to and understand one another. To the extent that the linguist's description is a true model of the speakers' linguistic competence, it will be a good or bad description of the grammar of the language, and of the language itself. Such a model is called **descriptive grammar.** It doesn't tell you how you *should* speak; it describes your basic linguistic knowledge; it explains how it is possible for you to speak and understand, and it explains what it is you know about the sounds, words, phrases, and sentences of your language.

We have used the word *grammar* in two ways: the first in reference to the grammar speakers have in their brains; the second as the model or description of this internalized grammar. Almost two thousand years ago the Greek grammarian Dionysius Thrax defined grammar as that which permits one to either speak a language or speak about a language. From now on we will not differentiate these two meanings, since the linguist's descriptive grammar is an attempt at a formal statement (or theory) of the speakers' grammar. That is, when we say in later chapters that there is a rule in the grammar such as: "every sentence has a noun phrase subject and a verb phrase predicate," this is posited as a rule in both the "mental" grammar and the model of it—the linguist's grammar. And when we say that a sentence is *grammatical* we mean that it is formed in keeping with the rules of both grammars; conversely, an *ungrammatical* (starred) sentence deviates in some way from these rules. If, however, we posit a rule for English which does not agree with your intuitions as a speaker, then there is something wrong with our grammar, or the grammar we are describing is in some way different from the grammar which represents your linguistic competence; that is, your language is not the one we are describing. If, however, there is a mistake, it must be in our descriptive grammar. Although the rules of your grammar may differ from the rules of someone else's grammar, there can't possibly be a mistake in your grammar. This is because according to linguists no language or variety of a language (called a dialect) is superior to any other in a *linguistic* sense. Every grammar is equally complex and logical and capable of producing an infinite set of sentences to express any thought one might wish to express. If something can be expressed in one language or one dialect, it can be expressed in any other language or dialect. You might use different means and different words, but it can be expressed. Since grammars are what determine the nature of the languages, no grammar is to be preferred except perhaps for nonlinguistic reasons.

This has not always been the view even of grammarians, or perhaps more correctly, particularly of grammarians. From ancient times until the present there have been "purists" who have believed that language change is corruption and that there are certain correct forms which all "educated" people should use in speaking and writing. The Greek Alexandrians in the first century, the Arabic scholars at Basra in the eighth century, and numerous English grammarians of the eighteenth and nineteenth centuries held this view. They wished to *prescribe* the rules of grammar rather than describe the rules. *Prescriptive grammars* were therefore written.

With the rise of capitalism and the emergence of a new middle class, there was a desire on the part of this new social group to have their children educated and to have them learn to speak the dialect of the "upper" classes. This led to the publication of many prescriptive grammars. In 1762 a very influential grammar, *A Short Introduction to English Grammar with Critical Notes,* was written by Bishop Robert Lowth. Lowth, influenced by Latin grammar and by personal preference, prescribed a number of new rules for English. Before the publication of his grammar, practically everyone—upper-, middle-, and lower-class speakers of English—said *I don't have none.*; *You was wrong about that.*; and *Mathilda is fatter than me.* Lowth, however, decided that "two negatives make a positive" and therefore one should say *I don't have any,* that even if *you* is singular it should be followed by the plural *were,* and that *I* not *me, he* not *him, they* not *them,* and so forth should follow *than* in comparative constructions. Because Lowth was very influential and because the rising new class wanted to speak "properly," many of these new "rules" were legislated into English grammar, at least for the "prestige" dialect. Note that grammars such as Lowth wrote are very different from the descriptive grammars we have been discussing. They are less interested in describing the rules people know than in telling them what rules they should know.

When we talk of the grammar of a language we are also differentiating the notion of grammar from **teaching grammars,** which are used to help speakers learn a second or foreign language, or even a second dialect. In some countries where it is economically or socially advantageous to speak a "prestige" dialect, people may wish to learn a dialect other than their own. Teaching grammars state explicitly the rules of the language, list the words and their pronunciations, and thus are aids in learning a new language or dialect.

In this book we shall not be primarily interested in either prescriptive or teaching grammars. We shall, however, discuss the question further in Chapter 10 when we discuss standard and nonstandard dialects.

The way we are using the word *grammar* differs in another way from its most common meaning. In our sense, the grammar includes everything speakers know about their language—the sound system, called **phonology,** the system of meanings, called **semantics,** and the rules of sentence formation, called **syntax.** Many people think of the grammar of a language as referring solely to the syntactic rules. This latter sense is what students usually mean when they talk about their class in "English grammar."

Our aim is more in keeping with that stated in 1784 by the grammarian John Fell in "Essay Towards an English Grammar": "It is certainly the business of a grammarian to find out, and not to make, the laws of a language." This is just what the linguist attempts to do—to find out the laws of a language, and the laws which pertain to *all* languages. Those laws which pertain to all human languages, representing the universal properties of language, constitute what may be called a **universal grammar.** We shall be discussing many of these "laws" in the chapters that follow. Some of these linguistic universals will be concerned with the sound systems of language. Every grammar, for example, includes discrete sound segments, like *p, n,* or *a,* which can all be defined by a finite set of "sound properties." Other phonological universals reveal that every language has both "vowels" and "consonants" and rules which determine the pronunciation of sentences.

There are also semantic universals which pertain to common semantic properties such as "male," "female," "animate," "human," and "concrete," which are found in all languages.

Finally, there are universals of syntax which reveal the ways in which sentences are formed. There is no language, for example, which cannot combine sentences in some way similar to the ways found in English. Every language has a way of forming sentences such as the following:

Linguistics is an interesting subject.
I know that linguistics is an interesting subject.
You know that I know that linguistics is an interesting subject.
Guinevere knows that you know that I know that linguistics is an interesting subject.
Is it a fact that Guinevere knows that you know that I know that linguistics is an interesting subject?

The linguist is also interested in seeing how these universal properties are expressed in particular languages like English, Zulu, Twi, Cherokee, Aztec, Eskimo, Russian, Arabic, and all the other languages in the world. That is, linguists are interested in writing descriptive grammars of languages.

The grammar of each language will include everything speakers know about their language to the extent that linguistic theory is capable of permitting the writing of adequate grammars. Since all speakers know how to produce sounds and pronounce sentences, one part of the grammar must describe the **phonology.** We will discuss these questions in Chapters 4 and 5.

Since knowing a language means knowing the words of the language and how to form new words, which is called **morphology,** the grammar must include a lexicon and morphological rules. This part of the grammar will be discussed in Chapter 6.

We have already noted that knowing a language means knowing how to relate sounds and meanings, how to produce sounds to represent our thoughts, and how to understand and comprehend the sounds others produce. Each grammar must then include **semantic** knowledge. This will be discussed in Chapter 7.

In addition, every grammar includes a **syntactic** part which determines how sentences are formed. The syntactic rules also explain how speakers know which sentences are grammatical and which are not, why some sentences have more than one meaning, and how sentences are related. The syntactic rules also permit speakers to produce and understand an infinite set of sentences. The syntactic parts of grammars will be discussed in Chapter 8.

Other topics, such as the language of animals, how languages change, languages of the world, dialects, writing systems, how children learn language, how language originated, and other more general questions will be discussed in the other chapters of the book.

SUMMARY

We are all intimately familiar with at least one language. Yet few of us ever stop to consider what we know when we know a language. There is no book which contains the English or Russian or Zulu language. One can list the words of a language in a dictionary, but not all the possible sentences, and a language consists of these sentences as well as words. Though we can't list all sentences, we can list the rules which a speaker uses to produce and understand an infinite set of "possible" sentences.

These rules comprise the **syntax** of a language. You learn these rules when you learn the language and you also learn the sound system of the language (the **phonology**) and the ways in which sounds and meanings are related (the **semantics**). The sounds and meanings of words are related in an **arbitrary** fashion. That is, if you had never heard the word *syntax* you would not, by its very sounds, know what it meant. Language, then, is a system which relates sounds with meanings, and when you know a language you know this system.

This knowledge (your linguistic **competence**) is different from your behavior (your linguistic **performance**). Even if you woke up one morning and decided to stop talking (as the Trappist monks did after they took a "vow of silence"), you would still have knowledge of your language. This ability or competence underlies linguistic behavior. If you didn't know the language, you couldn't speak, but if you know the language, you may choose not to speak.

The **grammar** of a language represents speakers' linguistic competence. It includes the basic sounds, words, and rules for the formation, pronunciation, and interpretation of sentences. Linguistic knowledge represented in the grammar is not conscious knowledge. An explicit description of competence is called a **descriptive grammar.** Such a grammar is a model of the "mental" grammar known by every speaker of the language. It doesn't teach the rules of the language; it describes the rules which are already known.

A grammar which attempts to legislate what your grammar should be is called a **prescriptive grammar.** It prescribes; it doesn't describe, except incidentally. Teaching grammars are also written to help people learn a foreign language or a dialect of their language which differs from their own.

Linguists are scientists who study the general properties of grammars—the universal properties found in all languages—and the specific properties of the grammars of individual languages. In this study they hope to provide a better understanding of the nature of human language, and to contribute to our understanding of the human mind.

EXERCISES

1. Part of your knowledge of English includes knowing what sound sequences occur in the language. When new products are put on the market the manufacturers have to think up new names for them, and these names must conform to the allowable sound patterns. Suppose you were hired by a manufacturer of soap products and your job was to name five new products. What names might you come up with? List them.

   We are not interested in the *spelling* of the words but in how they are pronounced. Therefore, describe in any way you can how the words which you list should be pronounced. Suppose for example you named one soap powder *Blick*. You can describe the sounds in any of the following ways:

   a. *bl* as in "blood," *i* as in "pit," *ck* as in "stick"
   b. *bli* as in "bliss," *ck* as in "tick"
   c. *b* as in "boy," *lick* as in "lick"
   and so on.

2. Anyone who knows a language knows what strings of words are grammatical sentences in the language and what strings are "starred," or ungrammatical. Construct five ungrammatical sentences. State, if you can, why you think they are ungrammatical.

3. Below are listed eight English words which are considered to relate sounds and meanings in a less arbitrary fashion than one finds in most words. State why

you might be able to figure out what each word means even if you did not know the word previously.

a. ding-dong	e. plop
b. tick-tock	f. cough
c. bang	g. bow-wow
d. zing	h. swish

4. We said that the sounds and meanings of most words are arbitrarily related. This is not necessarily true in all systems of communication in which the "signs" unambiguously reveal the "meaning."

   A. Describe (or draw) five different signs which directly show what they mean. Example: a road sign indicating an S curve.

   B. Describe any other communication system which, like language, consists of arbitrary form-meaning symbols. Example: traffic signals where *red* means *stop* and *green* means *go*.

5. State some "rule of grammar" which you have been taught in school but which you do not generally use in producing sentences. For example, you may have been taught that *It's me* is incorrect and that the correct form is *It's I*. But you always use *me* in such sentences. How does this show the difference between descriptive and prescriptive grammars?

6. Suppose you heard someone say *He made a tip of the slung* instead of *He made a slip of the tongue*. How would this reveal a difference between linguistic **competence** and **performance?** Would you expect anyone to err by saying *lpsi of the ngto?* If not, why not?

7. What does the following cartoon reveal about what speakers know about their language?

THE WIZARD OF ID   by Brant parker and Johnny hart

By permission of Johnny Hart and Field Enterprises, Inc.

8. Consider these two statements:

   a. I learned a new word today.
   b. I learned a new sentence today.

   One of these sentences may sound "odd" or "unusual" to you. Which one, and why?

References

Chomsky, Noam. *Language and Mind,* enlarged ed. New York: Harcourt Brace Jovanovich, 1972.

Chomsky, Noam. Review of B. F. Skinner's "Verbal Behavior" in J. A. Fodor and J. J. Katz, eds., *The Structure of Language.* Englewood Cliffs, N.J.: Prentice-Hall, 1964.

Langacker, Ronald. *Language and Its Structure,* 2nd ed. New York: Harcourt Brace Jovanovich, 1973.

Lyons, John. *Noam Chomsky.* New York: Viking, 1970.

Thomas, Owen, and Eugene Kintgen. *Transformational Grammar and the Teacher of English,* 2nd ed. New York: Holt, Rinehart and Winston, 1974.

CHAPTER

In the Beginning: Language Origin

God created the world by a Word, instantaneously, without toil and pains.
THE TALMUD

Nothing, no doubt, would be more interesting than to know from historical documents the exact process by which the first man began to lisp his first words, and thus to be rid for ever of all the theories on the origin of speech.
M. MÜLLER, 1871

The question of how language originated is a fascinating one. All religions and mythologies contain stories of language origin. Philosophers through the ages have argued the question. Scholarly works have been written on the subject. Prizes have been awarded for the "best answer" to this eternally perplexing problem. Theories of divine origin, evolutionary development, and language as a human invention have all been suggested.

Such widespread speculation is not surprising. Language is a unique human characteristic. Man's* curiosity about himself led to his curiosity about language. Many of the early theories on the origin of language resulted from man's interest in his own origins and his own nature. Since man and language are so closely related, it was believed that if one knew how,

---

* In English and in many (most?) other languages, the masculine forms of nouns and pronouns are used as the general, or generic, term. We would have liked to avoid this but found ourselves constrained by common usage. Had we said "Woman's curiosity about herself led to her curiosity about language," this would have been interpreted as referring only to women. Using the word "man" in this sentence, and other sentences throughout the book, we are sure that the interpretation will be "man and woman." Wherever "man" or "mankind" or a similar generic term is used, the reader is asked to consider these general terms embracing the whole of humanity, unless of course the meaning can specifically be related to the male members of the species.

16

when, and where language arose, perhaps one would know how, when, and where man arose.

The difficulties inherent in answering these questions about language are immense. Anthropologists think that man has existed for at least one million years, and perhaps for as long as five or six million years. But the earliest deciphered written records are barely six thousand years old, dating from the writings of the Sumerians of 4000 B.C. These records appear so late in the history of the development of language that they provide no clue at all to the origin of language.

One might conclude that the quest for this knowledge is doomed to failure. The only hard evidence we have about ancient languages is written, but speech precedes writing historically by an enormous period of time, and even today there are thousands of speech communities speaking perfectly "up-to-date" languages which lack writing systems. The language or languages used by our earliest ancestors are irretrievably lost.

For these reasons, scholars in the latter part of the nineteenth century, who were only interested in "hard science," ridiculed, ignored, and even banned discussions of language origin. In 1886, the Linguistic Society of Paris passed a resolution "outlawing" any papers concerned with this subject.[1]

This ban was reconfirmed in 1911 and was further supported by the president of the Philological Society of London, Alexander Ellis, who concluded in his address to the Society that:

> . . . We shall do more by tracing the historical growth of one single work-a-day tongue, than by filling wastepaper baskets with reams of paper covered with speculations on the origin of all tongues.

That such resolutions did not put an end to the interest is clear from the fact that just a few years ago the linguist John P. Hughes felt compelled to write:

> . . . a word or two should be said in any serious linguistic work to counter the arrant nonsense on this subject which is still circulated in Sunday supplement science features. According to this pseudo-evolutionary foolishness, based on nothing but rampant imagination, language originated among our caveman ancestors when someone tried to tell the hitherto speechless tribe about the wolf he had killed, and was forced to give an imitation of the wolf . . . or when he hit his thumb with the mallet while sharpening a stone spear, so that *ouch* became the word for "pain" . . . and similar fairy stories.[2]

This view sharply diverges from that put forth two hundred years earlier by Lord Monboddo, the Scottish anthropologist:

> The origin of an art so admirable and so useful as language . . . must be allowed to be a subject, not only of great curiosity, but likewise very important and interesting, if we consider, that it is necessarily connected

---

[1] *La Société n'admet aucune communication concernant . . . l'origine du langage . . ."* ("The Society does not accept any paper concerning the origin of language . . .") La Société de Linguistique, Section 2, Statuts (1886).

[2] John P. Hughes, *The Science of Language* (New York: Random House, 1969).

with an inquiry into the original nature of man, and that primitive state in which he was, before language was invented. . . .[3]

It is not just in Sunday supplements that one finds "pseudo-evolutionary foolishness." Some of the greatest linguists and philosophers continue to be interested in this question, and speculative theories on language origin have provided valuable insights into the nature and development of language. For these reasons, the learned scholar Otto Jespersen stated that "linguistic science cannot refrain forever from asking about the whence (and about the whither) of linguistic evolution."

In this chapter, some of the ideas about the origin of language will be examined, both because they may shed light on the nature of language and because there is continuing interest in the subject.

God's Gift to Mankind?

And out of the ground the Lord God formed every beast of the field, and every fowl of the air; and brought them unto Adam to see what he would call them: and whatsoever Adam called every living creature, that was the name thereof.
GENESIS 2:19

According to Judeo-Christian beliefs, God gave Adam the power to name all things. Similar beliefs are found throughout the world. According to the Egyptians, the creator of speech was the god Thoth. According to the Babylonians, the language giver was the god Nabû. According to the Hindus, we owe our unique language ability to a female god; Brahma was the creator of the universe, but language was given to man by his wife, Sarasvati.

The belief in the divine origin of language has continued through the ages. Cotton Mather wrote his M.A. thesis at Harvard on the question, providing a detailed defense in support of this theory. Almost three hundred years later, Lester Grabbe, pointing to the existence in far-removed cultures of stories similar to the Tower of Babel, concluded:

> . . . no acceptable theory has yet been propounded which can satisfactorily answer why man even has the faculty of speech—or language—if there is no Creator. On the other hand, the Genesis account is in complete agreement with all established scientific fact.[4]

Belief in the divine origin of language is closely intertwined with the magical properties man has associated with language and the spoken word. Children in all cultures utter "magic" words like *abracadabra* to ward off evil or bring good luck. Despite the childish jingle "Sticks and stones may break my bones, but names will never hurt me," name-calling is insulting, cause for legal punishment, and feared. In some cultures, when certain words are used, one is required to counter them by "knocking on wood." Language is used to bring down the curses of the gods. Prayers are offered,

[3] James Burnett, Lord Monboddo, *Of the Origin and Progress of Language* (1774).
[4] Lester Grabbe, "Origin of Languages," *The Plain Truth* (Aug.–Sept. 1970).

and thus man converses with his gods in language. According to the Bible, only the true God would respond when called upon; the false idols did not know the "word of God." The anthropologist Bronislaw Malinowski has pointed out that in many cultures words are used to control events and become sources of power when chanted over and over: "The repetitive statement of certain words is believed to produce the reality stated."

One finds taboo words all over the world. In western societies one is adjured not to "take the Lord's name in vain." In folk tales, forbidden names, such as *Rumpelstiltzkin,* can break spells if discovered. Personal names also carry special properties—a Jewish child is not to be named after a living person, and in some cultures it is forbidden to utter the name of someone who has died. In ancient Egypt every person was given two names, one of which was secret. If the secret name was discovered, the discoverer had power over the person. In Athens, in the fifth century B.C., a ventriloquist named Euricles pretended he had a demon in him; special powers were attributed to the ventriloquist's voice. In *The Wasps,* Aristophanes mentions the "sly prophet Euricles" who "hidden in other people's bellies produces much amusement."

The linguist David Crystal reports that someone is attempting to test the idea that the world will end when the billion names of God have been uttered by attaching a prayer wheel to an electronic speech synthesizer.[5]

The belief in the divine origin of language and its magical properties is also manifested by the fact that in many religions only special languages may be used in prayers and rituals. The Hindu priests of the fifth century B.C. believed that the original pronunciations of Vedic Sanskrit had to be used. This led to important linguistic study, since their language had already changed greatly since the hymns of the Vedas had been written. Until recently, only Latin could be used in the Catholic Mass. Among Moslems, the Koran was not to be translated and could be read only in Arabic; and Hebrew continues to be the one language used in the prayers of orthodox Jews throughout the world.

These myths and customs and superstitions do not tell us very much about language. They do tell us about the importance of language to men and the miraculous properties they attach to it. In addition, discussions of the divine origin of language, while not likely to settle the question to the satisfaction of anyone seeking "scientific proof," can provide insights into the nature of human language.

In 1756, a Prussian statistician-clergyman, Johann Peter Suessmilch, delivered a paper before the Prussian Academy in which he reasoned that man could not have invented language without thought, and that thought depends on the prior existence of language. The only escape from the paradox is to presume that God must have given language to man. Suessmilch, unlike other philosophers such as Rousseau (whose ideas will be discussed below), did not view primitive languages as "less developed" or "imperfect." He suggested just the opposite—that all languages are "perfect" and thus the reflection of God's perfection. He cites examples from the European languages, from Semitic languages, and from languages of "primitive" people to prove the perfection of all human language. To oppose the

[5] David Crystal, *Linguistics* (Middlesex, England: Penguin, 1971).

idea that there are primitive languages, he noted that the great and abstract ideas of Christianity can be discussed even by the "wretched Green-landers."

Suessmilch made other sophisticated observations. He pointed out that any child is able to learn perfectly the language of the Hottentots although adults cannot, revealing his awareness of the difference between acquisition of first and second languages. This observation anticipated the current "critical age hypothesis," which states that beyond a certain age a human being is incapable of acquiring a first language. He also pointed out, as did many philosophers of antiquity, that all languages have grammars which are highly regular, for otherwise children would be unable to learn them.

The arguments presented by Suessmilch were based on observations concerning the "universality" of linguistic properties, the relation between psychological and linguistic constraints, and the interdependence of reason and language. He presented powerful arguments, but ones which had less to do with language origin than with language itself.

At the present time there is no way to "prove" or "disprove" the divine-origin theory, just as one cannot argue scientifically for or against the existence of God.

The First Language

Imagine the Lord talking French! Aside from a few odd words in Hebrew, I took it completely for granted that God had never spoken anything but the most dignified English.
CLARENCE DAY, *Life with Father*

Among the proponents of the divine-origin theory a great interest arose in the language used by God, Adam, and Eve. Men have not always been pessimistic about discovering an answer to this question. For millennia, "scientific" experiments have reportedly been devised to verify particular theories of language origin. In the fifth century B.C. the Greek historian Herodotus reported that the Egyptian Pharaoh Psammetichus (664–610 B.C.) sought to determine the most primitive "natural" language by experimental methods. The monarch was said to have placed two infants in an isolated mountain hut, to be cared for by a servant who was cautioned not to utter a single word in their presence on pain of death. The Pharaoh believed that without any linguistic input the children would develop their own language and would thus reveal the original tongue of man. Patiently the Egyptian waited for the children to become old enough to talk. According to the story, the first word uttered was *bekos*. Scholars were consulted, and it was discovered that *bekos* was the word for "bread" in Phrygian, the language spoken in the province of Phrygia (the northwest corner of modern Turkey). This ancient language, which has long since died out, was thought, on the basis of this "experiment," to be the original language.

Whether James IV of Scotland (1473–1513) had read the works of Herodotus is not known. According to reports he attempted a replication of

Psammetichus's experiment, but his attempt yielded different results. The Scottish children matured and "spak very guid Ebrew," providing "scientific evidence" that Hebrew was the language used in the Garden of Eden.

Two hundred years before James's "experiment," the Holy Roman Emperor Frederick II of Hohenstaufen was said to have carried out a similar test, but without any results; the children died before they uttered a single word.

In the seventeenth century, a Swedish scholar, Andreas Kemke, is said to have refuted both views, asserting that God spoke Swedish, Adam Danish, and the serpent French. This view tells us more about the ideology of the scholar than it does about the origin of language. Since he mentions nothing at all about Eve, we are free to assume that she spoke either Phrygian or Hebrew, a most important conclusion since Eve's language would be our "mother tongue."

The legend of Psammetichus shows that the Pharaoh was willing to accept "evidence" even if it was contrary to national interests. It is clear that Kemke's nationalism influenced his views. A German scholar, J. G. Becanus (1518–1572), surpassed Kemke in his chauvinistic zeal. He argued that German must have been the primeval language, since the language given by God must have been a perfect language, and since, according to him, German was the most superior language in the world, it had to be the language used by God and by Adam. Becanus carried his arguments farther: German persisted as the perfect language because the early Cimbrians (who were Germans) did not contribute to the building of the Tower of Babel. Later, according to this theory, God caused the Old Testament to be translated from German into Hebrew.

Other proposals were put forth. In 1830 the lexicographer Noah Webster asserted that the "proto-language" must have been Chaldee (Aramaic), the language spoken in Jerusalem during the time of Jesus. In 1887, Joseph Elkins maintained in *The Evolution of the Chinese Language* that "there is no other language which can be more reasonably assumed to be the speech first used in the world's gray morning than can Chinese. . . . Hence, Chinese is regarded . . . as the . . . primeval language."

The belief that all languages originated from a single source is found in Genesis: ". . . the whole earth was of one language, and of one speech." The Tower of Babel story attempts to account for the diversity of languages. In this, and in similar accounts, the "confusion" of languages *preceded* the dispersement of peoples. (According to some Biblical scholars, *Babel* derives from the Hebrew *bilbel,* meaning "confusion"; others say it derives from the name Babylon.) Genesis continues: "Therefore is the name of it called Babel; because the Lord did there confound the language of all the earth: and from thence did the Lord scatter them abroad upon the face of all the earth."

A legend of the Toltecs, given by the native Mexican historian Ixtlilxochitl, also explains the diversity of languages by a similar account: ". . . after men had multiplied, their languages were confused, and not being able to understand each other, they went to different parts of the earth."

A study of the history of languages does indeed show that many languages develop from a single one, as will be discussed in later chapters.

But in these attested cases the "confusion" comes *after* the separation of peoples. Any view which maintains a single origin of language must provide some explanation for the number of language *families* which exist. The Bible explains this as an act of God, who at Babel created from one language many, all of which would eventually become individual multilanguage families. The monogenetic theory of languages—the single-origin theory—is related to a belief in the monogenetic origin of man. Many scientists today believe, instead, that man arose in many different places on earth. If this is the case, there were many proto-languages, out of which the modern language families developed.

It is clear that we are no farther along today in discovering the original language (or languages) than was Psammetichus when he attempted to use "experimental methods" to answer this question. Any such experiment is bound to fail. For obvious reasons, linguists would not attempt to duplicate such tests—while we may applaud the Pharaoh's motivation we must condemn his lack of humanity. But the misfortunes of life can be as cruel as a Pharaoh. There have been a number of cases of children reared in environments of extreme social isolation. Such reported cases go back at least to the eighteenth century. In 1758, Carl Linnaeus first included *Homo ferus* (wild or feral man) as a subdivision of *Homo sapiens*. According to Linnaeus, a defining characteristic of *Homo ferus* was his lack of speech or observable language of any kind. All the cases in the literature support his view.

The most dramatic cases of children raised in isolation are those described as "wild" or "feral" children, who have reportedly been reared with wild animals or have lived alone in the wilderness. In 1920 two feral children, Amala and Kamala, were found in India, supposedly having been reared with wolves. The most celebrated case, documented in François Truffaut's film *The Wild Child,* is that of Victor, "the wild boy of Aveyron," who was found in 1798. It was ascertained that he had been left in the woods when a very young child and had somehow survived. He was in his early teens when he was discovered. In addition, there are cases of children whose isolation resulted from deliberate efforts to keep them from normal social intercourse. As recently as 1970 a child, called Genie in the scientific reports, was discovered who had been confined to a small room under conditions of physical restraint, and who had received only minimal human contact from the age of eighteen months until almost fourteen years. None of these children, regardless of the cause of isolation, was able to speak or knew any language. Genie is, however, now learning to speak and understand.

Our unique genetic ability to acquire language is revealed only when we receive adequate linguistic stimulus. It is true that no one teaches us language, in the sense that we are taught arithmetic or a second language. We learn the language which is used in our environment when we are children. Without exposure to language, children do not speak at all—not even Phrygian, or "very guid Ebrew."

Despite the failure of the isolation method and the inability to prove or even test the various theories of language origin, the speculation continues.

Human Invention or the Cries of Nature?

Language was born in the courting days of mankind; the first utterances of speech I fancy to myself like something between the nightly love lyrics of puss upon the tiles and the melodious love songs of the nightingale.
OTTO JESPERSEN, *Language, Its Nature, Development and Origin*

The Greeks speculated about everything in the universe. It is therefore not surprising that the earliest surviving linguistic treatise which deals with the origin and nature of language should be Plato's *Cratylus* dialogue. A commonly held view among the classical Greeks was that at some ancient time there was a "legislator" who gave the correct, natural name to everything. Plato, in this dialogue, has Socrates express this idea:

> . . . not every man is able to give a name, but only a maker of names; and this is the legislator, who of all skilled artisans in the world is the rarest . . . only he who looks to the name which each thing by nature has, and is, will be able to express the ideal forms of things in letters [sounds] and syllables.

It was not one of their many gods who named all things, but this wise "legislator." The question of language origin was closely tied to the debate among the Greeks as to whether there is a truth or correctness in "names" regardless of the language, as opposed to the view that words or names for things result merely from an agreement—a convention—between speakers. This debate between the **naturalists** and the **conventionalists** was one of the first major linguistic arguments. In the *Cratylus* dialogue, Socrates analyzes and develops etymologies for the names of Homeric heroes, the Greek gods, mythological figures, the stars, the elements, and even abstract qualities—the proper and common nouns of language. In his attempt to justify the "trueness" or "naturalness" of these names, it is clear that he, at least in part, recognizes the humor in such an approach, for he says that "the heads of the givers of names were going round and round and therefore they imagined the world was going round and round."

In fact, it is clear from a reading of this delightful dialogue that Plato recognized the "arbitrariness" of certain words, and believed that both natural and conventional elements exist in language.

The naturalists argued that there is a natural connection between the forms of language and the essence of things. They pointed to onomatopoeic words—words which are imitative of the sounds they represent—and suggested that these form the basis of language, or at least the core of the basic vocabulary.

The idea that the earliest form of language was imitative, or "echoic," was reiterated by many scholars up to recent times. According to this view, a dog, which emits a noise that (supposedly) sounds like "bow-wow" would be designated by the word *bow-wow*. To refute this position one need merely point to the small number of such words in any language and, in addition, to the fact that words alone do not constitute language.

A parallel view states that language at first consisted of emotional ejac-

ulations of pain, fear, surprise, pleasure, anger, and so on. This theory—
that the earliest manifestations of language were "cries of nature" that man
shared with animals—was the view proposed by Jean Jacques Rousseau
in the middle of the eighteenth century. Rousseau, a founder of the Roman-
tic movement, became concerned with the nature and origin of language
while seeking to understand the nature of the "noble savage." Two of his
treatises deal with the origin of language.[6] According to him, both emotive
cries and gestures were used by man, but gestures proved to be too inefficient for communicating, and so man invented language. It was out of the
natural cries that man "constructed" words.

Rousseau's position was essentially that of the **empiricists,** who held
that all knowledge results from the perception of observable data. Thus,
the first words were names of individual things and the first sentences were
one-word sentences. General and abstract names were invented only later,
as were the "different parts of speech," and more complex sentences. Rousseau stated this in the following way: The more limited the knowledge, the
more extensive the dictionary. . . . General ideas can come into the mind
only with the aid of words, and the understanding grasps them only through
propositions.[7]

It is difficult to understand his reasoning. How was man able to acquire
the ability for abstract thought through his use of concrete words if he was
not, from the very beginning, equipped with special mental abilities? But,
according to Rousseau, it is not man's ability to reason which distinguished
him from animals (the view held by the earlier French philosopher Descartes); rather, it is his "will to be free." According to Rousseau, it is this
freedom which led to the invention of languages. He did not explain how
this freedom permitted speakers to associate certain sounds with certain
meanings and to construct a complex system of rules which permitted them
to construct new sentences. Rousseau based some of his ideas on the
assumption that the first languages used by humans were crude and
primitive languages "approximately like those which the various savage
nations still have today." It is interesting that this man, who spent his life
fighting inequality, should espouse such a position. Just one year after
Rousseau's treatise, Suessmilch, arguing against Rousseau and in favor of
the divine-origin theory, maintained the equality and perfection of all
languages.

Almost two hundred years after Rousseau suggested that both the
"cries of nature" and gestures formed the basis for language development,
Sir Richard Paget argued for an "oral gesture theory":

> Human speech arose out of a generalized unconscious pantomimic gesture
> language—made by the limbs and features as a whole (including the tongue
> and lips)—which became specialized in gestures of the organs of articula-
> tion, owing to the human hands (and eyes) becoming continuously occu-
> pied with the use of tools. The gestures of the organs of articulation were

[6] Jean Jacques Rousseau, "Discourse on the Origin and Foundations of Inequality
Among Men" (1755) and "Essay on the Origin of Languages" (published posthumously,
1822).

[7] Rousseau, "Essay on the Origin of Languages," in P. H. Salus, ed., *On Language:
Plato to Von Humboldt* (New York: Holt, Rinehart and Winston, 1969).

recognized by the hearer because the hearer unconsciously reproduced in his mind the actual gesture which had produced this sound.[8]

It is difficult to know exactly how the tongue and lips and other vocal organs were used as "pantomimic gestures." But it is of interest that there are a number of scholars today who accept a "motor theory of speech perception" which is a sophisticated version of Paget's last statement.

The view that human language developed out of an earlier gestural communication system is found in the current publications of Gordon Hewes.[9] He does not claim, however, that this was the only system utilized, but points to the cases where gestures are used where speech cannot be used (as for the deaf) or where speech is not feasible (under noisy conditions or where unknown languages are being spoken).

Another hypothesis concerning the development of human language suggests that language arose out of the rhythmical grunts of men working together. The Soviet aphasiologist A. R. Luria accepted this view in 1970:

> There is every reason to believe that speech originated in productive activity and arose first in the form of abbreviated motions which represented certain work activities and pointing gestures by which men communicated with one another. . . . Only considerably later, as shown by speech paleontology, did verbal speech develop. Only in the course of a very long historical period was the disassociation of sound and gesture accomplished.[10]

One of the more charming views on language origin was suggested by Otto Jespersen. He proposed a theory stating that language derived from song as an expressive rather than a communicative need, with love being the greatest stimulus for language development.

Just as with the theories of divine origin of language, many of these proposals in support of the idea that man invented language, or that it arose in the course of man's development—whether out of the cries of nature, the vocal mimicry of gestures, the songs of love, or the grunts of labor—are inconclusive. The debate is unsettled and it continues.

Mankind's Origin Is Language Origin

**But language just happened. It happened because
language is the most natural outcome in a world of people
where babies babble, and mothers babble back—and
where the baby also has the potential for metaphor.**
LOUIS CARINI

In 1769, fifteen years after Suessmilch's famous defense of the divine origin of language in opposition to the "invention" theory, the Prussian Academy reopened the discussion. They offered a prize for the best paper on the very same question. Johann Herder, the German philos-

[8] Richard Paget, *Human Speech* (New York: Harcourt, Brace, 1930).
[9] Gordon Hewes, "The Current Status of the Gestural Theory of Language," *Annals N. Y. Acad. Science* 280 (1976): 482–504.
[10] A. R. Luria, *Traumatic Aphasia* (New York: Humanities Press, 1970), p. 80.

opher and poet, won the prize with an essay which opposed both views. Herder argued against Rousseau's theory that language developed out of the "cries of nature" which man shared with animals by citing the fundamental differences between human language and the instinctive cries of animals. Herder felt that language and thought are inseparable, and that man must be born with a capacity for both. He agreed with Suessmilch that without reason, language could not have been invented by man, but he went further in stating that without reason, Adam could not have been taught language, not even by the Divine Father:

> Parents never teach their children language, without the latter at the same time inventing it themselves. The former only direct their children's attention to the difference between things, by certain verbal signs, and thus do not supply these, but by means of language only facilitate and accelerate for the children the use of reason.[11]

These very insightful remarks foreshadowed the view held by some present-day linguists that no one teaches children the rules of grammar—children discover them.

Herder's main point was that language ability is innate. One cannot talk of man existing before language. Language is part of our essential human nature and was therefore neither invented nor handed down as a gift. Herder drew on the universality, or uniformity, of all human languages as an argument to justify a monogenetic theory of origin. According to him, we have all descended from the same parents, and all languages therefore descended from one language. He put forth this theory to explain why languages, despite their diversity, have universal common properties. Even though the monogenetic theory is not widely accepted today, the universality of human language is accepted, and can be plausibly explained by Herder's argument that man, by nature, is everywhere the same. Herder accepted the Cartesian *rationalist* position that human languages and animal cries are as different from each other as human thought and animal instinct: "It is not the organization of the mouth which creates language for if a man were dumb all the days of his life, if he reflected, language must lie within his soul."[12]

Language and Evolution

Despite the earlier "bans" on speculation regarding the origin of human language, the interest in this question has been rekindled. Two scholarly societies, the American Anthropological Association and the New York Academy of Sciences, held forums to review recent research on the topic (in 1974 and 1976). Research being conducted in various disciplines is providing data which were unavailable earlier and which are directly related to the development of language in the human species.

Scholars are now concerned with how the development of language is related to the evolutionary development of the human species. There are those who view language ability as a difference in degree between humans

---

[11] J. G. Herder, "Essay on the Origin of Language," in Salus, op. cit.
[12] Herder, op. cit.

and other primates, and those who see the onset of language ability as a qualitative leap. The linguists who, in their evolutionary approach, take a "discontinuity" view believe that language is species-specific, and among these linguists there are those who further believe that the brain mechanisms which underlie this language ability are specific to language, rather than being a mere offshoot of more highly developed cognitive abilities. This latter view holds that all humans are innately or genetically equipped with a unique language learning ability or with genetically determined, specifically linguistic, neurological mechanisms. Such linguists agree with the earlier views of Herder.

In trying to understand the development of language, scholars past and present have debated the role played by the vocal tract and the ear. The linguist Philip Lieberman suggests that "nonhuman primates lack the physical apparatus that is necessary to produce the range of human speech." [13] He links the development of language with the evolutionary development of the speech production and perception apparatus. This, of course, would be accompanied by changes in the brain and the nervous system toward greater complexity. Lieberman's view implies that the languages of our human ancestors of millions of years ago may have been syntactically and phonologically simpler than any language known to us today. This still begs the question, however, because the notion "simpler" is left undefined. One suggestion is that this primeval language had a smaller phonetic inventory. But the reconstructed shape of the Neanderthal vocal tract (which Lieberman and the Yale anatomist Edmund Crelin constructed, based on fossil remains) on which this hypothesis is based has been questioned: F. L. Du Brul points out that if the Neanderthal vocal tract was as reconstructed, he would not have been able to open his mouth, let alone speak. [14]

Certainly one evolutionary step must have resulted in the development of a vocal tract capable of producing the wide variety of sounds utilized by human language, as well as the mechanism for perceiving and distinguishing them. That this step is insufficient to explain the origin of language is evidenced by the existence of mynah birds and parrots, which have this ability. Their imitations, however, are merely patterned repetitions. (See Chapter 3 on animal languages.)

Human language utilizes a fairly small number of sounds, which are combined in linear sequence to form words. Each sound is reused many times, as is each word. Suessmilch pointed to this fact as evidence of the "efficiency" and "perfection" of language. Indeed, the discreteness of these basic linguistic elements—these sounds—was noted in the earliest views of language.

Children learn very early in life that the continuous sounds of words like *bad* and *dad* can be "broken up" into discrete segments. In fact, children that know these two words may on their own produce the word *dab*, though they have never heard it before. Mynah birds can learn to produce

[13] Philip Lieberman, "Primate Vocalizations and Human Linguistic Ability," *J. Acoustical Soc. Am.* 44:1574–1584.
[14] E. L. Du Brul, "Biomechanics of Speech Sounds," *Annals N. Y. Acad. Science* 280 (1976): 631–642.

the sounds *bad* and *dad,* but no bird could ever produce the sound *dab* without actually hearing it.

On the other hand we also know that the ability to hear speech sounds is not a necessary condition for the acquisition and use of language. Humans who are born deaf learn the sign languages which are used around them, and these are as "creative" and complex as spoken languages. And deaf children acquire these languages in the same way as hearing children do—without being taught—by mere exposure.

Perhaps, then, the major evolutionary step in the development of language relates to evolutionary changes in the brain.

Language and the Brain

It only takes one hemisphere to have a mind.
A. W. WIGAN, 1844

Even if we completely understood the language acquisition process and the production and perception of speech (and we are just at the beginning of such knowledge), this would not tell us how the human animal is able to accomplish these feats. Why are we the only species that learns and uses language without being taught? What aspects of the human neurological makeup explain this ability? How did these brain mechanisms develop?

The attempts to understand the complexities of human cognitive abilities are as old and as continuous as the attempts to understand language. One way of investigating mental abilities and processes is by investigating language. As Fournier pointed out one hundred years ago, "Speech is the only window through which the physiologist can observe the workings of the cerebral life."

On the other hand, an investigation of the brain in humans and nonhuman primates, anatomically, psychologically, and behaviorally may help us to answer the questions posed above. The study concerned with the biological foundations of language and the brain mechanisms underlying its acquisition and use is called **neurolinguistics.**

Although neurolinguistics is still in its infancy, our understanding has progressed a great deal since a day in September 1848, when a foreman of a road construction gang named Phineas Gage became a famous figure in medical history. He achieved his "immortality" when a four-foot-long iron rod was blown through his head. Despite the gaping tunnel in his brain, Gage lived for twelve more years and, except for some personality changes (he became "cranky" and "inconsiderate"), Gage seemed to be little affected by this terrible accident. This seemed miraculous. How could so much damage to the brain have so little effect? Both Gage and science benefited from this explosion. Phineas gained monetarily by becoming a one-man touring circus; he traveled all over the country charging money to those curious enough to see him and the iron rod. Science benefited because brain researchers were stimulated to learn why his intelligence seemed to be intact.

Since that time we have learned a great deal about the brain—the most complicated organ of the body. It lies under the skull and consists of approximately 10 billion nerve cells (neurons) and all the billions of fibers which connect these cells. The nerve cells, or **gray matter,** form the surface of the brain, which is called the **cortex.** Under the cortex is the **white matter,** which consists primarily of the connecting fibers. The cerebral cortex is the decision-making organ of the body. It receives messages from all the sensory organs, and it initiates all voluntary actions. It is "the seat of all which is exclusively human in the mind." It is the storehouse of "memory" as well. Obviously, somewhere in this gray matter the grammar which represents our knowledge of language must reside.

The brain is divided into two parts (called **cerebral hemispheres**), one on the right and one on the left. These hemispheres are connected like Siamese twins right down the middle by the **corpus callosum,** which is a pathway leading from one side to the other, permitting the "two brains" to communicate with each other.

An interesting fact about these two hemispheres is that the left hemisphere controls the movements of the right side of the body and the right hemisphere the movements of the left side. That is, if you scratch your nose with your right hand, it is the left hemisphere which has "directed" your actions. If someone whispers into your left ear, the sound signal will go most directly to the right hemisphere before crossing over the pathway to get to the left.

The **cerebellum,** also divided into two halves, is located underneath the cerebral hemispheres and is responsible for controlling equilibrium. At the bottom of the brain is found the **brain stem,** which connects the brain to the spinal cord.

You might be wondering, at this point, why in a book on language we are going into all this anatomy. The details are not important, but, as Wallace Chafe pointed out: "The description of a language cannot be divorced from considerations of what is 'in people's heads.' "[15] We can't look into people's heads very easily, and even if we could we would not see the grammar which represents our linguistic knowledge. "We can only hypothesize what goes on there on the basis of indirect evidence," says Chafe. It is on the basis of such evidence that brain researchers and neurolinguists have found that different parts of the brain are responsible for different activities, abilities, and functions.

Accidents, disease, and surgery provided a great deal of information about the specific functions of different areas of the cortex. Damage (lesions) to one part of the brain causes certain malfunctions, and damage to other parts causes other kinds of pathological behavior.

In 1870, experiments on dogs were conducted by two German doctors who stimulated the cortex with electrodes. Later, the noted Montreal brain surgeon Dr. Wilder Penfield and his associates stimulated different parts of the cortex of patients who required brain surgery. They found that if a particular point in the cortex is electrically stimulated the little finger will twitch, if different neurons are stimulated the foot will move, and so on.

In these ways, the human cortex was "mapped," showing the areas responsible for motor activities of different parts of the body, sensations of

[15] Wallace Chafe, *Meaning and the Structure of Language* (Chicago: University of Chicago Press, 1970).

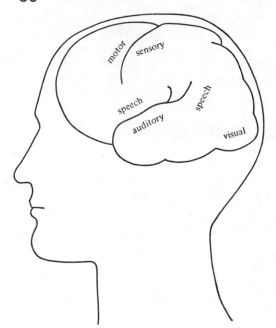

Figure 2-1 Specialized areas of the brain.

touch, visual perception, and so on. Figure 2-1 shows some of these areas.

One result of such studies is the realization that lesions in certain areas of the brain produce language disorders (called **aphasia**), while lesions in other areas do not. Patients with aphasia do not seem to have any impairment of general intelligence; they can produce sounds and the motor coordination of the vocal organs remains intact, but they have difficulties with language. There are many different kinds of language impairments found in aphasia patients; some produce long strings of "jargon" which "sound like" language but which are uninterpretable by anyone listening to them; others speak perfectly well but can't understand what is said to them; some find it difficult to "find the right word" or form "grammatical sentences"; some aphasics will substitute words in the same semantic class for the words they are asked to read (for example, they will read "liberty" for *democracy*, "chair" for *table*), while others substitute phonologically similar words ("pool" for *tool*, or "crucial" for *crucible*). All aphasics show some kind of language disorder.

Most of us have experienced some "aphasic symptoms," as did Alice when she said:

> "And now, who am I? I *will* remember, if I can. I'm determined to do it!" But being determined didn't help her much, and all she could say, after a great deal of puzzling, was "L, I *know* it begins with L."

This "tip-of-the-tongue" phenomenon is not uncommon. But if you *never* could find the word you wanted, you can imagine how serious a problem it would be. One aphasia patient appeared able to speak and understand perfectly well, but could not answer a direct question like "What is your wife's name?" After tremendous effort, he would grab a piece of paper and a pencil and write the answer to the question, but he could not speak the answer when a question was asked. This kind of problem is found in many aphasia patients.

The interest in aphasia goes far back in time. In the New Testament, St. Luke reports that Zacharias could not speak but could write. And in 30 A.D. the Roman writer Valerius Maximus describes an Athenian who was unable to remember his "letters" after being hit in the head with a stone.

But it was not until April 1861 that language disorders were specifically related to damage to the *left side of the brain*. At a scientific meeting in Paris, Dr. Paul Broca stated unequivocally that we speak with the left hemisphere.[16] Since Broca's time, extensive research has been conducted on language and the brain, including clinical aphasia studies, neurosurgical procedures, electrical stimulation of the brain, anesthetizing parts of the brain, studies of the electrical potentials and patterns emitted from the brain under various conditions, "split-brain" studies, dichotic listening studies, and tachistoscopic studies (discussed below). This research shows that while generally the nervous system is symmetrical—what exists on the left exists on the right, and vice versa—the two sides of the brain are an exception. As a child develops, the two sides of the brain become specialized for different functions; **lateralization** (one-sidedness) takes place. Until recently it was believed that this brain asymmetry was found only in humans. New evidence however shows that, both anatomically and functionally, canaries and zebra finches display lateralization of function. The view that language originated in humans because of the development of lateralization is therefore no longer viable.

As pointed out above, aphasia studies provide good evidence that language is a left-hemisphere function.[17] In the overwhelming number of cases, injuries to the left hemisphere result in aphasia but injuries to the right hemisphere do not. If both hemispheres were equally involved with language this could not be the case.

Other evidence is provided by patients who for various medical reasons have one of the hemispheres removed. If the right hemisphere is cut out, language remains intact. Because of the language impairments which would result from the removal of the left hemisphere, such surgery is performed only in dire cases.

"Split-brain" patients provide some of the most dramatic evidence. In recent years it was found that persons suffering from serious epilepsy could be treated by cutting the pathway connecting the two sides of the brain, with little effect on their lives. We mentioned above that the two cerebral hemispheres are connected by a membrane called the corpus callosum. This "freeway" between the two brain halves consists of tens of millions

[16] In 1836, in a paper unknown to Broca, Dr. Mark Dax had made a similar claim, but little attention had been paid to it.

[17] For some people—about a third of all left-handers—there is still lateralization, but it is the right side which is specialized for language. In other words, the special functions are switched, but asymmetry still exists.

of nerve fibers connecting the cells of the left and right hemispheres. If this pathway is split there is no "communication" between the "two brains." The psychologist Michael Gazzaniga states:

> With [the corpus callosum] intact, the two halves of the body have no se-
> crets from one another. With it sectioned, the two halves become two dif-
> ferent conscious mental spheres, each with its own experienced base and
> control system for behavioral operations. . . . Unbelievable as this may
> seem, this is the flavor of a long series of experimental studies first carried
> out in the cat and monkey.[18]

When the brain is split surgically, certain information from the left side of the body is received *only* by the right side of the brain and vice versa (because of the "split-brain" phenomenon discussed above). For example, suppose a monkey is trained to respond with its hands to a certain visual stimulus (a flashing light, say). If the brain is split after the training period, and the stimulus is shown only to the left visual field (the right brain), the monkey will perform only with the left hand, and vice versa. Many such experiments have been done on animals. These all show the distinctness of the two sides of the brain, as well as the fact that each side of the animal's brain is capable of performing the same tasks.

Persons with split brains have been tested by psychologists. Unlike the results of experiments conducted with cats and monkeys, tests with these human subjects showed that messages sent to the two sides of the brain resulted in different responses. If an apple is put in the left hand of a split-brain human and his vision is cut off, he cannot describe the object. The right brain senses the apple, and is able to distinguish the apple from other objects, but the information cannot be relayed to the left brain for linguistic description. But if the same experiment is repeated and in addition a banana is placed in the right hand, the subject is able to describe the banana verbally, though he is still unable to describe the apple (see Figure 2-2).

Various tests of this sort have been performed, all providing information as to the different capabilities of the "two brains." The right brain does much better than the left in "pattern-matching" tasks, or in recognizing faces, or in other kinds of spatial-perceptual tasks. The left hemisphere is superior for language, for rhythmic perception, for temporal-order judgments, for mathematical thinking. According to Gazzaniga, ". . . the right hemisphere as well as the left hemisphere can emote and while the left can tell you why, the right cannot."[19]

The evidence is overwhelming; the human brain is asymmetrical. The left brain is the language brain. But since all these cases involve "nonnormal" humans (in one way or the other), other experimental techniques to explore the specialized capabilities of the two hemispheres were developed which could be used with all human subjects. One such method, called **dichotic listening,** uses auditory signals. Subjects hear two different sound signals simultaneously through earphones. For example, a subject may hear "boy" in one ear and "girl" in the other, or "crocodile" in one ear and "alligator" in the other. Or the subject may hear a horn tooting

---

[18] Michael Gazzaniga, *The Bisected Brain* (New York: Appleton-Century-Crofts, 1970).
[19] Ibid.

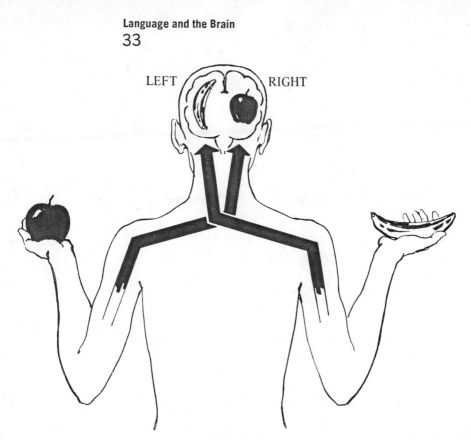

LEFT   RIGHT

Figure 2-2

in one ear and a toilet flushing in the other. When asked to state what she heard in each ear, the responses to the right-ear (left-brain) stimuli are more correct when the stimuli are linguistic in nature (words, nonsense syllables, and so on), but the left ear (right brain) does better with certain nonverbal sounds (musical chords, environmental sounds, and so on). That is, if the subject hears "boy" in the right ear and "girl" in the left ear, she is more likely to report the sound heard in the right ear correctly. But if she hears coughing in the right ear and laughing in the left, she is more apt to report the laughing stimulus correctly.

Notice that if the left hemisphere is "processing" the incoming verbal stimuli, any sounds going to the right hemisphere have to cross over the pathway (the corpus callosum) to get to the left side of the brain. These messages have longer to travel and so are weakened. If the right hemisphere was equally capable of processing (as well as receiving) the signal from the left ear no differences between ears would show up.

Figure 2-3 illustrates what is going on in a highly oversimplified fashion. (The situation is actually much more complex. The signals entering the right and left ears do have a path which goes to the right and left brains, respectively, but these are suppressed when there is another sound coming in from the crossed pathway.) In drawing A of Figure 2-3, "boy" coming in through the *right* ear goes directly to the *left* hemisphere, where it can

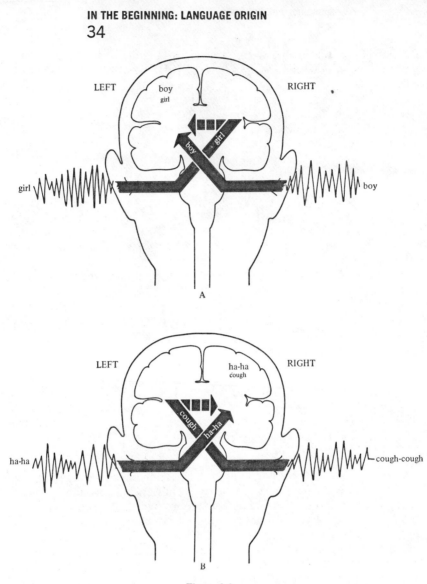

Figure 2-3

be processed, since this is the language-processing side of the brain; "girl" coming in through the *left* ear goes directly to the *right* hemisphere and then has to cross over to the left in order to be "understood." By the time it gets to the "language processor" it has been weakened, and so the subject makes more errors in reporting what she hears through this ear. In drawing B the reverse is true for nonlinguistic sounds—the laughing coming in through the *left* ear is heard more strongly.

The superior performance of the right ear for linguistic stimuli in such dichotic-listening tasks further reflects the left-hemispheric specialization for language.

These experiments were very important in that they showed that the left hemisphere is not superior for processing *all* sounds, but only for those which are linguistic in nature. That is, the left side of the brain is specialized for *language,* not sounds.

The lateralization of the brain is certainly connected with the language-learning abilities of children. It has long been noted that it is much more difficult to learn a language after a certain age. This "critical age" for first language acquisition seems to coincide with the period when lateralization is complete.[20] At birth the two sides of the brain do not seem to be specialized, although there is some evidence that even anatomically there are differences between the two hemispheres in humans (not found in other animals). Lateralization proceeds and is more or less complete by the age of five.[21] If you have ever listened to a five-year-old child, you know that the basic grammar of the language is also learned by this age. Language learning and lateralization seem to go hand in hand, but the relationship between the two is not clearly understood.

We are not certain whether language "input" conditions lateralization or whether lateralization precedes language acquisition. Nor are we sure of the extent to which our linguistic ability is distinct from other cognitive or intellectual abilities. Since children are capable of learning language (the most complex of all phenomena) before they are able to learn simpler logical operations, our language-learning ability may be "preprogrammed" in special ways. These are fascinating questions which may be answered in time.

It should not be surprising that we still have no definitive answers to the question of how human language arose in the course of evolution. Study of the human brain in comparison with the brains of other species allows us to see similarities and differences. There appears to have been both neural reorganization and a great expansion of brain size in humans, both of which may account in part for our linguistic ability. If one views language simply as one of many systems of communication, then one might be led to the "continuity" view of evolution. But when we examine the complexities of language, which is just one of the systems humans use to communicate with each other, a stronger case can be made for the "discontinuity" hypothesis. What seems to be quite clear no matter which view one holds is that the changes that occurred in the speech-producing and speech-receiving mechanisms of the species were accompanied or preceded by changes in the brain, showing that evolutionary restructuring of the brain played a significant role in the origin and development of human language.

Language was neither invented, nor was it a gift. It was ground out of the evolutionary mill and suffered the tests of survival. These tests were passed, the species "saw that it was good," and so we are blessed with language.

SUMMARY

Our curiosity about ourselves and our most unique possession, language, has led to numerous theories about language origin. There is no way at present

---

[20] Eric H. Lenneberg, *Biological Foundations of Language* (New York: Wiley, 1967).
[21] Stephen Krashen and Richard Harshman, "Lateralization and the Critical Period," *J. Acoustical Soc. Am.* 52 (1972): 174.

to "prove" or "disprove" these hypotheses, but they are of interest for the light they shed on the nature of human language.

The idea that language was God's gift to mankind is found in religions throughout the world. The continuing belief in the miraculous powers of language is tied to this notion. The assumption of the divine origin of language stimulated interest in discovering the first primeval language. There are legendary "experiments" in which children were isolated in the belief that their first words would reveal the original language. Children will learn the language spoken to them; if they hear no language they will speak none. Actual cases of socially isolated children show that language develops only when there is sufficient linguistic input.

Opposing theories suggest that language is a human invention. The Greeks believed that an ancient "legislator" gave the true names to all things. Others have suggested that language developed from "cries of nature," or "early gestures," or onomatopoeic words, or even from songs to express love.

There is at present a renewed interest among biologists and linguists in the question of language origin. Various evolutionary theories that are now proposed oppose both the divine-origin and the invention theory. Rather, it is suggested that in the course of evolution both the human species and language developed. Some scholars suggest that this occurred simultaneously, and that from the start the human animal was innately equipped to learn language. In fact there are those who believe that it is language which makes human nature human. Studies of the evolutionary development of the brain provide some evidence for physiological, anatomic, and "mental" preconditions for language development.

There is at present a considerable interest in the brain mechanisms which underlie linguistic competence and performance. This has given rise to a special area of study called **neurolinguistics,** which is concerned with the representation and processing of language in the brain.

The brain is the most complicated organ of the body, controlling motor activities and thought processes. Different parts of the brain control different body functions. The brain in all higher animals is divided into two hemispheres. Evidence from **aphasia,** surgical removal of parts of the brain, and **split-brain** patients shows that the "left brain" is the language hemisphere. **Dichotic listening** experiments on normal subjects confirm these findings. Thus, in the human animal, each brain is specialized for different tasks. This **lateralization** of functions develops from birth and is usually complete by five years of age. Developing lateralization coincides with the first language-learning years. It appears, then, that hemispheric specialization may be a precondition for human language.

EXERCISES

1. Suppose archeologists discovered an ancient document which they established to be 100,000 years old. Suppose further that the writing on this document was deciphered. How would you argue against the idea that this would tell us what man's earliest language was like?

2. List as many onomatopoeic English words as you can. Are such words sufficient evidence in favor of the "echoic" theory of language origin? If not, why not?

3. Compare the ideas of Rousseau, Herder, and Suessmilch on the origin of language. Note the similarities and the differences. Argue in favor of one of these theories.

4. Invent your own theory of language origin. For example, you might suggest that language arose because extraterrestrial creatures who already had a language possessed the bodies of cavewomen.

5. It has been shown that the left hemisphere of the brain is specialized (or lateralized) for the following: mathematical problem solving, judgments of the temporal order of events, analysis of a complex pattern into its component parts, determination of the sequencing of events, and, of course, language processing. Discuss what common factors may be said to "unite" these different tasks.

6. A. Some aphasic patients, when asked to read a list of words, substitute other words for those printed. In many cases there are similarities between the printed words and the substituted words that are read. The data given below are from actual aphasic patients. In each case state what the two words have in common and how they differ:

PRINTED WORD	WORD SPOKEN BY APHASIC
a. liberty	freedom
canary	parrot
abroad	overseas
large	long
short	small
tall	long
b. decide	decision
conceal	concealment
portray	portrait
bathe	bath
speak	discussion
remember	memory

B. What do the words in groups a and b reveal about how words are likely to be stored in the brain?

7. The following are some sentences spoken by aphasic patients collected and analyzed by Dr. Harry Whitaker of the University of Rochester. In each case state how the sentence deviates from normal nonaphasic language.

a. There is under a horse a new sidesaddle.
b. In girls we see many happy days.
c. I'll challenge a new bike.
d. I surprise no new glamour.
e. Is there three chairs in this room?
f. Mike and Peter is happy.
g. Bill and John likes hot dogs.
h. Proliferate is a complete time about a word that is correct.
i. Went came in better than it did before.

References

Curtiss, S. *Genie: A Psycholinguistic Study of a Modern-Day "Wild Child."* New York: Academic Press, 1977.

Dingwall, W. O. "The Evolution of Human Communication Systems" in H. Whitaker and H. A. Whitaker, eds., *Studies in Neurolinguistics,* vol 4. New York: Academic Press, 1977.

Fromkin, V. A., S. Krashen, S. Curtiss, D. Rigler, and M. Rigler. "Language Development Beyond the Critical Age," *Brain and Language,* vol. 1., no. 1 (1974).

Gazzaniga, Michael S. *The Bisected Brain.* New York: Appleton-Century-Crofts, 1970.

Itard, J. *The Wild Boy of Aveyron.* New York: Appleton-Century-Crofts, 1962.

Jesperson, O. *Language,* ch. XXI. New York: W. W. Norton & Co., reprinted 1964.

Kimura, Doreen. "The Asymmetry of the Human Brain," *Scientific American,* vol. 228, no. 3 (1973), pp. 70–80.

Lane, Harlan. *The Wild Boy of Aveyron.* Cambridge, Mass.: Harvard University Press, 1976.

Lenneberg, Eric. H. *Biological Foundations of Language.* New York: Wiley, 1967.

Lieberman, Philip. *On the Origins of Language.* New York: Macmillan, 1975.

Plato. *Cratylus.* Loeb Classical Library. Cambridge, Mass.: Harvard University Press, 1967.

Rousseau, J. J., and J. G. Herder. *On the Origin of Language,* trans. by J. H. Moran and A. Gode. New York: Frederick Ungar, 1966.

Stam, J. *Inquiries in the Origin of Language: The Fate of a Question.* New York: Harper & Row, 1976.

Animal "Languages"

No matter how eloquently a dog may bark, he cannot tell
you that his parents were poor but honest.
BERTRAND RUSSELL

The articulated signs of human language are not like the
expression of emotions of children or animals. Animal
noises cannot be combined to form syllables.
ARISTOTLE

If animals could talk, what wonderful stories they would
tell. The eagle already knew the earth was round when men were still afraid
of falling off its edge. The whale could have warned Columbus about a barrier between Europe and India and saved that explorer a lot of anxiety. Jus-
tice would be more properly served if animals could give testimony. There
would be a reduction in crime, no doubt, and quite possibly an increase
in the divorce rate. All of us would have to alter our behavior in some way
or another, for our environment would be considerably changed.

The idea of talking animals is as old and as widespread among human
societies as language itself. No culture lacks a legend in which some animal
plays a speaking role. All over West Africa, children listen to folk tales in
which a "spider-man" is the hero. "Coyote" is a favorite figure in many
American Indian tales. And there is hardly an animal who does not figure
in Aesop's famous fables. Many authors have exploited the idea success-
fully, among them Hugh Lofting, the creator of the famous Doctor Dolittle. The good doctor's forte was animal communication, and he is no doubt
fiction's most prodigious language learner. Still, Doctor Dolittle and his
adventures are fantasies for children, and the idea of communicating with
our fellow animal tenants of this globe as we communicate with our fellow
human tenants is absurd. Or is it?

Whether language is the exclusive property of the human species is an
interesting question. The answer depends on what properties of human language are considered. If language is viewed only as a system of communication, then obviously many species communicate. Humans also use

systems other than their language to relate to each other and to send "messages." To understand human language one needs to see what, if anything, is special and unique to language. If we find that there are no such special properties, then we will have to conclude that language, as we have been discussing it, is not, as claimed, uniquely human.

We have already mentioned a number of linguistic properties. All normal humans who acquire language utilize speech *sounds* to express meanings. Are such sounds a necessary aspect of language? Obviously not. Children who are born deaf cannot learn to speak vocally without very special training. These unfortunate children are nonetheless able to learn language. Many learn a sign language. Sign languages of the deaf will be discussed in Chapter 12. As we shall see, sign languages are actual human languages without sounds. Therefore, the use of speech sounds is not a key property of human language. If this is so, then the squeaking of dolphins, the dancing of bees, and the manipulation of plastic chips by chimpanzees may represent systems similar to human language. That is, if we decide that animal communication systems are *not* languages similar to human languages, it will not be because they fail to have speech sounds.

Conversely, if animals vocally imitate human utterances, this does not mean they possess language. We have already seen that language is a system by which sounds and meanings (or gestures and meanings) are related. "Talking" birds such as parrots and mynah birds are capable of flawlessly enunciating words and phrases of human language. The birds imitate what they have heard. But when a parrot says "Polly wants a cracker" she may really want a ham sandwich or a drink of water or nothing at all. A bird that has learned to say "hello" or "goodbye" is as likely to use one as the other, regardless of whether people are arriving or departing. The bird's "utterances" carry no meaning. They are neither speaking English nor their own language when they sound like us.

A mynah bird trained by the animal ethologist W. Thorpe "spoke" excellent English. Then a new laboratory assistant was hired who spoke English with a Hungarian accent. When the bird began to repeat his phrases, she sounded as though she were practicing for a part in a Hollywood Dracula movie. This illustrates the imitative nature of the bird's utterances. The parrot or mynah bird is not "dissecting" the sounds into discrete units. *Polly* and *Molly* do not "rhyme" for a parrot. They are as different as *hello* and *goodbye* (or as similar). One property of all human languages is the "discreteness" of the units which are ordered and reordered, combined and split apart. A parrot says what it is taught, or what it hears, and no more. If Polly learns "Polly wants a cracker" and "Polly wants a doughnut" and also learns to imitate the single words *whiskey* and *bagel,* she will not produce "spontaneously," as children do, "Polly wants whiskey" or "Polly wants a bagel." If she learns *cat* and *cats* and *dog* and *dogs* and then learns *parrot,* she will be unable to "form the plural" *parrots* (as in *cats*).

A parrot does not "take speech to pieces," nor can it form an unlimited set of utterances from a finite set of units. All humans can. We have already discussed this "creative" aspect of language use.

Thus, the ability to produce sounds similar to those used in human language cannot be equated with the ability to learn a human language.

In the seventeenth century, the philosopher and mathematician René Descartes pointed out what we have been discussing here: that the ability to use language is not based on the physiological abilities to produce speech or speech-like sounds. He concluded:

> It is not the want of organs that [prevents animals from making] . . . known their thoughts . . . for it is evident that magpies and parrots are able to utter words just like ourselves, and yet they cannot speak as we do, that is, so as to give evidence that they think of what they say. On the other hand, men who, being born deaf and dumb, are in the same degree, or even more than the brutes, destitute of the organs which serve the others for talking, are in the habit of themselves inventing certain signs by which they make themselves understood.[1]

We shall examine various animal communication systems to see whether other creatures share with humans the ability to learn and use languages creatively.

The Birds and the Bees

The birds and animals are all friendly to each other, and there are no disputes about anything. They all talk, and they all talk to me, but it must be a foreign language, for I cannot make out a word they say.
MARK TWAIN, *Eve's Diary*

Most animals possess some kind of "signaling" communication system. Among the spiders there is a complex system for courtship. The male spider, before he approaches his lady love, goes through elaborate gestures to inform her that he is indeed a spider and not a crumb or a fly to be eaten. These gestures are invariant. One never finds a "creative" spider changing or adding to the particular courtship ritual of his species.

A similar kind of "gesture" language is found among the fiddler crabs. There are forty different varieties, and each species uses its own particular "claw-waving" movement to signal to another member of its "clan." The timing, movement, and posture of the body never change from one time to another or from one crab to another within the particular species. Whatever the signal means, it is fixed. Only one meaning can be conveyed. There is not an infinite set of fiddler crab "sentences." Nor can the signal be "broken down" into smaller elements, as is possible in any utterance of human language.

The "language" of the honeybees is far more complex than that of the spiders or fiddler crabs. When a forager bee returns to the hive, if it has located a source of food it does a dance which communicates certain information about that source to other members of the colony.

The dancing behavior may assume one of three possible patterns:

---

[1] René Descartes, "Discourse on Method," part v, *The Philosophical Works of Descartes,* trans. by E. S. Haldane and G. R. T. Ross, Vol. I, p. 116.

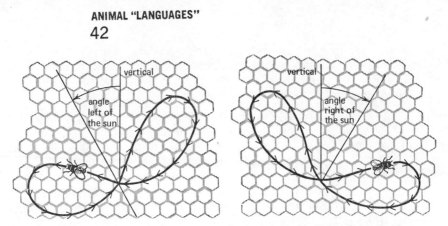

Figure 3-1 The sickle dance. In this case the food source is 20–60 feet from the hive.

round, sickle, and *tail-wagging*.[2] The determining factor in the choice of dance pattern is the distance of the food source from the hive. The round dance indicates locations near the hive, within twenty feet or so. The sickle dance indicates locations at an intermediate distance from the hive, approximately twenty to sixty feet. The tail-wagging dance is for distances that exceed sixty feet or so.

In all the dances the bee alights on a wall of the hive and literally dances on its feet through the appropriate pattern. For the round dance, the bee describes a circle. The only other semantic information imparted by the round dance, besides approximate distance, is the quality of the food source. This is indicated by the number of repetitions of the basic pattern that the bee executes, and the vivacity with which it performs the dance. This feature is true of all three patterns.

To perform the sickle dance the bee traces out a sickle-shaped figure-eight on the wall. The angle made by the direction of the open end of the sickle with the vertical is the same angle as the food source is from the sun. Thus the sickle dance imparts the information: approximate distance, direction, and quality (see Figure 3-1).

The tail-wagging dance imparts all the information of the sickle dance with one important addition. The number of repetitions per minute of the basic pattern of the dance indicates the precise distance: the slower the repetition rate, the longer the distance (see Figure 3-2).

The bees' dance is an effective system of communication, capable, in principle, of infinitely many different messages, and in this sense the bees' dance is infinitely variable, like human language. But unlike human language, the communication system of the bees is confined to a single subject, or thought. It is frozen and inflexible. For example, an experimenter forced a bee to walk to the food source. When the bee returned to the hive, it indicated a distance twenty-five times farther away than the food source actually was. The bee had no way of communicating the special circumstances or taking them into account in its message. This absence of *creativity* makes the bees' dance qualitatively different from human language.

The bees' dance does give us a chance to illustrate another very interesting property that every natural language of the world possesses, as al-

---

[2] A species of Italian honeybee is described here. Details differ from species to species. We might say that different species have different "dialects" of honeybee "language."

ready discussed in Chapter 1. We called this property the **arbitrariness** of the linguistic sign. In every system of communication that has a semantic system, each basic unit has two aspects, the **form** and the **meaning.** In the case of human language, the form is the actual string of sounds that make up the unit's pronunciation. Its meaning, or linguistic meaning, is of course determined by whatever language it belongs to. The sound and the meaning are like the head and tail of the same coin—distinct but inseparable. An example taken from the English language is the word *tree*. The linguistic form is the string of sounds *t-r-ee*; the linguistic meaning is the concept "tree." The same concept or meaning is expressed by different sounds in other languages. To take an example that does not involve language, consider a red traffic signal. The form is the physical object, a red light. The meaning is "stop—danger."

When we say that the linguistic sign is arbitrary, we mean that there is no connection between the linguistic form and its corresponding linguistic meaning. There is no connection between the sounds of the word *tree* and the concept "tree." Likewise there is no connection between a red light and the notion "stop—danger." The relationship in this case is a cultural matter. In all human languages the relationship between the sounds and meanings of the overwhelming majority of words is an arbitrary one.

What about the bees' dance? What are the forms of the sign, and to what meanings do they correspond? Are the relationships arbitrary or non-arbitrary? Consider the tail-wagging dance. One linguistic form is the vivacity of the dance, with a corresponding meaning "quality of food source." The relationship is clearly arbitrary, for there is nothing inherent about vivaciousness that indicates good or bad quality. In fact, we have been careful not to say whether more vivacity indicates a greater or lesser quality source of food. Because the relationship is arbitrary, there is no a-priori way of telling.

What about distance? The question here is more complicated. Remember that the slower the repetition rate, the greater the distance. On the surface this relationship may seem arbitrary, but let's use a little physics to reword the relationship: The longer it takes to complete the basic pat-

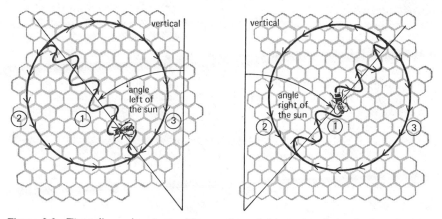

Figure 3-2 The tail-wagging dance. The number of times per minute the bee dances a complete pattern (1–2–1–3) indicates the distance of the food source.

tern, the longer it will take a bee to fly to the source. Thus we see that this sign is in some sense nonarbitrary. Similarly, the direction-determining aspect of the dance is perfectly nonarbitrary.

It should be remembered, however, that there are many communication systems, other than language, which contain signs that are arbitrarily related to the meanings they stand for. "Arbitrariness" is not enough to make a system a language in the sense of human language.

We have talked about the "language" systems of the spiders, the crabs, and the bees. What about the birds? It is known that the songs of certain species of birds have definite meanings. One song may mean "let's build a nest together," another song may mean "go get some worms for the babies," and so on. But the bird cannot make up a new song to cope with a new situation.

Two French scientists have studied the songs of the European robin.[3] They found that the songs are very complicated indeed. But, interestingly, the complications have little effect on the "message" which is being conveyed. The song which was studied was that which signaled the robin's possession of a certain territory. The scientists found that the rival robins paid attention only to the alternation between high-pitched and low-pitched notes, and which came first didn't matter at all. The message varies only to the extent of expressing how strongly the robin feels about his possession and how much he is prepared to defend it and start a family in that territory. The different alternations therefore express "intensity" and nothing more. The robin is creative in his ability to sing the same thing in many different ways, but not creative in his ability to use the same "units" of the system to express many different "utterances" all of which have different meanings.

Bird songs, then, seem to be no more similar to human language than are the movements of the spider, the claw-waving of the crab, or the dancing of the bees. All these systems are "fixed" in terms of the messages which can be conveyed. They lack the creative element of human language.

A study of higher animals also reveals no "language" systems that are creative in the way human language is. Wolves use many facial expressions, movements of their tails, and growls to express different degrees of threats, anxiety, depression, and submission. But that's all they can do. And the sounds and gestures produced by nonhuman primates, the monkeys and apes, show that their signals are highly stereotyped and limited in terms of the messages which they convey. Most importantly, studies of such animal communication systems reveal that the basic "vocabularies" produced by either sounds or facial expressions occur primarily as emotional responses to particular situations. They have no way of expressing the anger they felt "yesterday."

Descartes pointed out more than three hundred years ago that the communication systems of animals are qualitatively different from the language used by humans:

[3] R. G. Busnel and J. C. Bremond, "Recherche du support de l'information dans le signal acoustique de défense territoriale du Rougegorge," *C. R. Acad. Sci. Paris* 254 (1962): 2236–2238.

It is a very remarkable fact that there are none so depraved and stupid, without even excepting idiots, that they cannot arrange different words together, forming of them a statement by which they make known their thoughts; while, on the other hand, there is no other animal, however perfect and fortunately circumstanced it may be, which can do the same.[4]

Descartes goes on to state that one of the major differences between humans and animals is that human use of language is not just a response to external, or even internal, emotional stimuli, as are the grunts and gestures of animals. He warns against confusing human use of language with "natural movements which betray passions and may be . . . manifested by animals."

All the studies of animal communication systems provide evidence for Descartes' distinction between the fixed stimulus-bound messages of animals and the linguistic creative ability possessed by the human animal.

Dolphins

I kind of like the playful porpoise
A healthy mind in a healthy corpus
He and his cousin, the playful dolphin,
Why they like swimmin like I like golphin.
OGDEN NASH, "The Porpoise"[5]

Researchers are still trying to prove Descartes wrong. For a while the dolphin, the "monkey of the sea," appeared to be a good candidate for refuting the claim that language is unique to humans. The dolphin has a brain comparable in size to the human brain. Its surface, the cerebral cortex, is very wrinkled, like the surface of the human brain. However, the wrinkling is due to the thinness of the cerebral cortex; the dolphin's brain is even less complex than that of a rabbit, having fewer nerve cells.

But the dolphin does indeed use sounds to communicate. Dolphins produce clicking sounds. However, these are not produced to communicate with other dolphins. They are radar detection sounds; that is, dolphins produce them to help locate objects which may get in their way, just as bats do. Dolphins also produce squawky sounds and whistles. The analysis of these "sound units" shows that, like other animal signals, they are closely related to emotional situations. Thus a falling-pitch whistle represents the dolphin's call of distress, and also at times the mating call of the male.

A number of experiments have been conducted with dolphins. Jarvis Bastian developed an elaborate experiment to see if dolphins would communicate messages to each other.[6] A male and a female dolphin were kept in a special tank. The female was shown either a continuous light or a flash-

[4] René Descartes, op. cit.

[5] "The Porpoise," copyright 1942 by Ogden Nash. From *Verses from 1929 On* by Ogden Nash, by permission of Little, Brown and Co. Also by permission of The Estate of Ogden Nash and J. M. Dent and Sons.

[6] See Claire Russell and W. M. S. Russell, "Language and Animal Signals" in Noel Muhnis, ed., *Linguistics at Large,* (New York: Viking Press, 1971), pp. 159–194.

ing light. The male could see neither the lights nor the female. The task was as follows: If the continuous light was shown, the female had to press a right-hand paddle and "inform" the male by her calls to press his right-hand paddle too. If a flashing light appeared, the female had to press the left-hand paddle and again call out to the male to press his left-hand paddle. Only if both responded correctly would they be rewarded with fish. Remember that the male could not see either the light or the female. His response had to result solely from the signals he received from the female. It first appeared that the dolphins were indeed signaling each other. But later it became clear that they had learned their tasks as "conditioned responses," and had behaved more like Pavlov's dogs than communicating humans.

The great Russian physiologist Pavlov trained dogs to salivate when they heard a bell by giving them food whenever a bell rang, repeating this action over a long period of time. They became "conditioned" to salivate whenever they heard bells ringing, whether or not food followed the bells. Similarly, the female dolphin kept on pushing her paddles and producing her calls even when the male could see the lights for himself, and in fact even when the male was taken out of the tank. Her calls therefore had little to do with her desire to communicate with the male. She performed because she had been conditioned into believing the paddle-pressing and signal-giving would reward *her* with fish. She didn't really seem to care whether the male was fed or not. The male was no smarter. He had become conditioned to associate a certain paddle with a certain call, having learned that that would fill his stomach.

Such studies of animal communication systems provide evidence for Descartes' distinction between the fixed stimulus-bound messages of animals, and the creative linguistic ability possessed by the human animal.

The Chimpanzees

Children, behold the Chimpanzee:
  He sits on the ancestral tree
  From which we sprang in ages gone.
I'm glad we sprang: had we held on,
We might, for aught that I can say,
Be horrid Chimpanzees to-day.
OLIVER HERFORD, "A Child's Primer of Natural History"

The more nonprimate animal communication systems we examine, the more sure we become that language is a human characteristic. Those systems seem to be either a nonproductive limited set of fixed messages, or emotionally conditioned cries.

The attempt to teach animals to communicate failed in the case of the dolphins. There are other cases which have proved to be somewhat more successful. In the 1930s Winthrop and Luella Kellogg raised their infant son together with an infant chimpanzee named Gua.[7] Gua understood

---

[7] W. N. Kellogg and Luella A. Kellogg, *The Ape and the Child* (New York: McGraw-Hill, 1933).

about 100 words at sixteen months, more words than their son at that age. But she never went beyond that. And as we have already seen, comprehension of language involves much more than understanding the meanings of isolated words. When their son could understand the difference between *I say what I mean* and *I mean what I say,* Gua could not understand what either sentence meant.

A chimpanzee named Viki was raised by Keith and Cathy Hayes, and she too learned a number of individual words.[8] She even learned to "articulate" with great difficulty the words *mama, papa,* and *cup.* But that was the extent of her language production.

Allen and Beatrice Gardner recognized that one disadvantage suffered by the primates is the absence of a sufficiently complex system of articulatory organs necessary for producing aural contrasts. They therefore decided to teach sign language to a chimpanzee named Washoe.[9] By age 5, when the Gardners ended the experiment, Washoe understood and produced well over 100 signs with such meanings as "more," "eat," "listen," "gimme," "please," "key," "you," and "me." These results are remarkable and bring up the question of whether Washoe's accomplishments are comparable to a deaf child's learning sign language. There is much debate concerning this question. The answer depends to a great extent on what characteristics of human language are being considered. Washoe to this day does not seem to have acquired a grammar equivalent in complexity to the grammars of sign or spoken languages.

Another remarkable chimp, named Sarah, was taught a sort of language by David Premack, a psychologist at the University of California, Santa Barbara.[10] The units of Sarah's "language" consist of differently shaped and colored plastic symbols which are metal-backed. Sarah and her trainers "talk" to each other by arranging these symbols on a magnetic board. Sarah has been taught to associate particular symbols with particular meanings. These symbols are the "words" or "morphemes" of Sarah's language. Thus a small red square means "banana" and a small blue rectangle means "apricot." Some of these symbols are shown in Figure 3-3. These and others reveal that Sarah has words corresponding to English nouns, adjectives, and verbs. She even has symbols for abstract concepts like "same as" and "different from," "negation," and even a symbol to represent "question."

The forms of these symbols are *arbitrarily* related to their meanings. For example, the color red is represented by a gray chip, and the color yellow by a black chip. Sarah has learned the concepts "name of" and "color of." Premack is able to ask Sarah for "the color of name of blue" (that is, the color of the plastic chip that means "blue"). Sarah selects the gray plastic chip which means "red," since red is the color of the chip that means "blue." We can see that Sarah is even capable of using language as a metalanguage to describe her language. If you're confused, remember that a "dumb" chimpanzee named Sarah has no difficulty with this task.

[8] Catherine Hayes, *The Ape in Our House* (New York: Harper, 1951).
[9] R. A. Gardner and B. T. Gardner, "Teaching Sign Language to a Chimpanzee," *Science* 165 (Aug. 1969).
[10] Ann James Premack and David Premack, "Teaching Language to an Ape," *Scientific American* (Oct. 1972).

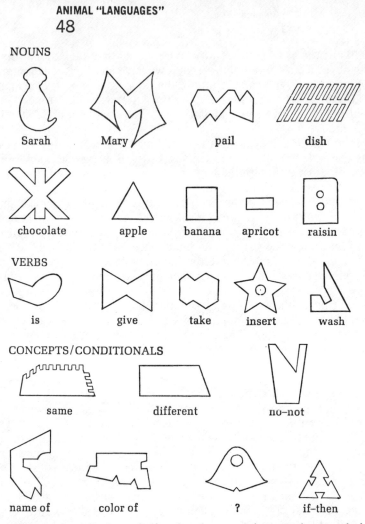

NOUNS

Sarah   Mary   pail   dish

chocolate   apple   banana   apricot   raisin

VERBS

is   give   take   insert   wash

CONCEPTS/CONDITIONALS

same   different   no–not

name of   color of   ?   if–then

Figure 3-3 Plastic symbols that varied in color, shape, and size were chosen as the language units to be taught to Sarah. The plastic pieces were backed with metal so they would adhere to a magnetic board. Each plastic symbol stood for a specific word or concept. A "Chinese" convention of writing sentences vertically from top to bottom was adopted because at the beginning of her training Sarah seemed to prefer it. Sarah had to put the words in proper sequence, but the orientation of the word symbols was not important. Actually, most of these symbols were colored. (Adapted from "Teaching Language to an Ape" by Ann James Premack and David Premack, *Scientific American,* Oct. 1972; copyright © 1972 by Scientific American, Inc.; all rights reserved)

Indeed, such "conversations" occasionally bore Sarah. During a particularly tedious drill one time, Sarah reached out and stole all the plastic tokens. Then, as if to suggest "let's get the whole thing over with," she wrote out all the questions she was being asked as well as the corresponding answers. This was very clever, showing that Sarah knew the questions and the answers. But she did not (and probably could not) write out "no questions" even though she had a "word" for "no" and for "question."

She is able to form new sentences, but only in the exact form of those she has been carefully taught.

Yet, Sarah seems to have mastered some rules of syntax. And, as with children, no one specifically taught her these rules. She generalized from the data. For example, given the sentence *If Sarah put red on green, Mary give Sarah chocolate,* Sarah will dutifully place a red card on top of a green card and collect her reward. The sentence *If Sarah put green on red, Mary give Sarah chocolate* also evokes the correct response. Sarah is quite obviously sensitive to word order—that is, the "syntax" of the sentences.

Sarah is also able to understand some complex sentence structures. She was taught to respond correctly to sentences such as *Sarah insert apple pail* (that is, "Sarah, insert the apple in the pail"), *Sarah insert banana pail, Sarah insert apple dish,* and *Sarah insert banana dish.* These sentences were then combined into *Sarah insert apple pail Sarah insert banana dish.* Sarah performed both tasks. Then a "transformational rule" was performed on this sentence by the trainer, which deleted the second occurrence of *Sarah insert* (see Chapter 8 on syntax for similar rules in our language). This transformed sentence given to Sarah was *Sarah insert apple pail banana dish.* Sarah still performed the complicated instruction, showing that she "understood" the "underlying" compound sentence. She correctly grouped together *apple* with *pail* and *banana* with *dish* rather than incorrectly grouping *pail* with *banana,* and she did not put the apple, pail, and banana in the dish, as the word order would suggest. Thus we see that when Sarah processes a sentence she does more than link words in simple linear order. She imposes subgroupings on the words, just as we do.

Does Sarah disprove the notion that only humans can learn language? Sarah's language certainly seems to include many of the properties of human language: arbitrariness of the linguistic sign, "open-endedness," subgrouping rules.

One major difference between the way Sarah has learned her language and the way children learn theirs is that each new rule was introduced in a deliberate, highly constrained way. When parents speak to children they do not confine themselves to a few words in a particular order for months, rewarding the child with a chocolate bar or a banana each time the child correctly responds to a command. Nor do they wait until the child has "mastered" one rule of grammar before going on to a different structure.

Young children require no special training. Children brought up with little adult "reinforcement" or encouragement will acquire all the complexities of their language. This is demonstrated by children brought up in orphan homes or institutions. Of course, exposure to language is required. Feral children such as those raised by animals do not learn language, as pointed out in Chapter 2. Normal children, while they require exposure to language, are not taught language the way Sarah is being taught.

The differences between Sarah's language acquisition and that of normal human children in no way negate the great achievement on Sarah's part and also on the part of Dr. Premack. At this time we do not know how much more Sarah will learn. We do know that a child by the age of four has already learned complex rules and a grammar qualitatively beyond what Sarah has mastered.

There were drawbacks to the Sarah experiment. Sarah was not allowed to "talk" spontaneously, but only in response to her trainers. And there was the possibility that her trainers unwittingly provided cues, which Sarah responded to rather than the plastic chips. To avoid these and other problems, Lana, a 2½-year-old chimpanzee, is being taught a language similar to Sarah's, but with some differences.[11]

Instead of being taught to arrange plastic chips, Lana is taught to push buttons on a computer console located in her room. On each button is drawn a symbol (called a *lexigram*) that represents a meaning similar to Sarah's plastic chips. The buttons have to be pushed in just the right order to produce a grammatical sentence in "Yerkish." A computer monitors the console twenty-four hours a day and records all "conversations" between Lana and her trainers. The computer is also programmed to respond to Lana's requests for food, water, ventilation, entertainment, and so on. An example of a sentence addressed to the machine is:

> please machine give Lana piece of apple

Like Sarah, Lana appears to have mastered some essential aspects of human language. She has learned that objects have names and that the name and the object are arbitrarily related. (The symbol for apple doesn't resemble an apple. Each lexigram is a composite of one or a combination of nine different geometric shapes placed on a background which can be one of three different colors.) She has also learned to regard word order as significant in producing composite meanings.

Despite the remarkable achievements of Sarah, Lana, and their trainers, it is still too early to say whether either chimp has mastered a human-language-like system. For one thing, neither the plastic-chip language nor the lexigram language is particularly human-language-like. For another, both Sarah and Lana were brought up in relative isolation, and rather than learning their language through natural social contact, interspersed with informal training sessions (as in the case of a human child), they were rigorously trained under stimulus-response techniques. Because of these and other drawbacks, many researchers feel that sign language—a human language—will provide the truest test of the linguistic abilities of chimpanzees.

At least ten chimpanzees and one gorilla have learned some sign language, including Washoe. One of the most promising of these is Nim Chimpsky[12] (named, we have no doubt, after the linguist Noam Chomsky). Nim's trainers are paying very close attention to his word order

[11] D. M. Rumbaugh and E. C. von Glasersfeld, "Reading and Sentence Completion by a Chimpanzee," *Science* 182 (1973), 731–733.

D. M. Rumbaugh and T. V. Gill, "The Mastery of Language-Type Skills by the Chimpanzee." Paper presented at Conference on Origins and Evolution of Language and Speech, New York Academy of Sciences, September 1975.

D. M. Rumbaugh, *Acquisition of Linguistic Skills by a Chimpanzee* (New York: Academic Press, 1977).

[12] H. S. Terrace and T. G. Bever, "What Might Be Learned from Studying Language in the Chimpanzee? The Importance of Symbolizing Oneself." Paper presented at Conference on Origins and Evolution of Language and Speech, New York Academy of Sciences, September 1975.

and the length of his sentences. They are also comparing Nim's acquisition of sign language with that of deaf children, something the Gardners did not do with Washoe.

At the time of this writing, many questions raised by these experiments remain unanswered. One important question is whether the ability to learn language is simply the result of greater general cognitive ability or whether it is due to a specific "language-learning" ability. The human animal appears to possess a brain capable of far greater analytic and synthetic abilities than does the chimpanzee, or any other animal. "Stupid" humans are far "smarter" than "smart" chimpanzees. And no animal language or communicative system has developed that is remotely as complex as human language, even with the intervention of human teachers. If other species have the ability equivalent to the human language-ability, one wonders why it has never been put to use. It thus seems that the kind of language learned and used by humans remains unique to the species.

SUMMARY

If language is defined merely as a system of communication, then language is not unique to humans. There are, however, certain characteristics of human language which are not found in the communication systems of any other species. A basic property of human language is its creative aspect—a speaker's ability to string together **discrete units** to form an **infinite** set of "well-formed" novel sentences. Also, children need not be taught language in any controlled way; they require only linguistic input to enable them to form their own grammar.

The fact that deaf children learn language shows that the ability to hear or produce sounds is not a necessary prerequisite for language learning. And the ability to "imitate" the sounds of human language is not a sufficient basis for the learning of language, since "talking" birds imitate sounds but can neither segment these sounds into smaller units nor understand what they are imitating.

Birds, bees, crabs, wolves, dolphins, and most other animals communicate in some way. Limited information is imparted, and emotions such as fear, and warnings, are emitted. But the communication systems are fixed and limited. They are **stimulus-bound.** This is not so of human language. Experiments to teach animals more complicated language systems have a history of failure. Recently, however, some primates have demonstrated an ability to learn more complex systems. It is possible that the higher primates have the limited ability to be taught *some* complex rules. To date, however, language still seems to be unique to humans.

EXERCISES

1. What do the barking of dogs, the meowing of cats, and the singing of birds have in common with human language? What are some of the basic differences?

2. What is meant by the "arbitrary nature of the linguistic sign"? Describe at least one animal system of communication which includes arbitrary signs. Describe

any communication system in which all the signs are nonarbitrary. State the reasons for your choices in all cases.

3. Suppose you heard someone say: "My parrot speaks excellent English. He even says such complicated sentences as *I want jam with my cracker*." Give reasons for or against this assertion.

4. A wolf is able to express very subtle gradations of expression by different positions of the ears, the lips, and the tail. There are eleven postures of the tail which express such emotions as self-confidence, confident threat, lack of tension, uncertain threat, depression, defensiveness, active submission, complete submission. This seems to be a complex system. Suppose there were a thousand different emotions which could be expressed in this way. Would you then say a wolf had language similar to a human? If not, why not?

5. Suppose you taught a dog to *heel, sit up, beg, roll over, play dead, stay, jump,* and *bark* on command, using the italicized words as cues. Would you be teaching it language? Why or why not?

6. What are the properties of Sarah's language which make it more like human language than like other animal languages?

7. Why is a normal, human-child-like social environment important for a chimpanzee learning sign language? Or why is it not?

8. Suppose that Nim and a female chimpanzee learn sign language, and later, bear offspring. Is the question of whether they teach their offspring sign language a crucial one?

References

Bronowski, J., and Ursula Bellugi. "Language, Name, and Concept," *Science* 168 (May 1970).

Busnel, R. H. G., ed. *Animal Sonar Systems: Biology and Bionics,* vol. 2. Jouy-en-Josas, France, 1966.

Gardner, R. A., and B. T. Gardner. "Teaching Sign Language to a Chimpanzee," *Science* 165 (Aug. 1969).

Hayes, Catherine. *The Ape in Our House*. New York: Harper, 1951.

Krough, August. "The Language of the Bees," in *Scientific American Reader*. New York: Simon and Schuster, 1953.

Lilly, John C. *Man and Dolphin*. New York: Pyramid Publications, 1969.

Lilly, John C. *The Mind of the Dolphin: A Nonhuman Intelligence*. New York: Avon Books, 1969.

Linden, Eugene. *Apes, Men, and Language*. New York: Penguin, 1974.

Premack, Ann J., and D. Premack. "Teaching Language to an Ape," *Scientific American* (Oct. 1972), pp. 92–99.

Premack, David. "The Education of Sarah: A Chimp Learns the Language," *Psychology Today* 4 (Sept. 1970).

Premack, David. "Language in the Chimpanzee?" *Science* 172 (May 1971), pp. 808–822.

Rumbaugh, D. M., *Acquisition of Linguistic Skills by a Chimpanzee*. New York: Academic Press, 1977.

Sebeok, T. A., and Alexandra Ramsay, eds. *Approaches to Animal Communica-tion*. The Hague: Mouton, 1969.

Thorpe, W. H. "Animal Vocalization and Communication," in C. H. Millikan and F. L. Darley, eds., *Brain Mechanisms Underlying Speech and Language*. New York: Grune and Stratton, 1967.

Von Frisch, K. *The Dance Language and Orientation of Bees,* trans. by L. E. Chadwick, Cambridge, Mass.: Belknap Press of Harvard University Press, 1967.

The Sounds of
Language: Phonetics

The voice is articulated by the lips and the tongue. . . .
Man speaks by means of the air which he inhales into his
entire body and particularly into the body cavities. When
the air is expelled through the empty space it produces a
sound, because of the resonances in the skull. The tongue
articulates by its strokes; it gathers the air in the throat
and pushes it against the palate and the teeth, thereby
giving the sound a definite shape. If the tongue would not
articulate each time, by means of its strokes, man would
not speak clearly and would only be able to produce a few
simple sounds.
HIPPOCRATES, *De Carnibus*, VIII

When we hear a language that we do not know, it sounds like gibberish. We don't know where one word ends and another begins. And even if we did we couldn't say what the sentence means.

In using language to speak or understand, the sounds produced or heard are related by the language system to certain meanings. Anyone who knows a language knows what sounds are in the language and how they are "strung" together and what these different sound sequences mean. Although the sounds of French or Xhosa or Quechua are uninterpretable to someone who does not speak those languages, and although there may be some sounds in one language that are not in another, all the languages of the world together comprise a limited set of sounds.

The study of these speech sounds, utilized by all human languages to represent meanings, is called **phonetics.** To describe speech sounds one has to decide what an "individual sound" is and how one sound differs from another.

This is not as easy as it may seem. You "know" there are three sounds in the word *cat,* one represented by *c,* one by *a,* and one by *t.* Yet, physically the word is just one continuous sound. You can *segment* the one sound into parts because you know the language. If you heard someone clearing his throat you would be unable to segment the sounds into a sequence of discrete units. When you speak you do not produce one sound, and then another, and then another. If you want to say *cat* you don't utter each sound separately; you move your organs of speech continuously, and you produce a continuous sound.

Despite the fact that the sounds we produce and the sounds we hear and comprehend are continuous signals, everyone who has ever attempted to analyze language has accepted the notion that speech utterances can be segmented into individual pieces. According to an ancient Hindu myth, the god Indra, in response to an appeal made by the other gods, attempted for the first time to break speech up into its separate elements. After he accomplished this feat, according to the myth, the sounds could be regarded as language. Indra thus was the first phonetician.

The early Greeks recognized the continual, ever-changing nature of the speech signal. Perhaps this is why they considered Hermes, the messenger of the gods who was always on the move, to be the god of speech. But the fleeting nature of the continually changing sound did not prevent the Greeks from attempting linguistic analysis. Hermogenes, one of the characters in Plato's *Cratylus* dialogue, asks if language can be analyzed by taking it to pieces, and Socrates answers that there is no better way to proceed.

In this sense music is similar to speech. A person who has not studied music cannot write the sequence of individual notes combined by a violinist into one changing continuous sound. A trained musician, however, finds it a simple task. Every human speaker, without special training, can segment a speech signal; when we learn the language we learn to segment an utterance into its basic discrete elements of sound.

To analyze speech into pieces one cannot start with just the acoustic physical signal, or even with the movements of the vocal organs used to produce speech. Where would the breaks come? The difficulties inherent in such an attempt would be complicated, in addition, because no two speakers ever say the "same thing" identically. In fact, the same speaker never says the "same thing" twice in exactly the same way. Yet speakers understand each other because they know the same language. One's knowledge of a language determines when physically different sounds are judged to be the same.

We have already asserted that language and speech are not identical. Our linguistic knowledge, or competence, imposes a system on the sounds produced and heard.

We are capable of making many sounds which we know instinctively (because we know the language) are not speech sounds in our language. An English speaker can and often does make a clicking sound which writers sometimes represent as *tsk tsk tsk*. But these sounds are not part of the English sound system. They never occur as part of the words of the sentences we produce. In fact, it is very difficult for many English speakers to combine this clicking sound with other sounds as Xhosa speakers do. But a click is a speech sound in Xhosa, Zulu, Sotho, Hottentot, just like the *k* or *t* or *b* in English.

Therefore, what is or is not an individual speech sound depends on the particular language. *Tsk* is a speech sound in Xhosa but not in English; *th* is a sound in English but not in French. But the sound we produce with our mouth closed when we have a tickle in our throats is not a speech sound in *any* language, nor is the sound we produce when we sneeze.

The science of phonetics attempts to describe all the sounds used in language—the sounds that constitute a small but extremely important fraction of the totality of sounds that human beings are capable of producing.

The process by which we use our linguistic knowledge to produce a meaningful utterance is a very complicated one. It can be viewed as a chain of events starting with an "idea" or message in the brain of the speaker and ending with the same message in the brain of the hearer. The message is put into a form that is dictated by the language we are speaking. It must then be transmitted by nerve signals to the organs of speech articulation which produce the different physical sounds heard by the listener.

Speech sounds can be described at any stage in this chain of events. The study of the physical properties of the sounds themselves is called **acoustic phonetics.** The study and description of the shapes of the vocal tract which produce the different sounds is called **articulatory phonetics.** One can also study and describe speech sounds in terms of the nerves and muscles used to produce the different articulatory shapes.

The Phonetic Alphabet

B.C.   by johnny hart

By permission of Johnny Hart and Field Enterprises, Inc.

Once a Frenchman who'd promptly said "Oui"
To some ladies who'd asked him if houi
Cared to drink, threw a fit
Upon finding that it
Was a tipple no stronger than toui.
ANONYMOUS

The one-l lama,
He's a priest.
The two-l llama,
He's a beast.

And I will bet
A silk pajama
There isn't any
Three-l lllama.
OGDEN NASH[1]

---

[1]"The Lama," copyright 1931 by Ogden Nash. From *Verses from 1929 On* by Ogden Nash, by permission of Little, Brown and Co. Also by permission of The Estate of Ogden Nash and J. M. Dent & Sons. This poem originally appeared in *The New Yorker*.

All languages contain sounds with different physical properties. So-called dead languages are no exception. We have approximate knowledge of the speech sounds produced by speakers of languages such as Sumerian, Sanskrit, and Latin because written records are extant. The written records represent the sounds which were used by speakers.

Alphabetic spelling represents the pronunciations of words. But it is often the case that the sounds of the words in a language are rather unsystematically represented by **orthography**—that is, by spelling.

Suppose all Earthlings were destroyed by some horrible catastrophe, and years later Martian astronauts exploring Earth discovered some fragments of English writing that included the following sentence:

Did h*e* bel*ie*ve that C*ae*sar could s*ee* the p*eo*ple s*ei*ze the s*ea*s?

How would a Martian linguist decide that *e, ie, ae, ee, eo, ei,* and *ea* all represented the same sound? To add to his confusion, he might later stumble across this sentence:

The sill*y* am*oe*ba stole the k*ey* to the mach*i*ne.

English speakers know the pronunciation of these words and know that *y, oe, ey,* and *i* also represent the same sound as the italicized letters in the first sentence. But how could a Martian know this?

This inconsistent spelling system prompted Ambrose Bierce to define *orthography* as "the science of spelling by the eye instead of the ear." When Mark Twain wrote: "They spell it Vinci and pronounce it Vinchy; foreigners always spell better than they pronounce,"[2] he was fully aware that it is not just "foreigners" whose spelling differs from pronunciation.

The discrepancy between spelling and sounds gave rise to a movement of English "spelling reformers." They wanted to revise the alphabet so that one letter would correspond to one sound, and one sound to one letter, thus simplifying spelling. This is a **phonetic alphabet.**

George Bernard Shaw followed in the footsteps of three centuries of spelling reformers in England. In typical Shavian manner he pointed out that we could use the English spelling system to spell *fish* as *ghoti*—the *gh* like the sound in *enough,* the *o* like the sound in *women,* and the *ti* like the sound in *nation.* Shaw was so concerned about English spelling that he included in his will a provision for a new "Proposed British Alphabet" to be administered by a "Public Trustee" who would have the duty of seeking and publishing a more efficient alphabet. This alphabet was to have at least forty letters to enable "the said language to be written without indicating single sounds by groups of letters or by diacritical marks." After Shaw's death in 1950, 450 designs for such an alphabet were submitted from all parts of the globe. Four alphabets were judged to be equally good, and the £500 prize was divided among their designers. An "expert" collaborated with these four to produce the alphabet designated in Shaw's will. Shaw also stipulated in his will that his play *Androcles and the Lion* be published in the new alphabet, with "the original Doctor Johnson's lettering opposite the transliteration page by page and a glossary of the two alphabets." This version of the play was published in 1962.

This new alphabet was not the first phonetic alphabet. In 1617, Robert

[2]Ambrose Bierce, *The Devil's Dictionary*; Mark Twain, *The Innocents Abroad.*

Robinson produced an alphabet which attempted to provide a relationship between "articulation" and the shapes of the letters. In 1657, Cave Beck produced *A Universal Character,* a publication described on its title page as "The Universal Character by which all the Nations in the World may understand one another's Conceptions, Reading out of one Common Writing their own Mother Tongues." In 1668, Bishop John Wilkins proposed a similar universal alphabet; and in 1686, Francis Lodwick published "An Essay Towards an Universal Alphabet," which he had worked out and circulated many years before. Lodwick's aim was to provide an alphabet "which should contain an Enumeration of all such Single Sounds or Letters as are used in any Language. . . . All single sounds ought to have single and distinct characters" and no one character shall "have more than one Sound, nor any one Sound be expressed by more than one Character." Lodwick, like Cave Beck before him and others who followed him, did not use Roman letters. He designed his own "letters" in such a way that similar sounds were represented by similar symbols. Even in Shaw's lifetime, the phonetician Henry Sweet, the prototype for Shaw's own Henry Higgins, produced a phonetic alphabet.

If we look at English spelling, it is easy to understand why there has been so much concern about spelling systems. Different letters may represent a single sound, as shown in the following:

  t*o* t*oo* tw*o* thr*ough* thr*ew* cl*ue* sh*oe*

A single letter may represent different sounds:

  d*a*me d*a*d f*a*ther c*a*ll vill*a*ge m*a*ny

A combination of letters may represent a single sound:

*sh*oot	*ch*aracter	*Th*omas	*ph*ysics
ei*th*er	de*a*l	rou*gh*	na*ti*on
*c*oat	gla*ci*al	*th*eater	pl*ai*n

Some letters have no sound at all in certain words in which they occur:

*m*nemonic	*w*hole	resi*g*n	*gh*ost
*p*terodactyl	*w*rite	hol*e*	corp*s*
*p*sychology	s*w*ord	de*b*t	*g*naw
bou*gh*	lam*b*	i*s*land	*k*nife

Some sounds are not represented in the spelling. In many words the letter *u* represents a *y* sound followed by a *u* sound:

  c*u*te (compare: l*oo*t)
  f*u*tile (compare: f*oo*l)
  *u*tility (compare: *oo*ze)

One letter may represent two sounds; the final *x* in *Xerox* represents a *k* followed by an *s*.

All these discrepancies between spelling and sounds seem to argue in favor of the spelling reformers. One may wonder why they didn't win their struggle. One may also wonder how such a chaotic spelling system arose.

The inventor of printing is a major culprit. When scribes used to write manuscripts they would often write words more or less as they pronounced them. But after the invention of printing, the spelling of words became relatively fixed. The present English spelling system is very much like that used in Shakespeare's time, although pronunciation has changed considerably. Pronunciation changes much more rapidly than spelling. What would we do with all the millions of books printed in English if we attempted to change all the spelling to conform to present pronunciation? Even if these books were reprinted and a law passed requiring all new books to conform to some new system of spelling, it would not be too long before the same problem would occur again.

To illustrate how spelling represents an older pronunciation, consider the words *knight* and *night*. They are pronounced identically today. At one time, the *k* was pronounced in the first word and the *gh* in both. At some point in the history of the English language we stopped pronouncing a *k* when it occurred at the beginning of a word and was followed by *n*. As for the sound spelled *gh* in words like *right,* it was once pronounced like the last sound in the German word *Bach*. This sound disappeared completely in many dialects of English, including most American English dialects.

If the spelling reformers could legislate an end to language change, then maybe their plan would be feasible. But this is impossible. Language is continually changing, and this change, apart from making spelling systems obsolete, also creates different dialects of the same language. An additional problem for the reformers is to determine which dialect the spelling should reflect. Should the same word of British and American English be spelled differently if pronounced differently? If not, how should a word like *schedule* be spelled? The British pronounce it as if it were spelled *shedyule* and the Americans pronounce it as if it were spelled *skedjule* or *skejual*. Such pronunciations lend some credence to Shaw's remark: "England and America are two countries separated by the same language." Even if the spelling reformers decided to spell British and American English differently, what would they do with the American dialects? Should *Cuba* be spelled *Cuber* with a final *r,* as President Kennedy pronounced it, or without the *r*? What about the words *cot* and *caught* or *horse* and *hoarse* or *pin* and *pen*? Some Americans pronounce these pairs identically, and others pronounce them differently.

There are further arguments against the spelling reformers, some of which will be discussed in later chapters. In any case, although English spelling does create some difficulties for children learning to read and write (as well as for many adult "poor spellers"), the system is not quite as chaotic as it appears to be.

But whether or not one wishes to take sides for or against spelling reform in English, it is clear that to describe the sounds of English, or any other language, one cannot depend on the spelling of words. In 1888 the International Phonetic Association (IPA) developed a phonetic alphabet which could be used to symbolize the sounds found in all languages. Since many languages use a Roman alphabet like that used in the English writing system, the IPA phonetic symbols are based on the Roman letters. These phonetic symbols have a consistent value, unlike ordinary letters, which

may or may not represent the same sounds in the same or different
languages.

It is of course impossible to construct any set of symbols which will
specify all the minute differences between sounds. Even Shaw recognized
this when in his will he directed his Trustee

> to bear in mind that the proposed British Alphabet does not pretend to be
> exhaustive as it contains only sixteen vowels whereas by infinitesimal
> movements of the tongue countless different vowels can be produced all
> of them in use among speakers of English who utter the same vowels no
> oftener than they make the same fingerprints.

Even if we could specify all the details of different pronunciations, we
would not want to. A basic fact about speech is that no two utterances are
ever physically the same. That is, if a speaker says "Good morning" on
Monday and Tuesday there will be some slight differences in the sounds
he produces on the two days. In fact if he says "Good morning" twice in
succession on the same day, the two utterances will not be physically identical. If another speaker says "Good morning" the physical sounds (that
is, the acoustic signal) produced will differ widely from that produced by
the first speaker. Yet all the "Good mornings" are considered to be repetitions of the same utterance.

This is an interesting fact about knowing a language. One knows that
some differences in the sounds of an utterance are important, and other differences can be ignored. Even though we never produce or hear exactly
the same utterance twice, we know when two utterances are linguistically
the same or different. Some properties of the sounds must be more important than others. In describing the sounds of a language, we want to reveal
those characteristics that all speakers of a language recognize as important
in understanding each other.

A phonetic alphabet should include enough symbols to represent the
"crucial" differences. At the same time it should not, and cannot, include
all noncrucial differences, since such differences are infinitely varied.

A list of phonetic symbols which can be used to represent all the basic
speech sounds of English is given on pages 61–63. The symbols omit many
details about the sounds and how they are produced in different words, and
in different places in words. These symbols are meant to be used by persons knowing English.

For example, in English the *p* in *pit* and the *p* in *spit* are physically
different sounds. The same difference occurs in the *t* in *tick* and the *t* in
stick, and the *k* in *kit* and the *k* in *skit.* When a *p, t,* or *k* occurs at the
beginning of a word, the consonant is followed by a puff of air (called **aspiration**). We can symbolize these **aspirated** sounds by p^h, t^h, and k^h. The
fact that most speakers of English do not realize that they produce different
sounds represented by *p, t,* or *k* reflects the rules of the English sound system which will be discussed in Chapter 5. In the list on pages 61–63 we will
omit phonetic details of this kind; thus, we will represent both the *p* and
the p^h as *p*.

To differentiate between the spelling of a word and the pronunciation
we will sometimes enclose the phonetic symbols in brackets [ ]. Thus the
word spelled *boat* would be **transcribed phonetically** as [bot]. As discussed

above, the phonetic transcription may omit some details, such as the aspiration of the first sound in *cake*. A more detailed phonetic transcription would be [kʰek] (which is sometimes called a **narrow** phonetic transcription); a less detailed phonetic transcription would be [kek] (which is sometimes called a **broad** phonetic transcription).

The list of phonetic symbols for consonants, vowels, and diphthongs includes a number of examples of English words given in English spelling. In all cases the different spellings represent the same sound in the American dialect being described. Some of these pronunciations may differ from yours, and in a number of cases where this is so the examples may be confusing. For example, some speakers of American English pronounce the words *cot* and *caught* identically. In the dialect described here, *cot* and *caught* are pronounced differently, so *cot* is given as an example for the symbol [a] and *caught* for the symbol [ɔ]. Many speakers who pronounce *cot* and *caught* identically pronounce *car* and *core* differently. If you use the vowel of *car* to say *cot* and the vowel of *core* to say *caught* you will be approximating the dialect that distinguishes the two words. There are a number of English dialects in which an *r* sound is not pronounced unless it occurs before a vowel. Speakers of this dialect would pronounce the word *bird* with a vowel not symbolized in the chart; that is [ɜ]. The phonetic transcription of *bird* for these speakers would thus be [bɜd]. The selection of the dialect described below is rather arbitrary; it is in fact a mixture of a number of dialects in the attempt to provide at least the major symbols which can be used to describe dialects of American English.

In the chart the first symbols given are those most widely used by American linguists and phoneticians; where these symbols differ from those of the International Phonetic Alphabet (IPA), the IPA symbols are given in parentheses. Although we believe that all phoneticians should adopt the IPA symbols, we will use the American symbols in this book because so many students will encounter these symbols in other American publications.

CONSONANTS

SYMBOLS	EXAMPLES
p	*p*at ta*p* *p*it s*p*it ti*p* hiccou*gh* a*pp*le am*p*le *p*rick *p*laque a*pp*ear
b	*b*at ta*b* am*b*le *b*rick *b*lack bu*bb*le
m	*m*at ta*m* s*m*ack a*m*nesia a*m*ple E*mm*y ca*m*p co*m*b
t	*t*ap pa*t* s*t*ick men*t*or p*t*erodac*t*yl scen*t*ing kiss*ed* kick*ed* stuff*ed*
d	*d*ip ca*d* *d*rip guar*d* sen*d*ing men*d*er love*d* cure*d* robbe*d* batte*d*
n	*n*ap ca*n* s*n*ow k*n*ow m*n*emonic a*n*y pi*n*t g*n*ostic desig*n* *p*neumatic sig*n* thi*n*
k	*k*it *c*at *ch*arisma *ch*arac*t*er sti*ck* *c*ritique *c*riti*c* *c*lose me*ch*anic e*x*ceed o*ch*er
g	*g*uard bur*g* ba*g* o*g*re a*g*nostic lon*g*er desi*g*nate Pitt*s*bur*gh*

SYMBOLS	EXAMPLES
ŋ	si*ng* lo*ng* thi*n*k fi*ng*er si*ng*er a*n*kle (the sound represented by the *n* in *think* is not produced in the same way as that represented by the *n* in *thin;* say the two words to yourself and notice that the tongue gestures are different)
f	*f*at *f*ish *ph*iloso*ph*y *f*racture *f*lat *ph*logiston co*ff*ee ree*f* cou*gh* com*f*ort
v	*v*at do*v*e ri*v*al gra*v*el an*v*il ra*v*age
s	*s*ap *s*kip *s*nip p*s*ychology pa*ss* pat*s* pack*s* democra*c*y *s*cissors fa*s*ten de*c*eive de*s*cent *s*clero*s*is p*s*eudo rhap*s*ody pea*c*e pota*ss*ium
z	*z*ip ja*zz* ra*z*or pad*s* ki*ss*es *X*erox *x*ylophone de*s*ign la*z*y mai*z*e lie*s* phy*s*ics pea*s* magne*s*ium
θ	*th*igh *th*rough wra*th* *th*istle e*th*er wrea*th* *th*ink mo*th* ari*th*metic Me*th*uselah tee*th* Ma*tth*ew
ð	*th*e *th*eir *th*en wrea*th*e la*th*e mo*th*er ei*th*er ra*th*er tee*th*e
š (ʃ)	*sh*oe *sh*y mu*sh* mar*sh* mi*ss*ion na*ti*on fi*sh* gla*ci*al *s*ure deduc*ti*on Ru*ss*ian logi*ci*an
ž (ʒ)	mea*s*ure vi*s*ion a*z*ure rou*ge* (for those who do not pronounce this word with the same ending sound as in *judge*) ca*s*ualty deci*s*ion Carte*s*ian
č, tš (tʃ)	*ch*oke *ch*ur*ch* ma*tch* fea*t*ure ri*ch* lun*ch* righ*te*ous consti*t*uent
ǰ, dž (dʒ)	*j*udge mid*g*et *G*eorge ma*g*istrate *j*ello *g*elatine re*g*ion resi*d*ual
l	*l*eaf fee*l* *l*ock ca*ll* pa*l*ace sing*l*e mi*l*d p*l*ant pu*l*p app*l*aud
r	*r*eef fea*r* *r*ock ca*r* Pa*r*is singe*r* p*r*une ca*r*p fu*r*l c*r*uel
y (j)*	*y*ou *y*es ba*y* pla*y*ing fe*u*d *u*se
w	*w*itch s*w*im mo*w*ing q*u*een
ʍ	*wh*ich *wh*ere *wh*at *wh*ale (for those dialects that do not pronounce *witch* and *which* the same)
h	*wh*o *h*at re*h*ash *h*ole *wh*ole
ʔ	bo*tt*le bu*tt*on La*t*in glo*tt*al (only for the dialect whose speakers substitute for the *tt* sound the sound which occurs between the vowels as in *uh-uh*)

VOWELS

SYMBOLS	EXAMPLES
i	b*ee*t b*ea*t w*e* s*ee* s*ea* rec*ei*ve k*ey* bel*ie*ve am*oe*ba p*eo*ple C*ae*sar vasel*i*ne ser*e*ne f*ie*nd mon*ey* lil*y*

* The American practice of representing this sound as [y] creates some problems: [y] is the IPA symbol to represent a vowel such as is found in the French word *tu*. It will be described below.

SYMBOLS	EXAMPLES
ɪ (ι)	b*i*t cons*i*st *i*njury mal*i*gnant b*i*n b*ee*n
e	b*a*te b*ai*t r*ay* prof*a*ne gr*ea*t *ai*r *eig*ht g*au*ge r*ai*n r*ei*gn th*ey*
ɛ	b*e*t s*e*renity rec*e*ption s*ay*s g*ue*st d*ea*d s*ai*d
æ	p*a*n *a*ct l*au*gh *a*nger l*a*boratory (American English) comr*a*de r*a*lly
u	b*oo*t wh*o* s*ew*er d*u*ty thr*ough* p*oo*r t*o* t*oo* tw*o* m*o*ve L*ou*
ʊ (ω)	p*u*t f*oo*t b*u*tcher c*ou*ld
ʌ	b*u*t t*ou*gh am*o*ng *o*ven d*oe*s c*o*ver fl*oo*d
o	b*oa*t g*o* b*eau* gr*ow* th*ough* t*oe* *ow*n *o*ver mel*o*dious
ɔ	b*ou*ght c*au*ght wr*o*ng st*a*lk c*o*re s*aw* b*a*ll *au*thor *aw*e
a	p*o*t f*a*ther p*a*lm c*a*r s*e*rgeant *ho*nor h*o*spital mel*o*dic
ə†	sof*a* *a*lone princ*i*pal sci*e*nce tel*e*graph symph*o*ny ros*e*s diffic*u*lt s*u*ppose mel*o*dy mel*o*di*ou*s want*e*d kiss*e*s th*e* f*a*ther b*i*rd h*e*rd w*o*rd f*u*r

DIPHTHONGS

SYMBOLS	EXAMPLES
ay	b*i*te s*i*ght b*y* d*ie* d*y*e St*ei*n *ai*sle ch*oi*r l*i*ar *i*sland h*eig*ht *si*gn
æw, aw‡	ab*ou*t br*ow*n d*ou*bt c*ow*ard
ɔy	b*oy* d*oi*ly

Using these symbols, we can now unambiguously represent the pronunciations of words. For example, words spelled with *ou* may have different pronunciations. To distinguish between the symbols representing sounds and the alphabet letters, we put the phonetic symbols between brackets, as discussed above and as is illustrated by the following:

SPELLING	PRONUNCIATION
though	[ðo]
thought	[θɔt]
tough	[tʌf]
bough	[baw]
through	[θru]
could	[kʊd]

Notice that only in *tough* do the letters *gh* represent any sound; that is, the sound [f]. Notice also that *ou* represents six different sounds, and *th*

†The vowel italicized in "ros*e*s" is phonetically more properly symbolized as [ɪ] or [i] to distinguish it from the italicized vowel in "Ros*a*'s." There are even finer distinctions that can be made for the unstressed, "reduced" vowels, but these may be ignored for our purposes. Some linguists symbolize the vowel before the *r* in words like *bird, burp, verb, verve,* and *purple* by the symbol [ʌ]; others represent the vowel and the following *r* by a single symbol, [ɚ].

‡The vowel of this diphthong varies from dialect to dialect. Therefore we have included two symbols which can be used to represent the sound.

two different sounds. The *l* in *could,* like the *gh* in all but one of the words above, is not pronounced at all.

Obviously, the symbols given in the list would not be sufficient to represent the pronunciation of words in all languages. We would need other symbols for the *ch* sound in the German word *Bach* (phonetically, this symbol is [x]) and for the French vowel sound in the word *tu* ([y] or [ü]) and for many other sounds not found in the English sound system.

All of the phonetic symbols represent different sounds. The science of phonetics is concerned with the ways in which these sounds differ, and the ways in which they may be similar.

A phonetic alphabet with symbols like those presented in this chapter is useful in a discussion of the sound patterns of language. We will be using these symbols whenever we wish to refer unambiguously to the sounds of words.

Articulatory Phonetics

HIGGINS Tired of listening to sounds?
PICKERING Yes. It's a fearful strain. I rather fancied myself because I can pronounce twenty-four distinct vowel sounds, but your hundred and thirty beat me. I can't hear a bit of difference between most of them.
HIGGINS Oh, that comes with practice. You hear no difference at first; but you keep on listening, and presently you find they're all as different as A from B.
G. B. SHAW, *Pygmalion*

To understand the nature of language, how it "works," and how children learn it, it is not enough merely to list all the individual sounds and provide a symbol for each one. As noted above, almost three hundred years ago Lodwick wished to devise his alphabet in such a way as to "sort [the sounds] into classes." Thousands of years before Lodwick, the Hindu grammarians classified the sounds of Sanskrit into groups according to the ways they were pronounced.

The ways in which sounds are classified may provide some clues as to how sounds are used in language. Before we examine the properties of speech sounds, let's look at how such sounds are used in a language such as English.

Children who learn English know how to form plural nouns from singular nouns at a very early age—usually by two or three years old. This is before they have learned to write, so they don't know that one adds an *s* to form a plural. In fact this is not what anyone does in speaking, even though in writing that may be the most general rule. Now that we know the difference between spelling and pronunciation, we can state the rules that form regular plurals:

(1) Add [s] after words that end in [p, t, k, θ, f]: caps   cats   sacks   myths   muffs.

(2) Add [z] after words that end in [b, d, g, v, ð, l, r, y, w, m, n, ŋ] and all vowels: cabs cads bags dives lathes mills cars boys cows cans rams things zoos.

(3) Add [əz] after words that end in [s, z, š, ž, č, ǰ]: buses causes bushes garages beaches badges.

Say these words out loud to yourself so you can see that the "plural ending" is either [s], [z], or [əz].

Do children really have to learn the plural rule in this way—by memorizing lists of sounds in each of these classes?

A look at how the past tense of English verbs is normally formed may help us to find some "regularity" in the classes of sounds. The past-tense rules can be stated as follows:

(1) Add [t] after verbs that end in [p, k, θ, f, s, š, č]: reaped peeked unearthed huffed kissed wished pitched.

(2) Add [d] after verbs that end in [b, g, ð, v, z, ž, ǰ, n, m, ŋ, l, r, y, w] and all vowels: grabbed hugged seethed loved buzzed rouged judged manned rammed longed killed cared tied bowed hoed.

(3) Add [əd] after verbs that end in [t, d]: stated clouded.

If you compare Rule (1) of the "plural formation" with Rule (1) of the "past-tense formation" you will notice that the sounds [p], [k], [θ], [f] are used in both rules; and if you compare Rule (2) in each formation you will notice that the classes of sounds are almost identical. If the sounds were just listed, but not analyzed, this similarity might be considered accidental. On the other hand, if there are indeed some common properties among the sounds which take an [s] in the plural and a [t] in the past tense, and among the sounds that take a [z] in the plural and a [d] in the past tense, then a child need not memorize long lists of sounds, but instead may learn just which properties of the classes of sounds distinguish one class from another.

When we analyze the sounds in the different rules we find that the ones that take either an [s] plural or a [t] past tense are phonetically "voiceless," and furthermore that [s] and [t] are also "voiceless." We also find that the sounds that take a [z] plural or a [d] past tense are phonetically "voiced" sounds, and that [z] and [d] are also phonetically "voiced."

You don't know *yet* what makes a sound "voiceless" or "voiced," but it is easy to see that there is some method in what first appeared as a lot of madness.

Leaving aside for the moment the classes of sounds that form plurals and pasts by adding [əz] or [əd], the rules become much simpler:

(1) Add [z] for the plural and [d] for the past to a word ending with a voiced sound.

(2) Add [s] for the plural and [t] for the past to a word ending with a voiceless sound.

Or, more simply, we can say:

> **(3)** Add the voiceless sound to a word ending with a voiceless sound and the voiced sound to a word ending with a voiced sound.

By this rule it would appear that we should add a [t] to a verb ending with a [t] and a [d] to a verb ending with a [d]. But then it would be hard to "hear" a difference between a present and a past form of the verb. To test this, try saying the past tense of *state* by adding a [t]—you would get [stett]. We find it difficult in English to distinguish between a single [t] and two [t]'s without a vowel in between. This is not true for speakers of all languages. To distinguish the present from the past tense of these verbs the short unstressed vowel [ə] is inserted between the end of the simple verb and the [d] which represents the past tense. We can also say that [əd] is added to the verb.

The reason an [əz] is added to nouns which end in [s], [z], [š], [ž], [č], and [ǰ] to form the plural is because all these sounds are *sibilants*. The plural endings [s] and [z] are also sibilants. In English it may be difficult to "hear" the difference between a single sibilant and a sequence of sibilants. Therefore, in order to distinguish the singulars and plurals of nouns ending in sibilants, [əz] is added instead of [s] or [z]. The vowel which is symbolized as [ə] is called a **schwa.**

Thus when we analyze sounds according to certain phonetic properties, the individual sounds fall into classes, and these classes are used by speakers to form "rules" of language.

Another example will show how we find the same kinds of classes in very different languages. In English we can change some words into their opposites by adding a prefix. Thus *intolerant* means *not tolerant, impossible* means *not possible,* and *incomplete* means *not complete.* The prefix meaning "not" is pronounced [ɪn] before [t], [ɪm] before [p], and [ɪŋ] before [k]. (You might not have realized that you pronounce the *n* in *incomplete* as [ŋ], but most speakers of English do. If you say the word in normal tempo without pausing after the *in* you may notice that your tongue is in the same position as in the final sound of *sing*.)

To form a negative sentence in the Ghanaian language Twi, you add either [n], [m], or [ŋ] before the verb, as shown below:

mɪ pɛ	"I like"	mɪ mpɛ	"I don't like"
mɪ tɪ	"I speak"	mɪ ntɪ	"I don't speak"
mɪ kɔ	"I go"	mɪ ŋkɔ	"I don't go"

Thus in Twi, as in English, you use [n] before [t], [m] before [p], and [ŋ] before [k]. This might appear to be just an accident. But when this same "accident" occurs in language after language, there should be some reason.

By understanding how sounds are produced and by classifying them according to their articulatory properties we can provide answers to why we find such similar processes in different languages.

Phonetic Features

AIRSTREAM MECHANISMS

The production of any speech sound (or any sound at all) involves the movement of an airstream. Most speech sounds are produced by pushing lung air out of the body through the mouth and sometimes also through the nose. Since lung air is used, these sounds are called **pulmonic** sounds; since the air is pushed *out,* they are called **egressive.** The majority of sounds used in languages of the world are thus produced by a **pulmonic egressive** airstream mechanism. All the sounds in English are produced in this manner.

Other airstream mechanisms are used in other languages to produce sounds called **ejectives, implosives,** and **clicks.** Instead of lung air, the body of air in the mouth may be moved. When this air is sucked in instead of flowing out, **ingressive** sounds, like implosives and clicks, are produced. When the air in the mouth is pushed out, ejectives are produced; they are thus also **egressive** sounds. Implosives and ejectives are produced by a **glottalic airstream mechanism,** while clicks are produced by a **velaric airstream mechanism.** A detailed description of these different airstream mechanisms goes beyond the requirements of an introductory text such as this. They are mentioned to show that sounds can be classified according to the airstream mechanism used to produce them. Ejectives are found in many American Indian languages as well as African and Caucasian languages. Implosives also occur in the languages of the American Indians and throughout Africa, India, and Pakistan. Clicks occur in the Southern Bantu languages like Xhosa and Zulu, and in the languages spoken by the Bushmen and Hottentots. In the rest of this chapter we will be discussing only sounds produced by a pulmonic egressive airstream mechanism.

VOICED AND VOICELESS SOUNDS

The airstream from the lungs moves up through the trachea, or windpipe, and through the opening between the vocal cords, which is called the **glottis** (see Figure 4-1).

If the vocal cords are apart, the airstream is not obstructed at the glottis and it passes freely into the **supraglottal** cavities (the parts of the vocal tract above the glottis). The sounds produced in this way are called **voiceless** sounds; [p], [t], [k], and [s] are voiceless sounds. All the sounds in the [s]-plural class and in the [t]-past-tense class are voiceless sounds.

If the vocal cords are together, the airstream forces its way through and causes them to *vibrate.* Such sounds are called **voiced** sounds. As we have said, all the sounds in the [z]-plural class are voiced sounds; all the sounds in the [d]-past-tense class are voiced sounds; [z] and [d] are also voiced sounds. If you put a finger in each ear and say "z-z-z-z-z-z" you can feel the vibrations of the sound as it goes through the vibrating vocal cords. If you now say "s-s-s-s-s" you will not feel these vibrations. When you whisper, you are making *all* the speech sounds voiceless.

As shown above, the voiced/voiceless distinction is a very important

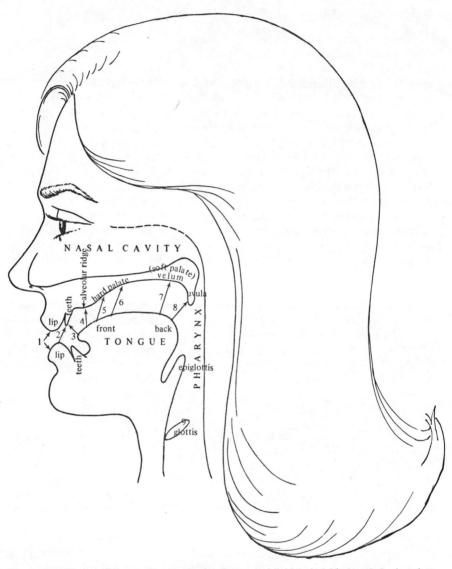

Figure 4-1 The vocal tract. *Places of articulation:* 1, bilabial; 2, labiodental; 3, dental or interdental; 4, alveolar; 5, palatoalveolar; 6, palatal; 7, velar; 8, uvular; 9, glottal.

one in English. Nouns and verbs ending with voiced sounds (excluding the exceptions noted) add a voiced [z] and [d], respectively, to form plurals and past tenses; those which end in voiceless sounds add [s] and [t].

The state of the vocal cords during speech permits us to classify speech sounds into two large classes: **voiced** and **voiceless.** We can also call these classes [+voiced] and [−voiced] since [−voiced] is equivalent to voiceless. The words in the pairs *fine* and *vine, pin* and *bin, tin* and *din, seal* and *zeal, cane* and *gain* may be distinguished by the fact that the initial consonant of the first word in each pair is [−voiced], while the second word begins with a consonant that is [+voiced]. The position of the lips and tongue is the same in the two paired words. The state of the vocal cords, however, differs in producing [f] and [v], [p] and [b], [t] and [d], [s] and [z], and [k] and [g].

Words may also be distinguished if the *final* sounds differ as to vocal cord position, as in *nap* and *nab, writ* and *rid, rack* and *rag, wreath* and *wreathe, rich* and *ridge*. Again the first words of the pairs end in voiceless sounds, and the second words end in corresponding voiced sounds. Except for voicing, the final sounds of each pair are identical.

Sounds must differ from each other in ways other than voicing. That is, [p], [t], [k] are all voiceless, and [b], [m], [d], [n], [g], [ŋ] are all voiced, yet all these sounds are distinct from one another in English. What further differences are there?

NASAL VS. ORAL SOUNDS

If you say *pad, bad,* and *mad* you will notice that the initial sounds are very similar. The [p], [b], and [m] are all produced by closing the lips. [p] differs from [b] because in producing the voiceless [p] the vocal cords are apart; the glottis is open. [b] is voiced because the vocal cords are together and vibrating. If you put your hands over your ears and keep your lips together for the [b] you will feel the hum of the vibrations. If you do the same and say "m-m-m-m" or *mad* you will see that [m] is also a voiced sound. What, then, distinguishes the [m] from the [b]?

[m] is a **nasal** sound. When you produce [m], air escapes not only through the mouth (when you open your lips) but also through the nose.

In Figure 4-1 notice that the roof of the mouth is divided into the **hard palate** and the **soft palate,** or **velum.** The hard palate is the bony structure at the front of the mouth. You can feel this hard palate with your finger. As you move your finger back you can feel the section of the palate where the flesh becomes soft and is movable. This soft, movable part is called the **velum.** At the end of the soft palate, or velum, is the **uvula,** which you can see in the mirror hanging down if you open your mouth wide and say "aaah." When the velum is raised all the way to touch the back of the throat, the passage through the nose is cut off. When the nasal passage is blocked in this way, the air can escape only through the mouth. Sounds produced this way are called **oral** sounds. [p] and [b] are oral sounds. When the velum is lowered, air escapes through the nose as well as the mouth. Sounds produced this way are called **nasal** sounds. [m], [n], and [ŋ] are the

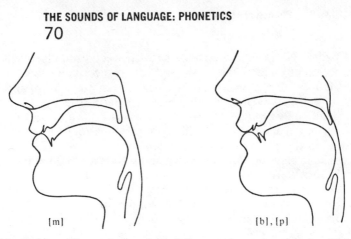

Figure 4-2 Position of lips and velum for [m] (lips together, velum down) and [p], [b] (lips together, velum up).

nasal consonants of English. The diagrams in Figure 4-2 show the position of the lips and the velum when [m] and [p] or [b] are articulated.

The difference between *bad* and *mad, dot* and *not,* is due only to the position of the velum in the first sounds of the words. In *bad* and *dot* the velum is raised, preventing air from entering the nasal cavity. [b] and [d] are therefore *oral* sounds. In *mad* and *not* the velum is lowered and air travels through the nose as well as the mouth. [m] and [n] are therefore *nasal* sounds. Note that [b], [d], [m], and [n] are all voiced.

Words with final consonants, alike in all other respects, may **contrast** with respect to the oral-nasal distinction. The final sounds of *rib* and *rim, mad* and *man, dig* and *ding* (the *ng* is the one sound [ŋ]) are identical except the first of each pair is oral, the second is nasal.

These **phonetic features,** or properties, enable us to classify all speech sounds into four classes: voiced, voiceless, nasal, oral. One sound may belong to more than one class, as shown in Table 4-1.

Table 4-1 Classes of speech sounds

	Oral (−nasal)	*Nasal* (+nasal)
Voiced (+voiced)	b d g	m n ŋ
Voiceless (−voiced)	p t k	All nasal consonants *in English* are voiced

We can also classify these sounds by specifying them as + or − for each phonetic property we have discussed:

	p	t	k	b	d	g	m	n	ŋ
Voiced	−	−	−	+	+	+	+	+	+
Nasal	−	−	−	−	−	−	+	+	+

It is easy, by this method, to determine the different classes of speech sounds. All sounds marked [+voiced] are in the class of voiced sounds, all sounds marked [−voiced] are in the class of voiceless sounds, all sounds marked [+nasal] are in the class of nasal sounds, and those marked [−nasal] are in the class of oral sounds.

Below we will discuss many other phonetic features. Each feature will determine a class of speech sounds. These classes will be most easily specified by using pluses and minuses, much as we did in the previous paragraph.

ARTICULATORY MODIFICATION OF SOUNDS (PLACES OF ARTICULATION)

If [b], [d], and [g] are all voiced nonnasal (oral) sounds, what distinguishes them? We know they are distinct because we recognize *brew*, *drew*, and *grew*, and *bash*, *dash*, and *gash* as different words, with different meanings. There must be other phonetic features which distinguish them besides those already discussed.

Labials

By moving the tongue and lips we are able to change the shape of the oral cavity and in this way produce different sounds. When we produce a [b], [p], or [m], we **articulate** by bringing both lips together. These sounds are therefore called **bilabials.**

We also use our lips to form [f] and [v], as in *fine* and *vine*. In this case we articulate by touching the bottom lip to the upper teeth. Hence these sounds are called **labiodental.** The five sounds that comprise the three bilabials [b], [p], and [m] and the two labiodentals [f] and [v] form the class of **labial** sounds.

Alveolars

When we articulate a [d], [n], or [t] we raise the tip of the tongue to the hard palate right at the point of the bony tooth ridge, called the **alveolar ridge** (see Figure 4-1). Sounds produced by raising the tongue tip to the alveolar ridge are called **alveolar** sounds. If you say *two, do, new, Sue, zoo* you will notice that the first sounds in all these words are produced by raising your tongue tip toward the alveolar ridge. The [t] and [s] are voiceless alveolar sounds, and the [d], [z], and [n] are voiced. Only [n] is nasal.

Velars

Another group of sounds is produced by raising the back of the tongue to the soft palate or velum. The sounds ending the words *back, bag,* and *bang* are produced this way and are called **velar** sounds.

Interdentals

To produce the sounds beginning the words *thin* [θ] and *then* [ð] you insert the tip of the tongue between the upper and lower teeth. These are **interdental** sounds. The [θ] in *thin* and *ether* is a voiceless interdental, and the [ð] in *then* and *either* is a voiced interdental.

Palatals (or Alveopalatals)

If you raise the front part of your tongue to a point on the hard palate, just behind the alveolar ridge, you can produce the sounds in the middle of the words *mesher* [mɛšər] and *measure* [mɛžər]. The voiceless [š] and the voiced [ž] are called **postalveolar, alveopalatal,** or **palatal,** sounds.

In English the voiced [ž] never begins words (except in words borrowed from the French which have retained the French pronunciation, like *genre* and *gendarme*); [š] is the sound which begins the words *shoe, shut, sure,* and *sugar.*

MANNERS OF ARTICULATION

Stops

We already have a number of distinct phonetic properties permitting many overlapping classes of sounds. Both [t] and [s], for example, are in the class of voiceless oral alveolar sounds. But what distinguishes the [t] from the [s]?

Once the airstream enters the oral cavity it may be stopped, it may be partially obstructed, or it may flow freely out of the mouth. Sounds which are stopped *completely* in the oral cavity for a brief period are, not surprisingly, called **stops.** All other sounds are called **continuants** because the stream of air continues without interruption through the mouth opening. [p], [b], [m], [t], [d], [n], [k], [g], and [ŋ] are stops which occur in English. In the production of nasal stops, the air does continue through the nose, but there is a blockage of the airflow in the oral cavity. Notice that when you produce these sounds the air is completely blocked either at the lips or where the tongue touches the alveolar ridge or velum. The nonnasal stops are also called **plosives** because the air that is blocked in the mouth "explodes" when the closure is released. This does not occur with nasal stops because the air has an "escape route" through the nose.

[b], [p], and [m] are bilabial stops. The airstream is stopped at the mouth by the complete closure of the lips.

[d], [t], [n] are alveolar stops. The airstream is stopped by the tongue making a complete closure with the alveolar ridge.

[g], [k], [ŋ] are velar stops. The airstream is stopped by the back of the tongue making a complete closure with the velum.

In Quechua one finds **uvular** stops as well. These are produced when the back of the tongue is raised and moved backward to form a complete closure with the uvula. The symbol for a voiceless uvular stop is [q].

We can classify all sounds into two classes (which of course intersect with other classes). Stops belong to the class specified as [−continuant] and nonstops belong to the class of [+continuant] sounds.

Aspirated vs. Unaspirated Sounds

When we distinguished above between voiced and voiceless sounds we pointed out that during the production of voiceless sounds the glottis is open and the air passes freely through the opening between the vocal cords. When the following sound is a voiced sound, which it often is, the vocal cords must close.

Voiceless sounds may differ among themselves, depending on the "timing" of the vocal cord closure. In English, when we pronounce the word *pit* there is a brief period of voicelessness *immediately after* the stop closure is released. That is, after the lips come apart the vocal cords are still kept open for a very short time. Such sounds are called **aspirated**. When we pronounce the [p] in *spit*, however, the vocal cords start vibrating as soon as the lips are opened. Such sounds are called **unaspirated**. Similarly, the [t] in *tick* and the [k] in *kin* are aspirated voiceless stops, while the [t] in *stick* and the [k] in *skin* are unaspirated. If you hold a strip of paper before your lips and say *pit*, the "aspiration" will be shown by the fact that the paper is pushed as if by a breeze. The paper, however, will not move or be pushed when you say *spit*.

Figure 4-3 shows in diagrammatic form the timing of the articulators (in this case the lips) in relation to the state of the vocal cords. Notice that

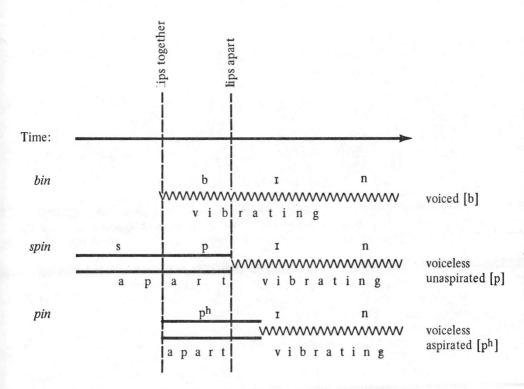

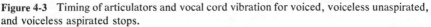

Figure 4-3 Timing of articulators and vocal cord vibration for voiced, voiceless unaspirated, and voiceless aspirated stops.

in the production of the voiced [b] the vocal cords are vibrating throughout the closure of the lips and continue to vibrate for the vowel production after the lips are opened. In the unaspirated [p] in *spin* the vocal cords are open during the lip closure and come together and start vibrating as soon as the lips open. In the production of the aspirated [pʰ] in *pin* the vocal cords remain apart for a brief period after the lip closure is released.

In English these two *p* sounds (or *k* or *t* sounds) are not used to change the meaning of words; that is, they are not used contrastively. If we aspirated the *p* in *spit*, it might sound "funny," as if we were actually spitting, but we would still know it meant "spit." In Thai the difference between an aspirated and an unaspirated voiceless stop is as important as the difference between a voiced or a voiceless stop. In French all the voiceless sounds are unaspirated. Whether two sounds are considered to be the same or different by speakers of the language depends upon the linguistic system, and not solely on the phonetic properties of the sounds.

Aspirated sounds are usually symbolized with a small raised *h* to distinguish them from unaspirated sounds. This is shown in the following Thai examples:

VOICELESS UNASPIRATED	VOICELESS ASPIRATED	VOICED
[pàa] "forest"	[pʰàa] "to split"	[bàa] "shoulder"
[tam] "to pound"	[tʰam] "to do"	[dam] "black"
[kàt] "to bite"	[kʰàt] "to interrupt"	

Fricatives

In the production of some sounds the airstream is not stopped completely but is obstructed from flowing freely. If you put your hand in front of your mouth when you produce an [s], [z], [f], [v], [θ], [ð], [š], or [ž], you will feel the air coming out of your mouth. The passage in the mouth through which the air must pass, however, is very narrow, and the narrowness of this passage causes turbulence. The air particles are pushed one against the other, producing *noise* because of the *friction*. Such sounds are called **fricatives**. (You may also hear them referred to as **spirants,** from the Latin word *spirare,* "to blow.")

In the production of the labiodental fricatives [f] and [v], the friction is created at the lips, where a narrow passage permits the air to escape.

In the production of the fricatives [s] and [z], the friction is created at the alveolar ridge.

In the production of the fricatives [š] and [ž], the friction or noise is created as the air passes through the narrow opening behind the alveolar ridge.

In the production of [θ] and [ð], the friction is created at the opening between the tongue and the teeth.

Most dialects of modern English do not include velar fricatives, although as mentioned previously they occurred in an earlier stage of English, in such words as *right, knight, enough,* and *through.* The velar fricative occurred where the *gh* occurs in the spelling. If you raise the back of the tongue as if you were about to produce a [g] or [k], but stop just short of touching the velum, you can produce a velar fricative. The voiced velar fricative is symbolized as [ɣ], and its voiceless counterpart as [x]. Some speakers of modern English substitute a [x] for a [k] and a [ɣ] for a [g] in words such as *bucket* and *wagon.* Both voiced and voiceless velar fricatives occur in many languages of the world.

Affricates

Some sounds are produced by a stop closure followed immediately by a slow release of the closure characteristic of a fricative. These sounds are called **affricates.** [č] and [ǰ] are such sounds. [č] occurs as the first and last sound of the word *church* [čərč]; [ǰ] occurs similarly in *judge* [ǰʌǰ]. Phonetically, an affricate is a sequence of a stop plus a fricative. Thus [č] is the same as the sound combination [t] + [š], and [ǰ] the same as [d] + [ž], as you can see by prolonging the pronunciation of either affricate.

This is also revealed by observing that very often in fast speech *white shoes* [wayt šuz] and *why choose* [way čuz] may be pronounced identically. In slower speech we might release the *t* in *white* before articulating the [š] in *shoes.*

Sibilants

The fricatives [s], [z], [š], [ž], and the affricates [č] and [ǰ] represent a class of sounds called **sibilants.** When you produce these sounds the friction causes a "hissing" noise. As pointed out above, it is just the nouns ending in these "sibilants" which add an [əz] to form the plural.

Obstruents

The nonnasal stops, the fricatives, and the affricates form a class of sounds which can be distinguished from all other sounds. Since the airstream cannot escape through the nose, it is obstructed only in its passage through the vocal tract. These sounds are called **obstruents;** all other sounds are called **sonorants.** Nasal stops are sonorants because although the air is blocked in the mouth it continues to "resonate" and move through the nose.

Fricatives are continuant obstruents because despite the obstruction which causes the friction the air is not completely stopped in its passage through the oral cavity. Nonnasal stops and affricates are noncontinuant obstruents because there is complete blockage of the air during the production of these sounds. The closure of a stop is released abruptly, as opposed to the closure of an affricate, which is released gradually, causing friction. All the affricates in English are sibilants.

Using these phonetic properties, we can form additional classes as shown in Table 4-2.

Table 4-2 Four classes of speech sounds specified by three features

Features	Oral Stops	Affricates	Fricatives	Nasal Stops
Sonorant	−	−	−	+
Continuant	−	−	+	−
Sibilant	−	+ ·	+ or −	−

Liquids

The sounds [l] and [r] are also sonorants. There is some obstruction of the airstream in the mouth, but not enough to cause friction. These sounds are called **liquids.**

[l] is a **lateral** sound. The front of the tongue makes contact with the alveolar ridge, but the sides of the tongue are down, permitting the air to escape laterally through the sides of the tongue.

The sound [r] is usually formed in English by curling the tip of the tongue back behind the alveolar ridge. Such sounds are called **retroflex** sounds. In some languages the "r" may be a **trill,** which is produced by the tip of the tongue vibrating against the roof of the mouth. It is possible that in an earlier stage of English the "r" was a trill. A trilled "r" occurs in many contemporary languages, such as Spanish, and is also represented as [r].

In addition to the alveolar trill [r], uvular trills also occur, as in French. A uvular trill, symbolized by [R], is produced by vibrating the uvula. In other languages the "r" is produced by a single **tap** instead of a series of vibrating taps. In Spanish both the alveolar trill and the alveolar tap occur. If you substitute one for the other in certain contexts you will change the meaning. (The usual symbol for the tapped "r" is [ɾ].) Thus [pero] in Spanish means "dog" while [peɾo] with the tap means "but." One may also produce an "r" by making the tongue **flap** against the alveolar ridge. The flapped "r" is symbolized by [ɾ] in IPA; some linguists use the symbol [D] instead. Some speakers of British English pronounce the "r" in the word *very* with a flap. It sounds like a "very fast" [d]. Most American speakers produce a flap instead of a [t] or [d] in words like *writer* and *rider,* and *latter* and *ladder*. For many speakers these pairs are pronounced identically in normal conversational style.

In English, [l] and [r] are regularly voiced. When they follow voiceless sounds, as in *please* or *price,* they may be automatically "de-voiced," at least partially. This may be symbolized by a small circle under the symbol, for example, [r̥]. (The same **diacritic** mark can be used to represent a voiceless nasal—for example, [n̥].) Many languages of the world have a voiceless [l̥]. Welsh is an example; the name *Lloyd* in Welsh starts with a voiceless [l̥].

Some languages may lack liquids entirely, or have only a single one. The Cantonese dialect of Chinese has the single liquid [l]. This fact has been the basis for many dialect jokes, in which, for example, *fried rice* is pronounced as *flied lice*. One need but listen to an American trying to speak Chinese, French, or Quechua to know that such humor can be in both directions.

Acoustically (that is, as physical sounds), [l] and [r] are very similar, which is why they are grouped together in the class of liquids and why they behave as a single class of sounds in certain circumstances. For example, the only two consonants permitted after an initial [k], [g], [p], or [b] in English are the liquids [l] and [r]. Thus we have *clear* [klir], *crop* [krap], *plate* [plet], *crate* [kret], *glad* [glæd], *grad* [græd], *bland* [blænd], and *brand* [brænd], but nothing beginning * [ks . . .], * [kp . . .], and so on. (Notice that in words like *psychology* the *p* is not pronounced.)

Glides

The sounds [y] and [w] are produced with little or no obstruction of the airstream in the mouth. When occurring in a word, they must always be either preceded or followed directly by a vowel. In articulating [y] or [w], the tongue moves rapidly in gliding fashion either toward or away from a neighboring vowel, hence the term **glide**. Glides are transition sounds, being partly like consonants and partly like vowels, and they are sometimes called **semivowels.**

In producing the glide [y], the blade of the tongue is raised toward the hard palate, so [y] is called a **palatal** glide. The tongue is in a position almost identical to that assumed in producing the [i] sound as in the word *beat.* In pronouncing *you* [yu] the tongue moves rapidly over the [y] to the [u].

The glide [w] is produced by both raising the back of the tongue toward the velum and simultaneously rounding the lips. It is thus a **labiovelar** glide. In the dialect of English where speakers have different pronunciations for *which* [ʍɪč] and *witch* [wɪč], the labiovelar glide in the first word is the voiceless [ʍ], and in the second word it is the voiced [w]. The position of the tongue and the lips when one produces a [w] is very similar to the positions for the production of a [u], but the [w] is a glide because the tongue moves quickly to the vowel which follows.

To produce the [h] which starts words such as *house, who,* and *hair,* the glottis is open as in the production of voiceless sounds. No other modification of the airstream mechanism occurs in the mouth. In fact, the tongue and lips are usually in the position for the production of the following vowel as the airstream passes through the open glottis. The air or noise produced at the glottis is heard as [h], and for this reason [h] is often classified as a **voiceless glottal fricative.** The [h] is also classified as a glide by some linguists, since it differs from "true" consonants in that there is no obstruction in the oral cavity and it also differs from vowels. When it is both preceded and followed by a vowel it is often voiced, as in *ahead* or *cohabit.*

If the air is stopped completely at the glottis by tightly closed vocal cords, the sound produced is a **glottal stop,** symbolized as [ʔ]. This is the sound often used instead of a [t] in words like *button* and *Latin.* It also may occur in colloquial speech at the end of words like *don't, won't,* or *can't.* In one New York dialect it regularly replaces the *tt* sound in words like *bottle*. If you say "ah-ah-ah-ah" with one "ah" right after another, but do not sustain the vowel sound, you will be producing glottal stops between the vowels. Like the [h], it differs from both consonants and vowels and is classified as a glide by some linguists. Because the air is completely blocked, other linguists classify it as a stop.

Table 4-3 presents a chart of the phonetic symbols which can be used for American English consonants.

Table 4-3   Phonetic symbols for American English consonants

When there are two symbols within a cell, the one to the left is voiceless, and the one to the right, voiced. The nasals, liquids, and [y] are voiced; [h] is voiceless.*

	Bilabial	Labiodental	Interdental	Alveolar	Palatal	Velar	Labiovelar	Glottal
Nasal	m			n		ŋ		
Stop	p b			t d		k g		ʔ
Fricative		f v	θ ð	s z	š ž			
Glide					y		ʍ w	h
Liquid				l r†				
Affricate					č ǰ			

* Nasals are also stops in that there is a complete blockage of air in the oral tract.
† r has various pronunciations in English and other languages.

In Table 4-4, each consonant given in the chart of phonetic symbols is specified by its phonetic features. Note that it is not necessary to include both the features "voiced" and "voiceless" or "oral" as well as "nasal," since any consonant marked [−voiced] must be "voiceless" and any consonant marked [−nasal] must be "oral." There are other features which can be used to group these consonants into larger, more inclusive classes. For example, the labial and alveolar sounds are all articulated at the front of the mouth, while the velar and glottal sounds are produced at the back. One could thus use the feature "back" and divide these sounds into the two classes [+back] and [−back]. The [−back] or "front" sounds have been called **anterior.** Similarly, the alveolar, postalveolar, and palatal sounds are all produced by raising the blade of the tongue. Such sounds have been called **coronal** sounds. Velars and labials would thus be [−coronal], while palatals and alveolars would be [+coronal].

Using a "feature" specification of this kind, one can easily group all the sounds into all the classes of which they are members; all sounds marked + for a certain feature belong in one class (for example, [+continuant] sounds) and all those marked − for a certain feature belong in another class (for example, [−continuant] sounds, which include all stops).

Table 4-4 Phonetic feature specification of American English consonants

Phonetic Segments

Phonetic Features	p	b	m	t	d	n	k	g	ŋ	f	v	θ	ð	s	z	š	ž	č	ǰ	l	r	y	ʍ	w	h	ʔ
Sonorant	–	–	+	–	–	+	–	–	+	–	–	–	–	–	–	–	–	–	–	+	+	+	+	+	–	–
Continuant	–	–	–	–	–	–	–	–	–	+	+	+	+	+	+	+	+	–	–	+	+	+	+	+	+	–
Voiced	–	+	+	–	+	+	–	+	+	–	+	–	+	–	+	–	+	–	+	+	+	+	–	+	–	–
Nasal	–	–	+	–	–	+	–	–	+	–	–	–	–	–	–	–	–	–	–	–	–	–	–	–	–	–
Sibilant	–	–	–	–	–	–	–	–	–	–	–	–	–	+	+	+	+	+	+	–	–	–	–	–	–	–
Liquid	–	–	–	–	–	–	–	–	–	–	–	–	–	–	–	–	–	–	–	+	+	–	–	–	–	–
Lateral	–	–	–	–	–	–	–	–	–	–	–	–	–	–	–	–	–	–	–	+	–	–	–	–	–	–
Glide	–	–	–	–	–	–	–	–	–	–	–	–	–	–	–	–	–	–	–	–	–	+	+	+	+	–/+
Labial	+	+	+	–	–	–	–	–	–	+	+	–	–	–	–	–	–	–	–	–	–	–	+	+	–	–
Interdental	–	–	–	–	–	–	–	–	–	–	–	+	+	–	–	–	–	–	–	–	–	–	–	–	–	–
Alveolar	–	–	–	+	+	+	–	–	–	–	–	–	–	+	+	–	–	–	–	+	+	–	–	–	–	–
Palatal	–	–	–	–	–	–	–	–	–	–	–	–	–	–	–	+	+	+	+	–	–	+	–	–	–	–
Velar	–	–	–	–	–	–	+	+	+	–	–	–	–	–	–	–	–	–	–	–	–	–	+	+	–	–
Glottal	–	–	–	–	–	–	–	–	–	–	–	–	–	–	–	–	–	–	–	–	–	–	–	–	+	+

VOWELS

In every language of the world, speech sounds can be divided into two major classes—**consonants** and **vowels.** In the production of consonants the flow of air is obstructed as it travels through the mouth. Vowels are produced with no oral obstruction whatsoever. Speakers usually know "intuitively" which sounds are vowels and which are consonants. Vowels usually constitute the "main core," or the **nucleus,** of syllables.

Some sounds do not fall easily into one of these two classes. Glides, for example, are like vowels in that there is little oral obstruction, but they are also like consonants in that their duration is very short; they always occur either before or after a vowel.

Liquids are like consonants in some ways and vowels in others. Because they are produced with obstructions in the oral cavity they are like consonants. But acoustically they have "resonances" like vowels.

To show the way all the sounds we have discussed group themselves into overlapping classes, we can use the two features—**vocalic** and **consonantal**—and mark each segment as being either plus or minus for each feature, as in Table 4-5.

Table 4-5   Vocalic and consonantal groupings

	Classes			
Features	Consonants	Vowels	Glides	Liquids
Consonantal	+	−	−	+
Vocalic	−	+	−	+

By such a system, consonants and vowels are distinct classes; they do not share any feature. Glides, however, are like consonants in that they are in the class of [−vocalic] segments, but they are like vowels in that they are in the class of [−consonantal] segments. Similarly, liquids are in the [+consonantal] class with consonants and the [+vocalic] class with vowels. In studying languages of the world we find this to be a helpful classification because it is true that glides and liquids can function like either consonants or vowels in certain contexts.

The quality of vowels is determined by the particular configuration of the vocal tract. Different parts of the tongue may be raised or lowered. The lips may be spread or pursed. The passage through which the air travels, however, is never so narrow as to obstruct free flow of the airstream.

Vowel sounds carry pitch and loudness; you can sing vowels. They may be long or short. Vowels can "stand alone"—they can be produced without any consonants before or after them. One can say the [i] of *beat,* the [ɪ] of *bit,* or the [u] of *boot,* for example, without the initial [b] or the final [t]. It is much more difficult to produce a [b] or a [t] without some kind of vowel attached.

There have been many different schemes used for describing vowel sounds. They may be described by articulatory features, as we have classified consonants. Many beginning students of phonetics find this method more difficult to apply to vowel articulations than to consonant articulations. When you make a [t] you feel your tongue touch the alveolar ridge. When you make a [p] you can feel your two lips come together or you can watch the lips move in a mirror. Since vowels are produced without any articulators touching or even coming very close together, it is often difficult to figure out just what is going on. One of the authors of this book almost gave up as a linguist and phonetician at the beginning of her graduate work because she couldn't understand what was meant by "front," "back," "high," and "low" vowels.

But these terms do have meaning. If you watched an x-ray movie of someone talking you would understand why vowels have traditionally been classified according to three questions:

1. How high is the tongue?
2. What part of the tongue is involved; that is, what part is raised? What part is lowered?
3. What is the position of the lips?

There are other distinguishing features, such as length, nasalization, and tenseness, which we will discuss below.

The three diagrams in Figure 4-4 show that in the production of [i] and

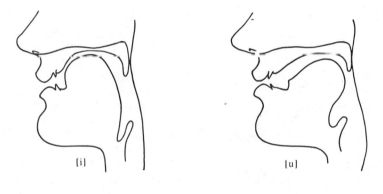

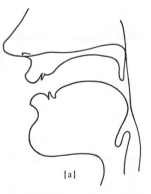

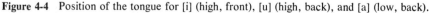

Figure 4-4 Position of the tongue for [i] (high, front), [u] (high, back), and [a] (low, back).

[u] the tongue is very *high* in the mouth. But in [i] it is the *front* part of the tongue which is raised and in [u] it is the *back* part of the tongue. In [a] the *back* of the tongue is *lowered*. (The reason a doctor asks you to say "ah" in examining your throat is because the tongue is "low" and he can thus see over it.)

[ɪ] is produced with the front part of the tongue raised slightly less than [i], and [ʊ] is produced with the back part of the tongue raised not quite as high as [u].

Using these "dimensions," we can plot the American English vowels (Table 4-6).

Table 4-6 Dimensional classification of vowels

	Part of the Tongue Involved		
	Front	*Central*	*Back*
High	i		u
	ɪ		ʊ
Mid	e		o
	ɛ	ə	ɔ
Low	æ	ʌ	a

This simple classification permits us to group vowels in the following way:

high vowels: i, ɪ, u, ʊ   front vowels: i, ɪ, e, ɛ, æ
mid vowels: e, ɛ, ə, o, ɔ   central vowels: ə, ʌ
low vowels: æ, ʌ, a   back vowels: u, ʊ, o, ɔ, a

Just as the classes of consonants show up again and again in language rules, so do these vowel classes.

Remember that these are "broad" descriptions which do not give all the phonetic details. Nor does the classification reveal the many varieties found in English. For many people, for example, the low vowel [a] is central rather than back. In many English dialects the vowels which we have symbolized as [i], [e], [u], and [o] would be symbolized in a narrower, more exact phonetic transcription as [iy], [ey], [uw], and [ow], respectively. They are not "simple" vowels but vowels followed by glides. Simple vowels are called *monophthongs* as opposed to *diphthongs*, which include both a vowel and a glide. In English, then, these are often diphthongs. In Spanish and other languages these vowels are true monophthongs. Thus the Spanish word *se* [se] differs in pronunciation from the English word *say* [sey].

In English we also have the diphthongs [ay] as in *bite*, [aw] (or [æw]) as in *bout* [bawt] ([bæwt]), and [ɔy] as in *boy* [bɔy].

Some linguists use the terms **tense** and **lax** to distinguish between [i] and [ɪ], [u] and [ʊ], [e] and [ɛ], and [o] and [ɔ]. The first vowel of each pair is tense, and the second lax. These terms are **cover terms** representing a number of phonetic properties which distinguish, for example, the tense [i] from the lax [ɪ]. The tense vowels in English are diphthongized, are longer in duration, and are produced by a slightly higher tongue position. One reason for classifying vowels as tense and lax in English is because we can state certain generalities about the classes instead of making statements about each particular vowel pair.

Vowels are differentiated not only by tongue height, tongue part, and tenseness (or diphthongization), but also by lip position. In the production of English vowels, we round our lips when we say [u], [ʊ], [o], and [ɔ]. It is true that some speakers use more lip rounding than others, but, generally speaking, the nonlow back vowels in English are produced with some lip rounding.

On the other hand, front vowels are never rounded in English. This is not true in all languages. French, for example, has both rounded and unrounded front vowels (and back rounded vowels as well). In the following examples the IPA symbol [y] represents the high front rounded vowel; it does not represent the palatal glide. We mentioned above that the traditional American use of [y] instead of [j] for the glide creates difficulties when we wish to represent the sounds of other languages.

[y] as in *tu* [ty] "you" (singular)	The tongue position is as for [i], but the lips are rounded
[ø] as in *bleu* [blø] "blue"	The tongue position is as in [e], but the lips are rounded
[œ] as in *heure* [œ] "hour"	The tongue position is as in [ɛ], but the lips are rounded

Another fact about the vowel system of the majority of English dialects is that there are no nonlow back vowels which are "unrounded." Some speakers of Southern English, or the special variety known as "Black English," use the high back unround vowel, symbolized as [ɯ], where other dialects use [l] as in words such as *help* [hɛɯp].

In Mandarin Chinese, in Japanese, in the Cameroonian language Feʔfeʔ, and in many other languages of the world we also find the high back unrounded vowel [ɯ]. The Chinese word meaning "four" is pronounced [sɯ]. The tongue position in producing the vowel is as for [u], but the lips are spread. This word in Mandarin contrasts with [su], "speed," where the high back vowel is rounded as in English.

This shows that certain combinations of phonetic features may or may not occur in all languages. That is, in English (but not in all languages) the lip rounding of vowels is *predictable*. If you know that a vowel is nonlow and back, you know (can predict) that it is rounded. Rounding is not a predictable feature in either French or Mandarin Chinese.

The monophthongal, or simple, vowels of English can be specified by using the + and − to show class membership in the same way as we specified the consonants. This is illustrated in Table 4-7.

Table 4-7 Phonetic feature specification of American English vowels

Phonetic Segments

Phonetic Features	i	ɪ	e	ɛ	æ	ə*	ʌ*	u	ʊ	o	ɔ	a
High	+	+	−	−	−	−	−	+	+	−	−	−
Low	−	−	−	−	+	−	+	−	−	−	−	+
Back	−	−	−	−	−	+	+	+	+	+	+	+
Round	−	−	−	−	−	−	−	+	+	+	+	−
Tense	+	−	+	−	−	−	−	+	−	+	−	+

*ə and ʌ are considered [+back] for purposes of feature classification.

Nasalized Vowels

Vowels, like consonants, can also be produced with a lowered velum permitting air to escape through the nose. Such vowels are called **nasal, or nasalized, vowels.**

In English nasal vowels always occur before nasal consonants. The nasality or nonnasality of vowels in English is predictable. The reason that vowels are usually nasalized in English and other languages when they immediately precede a nasal consonant is because the velum starts to lower during the vowel production in anticipation of the following nasal consonant. To specify that a vowel is nasalized, the diacritic mark ~ is placed over the vowel as shown below:

bomb [bãm]   *boon* [bũn]   *bean* [bĩn]

In French (and many other languages) nasalized vowels may occur when no nasal consonant is adjacent. In the French spelling system an *n* (which is silent in the words given below) is included to indicate that the preceding vowel is nasalized.

[ɛ̃] as in *vin* [vɛ̃] "wine"
[ã] as in *an* [ã] "year"
[õ] as in *son* [sõ] "sound"
[œ̃] as in *brun* [brœ̃] "brown"

Length

Vowels or consonants may be long or they may be short. In some languages of the world if you substitute a long vowel for a short vowel in a word (or a long consonant for a short consonant) you will produce a different word with a different meaning. Long sounds may be symbolized by placing a colon after the vowel or consonant—for example, [a:], [t:], or by doubling the symbol—[aa] or [tt]. When long vowels or consonants can be analyzed as sequences of two short sounds of identical phonetic quality they are called **geminates.** In slow speech in English, for example, the phrase *white tie* will be pronounced with a geminate [tt]—[wayt tay]—while the phrase *why tie* will have just one [t]—[way tay]. In fast speech both phrases will often be pronounced identically, with just one [t]. Within a word in English long consonants or geminate consonants do not occur.

In Italian, however, and other languages, one finds either long or short consonants within a word:

[nonnɔ] *nonno* "grandfather" vs. [nonɔ] *nono* "ninth"

Many other languages, such as Finnish, Luganda, Berber, Hungarian, Icelandic, Miwok, and Punjabi, to name just a few, also have both long or geminate consonants as well as short or nongeminate consonants.

Long and short vowels also occur. In Korean the word for "day" has a short vowel [il], while the word meaning "work" has a long vowel [i:l]. Some of the other languages with short and long vowels are Afrikaans, Altai, Arabic, Bembe, Crow, Menomini, and Tahitian.

In English when a vowel occurs before a voiced obstruent it is longer than when it occurs before voiceless sounds. The lengthening is automatic, or predictable. Thus the vowel in *cod* [ka:d] is longer than the vowel in *cot* [kat].

Natural Classes

We have now listed a number of phonetic properties which group all the speech sounds of all languages into overlapping classes. This enables us to show how one sound is both similar to and different from all other speech sounds in a language.

For example, [č] is like the voiceless sounds [p], [s], [k], and [θ] and functions together with this class in the formation of the past tense in English. One adds a [t] to form the past on a verb ending in [č] in the same way as one adds a [t] to form the past on verbs ending with those other voiceless sounds. Now [č] is distinguished from [ǰ] on the basis of voice. This distinction shows up in the rule of past-tense formation, where words ending in [ǰ] take the [d] past tense (for example, *fudged* [fʌǰd]).

But with respect to the plural rule in English, [č] and [ǰ] are in the same class. Both are sibilant affricates and are classed with the other sibilants [š], [ž], [s], [z]. Words ending in sounds that belong to the class of sibilants add [əz] to form plurals:

matches	[mæčəz]
ridges	[rɪǰəz]
kisses	[kɪsəz]
mazes	[mezəz]
lashes	[læšəz]
garages	[gəražəz]

It is clear that the phonetic symbols themselves do not reveal these facts. To understand how sounds "pattern" in languages, one needs to specify all the phonetic features which define the phonetic classes. We can do this by using pluses and minuses, as we have done above. This is further

Table 4-8 Sound groupings by phonetic classes

	s	z	t	d	p	b	k	g	š	ž
Voiced	−	+	−	+	−	+	−	+	−	+
Sibilant	+	.+	−	−	−	−	−	−	+	+
Alveolar	+	+	+	+	−	−	−	−	−	−
Stop	−	−	+	+	+	+	+	+	−	−

illustrated in Table 4-8. We see that [s] is in the class of [−voiced] sounds together with [t], [p], [k], and [š]; and is in the class of [+sibilant] sounds together with [z], [š], and [ž]; and is in the class of [+alveolar] sounds with [z], [t], and [d]; and is in the class of [−stop] sounds (or continuants) with [z], [š], [ž].

If we listed all the sounds of English and all the phonetic features that specify these sounds, we would have many more intersecting or overlapping classes of sounds. It is these classes that are utilized in the "phonological rules" which constitute one's knowledge of the sound patterns of one's language.

Pitch

Speakers of all languages change the pitch of their voices when they talk. The pitch produced depends upon how fast the vocal cords vibrate; the faster they vibrate, the higher the pitch.

The way pitch is used linguistically differs from language to language. In English, it doesn't much matter whether you say *cat* with a high pitch or a low pitch. It will still mean "cat." But if you say *ba* with a high pitch in Nupe (a language spoken in Nigeria), it will mean "to be sour," whereas if you say *ba* with a low pitch, it will mean "to count." The pitch "contour" *is* important in English; *John is going* as a statement is said with a falling pitch, but as a question the pitch rises at the end. Languages that use the pitch of *individual syllables* to contrast meanings are called **tone** languages. Languages that use pitch syntactically (for example, to change a sentence from a statement to a question) or in which the changing pitch of a *whole sentence* is otherwise important to the meaning are called **intonation** languages.

TONE

It is probably safe to say that most of the languages in the world are tone languages. There are more than 1000 tone languages in Africa alone; many languages of Asia, such as Chinese, Thai, and Burmese, are tone languages, as are many American Indian languages.

Thai is a language that has contrasting pitches, or tones. The same string of "segmental" sounds represented by [naa] will mean different things if one says the sounds with a low pitch, a mid pitch, a high pitch, a falling pitch from high to low, or a rising pitch from low to high. Thai therefore has five linguistic tones:

nàa	[＿]	low tone	"a nickname"
naa	[—]	mid tone	"rice paddy"
náa	[⌐]	high tone	"younger maternal uncle or aunt"
nâa	[＼]	falling tone	"face"
nǎa	[／]	rising tone	"thick"

In Nupe, there are three tones:

bá	[⌐]	high tone	"to be sour"
bā	[—]	mid tone	"to cut"
bà	[＿]	low tone	"to count"

In Twi we find contrasts between high and low pitch (tone):

dùà	[＿＿]	low + low	"tail"
dùá	[＿⌐]	low + high	"tree"
kòtó	[＿⌐]	low + high	"go buy"
kótò	[⌐＿]	high + low	"crab"

In some tone languages the pitch of each tone is "level"; in others, the direction of the pitch (whether it glides from high to low, or low to high) is important. Tones that "glide" are called **contour** tones; tones that don't are called **level**, or **register**, tones. In a tone language it is not the absolute pitch of the syllables which is important but the relations between the pitch of different syllables. This would have to be so, since some individual speakers have high-pitched voices, others low-pitched, and others medium-pitched. In fact, in many tone languages one finds a falling-off of the pitch, or a "downdrifting."

In the following sentence in Twi, we can see how it is the *relative* rather than the *absolute* pitch which is important:

Kòfí hwèhwé ádùàné kàkrá mà n'àdámfò bá.
"Kofi searches for a little food for his friend's child."

The tones can be specified as follows:

low high low high high low low high low high low low high low high

The actual pitches of these syllables would be rather different from each other, shown as follows (the higher the number, the higher the pitch):

8.		fí						
7.				hwé á				
6.	kò					né		
5.			hwè				krá		
4.					dùà			dám	
3.						kà			bá
2.							mà nà		
1.								fò	

The lowering of the pitch which occurs is called **downdrift**. In languages with downdrift—and many tone languages in Africa are downdrift languages—a high tone which occurs after a low tone, or a low tone after a high tone, is lower in pitch than the preceding similarly marked tone. Note that the first high tone in the sentence is given the pitch value 8. The next high tone (which occurs after an intervening low tone) is 7; that is, it is lower in pitch than the first high tone.

This example shows that in analyzing tones, just as in analyzing segments, all the physical properties need not be considered; only essential features are important in language—in this case, whether the tone is "high" or "low" in relation to the other pitches, but not the specific pitch of that tone.

INTONATION

In languages which are not tone languages, like English, pitch still plays an important role. The way we use pitch can be illustrated by a sign occasionally seen in men's lavatories:

We aim to please. You aim too, please.

Two sentences can be exactly the same phonetically except for the overall pitch contour of the utterance. The pitch contour, which is called the **intonation** of the sentence, can be used to distinguish between two different meanings. Note sentences *a* and *b*:

a. What did you put in my drink, Jane?

b. What did you put in my drink, Jane?

In sentence *a* the questioner is asking what Jane put in the drink. In sentence *b* the questioner is asking if someone put Jane in the drink. In sentence *a* the pitch rises sharply on the word *drink* and then falls off. In sentence *b* the sharp rise is on *Jane* and it continues to rise without any decrease.

Sentence *c* illustrates that a written sentence may be ambiguous (may have two meanings):

c. Tristram left directions for Isolde to follow.

When spoken, it can be disambiguated by changing the intonation. If it means that Tristram wanted Isolde to follow him, it is pronounced with the rise in pitch on the first syllable of *follow*, followed by a fall in pitch, as in *d:*

d. Tristram left directions for Isolde to follow.

The sentence can also mean that Tristram left a set of directions which he wanted Isolde to use. If this is the intention, the highest pitch comes on the second syllable of *directions,* as in *e:*

e. Tristram left directions for Isolde to follow.

The way we have indicated pitch is of course highly oversimplified. Before the big rise in pitch the voice does not remain on the same monotone low pitch. These pitch diagrams merely indicate when there is a special change in pitch.

Thus pitch plays an important role in both tone languages and intonation languages but functions in different ways.

Stress

B.C.   **by johnny hart**

By permission of Johnny Hart and Field Enterprises, Inc.

WORD STRESS

In English and many other languages, one or more of the syllables in each content word (words other than the little words like *to, the, a, of,* and so on) is **stressed.** The stressed syllable is marked by ´ in the following examples:

súbject	noun, as in "The subject of the story . . ."
subjéct	verb, as in "He'll subject us to his boring stories."
pérvert	noun, as in "My neighbor is a pervert."
pervért	verb, as in "Don't pervert the idea."

In some words, more than one vowel may be stressed, but if so, one of these stressed vowels receives greater stress than the others. The most highly stressed vowel is indicated by a ´ over the vowel (this is the vowel receiving the **accent,** or **primary** stress, or **main** stress); the other stressed vowels are indicated by marking a ` over the vowels (these vowels receive **secondary** stress).

rèsignátion	phònétic	sỳstemátic
fùndaméntal	ìntrodúctory	rèvolútion

Generally, speakers of a language know which syllable receives primary stress or accent, which receives secondary stress, and which are not stressed at all; it is part of their knowledge of the language. The stress pattern of a word may differ from dialect to dialect. For example, in most varieties of American English the word *láboratòry* has two stressed syllables; in one dialect of British English it receives only one stress [ləbɔ́rətri]. Because the vowel qualities in English are closely related to whether they are stressed or not, the British vowels differ from the American vowels in this word; in fact, in the British version one vowel "drops out" completely because it is not stressed.

One can then specify each vowel as either [+stress] or [−stress]. Vowels specified as [+stress] may be [+accent] or [−accent]. If there is only one stressed vowel in the word it will also be [+accent]. One can also designate stress by numbers. The primary stressed or accented vowel can be designated by placing a "1" over the vowel; secondary stress can be designated by a "2"; unstressed vowels are left unmarked.

$$
\begin{array}{cc}
\overset{2}{} \quad \overset{1}{} & \overset{2}{} \quad \overset{1}{} \\
\text{resignation} & \text{systematic}
\end{array}
$$

To stress a syllable, one may change the *pitch* (usually by raising it), make the syllable *louder,* or make it *longer*. We often use all three of these phonetic features to stress a syllable.

SENTENCE AND PHRASE STRESS

When words are combined into phrases and sentences, one of the syllables receives greater stress than all others. That is, just as there is only one primary stress in a word spoken in isolation (for example, in a list), only one of the vowels in a phrase (or sentence) receives primary stress or accent; all the other stressed vowels are "reduced" to secondary stress. A syllable which may have received the main stress when the word is not in a phrase may have only secondary stress in a phrase, as is illustrated by these examples:

hót + dóg	→ hótdòg	("frankfurter")
hót + dóg	→ hòt dóg	("an overheated dog")
réd + cóat	→ Rédcòat	("a British soldier")
réd + cóat	→ rèd cóat	("a coat that is red")
whíte + hóuse	→ Whíte Hòuse	("the president's house")
whíte + hóuse	→ whìte hóuse	("a house painted white")

In the next chapter, we shall see that there are some regular rules in English which determine where the primary stress is placed and where the secondary stress is placed.

In the English sentences used above to illustrate intonation contours, one may also describe the differences by referring to the word on which the main stress is placed. We can say, for example, that in *We àim to pléase* the primary stress is placed on the word *please,* and in *Yòu àim tóo, plèase* the primary stress is placed on the word *too*.

Perhaps it would be fitting to conclude this section of the chapter by writing in phonetic transcription the two sentences we have said could greatly complicate the research of Martian linguists. If they found the sentences as transcribed here, they would have a much easier time figuring out the English sound system:

[dɪd hì bəlìv ðæt sìzər kʊd sì ðə pìpəl sìz ðə síz]
[ðə sìli əmìbə stòl ðə kì tu ðə məšín]

Acoustic Phonetics: The Physical Properties of Speech Sounds

Throughout this chapter we have been describing speech sounds according to the ways they are produced. We have been describing their articulatory features, or properties—the position of the tongue, the lips, the state of the vocal cords, the airstream mechanisms, the position of the velum, whether the articulators obstruct the free flow of air, and so on. All of these articulatory characteristics are reflected in the physical characteristics of the sounds produced.

Speech sounds can also be described in physical or **acoustic** terms. Physically, a sound is produced whenever there is a disturbance in the position of air molecules. The ancient question asked by philosophers as to whether a sound is produced if a tree falls in the middle of the forest if no one is there to "hear" it has been answered by the science of acoustics. Objectively, a sound is produced; subjectively, there is no sound. In fact, there are sounds which we can't hear because our ears are not sensitive to all changes in air pressure (which result from the movement of air molecules). Acoustic phonetics is concerned only with speech sounds, all of which can be heard by the human ear.

When we push air out of the lungs, small pulses of air are pushed through the vibrating glottis, and these in turn push the mouth air. This creates small variations in the air pressure, due to the wavelike motion of the air molecules.

The sounds we produce can be described in terms of how fast the variations of the air pressure occur. This determines the **fundamental frequency** of the sounds, which for the hearer determines the **pitch**. We can also describe the extent of the variations; the larger the size of the variations in air pressure, the greater the **intensity**, which determines the **loudness** of the sound. The particular **quality** of the sound is determined by the shape of the vibrations, or wave; this in turn is determined by the shape of the vocal tract when the air is flowing through.

An important tool in acoustic research was provided by the invention of a machine called a **sound spectrograph**. When you speak into a microphone connected to this machine (or when a tape recording is plugged in), a "picture" is made of the speech signal. The patterns produced are called **spectrograms** or, more vividly, "visible speech." In the last few years these pictures have been referred to as **voiceprints**. A spectrogram of the words *heed, head, had,* and *who'd* is shown in Figure 4-5. Time in milliseconds moves horizontally from left to right; vertically, the "graph" represents pitch (or, more technically, frequency). Notice that for each vowel there are a number of very dark bands which differ in their placement according to their pitch. These represent the **overtones** produced by the shape

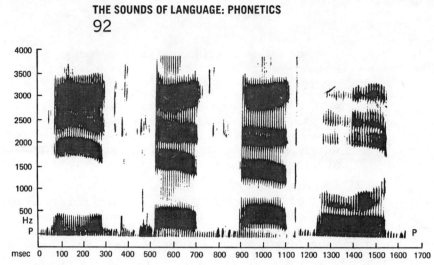

Figure 4-5 A spectrogram of the words *heed, head, had, who'd,* as spoken in a British accent (speaker: Peter Ladefoged, February 16, 1973).

of the vocal tract and are called the **formants** of the vowels. Since the tongue is in a different position for each vowel, the formant frequencies, or overtone pitches, differ for each vowel. It is the different frequencies of these formants which account for the different vowel qualities you hear. The pitch of the entire utterance (intonation contour) is shown by the "voicing bar" marked *P* on the spectrogram. When the striations are far apart the vocal cords are vibrating slowly and the pitch is low; when the striations are close together the vocal cords are vibrating rapidly and the pitch is high.

By studying spectrograms of all speech sounds and many different utterances, acoustic phoneticians have learned a great deal about the basic components which are used to synthesize speech.

A new interest in voiceprints has recently arisen. Spectrograms are being used in law courts as "evidence" to identify speakers. Spectrograms have been made from taped phone conversations, for example, and compared with spectrograms of the speech of individuals accused of making these phone calls. The claim that voiceprints are as conclusive as fingerprints has been challenged. A person cannot change his fingerprints, but a speaker may pronounce a word or a sentence very differently on two occasions and, in addition, his speech may be very similar to another speaker's. Because of such factors the opinion on the reliability of voiceprint identification is far from unanimous. In fact, a large section of the scientific community involved in speech research is concerned that popular opinion will accept voiceprints as infallible (influenced by Dick Tracy comic strips and various TV "who-done-it" programs). In March 1966, a meeting of the Speech Communication Committee of the Acoustical Society of America unanimously passed the following resolution: "The Technical Committee on Speech Communication is concerned that 'voiceprints' have been admitted as legal evidence on the basis of claims which have not yet been evaluated scientifically."

There have been attempts to make more definite judgments on the reliability of voiceprint identification, but scientific opinion remains divided, with the majority opinion still skeptical. Further research, improvement of methods, and more careful training of the "analysts" may in time make spectrograms a valuable aid in legal cases.

Talking Machines

Machines which, with more or less success, imitate human speech, are the most difficult to construct, so many are the agencies engaged in uttering even a single word—so many are the inflections and variations of tone and articulation, that the mechanician finds his ingenuity taxed to the utmost to imitate them.
Scientific American (Jan. 14, 1871)

In 1950, the English mathematician Alan M. Turing published a paper entitled "Computing Machinery and Intelligence." Turing began his paper: "I propose to consider the question, 'Can machines think?' " To answer this question one must decide the criteria to be considered. Turing decided that a machine can think if it can pass itself off as a human being to a real human being, not counting physical characteristics such as appearance, voice, mobility, and so on. Turing assumed that his thinking machine would understand and produce language.

The difficulties in automatic speech recognition and production are immense. Yet there are hundreds of scientists, including communication engineers, phoneticians, linguists, psychologists, and philosophers, who are now working in this research area.

The earliest efforts toward building "talking machines" were more concerned with machines that could produce sounds which sounded like human speech than with machines that could "think" of what to say. In 1779, Christian Gottlieb Kratzenstein won a prize for building such a machine ("an instrument constructed like the *vox humana* pipes of an organ which . . . accurately express the sounds of the vowels") and for answering a question posed by the Imperial Academy of St. Petersburg: "What is the nature and character of the sounds of the vowels *a, e, i, o, u* [which make them] different from one another?" Kratzenstein constructed a set of "acoustic resonators" similar to the shapes of the mouth when these vowels are articulated and set them resonating by a vibrating reed which produced puffs of air similar to those coming from the lungs through the vibrating vocal cords.

Twelve years later, Wolfgang von Kempelen of Vienna constructed a more elaborate machine with bellows to produce a stream of air, such as is produced by the lungs, and with other mechanical devices to "simulate" the different parts of the vocal tract. Von Kempelen's machine so impressed the young Alexander Graham Bell, who saw a replica of the machine in Edinburgh in 1850, that he, together with his brother Melville, attempted to construct a "talking head," making a cast from a human skull. They used various materials to form the velum, palate, teeth, lips, tongue, and so on, and constructed cheeks out of rubber and a metal larynx. The vocal cords were made by stretching a slotted piece of rubber over a structure. They used a keyboard control system to manipulate all the parts with an intricate set of levers. This ingenious machine produced vowel sounds and some nasal sounds and even a few short combinations of sounds.

With the advances in the acoustic theory of speech production and the technological developments in electronics, machine production of speech sounds has made great progress. We no longer have to build actual physical models of the speech-producing mechanism; we can now imitate the process by producing the physical signals by electronic means.

The research on speech has shown that all speech sounds can be reduced to a small number of acoustic components. One way to produce artificial or synthetic speech is to mix these important parts together in the proper proportions depending on the speech sounds one wishes to imitate. It is rather like following a recipe for making soup which might read: "Take two quarts of water, add one onion, three carrots, a potato, a teaspoon of salt, a pinch of pepper, and stir it all together."

This method of producing synthetic speech would include a recipe which might read: "Start with a buzzing noise corresponding to the puffs of air like those coming through the vibrating vocal cords, add different ingredients which correspond to the different vowel qualities (these being the 'overtones' resulting from the different vocal tract shapes), add the 'hissing' noise produced when fricatives occur, add nasal 'resonances' for any nasal sounds, cut off the 'buzz' to produce 'stops,' " and so on. This highly oversimplified "recipe" may be more confusing than enlightening. A more exact description would require technical knowledge of acoustic phonetics.

Although acoustic theory of speech production is very advanced, much of the speech which is synthesized still has a "machine quality." Some of it is highly intelligible despite this, and in a few cases it is hard to distinguish it from human speech. But it must be remembered that the machine only "talks" when we tell it *what* to say and *how* to say it and so is only imitating human speech on a phonetic level. This does, nevertheless, require a high level of knowledge about the important acoustic cues which listeners pay attention to in their "decoding" of spoken speech.

Much of the research aimed at achieving automatic speech recognition depends on our understanding of the acoustics of speech. To produce machines that can comprehend speech (or to program a computer to "understand" spoken language) is much more difficult than to produce machines that can synthesize speech. By now you should have some idea of why it is so difficult. It is even difficult for humans to "read" a spectrogram if they don't know the language, the speaker, and even what was said. Language is filled with redundancies which enable a human to "decode" a very noisy or distorted utterance. We can understand what is said to us because of our linguistic knowledge. The difficulty of programing a computer with the same linguistic competence that speakers possess and the ability to use this knowledge in comprehending the message is enormous.

The speech signal is not physically divided into discrete sounds. Our ability to "segment" the signal arises from our knowledge of the grammar, knowing what to consider important, what to ignore, how to pair certain sounds with certain meanings, what sounds or words may be "deleted" or "pushed together," when two different speech signals are linguistically "the same" and when two similar signals are linguistically "different." The difficulty may be illustrated by recalling how hard it is for a non-speaker of French even to divide an incoming French speech signal into separate words, let alone separate phonemic segments.

Yet, despite these problems, research on both automatic speech recognition and speech synthesis proceeds for practical and for "pure research" motives. We use synthetic speech in many "controlled" perception experiments to find out what features of the speech signal are important for perception. This knowledge then helps us to write "recognition" programs. A machine can only be programed to do what we tell it and can only "know" what we know. Thus we are pushed to learn more, to fill in all gaps in our knowledge of the communication process. As we gain more knowledge, recognition programs will be improved. "Recognition" research is proceeding along many lines—automatic speech analysis, automatic parsing, semantic programing, and so on. One cannot predict what the year will be—1984, 2000, 3000?—but one day we may be able to go up to a computer, ask it a question, and get an answer back in what sounds like human speech.

SUMMARY

The science of speech sounds is called **phonetics.** It aims to provide the set of **features,** or properties, which can describe all the sounds used in human language.

When we speak, the physical sounds we produce are continuous stretches of sound, which are the physical representations of strings of **discrete linguistic segments.** To describe these speech sounds we cannot depend on the way words are spelled. The conventional spellings represent the pronunciation of words only partially. Some spellings are archaic and represent earlier pronunciations. For this reason, a **phonetic alphabet** is used, in which each phonetic symbol stands for one and only one sound. The phonetic symbols which can be used to represent the sounds of English are presented in this chapter.

All human speech sounds fall into "natural" classes according to their phonetic properties or features; that is, according to how they are produced. It was shown that sounds may be either **voiced** or **voiceless; oral** or **nasal; labial, alveolar, palatal, velar, uvular,** or **glottal.** They may also be **fricatives** or **stops** and either **consonants, vowels, glides,** or **liquids.** In addition, vowels are distinguished according to the position of the tongue and lips: **high, mid,** or **low** tongue; **front, central,** or **back** tongue; **rounded** or **unrounded** lips. There are general and regular processes (rules) in languages which utilize these natural classes of sounds.

Pitch is also used phonetically. In some languages the pitch of individual syllables is as important as the phonetic properties of segments; these languages are called **tone** languages. Other **intonation** languages use pitch variations over a whole phrase or sentence. Chinese is a tone language, while English is an intonation language.

Stress is also used linguistically. Examples were provided from English to show how one may distinguish words and phrases by different stress placement. A stressed syllable is usually higher in pitch, longer in duration, and louder.

In some languages both long and short vowels and consonants occur. The **length** of a segment may also thus be phonetically important in describing speech sounds.

By means of these phonetic features one can describe all speech sounds, and in addition, see how the sounds are used in languages in regular patterns.

Speech sounds may be described by their physical properties. The study of the physical characteristics of speech sounds is called **acoustic phonetics.** Some of the major physical, or acoustic, features are **fundamental frequency** (or **pitch**), **intensity** (or **loudness**), and **formants** (overtone pitches for vowels).

As a step toward Turing's goal of constructing a "thinking machine," linguists and engineers are attempting to "teach" computers to speak and to understand spoken language. Attempts to produce **synthetic speech** by mechanical means—to produce noises which sound like human speech—go back at least 200 years. The advances in electronic technology and in the understanding of the acoustics of speech production have brought us close to our goal of synthesizing speech sounds. Our knowledge of the important acoustic properties of speech was aided greatly by the development of an instrument called a **sound spectrograph,** which produces a visual display of the physical acoustic signal called a **spectrogram.** Acoustic analysis of speech sounds can also be performed by computers.

Automatic **speech recognition** (or "understanding") is a much more difficult task. Humans use their linguistic knowledge to comprehend a spoken message. The physical signal alone is not enough to account for our ability to understand speech. At present, no machine can be programed to contain even a fraction of the knowledge that every speaker has about his or her language. There is, however, serious ongoing research in this field, which should also help to contribute to our understanding of speech production and perception.

EXERCISES

1. A. Write the phonetic symbol for the *first* sound in each of the following words, according to the way you pronounce it. Example: *ooze* [u], *psycho* [s].

a. though	f. judge
b. easy	g. Thomas
c. contact	h. physics
d. pneumonia	i. civic
e. thought	j. usury

B. Write the phonetic symbol for the *last* sound in each of the following:

a. fleece	f. cow
b. neigh	g. rough
c. long	h. cheese
d. health	i. bleached
e. watch	j. rags

C. Write the phonetic symbol for the vowel sound in each of the following:

a. coat	f. hot
b. steel	g. cut
c. play	h. put
d. fight	i. pat
e. cool	j. tease

2. Correct the phonetic description below. The speaker may not have exactly the same pronunciation as you; there are many alternate versions. But there is *one* major error in each line which is an impossible pronunciation for any American speaker. Write the word in which the error occurs; circle the wrong symbol and give the correct one. (Note: the writer of this limerick pronounced the word *didn't* as [dĩnt]; the lack of a [d] before the [n] in the transcription does not represent an error.)

a. θer wʌz wʌns
b. e lĩngwɪstɪks studĩnt
c. hu wʌz stupid
d. ænd not vɛri prudĩnt
e. ðə prõnawns hi yuzd
f. wər vɛri cʌnfyuzd
g. he wud se hũm dĩnt
h. ĩnstɛd ʌf hu dĩnt

3. Write the symbol which corresponds to each of the following phonetic descriptions; then give an English word which contains this sound. Example: voiced alveolar stop—[d], *d*og.

a. voiced bilabial stop
b. low front vowel
c. lateral liquid
d. lax high back rounded vowel
e. velar nasal consonant ŋ
f. voiceless alveolar fricative s
g. mid central vowel
h. voiced affricate
i. palatal glide w how
j. tense front mid vowel e
k. voiced interdental fricative ð the ð
l. voiceless labiodental fricative f

4. A phonetic symbol is actually a "cover term" for a composite of distinct phonetic properties or features. Define each of the symbols below by marking a + or a − for each given feature; a + if the property is present, a − if it is not.

A.	n	θ	z	g	t	f
stop	−		−	+	+	−
nasal	+		−	−	−	−
voiced	+		+	+	−	−
labial	−		−	−	−	+
alveolar	+		+	−	+	−
velar	−		−	+	−	−

B.	a	o	ɪ	u	i	æ	e
high		−			+		+ −
low		−			−		−
back		+			−		−
tense		+			+		+
round		+			−		−

5. Each of the following groups of sounds consists of members of a natural class of sounds plus one sound that is not a member of that class. A natural class of sounds all share one or more common properties; that is, voiced sounds, fricatives, bilabials, nasals, and so on. Identify the sound that does not belong to the class; name the feature or features that define the class.

a. [g], [p], [b], [d]
b. [f], [p], [m], [θ], [v], [b]
c. [æ], [u], [i], [e], [ɛ]
d. [z], [v], [s], [ž], [g]

e. [t], [z], [d], [n], [s]
f. [m], [n], [b], [ŋ]
g. [g], [k], [b], [d], [p], [v], [t]
h. [a], [u], [e], [w], [i], [o]

6. In each of the following pairs of words the italicized sounds differ by one or more phonetic properties (features). State the differences and, in addition, state what properties they have in common. Example: phone—phonic. The o in phone is mid, tense, round. The o in phonic is low, unround. Both are back vowels.

a. bath—bathe
b. reduce—reduction
c. cool—cold
d. wife—wives
e. face—facial

f. heal—health
g. cats—dogs
h. impolite—indecent
i. democrat—democracy
j. mouse—mice

7. Write the following in regular English spelling:

a. nom čamski ɪz ə lɪŋgwɪst hu tičəz æt ɛm ay ti.
b. fonɛtɪks ɪz ðə stʌdi əv spič sawndz.
c. ɔl læŋgwɪǰəz yuz sawndz produst bay ðə ʌpər rɛspərətɔri sɪstəm.
d. ɪn wʌn dayəlɛkt kat ænd kɔt ar pronawnst ðə sem.
e. sʌm pipəl θɪŋk fonɛtɪks ɪz ə bɪg bɔr.

8. A. Mark the primary stress on each of the following words by placing an acute accent (´) over the stressed syllable. Example: lánguage.

a. together
b. horrible
c. mystery
d. mysterious
e. phonetic
f. digest (noun)—digest (verb)
g. convert (noun)—convert (verb)
h. special
i. specific
j. specify

B. Mark the primary stress (as above) and the secondary stress by a grave accent (`) on the following. Example: fùndaméntal.

a. laboratory
b. medicine
c. specialize
d. professorial
e. conversation
f. general
g. generality
h. mystify
i. productivity
j. experience

C. Mark the *one vowel* which receives the primary stress in the following sentences (the meaning is given in parentheses). Example: It's a hótdog (it's a frankfurter); he's a hot dóg (the dog is overheated).

a. He's a lighthouse keeper. (He works in a lighthouse directing ships.)
b. She's a light housekeeper. (She is a housekeeper who is light.)
c. It's a blackboard eraser. (It's an eraser for a blackboard, e.g., a blackboard can be green.)
d. It's a black board eraser. (It's a black eraser for a board.)
e. She's a French literature teacher. (She's a teacher of French literature.)
f. She's a French literature teacher. (She's a teacher of literature who is French.)
g. He's a grandfather figure. (He's a figure of a grandfather.)
h. He's a grand father figure. (He's a father figure who is grand.)

9. The use of "voiceprints" for speaker identification is based on the fact that no two speakers ever talk *exactly* alike. List some of the differences you have observed in the speech of different individuals. What are some of the possible reasons why such differences exist?

10. Can you think of any practical uses for automatic speech recognition and synthesis? For example, one possible use would be in the postal service. Imagine a machine which would sort letters for individual states by being given verbal instructions. The mail clerk could put a letter on a conveyer belt and say "New Jersey," "Nevada," and so on, or "10028," "94619," and so on, and the computer would automatically send the letter to the correct bin. Another example would be in a library where someone could walk up to the computer and say, "Where will I find such and such a book?" and receive the answer "Section P. 3." Think up as many such uses as you can.

References

Abercrombie, David. *Elements of General Phonetics*. Chicago: Aldine, 1967. A good general introductory textbook.

Chomsky, N., and M. Halle. *The Sound Pattern of English,* ch. 8. New York: Harper & Row, 1968. An advanced treatment of phonetic theory, with a suggested set of universal distinctive features and their phonetic correlates.

Denes, P. B., and E. N. Pinson. *The Speech Chain*. New York: Anchor Books, 1973. An "easy to read and understand" discussion on the physics of sound and acoustics of speech.

Flanagan, J. L. "The Synthesis of Speech," *Scientific American,* vol. 226, no. 2 (Feb. 1972), pp. 48–58. A discussion on speech synthesis written for the general public.

International Phonetic Association. *Principles of the International Phonetic Association,* rev. ed. London: IPA, 1949. The phonetic alphabet used by the IPA is given with proposed diacritics for finer phonetic distinctions.

Jakobson, R., and M. Halle. "Fundamentals of Language," *Janua Linguarum* 1. The Hague: Mouton, 1956. One of the first treatments of distinctive feature theory as defined in acoustic terms.

Jones, Daniel. *An Outline of English Phonetics,* 8th ed. Cambridge, England: Heffer, 1956. A comprehensive summary of traditional phonetics from the British point of view.

Ladefoged, Peter. *Elements of Acoustic Phonetics*. Chicago: University of Chicago Press, 1962. The best introduction to acoustic phonetics for those who wish to understand the physical properties of speech sounds.

Ladefoged, Peter. *A Course in Phonetics*. New York: Harcourt Brace Jovanovich, 1975. A basic and comprehensive introduction to both articulatory and acoustic phonetics, with exercises to help the student understand basic concepts and gain production mastery of the speech sounds in all languages.

Sweet, Henry. *A Primer of Phonetics*. Oxford: The Clarendon Press, 1890. Those interested in one of the most famous founders of "modern phonetics" would find this book by the prototype of Henry Higgins of great historical interest.

5

Phonology: The Sound Patterns of Language

Phonology is the study of telephone etiquette.
A HIGH SCHOOL STUDENT[1]

I believe that phonology is superior to music. It is more variable and its pecuniary possibilities are far greater.
ERIK SATIE (from the cover of a record album)

Phonology is not the study of telephone etiquette nor is it the study of telephones. Phonology is rather the study of the sound patterns found in human language; it is also the term used to refer to the kind of knowledge that speakers have about the sound patterns of their particular language. Since everyone who knows a language knows (unconsciously of course) its phonology, it may indeed be superior to music, since there are many people who neither know nor care about music. But unlike Satie, we see no reason to compare the two in value. And we would certainly not encourage anyone to become a phonologist for the reasons given by Satie. We are not sure what "pecuniary possibilities" he had in mind (not knowing any rich phonologists), and the sound systems of the world's languages are less varied than they are similar. It is true that speech sounds as physical entities may be infinitely varied, but when they function as elements in a language, as phonological units, they are highly constrained. This is, in fact, one of the reasons why the study of the sound systems of language is a fascinating one, for it reveals how human linguistic ability enables one to extract regularities from the constantly varying physical sounds. Despite the infinite variations which occur when we speak, all speakers of a language agree that certain utterances are the "same" and others are "different." Phonology tells us why this is the case.

Linguists are interested in how sound systems may vary, and also in

---

[1] As reported in *Pullet Surprises* by Amsel Greene (Glenview, Ill.: Scott, Foresman & Co., 1969).

the phonetic and phonological universals found in all languages. We find that the same relatively small set of phonetic properties characterizes all human speech sounds, that the same classes of these sounds are utilized in languages spoken from the Arctic Circle to the Cape of Good Hope, and that the same kinds of regular patterns of speech sounds occur all over the world. When you learn a language you learn which speech sounds occur in your language and how they pattern according to regular rules.

Phonology is concerned with this kind of linguistic knowledge. Phonetics, as discussed in the previous chapter, provides the means for describing speech sounds; phonology studies the ways in which speech sounds form systems and patterns in human language. The phonology of a language is then the system and pattern of the speech sounds. We see that the word *phonology* is thus used in two ways, either as the *study* of sound patterns in language or as *the* sound pattern of a language.

Phonological knowledge permits a speaker to produce sounds which form meaningful utterances, to recognize a foreign "accent," to make up new words, to add the appropriate phonetic segments to form plurals and past tenses, to produce "aspirated" and "unaspirated" voiceless stops in the appropriate context, to know what is or is not a sound in one's language, and to know that different phonetic strings may represent the same "meaningful unit." Since the grammar of the language represents the totality of one's linguistic knowledge, knowledge of the sound patterns—the *phonology*—must be part of this grammar. In this chapter we shall discuss the kinds of things that speakers know about the sound system of their language—their phonological knowledge.

Phonemes: The Phonological Units of Language

In the physical world the naive speaker and hearer actualize and are sensitive to sounds, but what they feel themselves to be pronouncing and hearing are "phonemes."
EDWARD SAPIR, 1933

For native speakers, phonological knowledge goes beyond the ability to produce all the phonetically different sounds of their language. It includes this, of course. A speaker of English can produce the sound [θ] and knows that this sound occurs in English, in words like *thin* [θɪn] or *ether* [iθər] or *bath* [bæθ]. English speakers may or may not be able to produce a "click" or a velar fricative, but even if they can, they know that such sounds are not part of the phonetic inventory of English. Many speakers are unable to produce such "foreign" sounds. French speakers similarly know that the [θ] is not part of the phonetic inventory of French and often find it difficult to pronounce a word like *thin* [θɪn], pronouncing it as [sɪn].

An English speaker also knows that [ð], the voiced counterpart of [θ], is a sound of English, occurring in words like *either* [iðər], *then* [ðɛn], and *bathe* [beð].

Knowing the sounds (the phonetic units) of a language is only a small part of one's phonological knowledge.

In Chapter 1 we discussed the fact that knowing a language implies knowing the set of words which comprise the vocabulary, or lexicon, of that language. You might know fewer or more words than your next-door neighbor, but each word you have learned is stored in your brain or mind, in memory, as part of the grammar of the language. When you know a word, you know both its **form** (the sounds which represent it) and its **meaning.** We have already seen that the relationship between the form and the meaning of a word is arbitrary; one must learn *both*; knowing the meaning does not tell you its pronunciation, and knowing the sounds of a word does not tell you what it means (if you didn't know this already).

Consider the forms and meanings of the following words in English:

pill	till	kill
bill	dill	gill

Each word differs from all the other words in both form and meaning. The difference in meaning between *pill* and *bill* is "signaled" by the fact that the initial sound of the first word is *p* and the initial sound of the second word is *b*. The forms of the two words—that is, their sounds—are identical except for the initial consonants. *p* and *b* are therefore able to distinguish or **contrast** words. They are thus said to be **distinctive** sounds in English. Such distinctive sounds are called **phonemes.**

We see that *t* and *d*, *k* and *g* must also be phonemes in English for the same reasons, since if you substitute a *g* for a *k*, or a *d* for a *t*, the meaning of the word changes. Similarly, *p* is distinguished from *t*, and *t* from *k*, and *b* from *d*, and *d* from *g*. We can conclude that *p, t, k, b, d,* and *g* are all phonemes in English.

Even if we did not know what phonetic properties distinguished these sounds we would know that these sound segments represent phonemes in the English phonological system. Phonetics provides the means to describe the sounds, to show how they differ; phonology tells us that they function as phonemes, are able to contrast meanings of words.

A first rule of thumb which one can use to determine the phonemes of any language is to see if substituting one sound for another results in a change of meaning. If it does, the two sounds represent different phonemes. When two different forms are identical in every way except for one sound segment which occurs in the same place in the string, the two words are called **minimal pairs.** *Pill* and *bill* are minimal pairs, as are *pill* and *till, till* and *dill, till* and *kill, kill* and *gill.* All these words together constitute a **minimal set;** they are identical in form except for the initial consonants. Note that *lob* [lab] and *lead* [lid] are not minimal pairs because they differ in two sounds, the vowels and the final consonants. Similarly, *veal* [vil] and *leaf* [lif] are not minimal pairs because although only one sound differs in the two words, the [v] occurs initially and the [f] finally. Of course we can find a minimal pair which shows that [v] and [f] are phonemes in English: *veal* [vil] and *feel* [fil]. Substituting an [f] for the [v] changes the meaning of the word.

We have many minimal sets in English which make it relatively "easy" for us to know what the English phonemes are. All the following words are identical except for the vowels.

beat	[bit]	[i]	boot	[but]	[u]
bit	[bɪt]	[ɪ]	but	[bʌt]	[ʌ]
bait	[bet]	[e]	boat	[bot]	[o]
bet	[bɛt]	[ɛ]	bought	[bɔt]	[ɔ]
bat	[bæt]	[æ]	bout	[bawt]	[aw]
bite	[bayt]	[ay]			

In the minimal set above we do not find the vowels [a], [ʊ]; and [ɔy]. Does this mean they are not phonemes in English? Since we can find other minimal pairs in which these vowels contrast meanings, we see that they are phonemes.

seed	[sid]	sod	[sad]	[i] / [a]
hit	[hɪt]	hot	[hat]	[ɪ] / [a]
feet	[fit]	foot	[fʊt]	[i] / [ʊ]
fail	[fel]	full	[fʊl]	[e] / [ʊ]
sigh	[say]	soy	[sɔy]	[ay] / [ɔy]
bough	[baw]	boy	[bɔy]	[aw] / [ɔy]

Although [bat] and [bʊt] are not actual words in English, they are sequences or strings of sounds all of which represent phonemes, and the sequences of these phonemes are permissible in English. (We will discuss permissible sequences below.) One might then say that they are nonsense words (permissible forms with no meanings) or *possible* words. Note that until recently [bɪk] (spelled *Bic*) was not an English word. Before its introduction and before TV commercials talked about a "flick of the Bic," it must have been a possible word, for it is now a real one. One would hardly expect a new product to come on the market with the name [ɣik], since [ɣ] (the voiced velar fricative) does not represent an English phoneme. Possible but nonoccurring words, as *Bic* once was, are **accidental gaps** in the vocabulary. An accidental gap is a form which "obeys" all the phonological rules of the language—that is, it includes native phonemes in a permitted order—but which has no meaning. An actual, occurring word is a combination of both a permitted form and a meaning.

Some further examples of minimal pairs in English provide evidence for other contrasting phonemes. Note again that the change in the phonetic form produces a change in the meaning. When such a change in meaning is the result of the substitution of just one sound segment in the identical position in the string, the two different segments must represent distinctive phonemes. There is no other way to account for these particular meaning contrasts.

*s*in	*th*in	[s]	[θ]	me*s*her	mea*s*ure	[š]	[ž]	*ch*in	*g*in	[č]	[ǰ]
*d*o	*z*oo	[d]	[z]	*r*ink	*l*ink	[r]	[l]	*f*ine	*v*ine	[f]	[v]
*w*oo	*y*ou	[w]	[y]	e*th*er	ei*th*er	[θ]	[ð]	si*n*	si*ng*	[n]	[ŋ]
*m*ote	*n*ote	[m]	[n]	*h*igh	*w*hy	[h]	[w]	*d*en	*th*en	[d]	[ð]

We have said above that when the substitution of one sound segment for another results in a difference in meaning this is *sufficient* evidence that the two sounds represent two different phonemes. But note that *two different forms* may be *identical in meaning*, as shown by the fact that some speakers pronounce the word *economics* as [ìkənámɪks] and others as [ɛ̀kənámɪks]. These two forms are not minimal pairs, since the substitution of [i] for [ɛ] or vice versa does not change the meaning. Similarly, some speakers pronounce *ration* as [rešən] and others as [rǽšən]. Such pairs do not tell us whether [i] and [ɛ] or [e] and [æ] represent phonemes in the language. We know, however, that these are contrastive sounds from such pairs as *beat/bet* ([i]/[ɛ]) and *bait/bat* ([e]/[æ]). The different pronunciations of *economics* or *ration* are **free variations**; one meaning (of each word) is represented by two different phonemic forms.

Homonyms or homophones also show that two different meanings, two words, may have identical forms; that is, may be pronounced exactly alike. Thus [sol] can mean "sole," or "soul," and the sentence "Greta Garbo ate her cottage cheese with *relish* [rɛləš]" could mean she ate with "gusto" or with a particular kind of sauce.

Thus the determining fact is whether there is *both* a change in form (pronunciation) and a change in meaning. When this occurs we know that the substituted sound segments represent different phonemes.

In order for two phonetic forms to differ and to contrast meanings there must be some phonetic difference between the substituted sounds. We can conclude from the minimal pairs *seal* and *zeal* that [s] and [z] represent two contrasting phonemes in English. From the discussion of phonetics in Chapter 4 we know that the only difference between [s] and [z] is a voicing difference; [s] is voiceless or [−voiced] and [z] is voiced or [+voiced]. It is this phonetic feature which distinguishes the two words. Voicing thus plays a special role in English (and in many other languages). It also distinguishes *feel* and *veal* ([f]/[v]) and *ether* and *either* ([θ]/[ð]). It distinguishes one phoneme from another and in English is therefore a **distinctive feature** (or a **phonemic feature**). When two words are exactly alike phonetically except for one feature, the phonetic difference is distinctive, since this difference alone accounts for the meaning contrast. Note that a single feature has two values, + and −; for example, [± nasal], or [± voicing], or [± consonantal], and so forth. When we say that a phonetic feature is distinctive we are saying that the + value of that feature found in certain words contrasts with the − value of that feature in other words.

The minimal pairs given below illustrate some of the distinctive features in the phonological system of English.

bat	[bæt]	mat	[mæt]	The difference in meaning between *bat* and *mat* is due only to the difference in nasality between [b] and [m]. [b] and [m] are identical in all features except for the fact that [b] is oral ([−nasal]) and [m] is nasal ([+nasal]). Thus, nasality ([± nasal]) is a distinctive feature of English consonants.

rack	[ræk]	rock	[rak]	The two words are distinguished only because [æ] is a front vowel and [a] is a back vowel. They are both low, un-rounded vowels. [± back] is therefore a distinctive feature of English vowels.
see	[si]	zee	[zi]	The difference in meaning is due only to the voicelessness of the [s] in contrast to the voicing of the [z]. The two words are phonetically identical in all other re-spects. Therefore voicing ([± voiced]) is a distinctive feature of English conso-nants.

The method of substituting one sound for another to determine whether the new form creates a new meaning may also be used to show that all sounds which occur phonetically in a language may not represent separate phonemes. Again, this is a "tool" which may be helpful in analysis, but one must remember that it is the presence of contrast, not the lack of con-trast, that shows the phonemic distinctions.

In Chapter 4 we pointed out that *phonetically* both oral and nasalized vowels occur in English. The following examples show this.

bean	[bĩn]	bead	[bid]
roam	[rõm]	robe	[rob]

Nasalized vowels only occur in English before nasal consonants. If one substituted an oral vowel for the nasal vowels in *bean* and *roam* the mean-ings of the two words would not be changed. Try to say these words keep-ing your velum up until your tongue makes the stop closure of the [n] or your lips come together for the [m]. It will not be easy for you because in English we automatically lower the velum when producing vowels be-fore nasals.

Or try to produce a nasal vowel (lower your velum immediately after you articulate the consonant) in the words *by, see,* or *go* to produce [bãy], [sĩ], and [gõ]. If you spoke like this people would probably say you have a "nasal twang" but they would understand you to be saying *by, see,* and *go.* Changing the forms of the words by substituting nasalized vowels does not change the meanings.

We have seen above that a substitution of [i] for [ɛ] in *economics* does not change the meaning of the word. Thus, the fact that in one or more words the substitution of one sound for another may not change the mean-ing shows that this is not sufficient evidence for deciding whether two sounds represent two phonemes. But there is a difference between the sub-stitution of [i] and [ɛ] in *economics* and the substitutions we have observed between oral and nasalized vowels. [i] and [ɛ] were shown by a number of examples to represent different phonemes. We can find no such cases to demonstrate that [i] and [ĩ], for example, represent different phonemes.

A further, more important difference between [i] and [ɛ] and [i] and [ĩ] (or [u] and [ũ], [o] and [õ], [a] and [ã], and so on) is that there are no general principles in the phonology of English which tell us when [i] occurs and when [ɛ] occurs. One must learn, when learning the words, that [i] occurs in *beat* and [ɛ] occurs in *bet*.

There is, however, a general principle, or a *rule*, which tells us, or *predicts*, when a vowel will be oral and when the same vowel phoneme will be nasalized. Consider the following sets of words and nonwords:

WORDS						NONWORDS		
bee	[bi]	*bead*	[bid]	*bean*	[bĩn]	*[bĩ]	*[bĩd]	*[bin]
lay	[le]	*lace*	[les]	*lame*	[lẽm]	*[lẽ]	*[lẽs]	*[lem]
baa	[bæ]	*bad*	[bæd]	*bang*	[bæ̃ŋ]	*[bæ̃]	*[bæ̃d]	*[bæŋ]

The words show us where oral and nasal vowels can occur in English: oral vowels in final position and before nonnasal consonants; nasalized vowels only before nasal consonants. The "nonwords" show us where oral and nasalized vowels can*not* occur; where oral vowels can occur, nasalized vowels cannot occur, and vice versa. Thus the oral vowels and their nasalized counterparts never contrast. Nasalization of vowels in English is predictable by a rule which can be stated as:

(1) Nasalize a vowel when it occurs before a nasal consonant.

The value of the feature [±nasal] can be predicted for the class of vowel segments in English. When a feature is predictable by a general principle or rule it is not a distinctive, or phonemic, feature for that class of segments. Thus, the feature [±nasal] is not a distinctive feature for English vowels.

Yet we have seen that nasalized vowels do occur phonetically. We can conclude then that there is no one-to-one correspondence between phonetic segments and phonemes in a language. In fact, from the examples given above we see that one phoneme may be realized phonetically, or pronounced, as more than one phonetic segment. Each vowel phoneme in English is realized as either an oral vowel or a nasal vowel depending on its phonemic context.

Some new terminology may help to clarify things a bit. A phonetic unit or segment is called a **phone**. A **phoneme** is a more abstract unit. One must know the phonological rules of the language to know how to pronounce it, since in one context it may be realized as one phone (for example, [i]) and in another context as a different phone (for example, [ĩ]). To distinguish between phonemes and phones we will use slashes / / to enclose phonemic segments or phonemic transcriptions of words and will continue to use the square brackets [ ] for phonetic segments or phonetic transcriptions. Thus we will represent the vowel phoneme in *bead* and *bean* as /i/ in both words. This phoneme is pronounced (or realized) as [i] in *bead* and [ĩ] in *bean*.

We have seen that a single phoneme may be phonetically realized or pronounced as two or more phones. The different phones which "represent" or which are *derived* from one phoneme are called the **allophones** of that phoneme. Thus, in English, each vowel phoneme has both an oral and a nasalized allophone. The choice of the allophone is not random or haphazard in most cases; it is *rule-governed*. This was illustrated above by demonstrating that there is a general principle determining the occurrence of oral and nasalized vowels. No one explicitly teaches you these rules. You "construct" them yourself; language acquisition is to a great extent rule construction. You probably do not even know that you know these rules; yet you produce the nasalized allophones of the vowel phonemes automatically whenever they occur before nasal consonants.

When two or more allophones of one phoneme never occur in the same phonemic context or environment they are said to be in **complementary distribution**. The examples of the words and nonwords given on page 107 illustrate the way the oral and nasalized allophones of each vowel phoneme complement each other. We will repeat the environments in which the different allophones occur:

1. At the end of a word: only oral vowels; no nasal vowels
2. Before nasal consonants: only nasalized vowels; no oral vowels
3. Before nonnasal consonants: only oral vowels; no nasalized vowels

Where one variety occurs, the other doesn't. It is in this sense that the phones are said to complement each other or to be in complementary distribution.

This further illustrates that nasality is a predictable or **redundant** feature for vowels in English (but not consonants). Whether a vowel is [+nasal] or [−nasal] is said to be redundant because it depends on other aspects of the word. If the vowel occurs word-finally, you know that the vowel is oral or [−nasal]; the value of this feature is therefore redundant. It is not specific to any particular word but determined by a general rule.

The nasality feature, however, is not redundant for consonants in English; whether or not a consonant is [+nasal] cannot be predicted by a general rule but must be specified for each word. There is no rule which can predict that the word *bean* will have a final *n* rather than a *d*; in learning the word we must learn that the final consonant is the nasal consonant /n/ and not /d/, or /t/, or /k/, and so on. Similarly, the fact that *meat* begins with a bilabial nasal is an arbitrary fact about this particular word. Thus the first consonant must be specified as [+nasal] to distinguish it from the [−nasal] specification of the first consonant in the word *beat*.

But, the fact that the vowel in *bean* is nasalized is not a fact about just this word but about all the words in which the vowel is followed by a nasal consonant. If you didn't learn the rule you would not pronounce the words according to the normal English pronunciation.

The rule stated above is one found in many languages of the world. This is not surprising; it is a very plausible or "natural" rule, since it is more difficult to prevent nasalizing a vowel before a nasal consonant than it is to nasalize it in this context; to prevent nasalization, one's timing of the velic closure must be very precise.

This does not mean however that nasality cannot be distinctive for vowels in other languages. We have already seen some examples of nasalized vowels in French in Chapter 4. In Akan, the major language spoken in Ghana (also called Twi), nasalized and oral vowels occur both phonetically and phonemically, as the following examples illustrate; nasalization is a distinctive feature for vowels in Akan.

[ka]	"bite"	[kã]	"speak"
[fi]	"come from"	[fĩ]	"dirty"
[tu]	"pull"	[tũ]	"hole/den"
[nsa]	"hand"	[nsã]	"liquor"
[či]	"hate"	[čĩ]	"squeeze"
[pam]	"sew"	[pãm]	"confederate"

These examples show that vowel nasalization is not predictable. There is no rule which says that all vowels are nasalized before nasal consonants as shown by the last minimal pair. Furthermore, after the identical consonants one finds word-final oral vowels contrasting with word-final nasalized vowels; here we see that the change of form (that is, the substitution of nasalized for oral vowels, or vice versa) does change the meaning. Both oral and nasal vowel phonemes must therefore exist in Akan.

Notice that two languages may have the same phonetic segments (phones) but have two different phonemic systems. Both oral and nasalized vowels exist in English and Akan; English has no nasalized vowel phonemes but Akan does. The same phonetic segments function differently in the two languages. Nasalization of vowels in English is *redundant* and *nondistinctive*; nasalization of vowels in Akan is *nonredundant* and *distinctive*.

We can further illustrate the fact that two languages can have the same set of phonetic segments with different phonemic systems by examining the voiceless stops. In the previous chapter we pointed out that in English both aspirated and unaspirated voiceless stops occur. The aspirated stops [pʰ], [tʰ], and [kʰ] occur in the words *pill, till,* and *kill,* and the unaspirated voiceless stops [p], [t], and [k] occur in *spill, still,* and *skill.* Despite the phonetic difference between the unaspirated and aspirated phones, speakers of English (if they are not acting as linguists or phoneticians) usually consider the *p* in *pill* and *spill* to be the "same" sound, just as they consider the [i] and [ĩ] which represent the phoneme /i/ in *bead* and *bean* to be the "same." Again this is because the difference between them, in this case the feature "aspiration," is *predictable, redundant, nondistinctive, nonphonemic* (these are all equivalent terms). The aspirated and the nonaspirated phones are in complementary distribution. Voiceless stops are always aspirated when they occur at the beginning of a word before stressed vowels, and voiceless stops are always unaspirated after an initial /s/. This is a fact about English phonology. There are two *p* sounds (or phones) in English, but only one *p* phoneme. (This is also true of *t* and *k*). Remember that a phoneme is an abstract unit. We do not utter phonemes; we produce phones. /p/ is a phoneme in English which is realized phonetically (pronounced) as either [p] or [pʰ]. [p] and [pʰ] are allophones of the phoneme /p/. Another way of stating this same fact is to say that the [p] and [pʰ] are *derived* from /p/ by a rule which can be stated as:

(2) Aspirate a /p/ when it occurs word initially or syllable initially before a stressed vowel.

These same phonetic segments ([p] and [pʰ], [t] and [tʰ], [k] and [kʰ]) occur in Thai, but they function differently in Thai than in English. In the previous chapter we presented examples to show that the aspiration or nonaspiration of a voiceless stop is not predictable by a general rule in Thai. We can see from the following minimal pair that [p] and [pʰ] are contrastive and therefore must represent /p/ and /pʰ/, respectively, in Thai.

/paa/ [paa] "forest"   /pʰaa/ [pʰaa]   "to split"

Note that in the above examples the [p] and the [pʰ] are not in complementary distribution, since they both occur in the same "slot" or position in the two words, as the word-initial consonant.

In English it is not just the bilabial voiceless stop which is predictably aspirated in certain phonemic contexts. The phonological rule stated above applies to all voiceless stops, to the class of phonemes which are specified as $\begin{bmatrix} -\text{continuant} \\ -\text{voiced} \end{bmatrix}$. Similarly, the vowel nasalization rule applies to all vowels before nasal consonants, to the class of phonemes specified as $\begin{bmatrix} -\text{consonantal} \\ +\text{vocalic} \end{bmatrix}$

Some rules, however, are less general. Every speaker of English knows that an *l*-sound occurs in English. There must be a phoneme /l/, since *lake* means something different from *rake, make, bake, take, cake,* and so on. It comes as a surprise to most English speakers to discover that in most English dialects there are two phonetically different *l*'s. The *l* in *leaf* in these dialects differs from the *l* in *feel*. When you pronounce *leaf* the back of the tongue is not raised; in the pronunciation of *feel* the back of the tongue is raised toward the hard palate, or velum. If you say these words aloud and concentrate on the tongue position (and you speak this dialect) you may feel the difference. The *l* in *feel*, produced with the back of the tongue raised, is a "velarized" or "hard" *l*. In the English dialects where this difference occurs, the two *l*'s are in complementary distribution: the nonvelarized [l] occurs only before nonlow front vowels; the velarized [ɫ] occurs elsewhere (before back and low vowels and syllable finally). Thus [ɫ] occurs in *look, Luke, lock, load, feel, fool, pal, pull, pill,* and [l] occurs in *leak, lick, lake, let,* and so on. Thus, whether an /l/ is velarized or not is predictable by rule, and the two phonetic *l*-sounds [l] and [ɫ] are allophones of the single phoneme /l/ in English. In Russian there is a phonemic difference between these two sounds, but in English velarization is predictable, redundant, and nondistinctive. In Swedish only the nonvelarized *l* [l] occurs. There is only one lateral phone which represents or is derived from the phoneme /l/.

In learning a language, a child learns which features are distinctive in that language and which are not. One phonetic feature may be distinctive for one class of sounds but predictable or nondistinctive for another class, as, for example, the nasality feature for consonants as opposed to vowels.

Some features are nondistinctive for all the sounds of a particular language. Thus "aspiration" is totally predictable for voiceless stops and, since all voiced stops are by their very nature nonaspirated, this feature does not distinguish between any phonemes in English. Aspiration is in a sense neither distinctive nor nondistinctive for voiced stops (or any voiced sounds), since physiologically voiced sounds cannot be aspirated. This feature is thus irrelevant for voiced segments. The values of features may therefore be predictable either due to the phonological regularities or rules of a language or predictable because of universal constraints on feature combinations.

Some features are predictable because of the segments which precede or follow. That is, aspiration cannot be predicted in isolation but only when a voiceless stop occurs in a word, since the presence or absence of aspiration depends on *where* the voiceless stop occurs and *what precedes* or *follows* it. Its predictability depends on the environment. Similarly, the oral or nasal quality of a vowel depends on what follows the vowel in the word; for example, a vowel is nasalized if it is followed by a nasal consonant.

Some features, however, may be predictable or redundant due to the specification of the other features of that segment. That is, given the presence of certain features one can predict the value of other features without any reference to the surrounding segments.

In English, as pointed out in the preceding chapter, all front vowels are predictably nonround. Unlike French, there are no rounded front vowels in English. We can thus say that if a vowel in English is specified as [−back] it is also redundantly, predictably [−round].

Similarly, in Akan there is only one liquid phoneme /l/. ([l] exists only in a few loan words, like *London* and *U.C.L.A.*) Thus, laterality is not a distinctive feature in Akan; given that a segment is specified as $\begin{bmatrix} +\text{consonantal} \\ +\text{vocalic} \end{bmatrix}$ —that is, as a liquid—this segment is redundantly, predictably [−lateral].

Notice that a phonetic description of the sounds of a language is not enough to reveal the phonological system. The phonetic segments, or phones, pattern differently in different languages. Phonetic features that are distinctive in one language may be redundant in another.

Because of words like *pin* and *bin, rapid* and *rabid, rip* and *rib* we know that there is a phonemic contrast between /p/ and /b/. We also know that voicing is a distinctive feature of English, as shown by the following minimal pairs:

VOICELESS	VOICED
[f] *f*ine	[v] *v*ine
[s] *s*ink	[z] *z*inc
[š] me*sh*er	[ž] mea*s*ure
[č] *ch*in	[j] *g*in

/p/ and /b/ also differ in that /p/ is [−voiced] and /b/ is [+voiced]. But a third bilabial stop exists in English, the aspirated [pʰ]. Since we have already shown that aspiration is a nondistinctive feature of English and that [pʰ] can be derived from /p/, we can conclude that the phonemic difference between /p/ and /b/ is the voicing distinction. /p/ and /b/ (and all symbols of this kind) are cover symbols for **matrices** of distinctive features. The cover symbols by themselves do not reveal the phonetic distinctions which are shown by specifying the feature values. In a phonemic or phonetic matrix each column represents a segment and each row a feature.

	/p/	/b/	
Consonantal	+	+	
Vocalic	−	−	
Continuant	−	−	
Labial	+	+	
Voiced	−	+	← distinctive difference

The nondistinctive feature "aspiration" is not included in these phonemic representations because aspiration is predictable. The phonemic and phonetic differences between the bilabial stops in *pit, spit,* and *bit* illustrate this:

	pit /pɪt/	[pʰɪt]	*spit* /spɪt/	[spɪt]	*bit* /bɪt/	[bɪt]
Distinctive features						
Consonantal	+	+	+	+	+	+
Vocalic	−	−	−	−	−	−
Labial	+	+	+	+	+	+
Continuant	−	−	−	−	−	−
Voiced	−	−	−	−	+	+
Nondistinctive						
Aspirated		+		−		−

In the phonemic representations of all three words there is no feature value specified for the nondistinctive feature [±aspirated]. Phonemically, /p/ and /b/ are neither "aspirated" nor "unaspirated." The specification of this feature depends on the context of the /p/—where it occurs in a word. Rule (2) given above would apply only to the voiceless stops: /p/, /t/, and /k/. It would add the [+aspirated] designation to the voiceless stops in words like *pin, tin, kin, peal, teal,* and *keel,* but would do nothing to *spin, steal, skin,* and so on, or to any of the voiced stops.

In Thai, voicing is also phonemic, as is shown by the *three-way* contrast:

/pàa/ "forest"   /pʰàa/ "to split"   /bàa/ "shoulder"

The phonetic feature matrices for the labial stops in the three Thai words would be identical to the phonetic specifications of the labials in *spit, pit,* and *bit* in English. But the Thai phonemic specifications would differ in that the /p/ in "forest" would have to be marked [−aspirated] and the /pʰ/ in "to split" would have to be marked [+aspirated], since aspiration is contrastive.

We see that the same phonetic segments can form different phonemic patterns in languages.

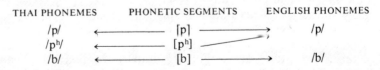

THAI PHONEMES	PHONETIC SEGMENTS	ENGLISH PHONEMES
/p/	←——— [p] ———→	/p/
/pʰ/	←——— [pʰ] ———↗	
/b/	←——— [b] ———→	/b/

The phonetic facts alone do not tell us what is distinctive or phonemic. The phonetic representation of utterances shows what speakers know about the *pronunciation* of utterances; the phonemic representation of utterances shows what the speakers know about the abstract underlying phonology. That *pot* /pat/ and *spot* /spat/ both include a /p/ reveals the fact that English speakers consider the [pʰ] in *pot* [pʰat] and the [p] in *spot* [spat] to be phonetic manifestations of the same phoneme /p/.

The phonology of a language includes rules which relate the phonemic representations of words to their phonetic representations. The phonemic representation need only include the *nonpredictable distinctive* features of the string of phonemes which represent the words. The phonetic representation includes all the *linguistically relevant phonetic* aspects of the sounds.

The phonetic representation does not include *all* the physical properties of the sounds of an utterance, since the physical signal may vary in many ways which have little to do with the phonological system. The absolute pitch of the sounds, or whether the utterance is spoken slowly or fast, or whether the speaker shouts or whispers is not linguistically significant. The phonetic transcription is thus also an abstraction from the physical signal; it includes the nonvariant phonetic aspects of the utterances, those features which remain relatively the same from speaker to speaker and from one time to another.

Given the phonemic representation of an utterance and the phonological rules of the language, one can unambiguously determine the phonetic representation:

	PHONEMIC REPRESENTATION	PHONOLOGICAL RULES	PHONETIC REPRESENTATION
"pot"	/pat/	/p/ → [pʰ] at the beginning of a word	[pʰat]

No rule can tell us that the word *pot* begins with a /p/. That is a unique characteristic of this sound-meaning unit in English. The fact that it begins with a /p/ differentiates it from *cot, not, rot, dot, sot, hot*, and so on. The grammar must then specify that English speakers know that the sound sequence that means "pot" begins with a voiceless bilabial stop, which is followed by a low back vowel and which ends with an alveolar voiceless stop. All three phonemes must be included, since *pot* also is distinguished from *pit, pat, put, pate*, and from *pod, pock, par*, and so on. But the phonemic representation of *pot* need not include anything about the aspiration of the /p/.

Suppose a linguist were attempting to analyze a language which she knew nothing about and wrote down in phonetic transcription the sounds of a number of different words in the language, including the following (n̥, m̥ are voiceless nasals):

[nat]	"girl"	[sn̥at]	"boy"
[nak]	"cat"	[sn̥ak]	"dog"
[mat]	"woman"	[sm̥at]	"man"
[mak]	"cow"	[sm̥ak]	"goat"
[tat]	"book"	[kat]	"tree"

From these few words it would be clear to the linguist (and hopefully to you at this point) that /n/ and /m/ are separate phonemes, since [nat] and [mat] contrast in meaning and this is due to the difference between the initial [n] and [m]. /t/ and /k/ are also phonemes as evidenced by the minimal pairs [nat] and [nak] and the minimal set [nat], [mat], [tat], and [kat]. But the linguist would also conclude that [n] and [n̥] were allophones of the phoneme /n/, and that [m] and [m̥] were allophones of the phoneme /m/. The two allophones are in complementary distribution; the voiceless nasals occur only after voiceless segments and the voiced nasals occur elsewhere. Thus the feature [±voiced] appears to be nondistinctive for nasals, since the devoicing is predictable. This can be revealed in the grammar of the language by including the rules:

> /n/ becomes [n̥] when it occurs after /s/.
> /m/ becomes [m̥] when it occurs after /s/.

This repetition seems needlessly cumbersome, and in fact would fail to reveal the generality which can be stated in just one rule:

> Nasal consonants become voiceless following voiceless segments.

If on further investigation the linguist found that [n̥at] did occur and meant "flower" and that [m̥at] meant "rain," she would have to change her analysis, since the occurrence of these words would show that voiced and voiceless nasals did contrast, so /n/ and /n̥/, and/m/ and /m̥/ would necessarily be phonemes in the language, and voicing would be a phonemic distinction for nasals.

This phonemic contrast does not occur in English but is found in other languages. In Burmese we find the following minimal pairs:

/ma/	[ma]	"health"	/ma/	[m̥a]	"order"
/na/	[na]	"pain"	/na/	[n̥a]	"nostril"

Minimal pairs and complementary distribution of phonetic units are helpful clues in the attempt to discover the inventory of phonemes in a language. By themselves, however, they do not determine the phonemic representation of utterances, as will be shown below in the discussion on phonological rules.

The grammar of a language includes the kind of information we have been discussing: what the distinctive phonemic units of the language are; which phonetic features are phonemic or distinctive; and which are nonphonemic or predictable. Thus, a grammar of French would not include a /θ/ as part of the phonemic representation of any word, just as a grammar of English would not include a /x/. English would have one voiceless labial stop phoneme, /p/, but Thai would have two, /p/ and /pʰ/. Both would include /b/. The grammar of English has no voiceless nasal phonemes, but the grammar of Burmese does. These examples illustrate that two languages may have the same phonetic segments but a different set of phonemes. The grammar must account for both the phonemes in the language and the way they are pronounced.

Sequences of Phonemes

If you were to receive the following telegram, you would have no difficulty in correcting the "obvious" mistakes:

BEST WISHES FOR VERY HAPPP BIRTFDAY

because sequences such as BIRTFDAY do not occur in the language.

COLIN CHERRY, *On Human Communication*

We demonstrated above that one's knowledge of the phonological system includes more than knowing the phonetic inventory of sounds in the language. It even goes beyond knowing the phonemes of the language.

Speakers also know that the phonemes of their language cannot be strung together in any random order to form words. The phonological system determines which phonemes can begin a word, end a word, and follow each other.

That speakers have knowledge of such sequential rules is not too difficult to demonstrate. Suppose you were given four cards, each of which had a different phoneme of English printed on it:

k	b	l	ɪ

If you were asked to arrange these cards to form all the "possible" words which these four phonemes could form, you might order them as:

b	l	ɪ	k
k	l	ɪ	b
b	ɪ	l	k
k	ɪ	l	b

These are the only arrangements of these phonemes permissible in English. */lbkɪ/, */ɪlbk/, */bkɪl/, */ɪlkb/, and so on are not possible words in the language. Although /blɪk/ and /klɪb/ are not *existing* words (you will not find them in a dictionary), if you heard someone say:

"I just bought a beautiful new *blick*."

you might ask: "What's a 'blick'?" But if you heard someone say:

"I just bought a beautiful new *bkli*."

you would probably just say "What?"

Your knowledge of English "tells" you that certain strings of phonemes are permissible and others are not. After a consonant like /b/, /g/, /k/, or /p/ another similar consonant is not permitted by the rules of the grammar. If a word begins with an /l/ or an /r/, every speaker "knows" that the next segment must be a vowel. That is why */lbɪk/ does not sound like an English word. It violates the restrictions on the sequencing of phonemes.

Other such constraints exist in English. If the initial sound of *church* begins a word, the next sound must be a vowel. [čat] or [čon] or [čækəri] are possible words in English, but *[člit] and *[čpæt] are not.

All languages have similar constraints on the sequences of phonemes which are permitted. Children learn these rules when they learn the language, just as they learn what the phonemes are and how they are related to phonetic segments. In Asante Twi, a word may end only in a vowel or a nasal consonant. /pik/ is not a possible Twi word, because it breaks the sequential rules of the language, and /ŋŋu/ is not a possible word in English for similar reasons, although it is an actual word in Twi.

Speakers of all languages have the same kinds of knowledge. They know what sounds are part of the language, what the phonemes are, and what phonemic and phonetic sequences may occur. The specific sounds and sound sequences may differ, but the phonological systems include similar *kinds* of rules.

The Rules of Phonology

No rule is so general, which admits not some exception.
ROBERT BURTON, *The Anatomy of Melancholy*

But that to come
Shall all be done by the rule.
SHAKESPEARE, *Antony and Cleopatra*

As discussed above, all who know a language know the basic vocabulary of that langauge. This means they know that an object like "pot" is represented by a given sequence of phonemes, /pat/. In other words, they know both the sounds and the meanings of these linguistic units. This knowledge must be part of the way they "store" these words in their mental dictionary, since when they want to refer to the concept "pot" they don't produce the sounds [tʰap]. But they needn't represent the sounds of this word by including all the phonetic features of these sounds as we saw in the discussion on phonemes, as long as the relationship between the phonemic representation they have stored and the phonetic pronunciation is "rule-governed." The rules which relate the minimally specified phonemic representation to the phonetic representation form part of a speaker's knowledge of the language. They are part of the grammar. One such rule in the grammar of English was given above:

(3) Aspirate voiceless stops at the beginning of a word or syllable before stressed vowels.

This rule makes certain predictions about English pronunciation. It specifies the *class of sounds* affected by the rule ("voiceless stops") and it specifies the context or phonemic environment of the relevant sounds ("at the beginning of a word before stressed vowels"). Both kinds of information must be given by a phonological rule, or we could apply it to the wrong class of sounds (for example, voiced stops) or in some environment where it is inapplicable (for example, after an /s/). Given this rule we can represent the words *pick, tick,* and *kick* phonemically as /pɪk/, /tɪk/, and /kɪk/ and *derive* the correct phonetic representation as follows:

/pɪk/ $\longrightarrow$ apply rule $\longrightarrow$ [pʰɪk]
/tɪk/ $\longrightarrow$ apply rule $\longrightarrow$ [tʰɪk]
/kɪk/ $\longrightarrow$ apply rule $\longrightarrow$ [kʰɪk]

We can also represent *stick*, for example, as /stɪk/. The rule will not apply, since the voiceless stop /t/ does not occur at the beginning of a word and the phonetic form is thus identical with the phonemic, [stɪk].

A separate rule was not necessary for each word or for each voiceless stop. In fact, had we given individual rules for /p/, /t/, and /k/ we would have obscured a generalization about English—that the rule applies to a *class* of phonemes.

As one examines the phonological regularities in language after language the importance of natural classes of speech sounds is revealed. Rule (3) applies to the natural class of sounds specified as $\begin{bmatrix} -\text{continuant} \\ -\text{voiced} \end{bmatrix}$. A **natural class of speech sounds** is one in which the number of features which must be specified is smaller than the number of features which is required to distinguish any member of that class. It is easy to see that if the rule above applied only to /p/ and /t/ we would have to add the feature [−velar]. More importantly, this fact about phonological rules illustrates why individual phonemes are better regarded as combinations of features than as indissoluble whole segments. If such segments are not composites of features, the similarities among /p/, /t/, and /k/ are not revealed. One can expect rules to apply to natural classes of sounds, since rules often have phonetic explanations and the classes of sounds are defined by phonetic features. The vowel nasalization rule illustrates this. We have stated that there is a plausible phonetic explanation for why vowels in many languages are nasalized before nasal consonants. The rule applies to the entire class of vowels in English. It would be a less "natural" rule if it applied only to the vowels /i/ and /o/. The statement of the rule would also have to be much more complex, since it could no longer apply to the class specified by only the two features $\begin{bmatrix} +\text{vocalic} \\ -\text{consonantal} \end{bmatrix}$.

The vowel nasalization rule is an **assimilation rule**; it *assimilates* one segment to another by "copying" a feature of a sequential phoneme, thus making the two phones more similar. Assimilation rules are, for the most part, caused by articulatory or physiological processes. There is a tendency when we speak to increase the *ease of articulation*. This "sloppiness" tendency may become regularized as rules of the language.

The rule we cited above for our make-believe language which devoiced nasals after voiceless segments is also an assimilation rule. The feature [−voiced] carries over onto the following segment. This is also an optional rule in English. Many speakers, particularly in fast speech, devoice the nasals (and liquids) in words like *snow* [sno̥], *slow* [sl̥o], *smart* [sm̥art], and so on.

Vowels may also become devoiced or voiceless in a voiceless environment. In Japanese the high back vowel /u/ when preceded and followed by voiceless obstruents is devoiced in words like *sukiyaki*. The /u/ becomes [u̥]. This is also an assimilation rule.

The rule which specifies when an /l/ is velarized and when it is not is also partially explainable on phonetic grounds. When the /l/ occurs before back vowels the back of the tongue is raised in anticipation of the back vowel articulation. The fact that we also velarize an /l/ at the end of a word is less easily explained. One could also say, instead, that the phoneme in English is /ɫ/, which loses its velarization, becoming [l] before front vowels by a lowering of the back of the tongue in anticipation of the following front vowels.

The assimilation rules we have discussed are just a small subset of these kinds of rules found in the world's languages. The above rules add nondistinctive features to phonemic segments. That is, nasalization is nondistinctive for vowels and the rule makes the vowels [+nasal]; vowels in Japanese are phonemically voiced and the rule changes certain vowels into voiceless segments. We shall see that phonological rules have other functions in addition to that of adding nondistinctive features.

Although the rules we have discussed are phonetically plausible as are other assimilation rules and can be explained by natural phonetic processes, this does not mean that all these rules occur in all languages. For example, there is a nasal assimilation rule in Akan which nasalizes voiced stops when they follow nasal consonants, as shown in the following example:

/ɔ ba/ [ɔba] "he comes" /ɔm ba/ [ɔmma] "he doesn't come"

The /b/ of the verb "come" becomes an [m] when it follows the negative prefix [m].

This rule has a phonetic explanation; the velum is lowered to produce the nasal consonant and remains down during the following stop. While it is a phonetically "natural" assimilation rule, it does not occur in the grammar of English; the word *amber*, for example, shows an [m] followed by a [b]. A child learning Akan must learn this rule, just as a child learning English learns to nasalize all vowels before nasal consonants, a rule which does not occur in the grammar of Akan.

Note that the Akan rule did not add a nondistinctive feature to the /b/, since the phoneme /m/ occurs; rather, it changed the features of /b/ from [−nasal] to [+nasal]. Thus we see that phonological rules can also *change feature specifications*.

In the previous chapter we pointed out that the phonetic form of the prefix meaning "not" is phonetically variant; it is [ɪn] before a vowel or an alveolar consonant, [ɪm] before a labial consonant, and [ɪŋ] before a velar, as illustrated in the following words:

*in*operable	[ɪnapərəbəl]
*in*discrete	[ɪndəskrit]
*im*plausible	[ɪmplɔzəbəl]
*in*conceivable	[ɪŋkənsɪvəbəl]

Since in all these cases the same prefix is added, one would expect it to have the same **phonemic** representation. If it is represented phonemically as /ɪn-/, the phonetic forms are predictable by one rule:

(4) Within a word, a nasal consonant assumes the same place of articulation as a following consonant.

The rule states the class of phonemes to which it applies (all nasal consonants) and where it is to be applied (before another consonant). Like the vowel nasalization rule, this is an *assimilation* rule; the nasal assimilates its place of articulation to agree with the articulation of the following consonant. When two consonants have the same place of articulation they are called **homorganic** consonants. We can call Rule (4) the "homorganic nasal" rule.

In the examples above, *inoperable* is composed of the prefix /ɪn-/ plus *operable*, which begins with a vowel. The rule cannot apply because it specifically mentions that it is only relevant if the nasal is followed by a consonant. Thus /ɪn-/ is phonetically [ɪn]. When /ɪn-/ is prefixed to *discrete*, since the /n/ and /d/ are already homorganic (that is, they are both [+alveolar]), the rule applies vacuously; it does not change the /n/, and the phonetic form of the prefix is [ɪn-]. The /ɪn-/ is changed to [ɪm-] before *plausible*, since /n/ is alveolar and /p/ is labial, and the /n/ becomes a velar [ŋ] before the initial velar /k/ in *conceivable*. The phonetic representation of these words should also include the nasalization of the vowels that occurs before nasal consonants; this nasalization would be added by the nasalization rule given above as Rule (1).

In the previous chapter it was pointed out that the same "homorganic nasal" rule occurs in Twi, and, in fact, this rule is found in many languages of the world. A rule such as this does not add a phonetic feature to a phoneme but *changes the feature specification* of that phoneme.

The spelling of *implausible* (or *impossible*) reflects the phonetic representation of these words, while the spelling of *incommunicable* (or *incompetent*) represents the phonemic representation. If *impossible* were spelled *inpossible*, it would still be pronounced with an [m].

It is interesting that a very common spelling error in English is the spelling **imput* for *input*. People who substitute the *m* for the *n* are drawing on their knowledge of the pronunciation of the word; the spelling represents the phonemic representation. There are many cases where the English spelling represents the more abstract phonemic representation of words. This does not present problems for anyone who knows the grammar of English, since part of that grammar includes those phonological rules which relate phonemic representations to phonetic pronunciation. The spelling in these cases may actually be more efficient, as it represents more directly the fact that speakers store words phonemically in their mental dictionaries.

The phonological rules of the language "tell" us how to pronounce the "same item" (like /ɪn-/) differently in different contexts. These rules apply to whole sets of words, not to just one single item, as is further illustrated by the following examples:

A	B
sign [sayn]	signature [sɪgnəčər]
design [dəzayn]	designate [dɛzɪgnet]
paradigm [pærədaym]	paradigmatic [pærədɪgmæDək]

In none of the words in column A is there a phonetic [g], but in each corresponding word in column B a [g] occurs. Our knowledge of English phonology accounts for these phonetic differences. The "[g]—no [g]" alternation is regular and applies to words which one might never have heard before. Suppose someone said:

He was a *salignant* [səlɪgnənt] man.

Even if you didn't know what the word meant, you might ask (perhaps to hide your ignorance):

Why, did he *salign* [səlayn] somebody?

It is highly doubtful that you would pronounce the verb form with the *-ant* dropped as [səlɪgn]. Your knowledge of the phonological rules of English would "delete" the /g/ when it occurred in this context. The rule can be stated as:

(5) Delete a /g/ when it occurs before a final nasal consonant.[2]

Given this rule, the phonemic representation of the stems in *sign/signature, design/designation, resign/resignation, repugn/repugnant, phlegm/phlegmatic, paradigm/paradigmatic, diaphragm/diaphragmatic* will include a *phonemic* /g/ which will be deleted by the regular rule if a suffix is not added. Notice that by stating the *class* of sounds which follow the /g/ (nasal consonants) rather than specifying any specific nasal consonant, the rule deletes the /g/ before both /m/ and /n/.

Phonological rules can therefore *delete whole segments* as well as add segments and features and change features.

There are other rules which delete segments in English. Consider the following words:

A		B	
bomb	[bam]	bombardier	[bambədir]
iamb	[ayæm]	iambic	[ayæmbɪk]
crumb	[krʌm]	crumble	[krʌmbəl]

A speaker of English knows when to pronounce a final /b/ and when not to. The relationship between the pronunciation of the A words and their B counterparts is regular and can be accounted for by Rule (6):

(6) Delete a word-final /b/ when it occurs after an /m/.

The underlying phonemic representation of the A and B stems is the same. (NA means "nonapplicable" or "does not fit the specifications of the rule.")

---

[2] The /g/ may be deleted under other circumstances as well, as indicated by its absence in *signing* and *signer*.

PHONEMIC REPRESENTATION	/bamb/	/bamb + adir/	/bʌlb/
/b/ deletion rule	ø	NA	NA
vowel schwa rule[3]	NA	ə	NA
PHONETIC REPRESENTATION	[bam]	[bambədir]	[bʌlb]

"Deletion rules" also show up as **optional** rules in fast speech or more casual speech in English. They result, for example, in the common contractions changing *he is* [hi ɪz] to *he's* [hiz] or *I will* [ay wɪl] to *I'll* [ayl]. In ordinary everyday speech most of us also "delete" the unstressed vowels which are italicized in words like the following:

> myst*e*ry gen*e*ral mem*o*ry fun*e*ral pers*o*nal vig*o*rous Barb*a*ra

Phonological rules which can delete whole segments can thus be either optional or obligatory. They are optional for words like *general* and obligatory for "g-deletion" in words like *sign*.

Phonological rules which delete whole segments are found in languages throughout the world. In French, for example, as demonstrated by Sanford Schane,[4] word-final consonants are deleted when the following word begins with a consonant or a liquid, but are retained when the following word begins with a vowel or a glide:

Before a consonant:	petit tableau	[pəti tablo]	"small picture"
	nos tableaux	[no tablo]	"our pictures"
Before a liquid:	petit livre	[pəti livr]	"small book"
	nos livres	[no livr]	"our books"
Before a vowel:	petit ami	[pətit ami]	"small friend"
	nos amis	[noz ami]	"our friends"
Before a glide:	petit oiseau	[pətit wazo]	"small bird"
	nos oiseaux	[noz wazo]	"our birds"

This is a general rule in French applying to all word-final consonants.[5] In the chapter on phonetics we distinguished these four classes of sounds by the following features:

	CONSONANTS	LIQUIDS	VOWELS	GLIDES
Consonantal	+	+	−	−
Vocalic	−	+	+	−

Using these classes, we can state the French rule very simply:

(7) Delete a word-final consonant when it occurs before the class of [+consonantal] segments (that is, consonants and liquids).

---

[3] This rule is discussed below.

[4] Sanford Schane, *French Phonology and Morphology* (Cambridge, Mass.: M.I.T. Press, 1968).

[5] In Schane's complete analysis, many words that are pronounced with a final consonant actually have a vowel as their word-final segment in phonemic representation. The vowel prevents the rule of word-final consonant deletion—Rule (7)—from applying. The vowel itself is deleted by another, later rule.

In the grammar of French, *petit* would be phonemically /pətit/. It need not be represented additionally as /pəti/, since the rule determines the phonetic shape of the word.

We see then that it is not only in English that rules may delete segments. All the kinds of rules discussed so far are found in languages throughout the world.

Phonological rules may also move phonemes from one place in the string to another. Such rules are called **metathesis rules**. They are less common, but they do exist. In some dialects of English, for example, the word *ask* is pronounced [æks] but the word *asking* is pronounced [æskɪŋ]. In these dialects a metathesis rule "switches" the /s/ and /k/ in certain contexts. It is interesting that at an earlier stage of English the Old English verb was *aksian* with the /k/ preceding the /s/. An historical metathesis rule switched these two consonants, producing *ask* in most dialects of English. Children's speech shows many cases of metathesis (which are then later corrected as the child approaches the adult grammar): *aminal* for *animal* and *pusketti* for *spaghetti* are common children's pronunciations.

In Hebrew there is a metathesis rule which reverses a pronoun-final consonant with the first consonant of the following verb if the verb starts with a sibilant. These are in reflexive verb forms, as shown in the following examples:

NONSIBILANT INITIAL VERBS		SIBILANT INITIAL VERBS	
kabel	lehit-kabel	tsadek	lehits-tadek
"to accept	"to be accepted"	"to justify"	"to apologize" (not *lehit-tsadek)
pater	lehit-pater	sames	lehis-tames
"to fire"	"to resign"	"to use for	"to use" (not *lehit-sames)
bayes	lehit-bayes	sader	lehis-tader
"to shame"	"to be ashamed"	"to arrange"	"to arrange oneself" (not *lehit-sader)

Phonological rules may also add whole segments. In the next chapter we will discuss some rules of this kind in English, in which a schwa vowel is inserted between the end of a noun and the plural ending in words like *base* (singular), *bases* (plural). In Greenlandic there is a rule which inserts a vowel between two consonants when these come at the end of a word or when followed by a suffix that begins with a consonant.

We see then that phonological rules may do the following things:

1. Add new features (e.g., aspiration in English)
2. Change feature values (e.g., homorganic nasal rule)
3. Delete segments (e.g., g-deletion rule in English)
4. Reorder segments (e.g., metathesis rule in Hebrew)
5. Add segments (e.g., Greenlandic vowel insertion)

These rules when applied to the phonemic representations of words and phrases result in phonetic forms which differ (or may differ) substantially from the phonemic forms. If such differences were unpredictable one would find it difficult to explain how we as speakers can understand what we hear or how we produce utterances that represent the meanings we wish to convey. The more we look at languages, however, the more we see that many aspects of the phonetic forms of utterances which appear at first to be irregular and unpredictable are actually rule-governed. We learn, or construct, these rules when we are learning the language as children. The rules represent "patterns," or general principles.

In the *sign/signature* examples we showed that the presence or absence of a [g] was determined by rule. Similarly, the vowel differences in the pairs are predictable. Notice that in all the words in the first column below, the italicized vowel is pronounced [ay] and in the second column [ɪ].

[ay]	[ɪ]
s*i*gn	s*i*gnature
l*i*ne	l*i*near
subl*i*me	subl*i*mation
d*i*ne	d*i*nner
r*i*te	r*i*tual
sacrif*i*ce	sacrif*i*cial
suff*i*ce	suff*i*cient
div*i*de	div*i*sion

These words are just a few of such pairs which show the regular **alternation** between phonetic [ay] and [ɪ].

Other regular vowel alternations also occur in English.

The rules which account for the [ay]/[ɪ] substitutions apply generally, not just to the words listed. They also, for example, account for the [i]/[ɛ] phonetic vowels in such words as these:

ser*e*ne/ser*e*nity   obsc*e*ne/obsc*e*nity   perc*ei*ve/perc*e*ption

The explicit statement of this vowel rule is quite complex and goes beyond the introductory level of this discussion. But the regularities are clearly seen and illustrate the fact that a single stem may be pronounced differently when different suffixes are added to it. They further illustrate that English spelling is not as irregular as some spelling reformers would lead one to think. That *sign* is spelled with a *g* presents no problem for speakers who know English, since part of their knowledge includes the fact that the /g/ is not always pronounced. This "silent letter" (or silent phoneme) shows the relationship between *sign* and *signature*. The pronunciation of the words is accounted for by regular rules, rules which you know even if you cannot state them explicitly (unless of course you are taking a linguistics course). They are not part of your conscious knowledge. They represent highly abstract principles which are expressed as phonological rules.

It is not the purpose of this chapter (or this book) to describe the complex phonology of English. Examples from English are used only to illustrate the kinds of phonological rules found in languages of the world.

In the discussion on how phonemic representations of utterances are realized phonetically, it might have been concluded that each phoneme is represented by a set of allophones which "belong" only to that phoneme. That is, phoneme A is represented by the phonetic segments [a] and [a'], phoneme B by [b] and [b'], phoneme C by [c] and [c'], and so on, and phoneme A can never be realized as [b] or [c]. This would be a neat and tidy mapping of phonemic representations onto phonetic representations. But the mind is capable of greater complexities, which show up in the phonological rules of grammars. Consider the italicized vowels in the following pairs of words:

A			B	
/i/	comp*e*te	[i]	comp*e*tition	[ə]
/ɪ/	med*i*cinal	[ɪ]	med*i*cine	[ə]
/e/	maint*ai*n	[e]	maint*e*nance	[ə]
/ɛ/	t*e*legraph	[ɛ]	t*e*legraphy	[ə]
/æ/	an*a*lysis	[æ]	an*a*lytic	[ə]
/a/	s*o*lid	[a]	s*o*lidify	[ə]
/o/	ph*o*ne	[o]	ph*o*nology	[ə]
/ʊ/	Talm*u*dic	[ʊ]	Talm*u*d	[ə]

In column A all the italicized vowels are stressed vowels and show a variety of different vowel phones; in column B all the italicized unstressed vowels are pronounced [ə]. Yet the "reduced" vowels of column B must be derived from different underlying phonemes, since when they are stressed they show up as different vowels in column A. If the italicized vowel of *compete* were not phonemically /i/, there would be no way to account for the particular quality of the stressed vowel. Thus, one might say that [ə] is an allophone of all English vowel phonemes. The rule to derive the schwa can be stated simply as:

(8) Change a vowel into a [ə] when it is unstressed.

This rule is also oversimplified because when an unstressed vowel occurs as the final segment of a word it retains its full vowel quality, as shown in words like *confetti, cocoa,* or *democracy.*

The rule which "reduces" unstressed vowels to schwas is another example of a rule which changes feature values.

In a phonological description of a language we do not know, we can't always tell from the phonetic transcription what the phonemic representation is. But given the phonemic representation and the phonological rules, one can always derive the correct phonetic transcription. Of course in our internal, mental grammars this is no problem, since the words are listed phonemically and we know the rules of the language.

Another example may help to illustrate this aspect of phonology.

In English, /t/ and /d/ are both phonemes, as is illustrated by the minimal pairs *tie/die* and *bat/bad.* When /t/ or /d/ occurs between a stressed and an unstressed vowel they both become a flap [D]. For many speakers of English, *writer* and *rider* are pronounced identically as [rayDər]. Yet speakers know that *writer* has a *phonemic* /t/ because of *write* /rayt/, and that *rider* has a *phonemic* /d/ because of *ride* /rayd/. The "flap rule" may be stated as:

(9) An alveolar stop becomes a voiced flap when preceded by a stressed vowel and followed by an unstressed vowel.

The application of this rule is illustrated as follows:

	write	writer	ride	rider
PHONEMIC REPRESENTATION	/rayt/	/rayt + ər/ ↓	/rayd/	/rayd + ər/ ↓
"flap rule"	NA	D	NA	D
PHONETIC REPRESENTATION	[rayt]	[rayDər]	[rayd]	[rayDər]

We are omitting other phonetic details which are also determined by phonological rules, such as the fact that in *ride* the vowel is slightly longer than in *write* because it is followed by a voiced [d]. We are using the example only to illustrate the fact that two distinct phonemes may be realized phonetically as the same sound.

Such cases show that one cannot arrive at a phonological analysis by simply inspecting the phonetic representation of utterances. If we just looked for minimal pairs as the only evidence for phonology, we would have to conclude that [D] was a phoneme in English because it contrasts phonetically with other phonetic units: *riper* [raypər], *rhymer* [raymər], *riser* [rayzər], and so forth. Grammars are much more complex than this. The fact that *write* and *ride* change their phonetic forms when suffixes are added shows that there is an intricate mapping between phonemic representations of words and phonetic pronunciation.

Note that in the case of the "schwa rule" and the case of the "flap rule" the allophones derived from the different phonemes by rule are different in features from all other phonemes in the language. That is, there is no /D/ phoneme, but there is a [D] phone.

The homorganic nasal rule discussed above also reveals that two phonemes may be realized by the same phone, but it differs somewhat from the examples given above. We know that the phoneme /n/ is realized as [n] in words like *knight* [nayt] and the phoneme /m/ is realized as [m] in words like *might* [mayt]. Yet we saw that the prefix which we represented phonemically as /ɪn-/ (meaning "not") was phonetically [ɪn] or [ɪm] or [ɪŋ] depending on the place of articulation of the following consonant. In this case the realization of the /n/ is [m] in words like /ɪn-/ + *possible* and is identical to the phonetic realization of the phoneme /m/ in words like *might*. The homorganic nasal rule is another example of a rule which changes the feature specification of a phoneme.

Similar rules are found in other languages. In both Russian and German, when voiced obstruents occur at the end of a word (or syllable) they become voiceless. Both voiced and voiceless obstruents do occur in German as phonemes, as is shown by the following minimal pair:

Tier [ti:r] "animal" *dir* [di:r] "to you"

At the end of a word, however, only [t] occurs; the words meaning "league," *Bund*, and "colorful" (singular), *bunt*, are phonetically identical and pronounced [bʊnt]. Should they then be phonemically identical; that is, /bʊnt/?

If *Bund* and *bunt* were represented phonemically as /bʊnt/, identically with the phonetic pronunciation, there would be no way of deriving the [d] in the plural of *Bunde* [bʊndə]. If, however, the singular and plural stems are represented phonemically as /bʊnd/ and /bʊnt/ and there is a rule in the grammar of German which says "devoice obstruents at the end of a word," we would get the following derivations:

PHONEMIC REPRESENTATION	/bʊnd/	/bʊndə/	/bʊnt/	/bʊntə/
devoicing rule	t	NA	NA	NA
PHONETIC REPRESENTATION	[bʊnt]	[bʊndə]	[bʊnt]	[bʊntə]

This is another example to show that the phonetic realization of two distinct phonemes may be identical in certain environments. The rule is one which, like the vowel reduction rule in English and the homorganic nasal rule, changes the specifications of features. In the case of German, the phonemic representation of the final stop in *Bund* is /d/, specified as [+voiced]; this is changed by the rule above to [−voiced] to derive the phonetic [t] in word-final position.

This rule in German further illustrates that one cannot decide what the phonemic representation of a word is, given only the phonetic form, since [bʊnt] can be derived from either /bʊnd/ or /bʊnt/. But given the phonemic representations and the rules of the language, the phonetic forms are automatically determined.

In many cases one even requires nonphonological information in phonological rules; that is, the phonology is not totally independent of the rest of the grammar. In English we place primary stress on an adjective followed by a noun when the two words are combined in a compound noun, but we place the stress on the noun when the words are combined in a noun phrase in which the noun is modified by the adjective:

NOUN COMPOUNDS	ADJECTIVE + NOUN PHRASE
Whíte House	white hóuse
Rédcoat	red cóat
hót dog	hot dóg
bláckboard	black bóard
blúebird	blue bírd

In the previous chapter we also illustrated the stress difference in noun-verb pairs in English, as shown by :

NOUN	VERB
pérvert	pervért
pérmit	permít
cónvert	convért
réject	rejéct

The stress placement is predictable (that is, nonphonemic), given knowledge of the "word class." Actually, the stress rules are more complicated than this. These examples, as well as the others discussed above, are provided only to illustrate the *kind* of knowledge accounted for by the phonological rules of a grammar.

Such rules illustrate that their function in a grammar is to provide the phonetic information necessary for the pronunciation of utterances. One may illustrate the function of phonological rules in the following way:

input   PHONEMIC (DICTIONARY) REPRESENTATION OF WORDS
IN A SENTENCE
↓
Phonological rules (P-rules)
↓
output   PHONETIC REPRESENTATION OF WORDS IN A SENTENCE

That is, the input to the P-rules is the **phonemic representation**; the P-rules apply or operate on the phonemic strings and produce as output the **phonetic representation.**

This should not be interpreted as meaning that when we speak we necessarily apply one rule after another. Speaking is part of linguistic performance; phonological rules represent part of one's grammar, which in turn is equivalent to one's knowledge of the language. The rules reveal the more abstract relationship between phonemic and phonetic representations. The grammar does not describe how we use this grammar in speech production or comprehension.

Thus, to state that there is a phonological rule which nasalizes vowels before nasal consonants in English is to state an abstract rule or principle or formula. This doesn't mean that you necessarily start with a nonnasal vowel and then apply the rule when you are speaking. It means that your knowledge of the distribution of oral and nasal vowels in English is represented by this statement.

The rules however may indeed be applied in performance. "Slips of the tongue," where we deviate in some way from the intended utterance, show that such rules are applied or are "real."

For example, someone who intended to say *gone to seed* [gãn tə sid] said instead *god to seen* [gad tə sĩn]. The final consonants of the first and third words were reversed. But, notice that the reversal of the consonants also changed the nasality of the vowels. The first vowel /a/ was a nasalized [ã] in the intended utterance; in the actual utterance the nasalization was "lost," since it no longer occurred before a nasal consonant. But the vowel in the third word which was the nonnasal [i] in the intended utterance became [ĩ] in the error, since it was followed by *n*. The nasalization rule applied.

Another speech error shows the application of the aspiration rule. For the intended *stick in the mud* [stɪk ĩn ðə mʌd], the speaker said *smuck in the tid* [smʌk ĩn ðə tʰɪd]. When the /t/ occurred incorrectly as the initial consonant of the last word it was pronounced as an aspirated [tʰ], although in the intended utterance after the /s/ it would have been pronounced as a [t].

An examination of the phonologies of different languages shows rules which add features, change features, add segments, delete segments, and transpose or switch segments. This must mean that human linguistic ability permits us to form such rules. Just as all possible sounds are not found in languages, so all conceivable rules are not. No language has ever been found which includes a rule specifying that all the phonemes in a word should be reversed or that every third phoneme should be deleted or that one should add an /l/ before a word just in case the word has thirteen phonemes. These rules are logically possible but not phonologically possible. We see then that the forms of grammars, and their phonological parts, are not as variable as Satie seemed to think. There are universal constraints on the phonological systems which humans can learn.

The Formalization of Phonological Rules

Form follows function.
Slogan of the Bauhaus school of architecture

In this chapter all the examples of phonological rules we have considered have been stated in words. That is, we have not used any special "formal devices" or "formal notations." We could, however, have stated the rules using special symbols which would make the rules look more like "mathematical" formulas.

A number of such notational devices are used as part of the theory of phonology. They do more than merely save paper or abbreviate long statements. They provide a way to express the generalizations of the language which may be obscured otherwise.

For example, if we used our + and − feature value notation in the rule which nasalizes vowels before nasal consonants, it could be stated as:

(10) $\begin{bmatrix} +\text{vocalic} \\ -\text{consonantal} \end{bmatrix}$ becomes [+nasal] before a [+nasal]

This clearly shows that just one feature is changed and that it is an assimilatory rule.

Suppose we wished to write a rule which nasalized a vowel before, and only before, a /p/. By stating this without features, we could say: Nasalize a vowel before a /p/. This seems to be as simple and general a rule as the nasalization rule. Yet it is a strange and highly unlikely rule. To state this rule with features, we would have to write:

(11) $\begin{bmatrix} +\text{vocalic} \\ -\text{consonantal} \end{bmatrix}$ becomes [+nasal] before a $\begin{bmatrix} +\text{consonantal} \\ -\text{vocalic} \\ +\text{labial} \\ -\text{voiced} \\ -\text{continuant} \end{bmatrix}$

We can see at a glance that Rule (11) is more complex (you have to mention more features) and that the features mentioned have nothing in common.

Rule (10) seems like a "natural" rule and Rule (11) does not. But that is exactly what we want to reveal. Without the use of features the difference between the two rules is hidden. The use of such feature notation to represent phonemes is then part of the theory of phonology. The formal notation is not used merely because it is somehow more "elegant" but because it better represents what we know about phonological rules.

Instead of writing "becomes" or "occurs," we can use an arrow, →, to show that the segment on the left of the arrow is or becomes whatever is on the right of the arrow:

(12) $\begin{bmatrix} +\text{vocalic} \\ -\text{consonantal} \end{bmatrix}$ → [+nasal] before a [+nasal]

The phonological environment, or context, is also important to specify in a rule. In many languages vowels are nasalized before but not after a nasal. We can formalize the notions of "environment" or "in the environment" and the notions of "before" and "after" by the following notations:

  a slash, /, to mean "in the environment of"
  a dash, —, placed before or after the segment(s) which determine the
      change

Using these notations we can write the above rule:

(13) $\begin{bmatrix} +\text{vocalic} \\ -\text{consonantal} \end{bmatrix}$ → [+nasal] / — [+nasal]

This rule reads: "A vowel (that is, a segment which is specified as vocalic and nonconsonantal) becomes (→) nasalized in the environment (/) before (—) a nasal segment.

If we write the rule as

(14) $\begin{bmatrix} +\text{vocalic} \\ -\text{consonantal} \end{bmatrix}$ → [+nasal] / [+nasal] —

it reads: "A vowel becomes nasalized in the environment *after* a nasal." The fact that the dash follows the [+nasal] shows that a vowel which comes *after* it is changed.

Some of the rules discussed above state that the segment to be changed by the rule occurs at the beginning or end of a word. We can use a double cross, #, to signify a word boundary.

See if you can read the following rule:

(15) $\begin{bmatrix} -\text{continuant} \\ -\text{voiced} \end{bmatrix}$ → [+aspirated] / # — $\begin{bmatrix} -\text{consonantal} \\ +\text{vocalic} \\ +\text{stressed} \end{bmatrix}$

If the formal devices and notational system we have been discussing haven't completely confused you, you should be able to see that this is our old friend the "aspiration rule" and should be read: "A voiceless stop (a segment that is [−continuant] and [−voiced]) becomes (→) aspirated in the environment (/) after a word boundary (#—) (that is, at the beginning of a word) before a stressed vowel (a segment that is [−consonantal] and [+vocalic] and [+stressed])." Note that the environment dash occurs between the # and the vowel segment.

The rule which velarizes an /l/ in English must state all the environments where this occurs: before back vowels, before low front vowels, at the end of a word. We can state this formally as:

(16a) [+lateral] → [+velarized] / — $\begin{bmatrix} +\text{vocalic} \\ -\text{consonantal} \\ +\text{back} \end{bmatrix}$

(16b) [+lateral] → [+velarized] / — $\begin{bmatrix} +\text{vocalic} \\ -\text{consonantal} \\ +\text{low} \end{bmatrix}$

(16c) [+lateral] → [+velarized] / — #

By writing three rules, we seem to miss some generalization, since they all apply to /l/ and all add the feature [+velarized]. To **collapse** (or combine) two or more rules which have *identical parts* we can use another device, braces { }, and can collapse Rules **(16a, (16b), and (16c)** into Rule **(16d).**

(16d) [+lateral] → [+velarized] / — $\left\{ \begin{matrix} \begin{bmatrix} +\text{vocalic} \\ -\text{consonantal} \\ +\text{back} \end{bmatrix} \\ \begin{bmatrix} +\text{vocalic} \\ -\text{consonantal} \\ +\text{low} \end{bmatrix} \\ \# \end{matrix} \right\}$

The braces signify that the rule applies *either* before back vowels, *or* before any low vowel, *or* before a word boundary. Thus the brace notation permits us to express a general rule in a general fashion.

We noted above that the complementary distribution between velarized and nonvelarized *l*'s could also be revealed in the grammar by positing a phoneme which has the feature [+velarized]. We would then need a rule to delete this feature before nonlow front vowels:

(17) [+lateral] → [−velarized] / — $\begin{bmatrix} -\text{consonantal} \\ +\text{vocalic} \\ -\text{back} \\ -\text{low} \end{bmatrix}$

Note that all we need to specify on the left on the arrow (that is, the segment to which the rule applies, the segment to be changed) is that it is a lateral. We don't have to state that it is [+velarized] to begin with, since all laterals will be so specified. This rule is a much simpler rule than **(16d)** and seems also to be more "natural." Instead of the feature [±velarized], we could specify the velarized *l* as [+back]. The statement would then clearly reveal it as an assimilation rule.

(18) $[+\text{lateral}] \rightarrow [-\text{back}] / — \begin{bmatrix} -\text{consonantal} \\ +\text{vocalic} \\ -\text{back} \\ -\text{low} \end{bmatrix}$

Can you "read" the following rule?

(19) $\begin{bmatrix} -\text{consonantal} \\ +\text{vocalic} \end{bmatrix} \rightarrow [+\text{long}] / — \left\{ \begin{matrix} \begin{bmatrix} +\text{consonantal} \\ -\text{vocalic} \\ +\text{voiced} \end{bmatrix} \\ \# \end{matrix} \right\}$

You should have read it as: "A vowel becomes long in the environment before either a voiced consonant or at the end of a word (before a word boundary)."

We mention just one other "notational device" that helps reveal generalizations in phonology. Suppose there was a rule in some language to shorten a vowel when the vowel occurs before three consonants or two consonants. We could write this rule using the brace notation:

(20) $\begin{bmatrix} +\text{vocalic} \\ -\text{consonantal} \end{bmatrix} \rightarrow [-\text{long}] / —$

$$\left\{ \begin{matrix} \begin{bmatrix} -\text{vocalic} \\ +\text{consonantal} \end{bmatrix} \begin{bmatrix} -\text{vocalic} \\ +\text{consonantal} \end{bmatrix} \begin{bmatrix} -\text{vocalic} \\ +\text{consonantal} \end{bmatrix} \\ \begin{bmatrix} -\text{vocalic} \\ +\text{consonantal} \end{bmatrix} \begin{bmatrix} -\text{vocalic} \\ +\text{consonantal} \end{bmatrix} \end{matrix} \right\}$$

If we use V for vowels and C for consonants, this can be written as:

(21) $V \rightarrow [-\text{long}] / — \left\{ \begin{matrix} \text{CCC} \\ \text{CC} \end{matrix} \right\}$

This rule gives us the result we want; by using the braces we have collapsed two rules, both of which apply to vowels and both of which shorten the vowels. But there are identical parts in the two rules which are repeated. This seems to miss a generalization that we would want to capture. That is, we should have some notational device which clearly and simply shows that the rule applies before three or two consonants. To collapse rules like this, we use parentheses, ( ), around an "optional" segment or segments. That is, the rule really states that a vowel is always shortened before two consonants and there may or may not be a third consonant. The presence of the third consonant does not affect the rule. Using parentheses, we can state the rule as:

(22) $V \rightarrow [-\text{long}] / — \text{CC (C)}$

This rule then reads: "A vowel is shortened in the environment before three consonants (with the C in parentheses included) or before two consonants."

The importance of formal devices like feature notations, arrows, slashes, dashes, braces, and parentheses is that they enable us to express linguistic generalizations. Since the grammar that linguists write for any particular language aims to express in the most general fashion a speaker's linguistic competence, the notations which permit them to do this are part of the theory of phonology.

We have not discussed all the formalisms used in phonology to capture linguistic generalizations. Actually, our main purpose here is to help you understand the *kinds* of phonological processes (rules) found in the languages of the world. Thus, this discussion of formal notations as such is brief, since it is intended mainly for those who wish to read further in phonology and who may come across rules written in this way.

SUMMARY

Part of one's knowledge of a language is knowledge of the sound system—the **phonology** of that language. The phonology of the language includes the inventory o basic **phonemes** (those segments which are used to differentiate between the meanings of words) and the permissible sequences of these units. A phoneme may have different phonetic representations. The relationship between the phonemic representation of words or utterances and the phonetic representation (the pronunciation of these utterances) is determined by general **phonological rules.**

Phonological rules in a grammar apply to phonemic strings and may alter them in various ways:

1. They may add nondistinctive features which are predictable from the context. The rule which aspirates voiceless stops at the beginning of words in English is such a rule, since aspiration is a nonphonemic feature.
2. They may change the feature specification of phonemes. The "homorganic nasal" rule which changes an /n/ to an [m] or an [ŋ] before labials and velars, respectively, is such a rule.
3. They may add segments which are not present in the phonemic string.
4. They may delete phonemic segments in certain contexts. The "g-deletion" rule which accounts for the pronunciation of *sign* without a [g] but of *signature* with a [g] is a deletion rule.
5. They may "transpose" or move segments around in a string, as illustrated by the /sk/ to [ks] rule in certain American dialects.

Such rules show that the phonemic shape of words or phrases is not identical with their phonetic form. While the rules may be very complex, they are never too complex to be learned, since these rules represent what speakers of a language know. We all learn the basic phonological units of our language—the phonemic segments—and the phonemic representation of words. The phonemes are not the actual phonetic sounds, but are abstract mental constructs which are realized as sounds by the operation of rules such as those described above. No one teaches us these rules. And yet, all speakers of a language know the phonology of their language better than any linguist who tries to describe it. The linguist's job is to make explicit what we know unconsciously about the sound pattern of our language.

In the writing of rules, linguists use certain formal devices to permit better generalizations of the phonological processes which occur. Features are used rather than whole segments, and other devices such as braces and parentheses collapse rules when the rules contain similar parts. Such devices are used only if they are able truly to represent what speakers know about the sound patterns of their language.

EXERCISES

1. The following sets of minimal pairs show that English [p] and [b] contrast in initial, medial, and final positions. Minimal pairs are pairs of words which contrast in only one sound segment; all other sounds are identical and the segments are in the same order. That is, *pan* and *tan* are minimal pairs; *pan* and *tin* are not, and *tam* and *mat* are not.

INITIAL	MEDIAL	FINAL
pit/bit	rapid/rabid	cap/cab

    Find similar sets of minimal pairs involving each of the following pairs of consonants in word-initial, word-medial, and word-final position:

    a. [k] — [g]   f. [θ] — [ð]
    b. [b] — [v]   g. [l] — [r]
    c. [s] — [š]   h. [č] — [j]
    d. [m] — [n]   i. [p] — [f]
    e. [b] — [m]   j. [s] — [z]

2. The indefinite singular article in English is either *a* or *an*, as shown in the following phrases:

    > a hotel, a boy, a use, a wagon, a big man, a yellow rug, a white house, an apple, an honor, an orange curtain, an old lady

    State the rule which determines when *a* is used and when *an* is used. If possible do not list individual sound segments but make the rule as general as possible, referring to *features* or *classes* of segments.

3. Below are given some data (in *phonetic* transcription) from a hypothetical language called Hip.

[tip]	"girl"	[tiben]	"girls"
[pit]	"boy"	[piden]	"boys"
[kip]	"child"	[kiben]	"children
[pik]	"policeman"	[pigen]	"policemen"
[tab]	"teacher"	[taben]	"teachers"
[bid]	"dog"	[biden]	"dogs"
[gip]	"car"	[giben]	"cars"
[dag]	"cat"	[dagen]	"cats"
[tap]	"house"	[giden]	"lions"

A. What are the stop *phonemes* in Hip? Justify your answer.

B. What is the *phonemic* form for the word meaning "children"?

C. What is the *phonetic* form for "houses"?

D. What is the *phonemic* form for "lions"?

E. State the rule which accounts for the phonetic differences between the singular and plural forms where they occur.

4. Here are some phonetic forms from another language. The words in the first column are singular nouns; those in the second column are the corresponding plurals.

SINGULAR	PLURAL
[orat]	[ēmorat]
[laz]	[ēmlaz]
[bole]	[ēmbole]
[dus]	[ēndus]
[sar]	[ēnsar]
[kipo]	[ēŋkipo]
[gola]	[ēŋgola]
[gũn]	[ēŋgũn]

A. Which of the following is the most likely phonemic representation for the plural prefix?

a. /ēm/   b. /em/   c. /ēn/   d. /en/   e. /ēŋ/   f. /eŋ/

State the reasons for your choice.

B. If the phonetic form for "girl" is [tabo], what would the *phonetic* form for "girls" be?

C. What is the *phonemic* representation for [ēŋgũn]?

D. State the phonological rules which can account for the phonetic forms.

5. In some dialects of English the following words have different vowels, as is shown by the phonetic transcriptions.

A		B		C	
bite	[bʌyt]	bide	[bayd]	tie	[tay]
rice	[rʌys]	rise	[rayz]	by	[bay]
type	[tʌyp]	bribe	[brayb]	sigh	[say]
wife	[wʌyf]	wives	[wayvz]	die	[day]
tyke	[tʌyk]	time	[taym]		
		nine	[nayn]		
		tile	[tayl]		
		tire	[tayr]		
		writhe	[rayð]		

A. How may the classes of sounds which end the words in columns A and B be characterized? That is, what feature specifies all the final segments in A and all the final segments in B?

B. How do the words in column C differ from those in columns A and B?

C. Are [ʌy] and [ay] in complementary distribution? Give your reasons.

D. If [ʌy] and [ay] are allophones of one phoneme, should they be derived from /ʌy/ or /ay/? Why?

E. What is the *phonetic* representation of *life* and *lives*?

F. What would the *phonetic* representations of the following words be?

    a. trial   b. bike   c. lice   d. fly   e. mine

G. State the rule which will relate the phonemic representations to the phonetic representations of the words given above.

6. Below are some data from Twi, a language spoken in Ghana. The phonemic representation of the verbs is given, followed by the phonetic transcription of these verbs in affirmative and negative constructions.

"pour"	/gu/	"he pours"	[o gu]	"he doesn't pour"	[o ŋŋu]
"kill"	/kum/	"he kills"	[o kum]	"he doesn't kill"	[o ŋkum]
"break"	/bu/	"he breaks"	[o bu]	"he doesn't break"	[o mmu]
"appear"	/pue/	"he appears"	[o pue]	"he doesn't appear"	[o mpue]
"eat"	/dĺ/	"he eats"	[o dĺ]	"he doesn't eat"	[o nniĺ]
"scratch"	/tĩ/	"he scratches"	[o tĩ]	"he doesn't scratch"	[o ntĩ]

What are the rules that change the phonemic forms of the verbs to the phonetic forms, where the phonetic forms differ from the phonemic?

7. A. The English verbs in column A have stress on the next-to-last syllable (called the **penultimate**), while the verbs in column B have their last syllable stressed. State a rule which can predict where stress occurs in these verbs.

A	B
astónish	collápse
éxit	exíst
imágine	tormént
cáncel	revólt
elícit	adópt
práctice	insíst
solícit	contórt

B. In the verbs in column C, stress also occurs on the final syllable. What do you have to add to your rule which will account for this? In the forms in columns A and B the final consonants had to be considered; in the forms in column C consider the vowels.

C

expláin
eráse
surpríse
combíne
caréen
atóne
equáte

8. Below are listed fifteen "words." Some of them could be English "words" and others are definitely "foreign." For each "word" state whether it could or could not be an English word. For those which you mark as "foreign" give all the reasons you can think of for making this decision.

a. [klǽnp] f. [fɔlərayt] k. [žoli]
b. [tligɪt] g. [splad] l. [šɛktər]
c. [prɪsk] h. [vuzapm] m. [θemərɛt]
d. [trigã̃] i. [ŋar] n. [jrʊdki]
e. [æləposg] j. [skwɪɬ] o. [mlop]

9. State the following rules using the "formal devices" discussed at the end of the chapter.

Example: A consonant becomes zero (is deleted) after one or two consonants.

$$C \rightarrow \emptyset \ /C \ (C) \ —$$

Example: Aspirate a voiceless stop consonant at the end of a word.

$$\begin{bmatrix} C \\ -\text{continuant} \\ -\text{voice} \end{bmatrix} \rightarrow [+\text{aspirated}] \ / \ — \ \#$$

A. A vowel is stressed in the environment after a word boundary (at the beginning of a word).

B. A voiced consonant becomes nasal before a nasal.

C. A voiceless segment becomes voiced between two vowels.

D. A voiced consonant becomes voiceless either before a voiceless consonant or at the end of a word.

E. A vowel is lengthened before one or two voiced consonants.

10. Consider these *phonetic* forms of the following Hebrew words:

[v] – [b]		[f] – [p]	
bika	"lamented"	litef	"stroked"
mugbal	"limited"	sefer	"book"
šavar	"broke" (masc.)	šataf	"washed"
šavra	"broke" (fem.)	para	"cow"
ʔikev	"delayed"	mitpaxat	"handkerchief"
bara	"created"	haʔalpim	"the Alps"

(In answering the questions below, you should consider these words and the phonetic sequences as representative of what may occur in Hebrew. In your answers consider classes of sounds rather than just individual sounds.)

A. Are [b] and [v] allophones of one phoneme, and therefore in complementary distribution?

B. Does the same rule, or lack of a rule, which describes the distribution of [b] and [v] apply to the distribution of [p] and [f]?

C. Here is a word with one phone missing. A blank appears in place of the missing sound: hid__ik. Which *one* of the following statements is correct? (Only one is correct.)

   a. [b] but not [v] could occur in the empty slot.
   b. [v] but not [b] could occur in the empty slot.
   c. Either [b] or [v] could occur in the empty slot.
   d. Neither [b] nor [v] could occur in the empty slot.

D. Which one of the following statements is correct about the incomplete word __ana?

   a. [f] but not [p] could occur in the empty slot.
   b. [p] but not [f] could occur in the empty slot.
   c. either [p] or [f] could fill the blank
   d. Neither [p] nor [f] could fill the blank.

11. Now consider the following imaginary words (in *phonetic* transcription):

laval   surva   labal   palar   falu   razif

If these words were found to actually occur in Hebrew, would they:

A. Force you to revise your conclusions about the distribution of labial stops and fricatives you reached on the basis of the first group of words given above?

B. Support your original conclusions?

C. Neither support nor disprove your original conclusions?

References

Anderson, Stephen R. *The Organization of Phonology*. New York: Academic Press. 1974. A thorough, advanced textbook dealing with current "generative" phonological theory.

Chomsky, N., and M. Halle. *The Sound Pattern of English*. New York: Harper & Row, 1968. The first comprehensive statement of the formal and substantive principles of generative phonology. Only for the advanced student.

Hyman, Larry M. *Phonology: Theory and Analysis*. New York: Holt, Rinehart and Winston, 1975. An excellent textbook for the beginning student which deals with both phonological theory and descriptive analysis.

Schane, S. A. *Generative Phonology*. Englewood Cliffs, N.J.: Prentice-Hall, 1973. A summary of the main ideas present in Chomsky and Halle, 1968.

CHAPTER 6

The Wonder of Words

B.C.   by johnny hart

By permission of Johnny Hart and Field Enterprises, Inc.

A word is dead
When it is said,
Some say.
I say it just
Begins to live
That day.
EMILY DICKINSON, "A Word"

POLONIUS   What do you read, my lord?
HAMLET   Words, words, words.
WILLIAM SHAKESPEARE, *Hamlet*, II, ii

Every speaker of a language knows thousands, even tens of thousands, of words. Knowing a word means knowing both its sound and its meaning. Someone who doesn't know English would not know where one word begins or ends in hearing an utterance like [ðəkʰǽtèt-ðərǽt]. It isn't even possible to tell how many words have been said. If you are a speaker of English, however, you will have no difficulty in segmenting the sounds into the individual words *the cat ate the rat*. Similarly, someone who doesn't know Potawatomi would not know whether [kwapmuknanuk] (which means "They see us.") was one, two, or more words. It is, in fact, only one word, as any speaker of Potawatomi could tell you.

The sounds (pronunciation) and the meaning of a word are inseparable. This was pointed out by the great nineteenth-century Swiss linguist Ferdinand de Saussure, who discussed the *arbitrary* union between the sounds (form) and meaning (concept) of the **linguistic sign**. It is in this sense that a word is a linguistic sign.

We have already seen that speakers of a language by virtue of their phonological knowledge know whether a string of sounds *could* be a word in their language. If they did not know the meaning of *plarm*, they would conclude either that it was a word they didn't know or that it wasn't a word in English. They would know, however, that it was a possible English word. If someone told them that a *plarm* was a particular kind of water rat, *plarm* would become a sound-meaning unit, a linguistic sign, a word.

Just as a particular string of sounds must be united with a meaning for it to be a word, so a concept or meaning must be united with specific sounds. Before 1955 the word *googol* [gugəl] did not exist as an English word. Now, at least among mathematicians and scientists, it is a word. The word was "coined" by the 9-year-old nephew of Dr. Edward Kasner, an American mathematician, to mean "the number 1 followed by 100 zeros," a number equal to 10^{100}. The number existed before the word was invented, but no word represented this particular numerical concept. When the concept and sounds were united, a word came into being. In fact, from this word another word, *googolplex*, was formed to mean "1 followed by a googol of zeros."

The words we know form part of our linguistic knowledge, part of our internalized grammars. Since each word is a sound-meaning unit, each word which is stored in our mental dictionaries must be stored with its unique phonological representation which determines its pronunciation (when the phonological rules are applied) and with its meaning.

Each word must include other information as well. Part of the dictionary representation of a word must include whether it is a noun, a verb, an adjective, an adverb, a preposition, a conjunction. That is, it must specify what **grammatical category**, or **syntactic class**, it is in. If this were not so, speakers of English would be unable to distinguish between a grammatical, well-formed sentence like *The solution to the problem is simple* and an ungrammatical, ill-formed string of words like *The solve to the problem is simply*. *Solve* is a verb and cannot occur in a sentence where a noun like *solution* belongs, and *simply* is an adverb, whereas a modifying adjective is required instead in this position in the sentence. You, as speakers of English, know this unconsciously, since your grammar includes the rules of sentence formation which in turn require information about the syntactic properties of each word. Some words, like *love*, may be either a noun or a verb, as shown by the sentences *I love you* and *You are the love of my life*. The classes of words, the syntactic categories—such as nouns, verbs, adjectives, and so on—will be discussed in more detail in Chapter 8. The semantic properties of words, which represent their meanings, will be discussed in Chapter 7.

In English, nouns, verbs, adjectives, and adverbs make up the largest part of the vocabulary. They are "open" classes, since we can and regularly do add new words to these classes. *Googol*, for example, was added to the class of nouns. Recently, from the name *Watergate*, a new verb, *to watergate*, entered the language. New adverbs like *weatherwise* and *saleswise* have been added, as well as adjectives like *biodestructible*.

The other syntactic categories are, for the most part, "closed" sets. It is not easy to think of new conjunctions or prepositions or pronouns that have entered the language recently. There is a small set of personal pronouns such as *I, me, mine, he, she*, and so on. With the growth of the feminist movement some proposals have been made for adding a new neutral singular pronoun, which would be neither masculine nor feminine, and which could be used as the general, or **generic**, form. If such a pronoun existed it might have prevented the department chairperson in a large university from making the incongruous statement: "We will hire the best person for the job regardless of his sex." The UCLA psychologist Donald MacKay has suggested that we use "e" [i] for this pronoun with various alternative forms; others suggest that *they* is already being used as a neutral third-person singular, as in the sentence "Anyone can do it if they try hard enough." Because of the "closed" nature of the set of pronouns, we would predict that *they* has a better chance to serve this need than a completely new pronoun.

Another interesting thing about the words we know is that some words seem to be related to each other in a special way. The short story writer O. Henry once said: "Most wonderful of all are words, and how they make friends one with another. . . ." Perhaps he was thinking of words like the following:

phone	phonic
phonetic	phoneme
phonetician	phonemic
phonetics	allophone
phonology	telephone
phonologist	telephonic
phonological	euphonious

All the above words are related in both sound and meaning. They all include the same phonological form with the identical meaning of the first word, *phone*. *Phone* seems to be a minimal form in that it can't be divided into more elemental structures. *ph* doesn't mean anything, and *pho* [fo] has no relation in meaning to the identical sounds in the word *foe*, and -*one* [on] is not related to the sound units [on] meaning "own." But all the other words on the list contain as part of their structure this same word. The phonological rules of English "tell us" that in *phonetic, phonetics, phonology, phonologist, phonemic* the pronunciation is [fən] instead of [fon], but the same element *phone* /fon/ is present, with its identical meaning, "pertaining to sound," in all these words.

Notice further that in the following pairs of words the meanings of all the words in column B consist of the meanings of the words in column A plus the meaning "not":

A	B
desirable	undesirable
likely	unlikely
inspired	uninspired
happy	unhappy
developed	undeveloped
sophisticated	unsophisticated

Webster's Third New International Dictionary lists about 2700 adjectives beginning with *un-*, the meaning of which speakers of English would know if they knew the word without the *un-*.

If the most elemental units of meaning, the basic linguistic signs, are assumed to be the words of a language, it would be a coincidence that *un* has the same meaning in all the column B words above, or that *phone* has the same meaning in all the words in the preceding list. But this is obviously no coincidence. The words *undesirable, unlikely, uninspired, unhappy,* and the others in column B consist of at least two meaningful units: *un + desirable, un + likely,* and so on.

It is also a fact about English words that their internal structure is subject to rules. Thus *uneaten, unadmired, ungrammatical* are words in English, but **eatenun, *admiredun, *grammaticalun* (to mean "not eaten," "not admired," "not grammatical") are not, because we do not form a negative meaning of a word by suffixing *un* (that is, by adding it to the end of the word), but by prefixing it (that is, by adding it to the beginning).

The study of the internal structure of words, and of the rules by which words are formed, is called **morphology**. Just as knowledge of a language implies knowledge of the phonology, so it also implies knowledge of the morphology.

In this chapter we will be discussing how words are formed in English and other languages and what it is speakers of a language know about word formation, about the morphology of their language.

Morphemes: The Minimal Units of Meaning

"They gave it me," Humpty Dumpty continued . . . ,
"for an un-birthday present."
"I beg your pardon?" Alice said with a puzzled air.
"I'm not offended," said Humpty Dumpty.
"I mean, what *is* an un-birthday present?"
"A present given when it isn't your birthday, of course."
LEWIS CARROLL, *Through the Looking-Glass*

LUTHER   BY BRUMSIC BRANDON, JR.

When Samuel Goldwyn, the pioneer moviemaker, announced: "In two words: *im-possible*." he was reflecting the common view that words are the basic meaningful elements in a language. We have already seen that this cannot be so, since some words are formed by combining a number of distinct units of meaning. The traditional term for the most elemental unit of grammatical form is **morpheme**. The word is derived from the Greek word *morphē*, meaning "form." Linguistically speaking, then, Goldwyn should have said: "In two morphemes: *im-possible*."

A single word may be composed of one or more morphemes:

one morpheme	boy, desire
two morphemes	boy + ish, desire + able
three morphemes	boy + ish + ness, desire + able + ity
four morphemes	gentle + man + li + ness, un + desire + able + ity
more than four morphemes	un + gentle + man + li + ness anti + dis + establish + ment + ari + an + ism[1]

A morpheme may be defined as the **minimal linguistic sign**, a grammatical unit in which there is an arbitrary union of a sound and a meaning and which cannot be further analyzed. As we shall see below, this may be too simple a definition, but it will serve our purposes for now. Every word in every language is composed of one or more morphemes.

If we look at the examples given above we can see that some morphemes like *boy, desire, gentle,* and *man* can constitute words by themselves. Other morphemes like *-ish, -able, un-, -ness,* and *-li* are never words but always parts of words. Thus, *un-* is like *pre-* (*prefix, predetermine, prejudge, prearrange*), and *dis-* (*disallow, disobey, disapprove, dislike*), and *bi-* (*bipolar, bisexual, bivalved*), and occurs only before other morphemes. Such morphemes are called **prefixes**. Other morphemes occur only as **suffixes**, after other morphemes. English examples of such morphemes are *-er* (*singer, performer, reader, beautifier*), *-ist* (*typist, copyist, pianist, novelist, collaborationist, Marxist*), and *-ly* (*manly, bastardly, sickly, orderly, friendly*), to mention just a few.

These prefix and suffix morphemes have traditionally been called **bound morphemes**, since they can not occur "unattached," as distinct from **free morphemes** like *man, bastard, sick, prove, allow, judge,* and so on. Of course in speaking we seldom use even free morphemes alone. We combine all morphemes into larger units—phrases and sentences.

In all languages morphemes are the minimal linguistic signs. In Turkish, if you add *-ak* to a verb, you derive a noun, as in:

dur, "to stop"	*dur+ak,* "stopping place"
bat, "to sink"	*bat+ak,* "sinking place" or "marsh/swamp"

In English, in order to express reciprocal action we use the phrase *each other* as in *understand each other, love each other.* In Turkish, one simply adds a morpheme to the verb: *anla* "understand," *anla+š* "understand each other," *sev* "love," *sev+iš* "love each other."

In Piro, an Arawakan language spoken in Peru, a single morpheme, *kaka,* can be added to a verb to express the meaning "cause to": *cokoruha*

---

[1] Some speakers of English would have even more morphemes than this.

"to harpoon," *cokoruha+kaka* "to cause to harpoon"; *salwa* "to visit," *salwa+kaka* "to cause to visit."

In Karok, an American Indian language spoken in the Pacific northwest, if you add -*ak* to a noun, it forms a locative adverbial meaning "in, on, or at": *ikrivra:m* "house," *ikrivra:m+ak* "in a house"; *2a:s* "water," *2a:s+ak* "in water." Note that it is accidental that both Turkish and Karok have a suffix -*ak*. Despite the similarity in form, the meanings are different.

Also in Karok, the suffix -*ara* has the same meaning as our suffix -*y*, that is, "characterized by," as in *2a:x* "blood," *2ax+ara* "bloody"; *apti:k* "branch," *aptik+ara* "branchy."

The examples illustrate "free" morphemes like *boy* in English, *dur* in Turkish, *salwa* in Piro, and *2a:s* in Karok. Prefix and suffix morphemes were also illustrated. Some languages also have **infixes**, morphemes which are conjoined to other morphemes by inserting them into a morpheme. Bontoc, a language spoken in the Philippines, is such a language, as is illustrated by the following:

NOUNS/ADJECTIVES		VERBS	
fikas	"strong"	f*um*ikas	"to be strong"
kilad	"red"	k*um*ilad	"to be red"
fusul	"enemy"	f*um*usul	"to be an enemy"

In this language the infix -*um*- is inserted after the first consonant of the noun or adjective. Knowing that *pusi* means "poor," what do you think would be the most likely meaning of *pumusi*? And if *gumitad* means "to be dark," what would the Bontoc word for the adjective "dark" be?

Crans and Huckles and Other Such Morphemes

B.C. by johnny hart

By permission of Johnny Hart and Field Enterprises, Inc.

We have already defined a morpheme as the most basic element of meaning, as a phonological form which is arbitrarily united with a particular meaning and which cannot be analyzed into simpler elements. This definition has presented problems for linguistic analysis for many years, although it holds for most of the morphemes in a language. Consider words like *cranberry, huckleberry,* and *boysenberry.* The *berry* part is no problem, but *huckle* and *boysen* occur only with *berry*, as did *cran* until the drink *cranapple* juice came on the market. To account for such forms, and others which we will discuss briefly below, we have to redefine the notion "morpheme." Some morphemes are not meaningful in isolation, but acquire meaning by virtue of their connection with other morphemes in words. Thus the morpheme *cran* when joined with *berry* has the meaning of a special kind of berry which is small, round, red, and so on.

Just as there seem to be some morphemes which occur only in a single word (that is, combined with another morpheme), there are other morphemes that occur in many words, combining with different morphemes, but for which it is very difficult to find a constant meaning. How would you define the -*ceive* in *receive, perceive, conceive,* or the *mit* in *remit, permit, commit, submit*? There are also words which seem to be composed of prefix + stem morpheme in which the stem morphemes, like the *cran* above, never occur alone. Thus we find *inept* but no **ept, inane* but no **ane, incest* but no **cest, inert* but no **ert, disgusted* but no **gusted, lukewarm* but no *luke.

To complicate things a little further, there are words like *strawberry* where the *straw* has no relationship to any other kind of *straw*, and *gooseberry*, which is unrelated to *goose*, and *blackberries*, which may be blue or red.

We do not expect to try to solve this problem which has been troubling linguists for many years. Different linguists have provided different solutions. We will treat these "funny" forms as morphemes, recognizing that some morphemes acquire their meaning only by the connection to the conjoined morphemes in the words in which they occur.

Even though linguists have not been able to solve this problem to the satisfaction of all, we must remember that speakers of a language do not seem to have any problem with it. The difficulty is that our linguistic knowledge is unconscious knowledge and that as language learners and users we have greater ability to formulate grammars (without knowing that we do) than linguists have in discovering what these grammars are.

Morphological Rules of Word Formation

© 1974 United Feature Syndicate, Inc.

When the Mock Turtle listed the different branches of Arithmetic for Alice as "Ambition, Distraction, Uglification, and Derision," Alice was very confused:

> "I never heard of 'Uglification,' " Alice ventured to say. "What is it?"
>
> The Gryphon lifted up both its paws in surprise. "Never heard of uglifying!" it exclaimed. "You know what to beautify is, I suppose?"
>
> "Yes," said Alice doubtfully: "it means—to make—anything—prettier."
>
> "Well, then," the Gryphon went on, "if you don't know what to uglify is, you *are* a simpleton.

Alice wasn't really such a simpleton, since *uglification* was not a common word in English until Lewis Carroll used it. We have already noted that there are gaps in the lexicon, words which do not exist but which could exist. Some of the gaps are due to the fact that a permissible sound sequence has no meaning attached to it (like *blick* or *slarm* or *krobe*). Other gaps are due to the fact that possible combinations of morphemes have not been made (like *ugly + ify* or possibly *linguistic + ism*). The reason morphemes can be combined in this way is that there exist, in every language, rules which relate to the formation of words, **morphological rules**, which determine how morphemes combine to form new words.

The Mock Turtle added *-ify* to the adjective *ugly* and formed a verb. Many verbs in English have been formed in this way: *purify, amplify, simplify, falsify. -ify* conjoined with nouns also forms verbs: *objectify, glorify, personify*. Notice that the Mock Turtle went even further; he added the suffix *-cation* to *uglify* and formed a noun, *uglification*, as in *glorification, simplification, falsification, purification*.

There are other morphemes in English which change the category, or grammatical class, of words. These are sometimes called **derivational morphemes** because when they are conjoined to other morphemes (or words) a new word is **derived**, or formed. And, as noted, the derived word may be in a different grammatical class than the underived word. Thus, when a verb is conjoined with the suffix *-able*, the result is an adjective, as in *desire + able* or *adore + able*. A few other examples are: (noun to adjective) *boy + ish, virtu + ous, Elizabeth + an, pictur + esque, affection + ate, health + ful, alcohol + ic, life + like;* (verb to noun) *acquitt + al, clear + ance, accus + ation, confer + ence, sing + er, conform + ist;* (adjective to adverb) *exact + ly, quiet + ly;* (noun to verb) *moral + ize, vaccin + ate, brand + ish*.

Other derivational morphemes do not cause a change in grammatical class. Many prefixes fall into this category: *a + moral, auto + biography, ex + wife, mono + theism, re + print, semi + annual, sub + minimal*. There are also suffixes of this type: *vicar + age, fad + ism, Trotsky + ite, Commun + ist, Americ + an, music + ian*.

New words may enter the dictionary in this fashion, created by the application of morphological rules. It is often the case that when such a word as, for example, *Commun + ist* enters the language, other possible complex forms will not, such as *Commun + ite* (as in *Trotsky + ite*) or *Commun + ian* (as in *grammar + ian*). There may however exist alternative forms: *Marxian/Marxist*. The redundancy of such alternative forms, all of which conform to the regular rules of word formation, may explain some of the accidental gaps in the lexicon. This further shows that the actual words in the language constitute only a subset of the possible words.

Some of the morphological rules are very **productive** in that they can be used quite freely to form new words from the list of free and bound morphemes. The suffix -*able* appears to be a morpheme which can be freely conjoined with verbs to derive an adjective with the meaning of the verb and the meaning of -*able*, which is something like "able to be" as in *accept+able, blam(e)+able, pass+able, change+able, breath+able, adapt +able*, and so on. The meaning of -*able* has also been given as "fit for doing" or "fit for being done."[2]

Such a rule might be stated as:

(1) VERB + able = "able to be VERB-ed"

accept + able = "able to be accepted"

The productivity of this rule is illustrated by the fact that we find -*able* in such morphologically complex words as *un+speakabl(e)+y* and *un+ come+at+able*.

We have already noted that there is a morpheme in English meaning "not" which has the form *un-* and which when combined with adjectives like *afraid, fit, free, smooth, American,* and *British* forms the antonyms, or negatives, of these adjectives; for example, *unafraid, unfit, unfree, unsmooth, unAmerican, unBritish*.

We can also add the prefix *un-* to derived words that have been formed by morphological rules:

un + believe + able
un + accept + able
un + talk + about + able
un + keep + off + able
un + speak + able

The rule which forms these words may be stated as:

(2) un + ADJECTIVE = "not − ADJECTIVE"

This seems to account for all the examples cited. Yet we find *happy* and *unhappy, cowardly* and *uncowardly*, but not *sad* and **unsad* or *brave* and **unbrave*.

These starred forms may of course just be accidental gaps in the lexicon. Certainly if someone refers to a person as being **unsad* we would know that the person referred to was "not sad," and an **unbrave* person would not be brave. But as the linguist Sandra Thompson points out, it may be the case that the "un Rule" is not as productive for adjectives composed of just one morpheme as for adjectives that are themselves de-

[2] Hans Marchand, *The Categories and Types of Present-Day English Word-Formation*, 2nd ed. (Munich: C. H. Beck'sche Verlagsbuchhandlung, 1969).

rived from verbs.[3] The rule seems to be freely applicable to an adjectival form derived from a verb, as in *unenlightened, unsimplified, uncharacterized, unauthorized, undistinguished,* and so on.

Morphological rules may thus be productive (constantly used to form new words) or less productive. The rule which adds an *-er* to verbs in English to produce a noun which means "one who performs an action (once or habitually)"[4] appears to be a very productive morphological rule; most English verbs accept this suffix: *lover, hunter, predictor* (note that *-or* and *-er* have the same pronunciation), *examiner, examtaker, analyzer, programer,* and so forth.

Now consider the following:

sincerity	from	*sincere*
warmth	from	*warm*
moisten	from	*moist*

The suffix *-ity* is found in many other words in English, like *chastity, scarcity, curiosity.* And *-th* occurs in *health, wealth, depth, width, growth.* We find *-en* in *sadden, ripen, redden, weaken, deepen.*

Yet the phrase **The fiercity of the lion* sounds somewhat strange, as does the sentence **I'm going to thinnen the sauce.* Someone may use the word *coolth,* but, as Thompson points out, when such words like *fiercity, thinnen, fullen,* or *coolth* are used, usually it is either a speech error or the speaker is attempting humor.

It is possible that this is because a morphological rule which was once productive as shown by the existence of related pairs like *scarce/scarcity* is no longer a productive rule. Our knowledge of the related pairs, however, may permit us to use these examples in forming new words, on **analogy** with the existing lexical items.

"PULLET SURPRISES"

That speakers of a language know the morphemes of that language and the rules for word formation is shown as much by the "errors" made as by the nondeviant forms produced. Morphemes combine to form words. These words form our internal dictionaries. No speaker of a language knows all the words. Given our knowledge of the morphemes of the language and the morphological rules, we can often guess the meaning of a word which we do not know. Sometimes, of course, we guess wrong. Amsel Greene collected errors made by her students in vocabulary-building classes and published these in a delightful book called *Pullet Surprises.*[5] The title is taken from a sentence written by one of her high-school students: "In 1957 Eugene O'Neill won a Pullet Surprise." What is most interesting about these errors is how much they reveal about the students' knowledge of English morphology. Consider the creativity of these students in the following examples.

[3] S. A. Thompson, "On the Issue of Productivity in the Lexikon," *Kritikon Litterarum* 4 (1975): 332–349.

[4] Marchand, op. cit., p. 215.

[5] Amsel Greene, *Pullet Surprises* (Glenview, Ill.: Scott, Foresman & Co., 1969).

WORD	STUDENT'S DEFINITION
deciduous	"able to make up one's mind"
longevity	"being very tall"
fortuitous	"well protected"
gubernatorial	"to do with peanuts"
bibliography	"holy geography"
adamant	"pertaining to original sin"
diatribe	"food for the whole clan"
polyglot	"more than one glot"
gullible	"to do with sea birds"
homogeneous	"devoted to home life"

The student who used the word *indefatigable* in the sentence *She tried many reducing diets, but remained indefatigable* clearly shows morphological knowledge: *in*, meaning "not" as in *ineffective*; *de*, meaning "off" as in *decapitate*; *fat*, as in "fat"; *able*, as in *able*; and combined meaning, "not able to take the fat off."

Compounds

... the Houyhnhnms have no Word in their Language to express any thing that is *evil*, except what they borrow from the Deformities or ill Qualities of the Yahoos. Thus they denote the Folly of a Servant, an Omission of a Child, a Stone that cuts their Feet, a Continuance of foul or unseasonable Weather, and the like, by adding to each the Epithet of Yahoo. For instance, Hhnm Yahoo, Whnaholm Yahoo, Ynlhmnawihlma Yahoo, and an ill contrived House, Ynholmhnmrohlnw Yahoo.
JONATHAN SWIFT, *Gulliver's Travels*

She played upon her music-box a fancy air by chance,
And straightway all her polka-dots began a lively dance.

"A milkweed and a buttercup, and cowslip," said sweet Mary,
"Are growing in my garden-plot, and this I call my dairy."
PETER NEWELL, *Pictures and Rhymes*

We have seen how the combination of "derivational" and "free" morphemes produces new words. Words may also be formed by stringing together other words to create **compound** words. There is almost no limit on the kinds of combinations which occur in English, as can be seen by the examples in the following list of compounds:

	-ADJECTIVE	-NOUN	-VERB	-PREPOSITION
ADJECTIVE-	bittersweet	poorhouse	highborn	blackout
NOUN-	headstrong	rainbow	spoonfeed	handsoff
VERB-	carryall	pickpocket	sleepwalk	cutup
PREPOSITION-	underripe	outhouse	overdo	without

When the two words are in the same grammatical category, the compound will be in this category: noun + noun—*girlfriend, fighter-bomber, paper clip, elevator-operator, landlord, mailman*; adjective + adjective—*icy-cold, red-hot, lukewarm, worldly-wise*. In many cases, where the two words fall into different categories the class of the second or final word will

be the grammatical category of the compound. noun + adjective—*head-strong, watertight, lifelong*; verb + noun—*pickpocket, pinchpenny, dare-devil, sawbones*. This is not always true, and compounds with a preposition are in the category of the nonprepositional part of the compound: *overtake, hanger-on, undertake, backdown, afterbirth, downfall, uplift*.

Though two-word compounds are the most common in English, it would be difficult to state an upper limit: *three-time loser, four-dimensional space time, sergeant-at-arms, mother-of-pearl, man about town, master of ceremonies, daughter-in-law*.

Spelling does not tell us what sequence of words constitutes a compound, since some compounds are spelled with a space between the two words, others with a hyphen, and others with no separation at all, as shown for example in *blackbird, gold-tail, smoke screen*.

It is very often the case that compounds have different stress patterns from non-compounded word sequences, as we saw in Chapter 5. Thus *Rédcoat, gréenhouse, líghthouse keeper* have the primary stress on the first part of the compound, whereas *red cóat, green hóuse, light hoúse-keeper* do not. There are exceptions to this: *Fífth Street vs. Fifth Ávenue, máilmán* vs. *póstman*, among others. Even in complex compounds like *síx-cornered hen house annex door* we find the compound stress pattern.

One of the interesting things about a compound is that you can't always tell by the words it contains what the compound means. The meaning of a compound is *not* always the sum of the meanings of its parts.

Everyone who wears a red coat is not a Redcoat. There is quite a difference between the sentences *She has a red coat in her closet* and *She has a Redcoat in her closet*. It is true, as noted above, that the two sentences sound different. But in *bedchamber, bedclothes, bedside,* and *bedtime, bed* is stressed in all of the compounds; yet a *bedchamber* is a room where there is a bed, *bedclothes* are linens and blankets for a bed, *bedside* does not refer to the physical side of a bed but the place next to it, and *bedtime* is the time one goes to bed.

Other similarly constructed compounds show that underlying the juxta-position of words, different grammatical relations are expressed. A *house-boat* is a boat which is a house, but a *housecat* is not a cat which is a house. A *boathouse* is a house for boats, but a *cathouse* is not a house for cats, though by coincidence some cats live in cathouses. A *jumping bean* is a bean that jumps, a *falling star* is a "star" that falls, and a *magnifying glass* is a glass that magnifies. But a *looking glass* isn't a glass that looks, nor is an *eating apple* an apple that eats, nor does *laughing gas* laugh.

In all the examples given, the meaning of each compound includes at least to some extent the meanings of the individual parts. But there are other compounds which don't seem to relate to the meanings of the individual parts at all. A *jack-in-a-box* is a tropical tree, and a *turncoat* is a traitor. A *highbrow* doesn't necessarily have a high brow, nor does a *bigwig* have a big wig, nor does an *egghead* have an egg-shaped head.

The meaning of many compounds must therefore be learned, as if they were individual simple words. Some of the meanings may be figured out, but not all. Thus, if one had never heard the word *hunchback*, it might be possible to infer the meaning. But if you had never heard the word *flatfoot* it is doubtful you would know it was a word meaning "detective" or "policeman," even though the origin of the word, once you know the meaning, can be figured out.

It is also true that in morphologically complex words consisting of free morphemes and derivational morphemes one cannot always know the meaning from the morphemes themselves. As pointed out by Thompson,[6] the *un-* forms of the following have unpredictable meanings:

unloosen	"loosen, let loose"
unrip	"rip, undo by ripping"
undo	"reverse doing"
untread	"go back through in the same steps"
unearth	"dig up"
unfrock	"deprive (a cleric) of ecclesiastic rank"
unnerve	"fluster"

Thus, although the words in a language are not the most elemental sound-meaning units, they (plus the morphemes) must be listed in our dictionaries. The morphological rules also are in the grammar, revealing the relation between words and providing the means for forming new words.

The fact that such rules exist makes it possible for us to coin new words, such as *teach-in* and *space-walk*. Dr. Seuss uses the rules of compounding when he explains that ". . . when tweetle beetles battle with paddles in a puddle, they call it a *tweetle beetle puddle paddle battle*."[7]

It is of course not only English that has rules for conjoining words to form compounds, as is shown in the examples from these other languages: French *cure-dent*, "toothpick"; German *Panzerkraftwagen*, "armored car"; Russian *četyrexetažnyi*, "four storied"; Spanish *tocadiscos*, "record-player." In the American Indian language Papago the word meaning "thing" is *haʔichu*, and when combined with *doakam*, "living creature," the compound *haʔichu doakam* means "animal life."

[6] Thompson, op. cit., p. 338.
[7] T. S. Geisel, *Fox in Sox* (New York: Random House, 1965), p. 51.

In Twi if one combines the word meaning "son" or "child," ɔba, with the word meaning "chief," ɔhene, one derives the compound ɔheneba, meaning "prince." Or if you add the word for "house," ofi, to ɔhene, you have a word meaning "palace," ahemfi. The other changes which occur in the Twi compounds are due to phonological and morphological rules in the language.

In Thai the word for "cat" is mɛɛw, the word for "watch" (in the sense of "to watch over") is fâw, and the word for "house" is bâan. The word for "watch cat" (like a watch dog) is the compound mɛɛwfâwbâan—literally, "catwatchhouse."

Compounding is thus a very common and frequent process for enlarging the vocabulary of all languages.

In Chapter 7 other ways of forming new words which become part of the lexicon are discussed.

Morphology and Syntax: Inflectional Morphology

". . . and even . . . the patriotic archbishop of Canterbury found it advisable—"

"Found *what*?" said the Duck.

"Found *it*," the Mouse replied rather crossly: "of course you know what 'it' means."

"I know what 'it' means well enough, when *I* find a thing," said the Duck: "it's generally a frog or a worm. The question is, what did the archbishop find?"

LEWIS CARROLL, *Alice's Adventures in Wonderland*

"*My boy, Grand-père is not the one to ask about such things. I have lived eighty-seven peaceful and happy years in Montoire-sur-le-Loir without the past anterior verb form.*"

Drawing by Opie; © 1973 The New Yorker Magazine, Inc.

B.C.   BY JOHNNY HART

By permission of Johnny Hart and Field Enterprises, Inc.

Linguists traditionally have made a distinction between *morphology*, the combining of morphemes into words, and *syntax*, the combining of words into sentences. In the discussion of derivational morphology and compounding, we saw that certain aspects of morphology have syntactic implications in that nouns can be derived from verbs, verbs from adjectives, adjectives from nouns, and so on. There are other ways in which morphology is dependent on syntax, as we shall see in the discussion of *inflection*.

We also saw above that the definition of a morpheme as a minimal unit of meaning was too simple, since some morphemes have constant form but become meaningful only when combined with other morphemes. That is, the morpheme *-ceive* or *-mit* cannot be assigned an intrinsic meaning, yet, as speakers of English, we recognize it as a separate grammatical unit. When we combine words to form sentences, these sentences are combinations of morphemes. It is not always possible to assign a meaning to some of these morphemes, however. For example, what is the meaning of *it* in the sentence *It's hot in July* or in *The Archbishop found it advisable?* What is the meaning of *to* in *He wanted her to go?* *To* has a grammatical "meaning" as an infinitive marker, and *it* is also a morpheme required by the syntactic, sentence-formation rules of the language.

Similarly, there are "bound" morphemes which, like *to*, are for the most part purely grammatical markers, representing such concepts as "tense," "number," "gender," "case," and so forth.

Such "bound" grammatical morphemes are called **inflectional** morphemes; they never change the syntactic category of the words or morphemes to which they are attached. They are always attached to complete words. Consider the forms of the verb in the following sentences:

- a. I sail the ocean blue.
- b. He sail*s* the ocean blue.
- c. John sail*ed* the ocean blue.
- d. John has sail*ed* the ocean blue.
- e. John is sail*ing* the ocean blue.

In sentence *b* the *s* at the end of the verb is an "agreement" marker; it signifies that the subject of the verb is "third-person," is "singular," and that the verb is in the "present tense." It doesn't add any "lexical meaning." the *-ed* and *-ing* endings are morphemes which are required by the syntactic rules of the language to signal "tense" or "aspect."

English is no longer a highly inflected language. But we do have other inflectional endings. The plurality of a count noun,[8] for example, is usually marked by a plural suffix attached to the singular noun, as in *boy/boys, cat/cats,* and so on.

An interesting thing about inflectional morphemes in English is that they always "surround" derivational morphemes. Thus, to the derivationally complex word *un + like + ly + hood*, one can add a plural ending to form *un + like + ly + hood + s* but not **unlikeslyhood.*

Some grammatical relations can be expressed either inflectionally (morphologically) or syntactically. We can see this in the following sentences:

The boy'*s* book is blue.   The book *of* the boy is blue.
He love*s* books.   He is a lov*er* of books.
The planes *which* fly are red.   The fl*ying* planes are red.
He is hungri*er* than she.   He is *more* hungry than she.

Perhaps some of you form the comparative of *beastly* only by adding *-er. Beastlier* is often used interchangeably with *more beastly.* There are speakers who say either. We know the rule that determines when either form of the comparative can be used or when just one can be used. So does Alice: " 'Curiouser and curiouser!' cried Alice (she was so much surprised, that for the moment she quite forgot how to speak good English)."

Some languages are highly inflective. The noun in Finnish,[9] for example,

---

[8] "Count" nouns can be counted: *one boy, two boys,* and so forth. Noncount nouns cannot be counted: **one rice, *two rices,* and so on.

[9] Examples from L. Campbell, "Generative Phonology vs. Finnish Phonology: Retrospect and Prospect," *Texas Linguistic Forum* 5 (1977): 21–58.

has many different inflectional endings, as shown in the following example (don't be concerned if you don't know what all the specific case endings mean):

"continent, mainland"

mantere	nominative singular (sg.)
mantereen	genitive (possessive) sg.
manteretta	partitive sg.
mantereena	essive sg.
mantereeseen	illative sg.
mantereita	partitive plural (pl.)
mantereisiin	illative pl.
mantereiden	genitive pl.

These forms of the noun meaning "continent" are just some of the inflected forms of this noun.

In discussing derivational and compounding morphology, we noted that knowing the meaning of the distinct morphemes may not always reveal the meaning of the morphologically complex word. Such words, in addition to the morphemes, must be listed in our dictionaries with their meanings. This is not true of the words formed by the rules of inflectional morphology. If one knows the meaning of *linguist*, one also knows the meaning of *linguists*; if one knows the meaning of *analyze*, one knows the meaning of *analyzed* and *analyzes* and *analyzing*. One might then suggest that the difference between inflectional morphology and derivational morphology is that the inflected words are determined by the syntax of the language, and the derived words are part of the lexicon or dictionary.

The Pronunciation of Morphemes

Speak the speech, I pray you, as I pronounced it to you, trippingly on the tongue.
WILLIAM SHAKESPEARE, *Hamlet*, III, ii

In the discussion of phonetics in Chapter 4, the formation of noun plurals was considered. To form a regular plural in English one adds either a [z], [s], or [əz]. The particular sound added depends on the final phoneme of the noun. It was further pointed out that it is not necessary to learn or memorize all the sounds in each class as a list. There are regularities—"rules"—which determine the proper plural ending. That is, the addition of [s] to *cat*, and [z] to *dog*, and [əz] to *bus* is determined by the same rule as that which adds [s] to *cap, book, myth, cuff*, and which adds [z] to *cab, cad, dive, cow*, and which adds [əz] to *pause, bush, beach, judge*. A grammar which included lists of these sounds would not reveal the regularities in the language and would fail to reveal what a speaker knows about the plural formation.

The regular plural rule does not work for a word like *child*, which in the plural is *children*, or for *ox*, which becomes *oxen*, or for *sheep*, which is unchanged phonologically in the plural. *Child, ox*, and *sheep* are **exceptions** to the regular rule. One learns these exceptional plurals when learning the language. If the grammar represented each unexceptional or regular word in both its singular and plural forms—for example, *cat* /kaet/, *cats* /kæts/; *cap* /kæp/, *caps* /kæps/; and so on, it would imply that the plurals of *cat* and *cap* were as irregular as the plurals of *child* and *ox*. But this is not the case. If a new toy appeared on the market called a *glick* /glɪk/, a young child who wanted two of them would ask for two *glicks* /glɪks/ and not two *glicken*, even if the child had never heard anyone use the plural form. This is because the child would know the regular rule to form plurals. A grammar that describes such knowledge (the internalized mental grammar) must then include the general rule.

Notice that this rule which determines the phonetic representation or pronunciation of the plural morpheme is somewhat different from some of the other phonological rules we have discussed. The "aspiration rule" in English applies to a word whenever the phonological description is met; it is not the case, for example, that a /t/ is aspirated only if it is part of a particular morpheme. But the plural rule applies only to the inflectional plural morpheme. To see that it is not "purely" phonological in nature, consider the following words:

race	[res]	ray	[re]	ray+pl.	[rez]	*[res]
souse	[saws]	sow	[saw]	sow+pl.	[sawz]	*[saws]
rice	[rays]	rye	[ray]	rye+pl.	[rayz]	*[rays]

It is only when the final sibilant represents the plural morpheme that an [s] is not permitted after a vowel or diphthong.

The rule that determines the phonetic form of the plural morpheme is a rule which has traditionally been called a **morphophonemic rule**, in that its application is determined by both the morphology and the phonology.

This illustrates another important fact about morphemes which was mentioned very briefly above; a single morpheme may have different pronunciations. We saw in Chapter 5 that the derivational morpheme *in-* (meaning "not") was pronounced with an [n] or [m] or [ŋ] depending on the initial phoneme of the morpheme which followed it. We also saw that *phone* was phonetically [fon] or [fən], as shown by *phoneme* [fónim] vs. *phonemic* [fənímɪk].

When a morpheme has alternate phonetic forms, these forms are called **allomorphs** by some linguists. Thus [əz], [z], and [s] would be allomorphs of the regular plural morpheme.

The different pronunciations, the phonetic representations, of some morphemes are determined by regular phonological rules. This is true of the alternate forms of *phone* /fon/; the phonological stress rules and vowel reduction rules of English determine the different phonetic forms.

But for morphemes like "plural" the rules require morphological information. Given this information, the rules apply regularly.

Suppose, for example, that the regular, productive, plural morpheme has the phonological form /z/ with the meaning "plural." The regular "plural rule" can be stated in a simple way:

(3) (a) Insert an [ə] before the plural ending when a regular noun ends in a sibilant (/s/, /z/, /š/, /ž/, /č/, or /ǰ/).

    (b) Change the voiced /z/ to voiceless [s] when it is preceded by a voiceless sound.

If neither (3a) nor (3b) applies, then /z/ will be realized as [z]; no segments will be added and no features will be changed.

The "plural rule" will derive the phonetic forms of plurals for all regular nouns (remember, this is the *plural* /z/):

PHONEMIC	*bus+pl.*	*bat+pl.*	*bag+pl.*
REPRESENTATION	/bʌs+z/	/bæt+z/	/bæg+z/
	↓		
rule (3a)	ə	NA ↓	NA
rule (3b)	NA	s	NA
PHONETIC			
REPRESENTATION	[bʌsəz]	[bæts]	[bægz]

(NA means "not applicable.")

As we have formulated these rules, (3a) must be applied before (3b). If we applied the two parts of the rule in reverse order, we would derive incorrect phonetic forms:

PHONEMIC REPRESENTATION	/bʌs+z/
rule (3b)	s
rule (3a)	ə
PHONETIC REPRESENTATION	*[bʌsəs]

This "plural-formation" rule illustrates what we said in Chapter 5 concerning the function of phonological rules; that is, that such rules can insert *entire segments* into the phonemic string. An [ə] is added by the first rule.

In Chapter 4 we saw many other examples of the fact that a single morpheme may have different, alternate phonetic representations. The rules, whether strictly phonological, or morphophonemic (sometimes called morphophonological), which can add features, change feature values, delete segments, reorder segments, and add segments, all operate on the underlying, phonemic representations of morphemes.

Since a single morpheme is a constant phonemic form-meaning unit, there may be different morphemes which have the same meaning but different phonological form. We have suggested that the regular plural morpheme has the form /z/ with its alternate phonetic forms. There are other plural morphemes in English, as can be seen by the following "irregular" singular/plural pairs:

ox	oxen
child	children
man	men
sheep	sheep
criterion	criteria

Similarly, the productive regular past-tense morpheme in English is /d/, phonemically, but [əd] or [t] or [d] phonetically, again depending on the final phoneme of the verb to which it is attached. Some verbs, however, are exceptional:

go	went
sing	sang
hit	hit

There are no regular rules to specify these past-tense forms and the irregular plural forms listed above. When, as children, we are acquiring (or constructing) the grammar, we have to learn specifically that the plural of *man* is *men* and that the past of *go* is *went*. This is the reason why we often hear children say *mans* and *goed*; they first learn the regular rules, and before they learn the exceptions to these rules they apply the rules generally to all the nouns and verbs. These children's errors, in fact, support our position that the regular rules exist.

The irregular forms then must be listed separately in our mental dictionaries, as **suppletive** forms. It is interesting to note that when a new word enters the language it is the regular inflectional rules which apply. The plural of *Bic* is thus *Bics*, not **Bicken*.

The past tense of the verb *hit*, as in the sentence *Yesterday, John hit the roof*, and the plural of the noun *sheep*, as in *The sheep are in the meadow*, show that some morphemes seem to have no phonological shape at all. We know that *hit* in the above sentence is *hit*+past because of the time adverb *yesterday*, and we know that *sheep* is the phonetic form of *sheep*+plural because of the plural verb form *are*. Thousands of years ago the Hindu grammarians suggested that some morphemes have a zero-form; that is, they may not have any phonological representation. In our view, however, since we would like to hold to the definition of a morpheme as a sound-meaning constant form, we will suggest that the morpheme *hit* is marked as both present and past in the dictionary, and the morpheme *sheep* is marked as both singular and plural. Other linguists would analyze these differently.

Just as we find more than one morpheme with the same meaning, due to the different phonemic forms—like *in-*, *un-*, and *not* (all meaning "not") —we also find different morphemes with the same phonological form but different meanings. This follows from the concept of the morpheme as a sound-meaning unit. The morpheme *-er* means "one who does" in words like *singer, painter, lover, worker*. The same sounds represent the "comparative" morpheme, meaning "more," in *nicer, prettier, taller*. But notice that in *butcher* the sounds *-er* do not represent any morpheme, since a *butcher* is not one who **butches*. (In an earlier form of English the word *butcher* was *bucker*, "one who dresses bucks." The *-er* in this word was then a separate morpheme.) Similarly, in *water* the *-er* is not a distinct morpheme ending; *butcher* and *water* are single morphemes, or monomorphemic words.

We can therefore summarize what we have been discussing regarding the morpheme as a sound-meaning unit:

1. A morpheme may be represented by a single sound, like the "without" morpheme *a-* in *amoral* or *asexual*.

2. A morpheme may be represented by a syllable, like *child* and *-ish* in *child+ish*.
3. A morpheme may be represented by more than one syllable: by two syllables, as in *aardvark, lady, water*; or by three syllables, as in *Hackensack* or *crocodile*; or by four or more syllables, as in *salamander*.
4. Two different morphemes may have the same phonological representation: *-er* as in *singer* and *-er* as in *skinnier*.
5. A morpheme may have alternate phonetic forms: the regular plural /z/, which is either [z], [s], or [əz]; *sign* in *sign* [sayn] and *signature* [sɪgn]; or the different pronunciations of the morphemes *harmony, melody, symphony* in *harmonic/harmonious, symphonic/symphonious, melodic/melodious*.
6. For most of the lexicon, the different pronunciations can be predicted from the regular phonological rules of the language.

The grammar of the language which is internalized by the language learner includes the morphemes and the derived words of the language. The morphological rules of the grammar permit you to use and understand the morphemes and words in forming sentences and understanding sentences, and in forming and understanding new words.

SUMMARY

Knowing a language means knowing the words of that language. When you know a word you know both its sound and its meaning; these are inseparable—they are the inseparable parts of the **linguistic sign**. Each word is stored in our mental dictionaries with its phonological representation, its meaning (semantic properties), and its syntactic class, or category, specification.

Words are not the most elemental sound-meaning units; some words are structurally complex. The most elemental grammatical units in a language are **morphemes**. Thus, *moralizers* is an English word composed of four morphemes: *moral+ize+er+s*.

The study of word formation and the internal structure of words is called **morphology**. Part of one's linguistic competence includes knowledge of the morphemes, words, their pronunciation, their meanings, and how they are combined. Morphemes combine according to the morphological rules of the language.

Some morphemes are **bound**, in that they must be joined to other morphemes, are always parts of words and never words by themselves. Other morphemes are **free**, in that they need not be attached to other morphemes. *Free, king, serf, bore* are free morphemes; *-dom*, as in *freedom, kingdom, serfdom*, and *boredom*, is a bound morpheme. Bound morphemes may be **prefixes, suffixes, or infixes**.

Some morphemes, like *huckle* in *huckleberry* and *-ceive* in *perceive* or *receive*, have constant phonological form but have meanings determined only by the words in which they occur.

Morphemes may also be classified as **derivational** or **inflectional**. Derivational morphological rules are lexical rules of word formation. *Inflectional morphemes* are determined by the rules of syntax. Unlike derivational morphemes, they are only added to complete words; they never change the syntactic category of the word.

Grammars also include morphological **compounding** rules. These rules account for the combinations of two or more "free" morphemes or words to form complex **compounds**, like *lamb chop, deep-sea diver, ne'er-do-well.* Frequently the meaning of compounds cannot be predicted from the meanings of their individual morphemes or words. Many compounds must therefore be included in our internalized dictionaries, each with its phonological form and its meaning.

A morpheme may have different phonetic representations; these are determined by the **morphophonemic** and phonological rules of the language. Thus, the regular plural morpheme is phonetically [z] or [s] or [əz], depending on the final phoneme of the noun to which it is attached. In some cases the alternate forms are not predictable by regular or general rules; such forms are called **suppletive** forms, as for example, *man/men, datum/data,* or *go/went, bring/ brought.* These constitute a small set of the lexical items in a language; most of the morphemes are subject to regular rules.

While the particular morphemes and the particular morphological rules are language-dependent, the same general processes occur in all languages.

EXERCISES

1. Divide these words into their separate morphemes by placing a + between each morpheme and the next:

   a. retroactive   f. psycholinguistics
   b. befriended   g. irreplaceable
   c. televise   h. grandmother
   d. endearment   i. tourists
   e. predetermination j. morphophonemic

2. Think of five morpheme suffixes. Give their meaning, what types of stems they may be suffixed to, and at least two examples of each.
   Example: *-er*   meaning: "doer of"; makes an agentive noun
                   stem type: added to verbs
                   examples: *rider,* "one who rides"
                               teacher, "one who teaches"

3. Think of five morpheme prefixes. Give their meaning, what types of stems they may be prefixed to, and at least two examples of each.
   Example: *-a*   meaning: "lacking the quality"
                   stem type: added to adjectives
                   examples: *amoral,* "lacking morals"
                               asymmetric, "lacking symmetry"

4. Consider the following data from Ewe, a West African language. (Ewe is a tone language, but the tones are unmarked in these examples, since tone is not relevant to the problem.)

EWE	ENGLISH
uwa ye xa amu	"The chief looked at a child."
uwa ye xa ufi	"The chief looked at a tree."
uwa xa ina ye	"A chief looked at the picture."
amu xa ina	"A child looked at a picture."
amu ye vo ele ye	"The child wanted the chair."
amu xa ele ye	"A child looked at the chair."
ika vo ina ye	"A woman wanted the picture."

A. The morpheme meaning "the" is _____ .

B. The morpheme meaning "a" is: (Choose one)

    a. xa b. amu c. ye d. none of these

C. List all the other morphemes occurring in the Ewe sentences above. (Give the Ewe morpheme and the English "gloss.")

D. How would you say in Ewe "The woman looked at the tree"?

E. If *oge de abo* means "A man drank wine," what would the Ewe sentence meaning "A man wanted the wine" be?

5. Below are some data from Samoan:

manao	"he wishes"	mananao	"they wish"
matua	"he is old"	matutua	"they are old"
malosi	"he is strong"	malolosi	"they are strong"
punou	"he bends"	punonou	"they bend"
atamaki	"he is wise"	atamamaki	"they are wise"
savali	"he travels"	pepese	"they sing"
laga	"he weaves"		

A. What is the Samoan for:

    a. they weave —————————————————

    b. they travel —————————————————

    c. he sings —————————————————

B. Formulate a general statement (a morphological rule) which states how to form the plural verb form from the singular verb form.

6. Below are listed some words followed by the incorrect definitions provided by high-school students. (All these errors are taken from Amsel Greene's *Pullet Surprises*.)

WORD	STUDENT DEFINITION
stalemate	"husband or wife no longer interesting"
effusive	"able to be merged"
tenet	"a group of ten singers"
dermatology	"study of derms"
ingenious	"not very smart"
finesse	"a female fish"

For each of these incorrect definitions provide the possible reasons why the students made the guesses they did. Where you can exemplify by reference to other words or morphemes, giving their meanings, do so.

7. Look at the following conjugation of a Luiseño verb. (Luiseño is a Native American Indian language spoken in California.)

([q] is a uvular stop.)

no: čoriq	"I chop"	ča:m čoriwan	"We chop"
ʔom čoriq	"You (sg.) chop"	ʔomom čoriwun	"You (pl.) chop"
wuna:l čoriq	"He chops"	wuna:lum čoriwun	"They chop"

A. List the different morphemes and state what they mean.

B. Here are some more Luiseño verbs:

čuŋi "kiss"   pati "shoot"   koʔi "bite"

How would you say in Luiseño:

a. we kiss —————————————————————

b. you (pl.) bite —————————————————————

c. they bite —————————————————————

d. I shoot —————————————————————

e. you (sg.) shoot —————————————————————

f. he kisses —————————————————————

8. Below are some sentences in Swahili:

mtoto	amefika	"The child has arrived."
mtoto	anafika	"The child is arriving."
mtoto	atafika	"The child will arrive."
watoto	wamefika	"The children have arrived."
watoto	wanafika	"The children are arriving."
watoto	watafika	"The children will arrive."
mtu	amelala	"The man has slept."
mtu	analala	"The man is sleeping."
mtu	atalala	"The man will sleep."
watu	wamelala	"The men have slept."
watu	wanalala	"The men are sleeping."
watu	watalala	"The men will sleep."
kisu	kimeanguka	"The knife has fallen."
kisu	kinaanguka	"The knife is falling."
kisu	kitaanguka	"The knife will fall."
visu	vimeanguka	"The knives have fallen."
visu	vinaanguka	"The knives are falling."
visu	vitaanguka	"The knives will fall."

kikapu	kimeanguka	"The basket has fallen."
kikapu	kinaanguka	"The basket is falling."
kikapu	kitaanguka	"The basket will fall."
vikapu	vimeanguka	"The baskets have fallen."
vikapu	vinaanguka	"The baskets are falling."
vikapu	vitaanguka	"The baskets will fall."

One of the characteristic features of Swahili (and Bantu languages in general) is the existence of noun classes. There are specific singular and plural prefixes which occur with the nouns in each class. These prefixes are also used for purposes of agreement between the subject-noun and the verb. In the sentences given, two of these classes are included (there are many more in the language).

A. Identify all the morphemes you can detect (and give their meanings). Example:

-toto   "child"
m-   noun prefix attached to singular nouns of Class I
a-   prefix attached to verbs when the subject is a singular noun of class I.

Be sure to look for the other noun and verb markers, including tense markers.

B. How is the "verb" constructed? That is, what kinds of morphemes are strung together and in what order?

C. How would you say in Swahili:

a. The child is falling. ————————————————

b. The baskets have arrived. ——————————————

c. The man will fall. ————————————————

References

Aronoff, Mark. *Word Formation in Generative Grammar*. Linguistic Inquiry, Monograph 1. Cambridge, Mass.. M.I.T. Press, 1976.
Greene, Amsel. *Pullet Surprises*. Glenview, Ill.: Scott, Foresman & Co., 1969.
Marchand, Hans. *The Categories and Types of Present-Day English Word-Formation*, 2nd ed. Munich: C. H. Beck'sche Verlagsbuchhandlung, 1969.
Matthews, P. H. *Morphology: An Introduction to the Theory of Word Structure*. Cambridge, England: Cambridge University Press, 1976.
Nida, Eugene A. *Morphology: The Descriptive Analysis of Words*, 2nd ed. Ann Arbor: University of Michigan Press, 1949.

CHAPTER
What Does It Mean?

B.C.

by johnny hart

Language without meaning is meaningless.
ROMAN JAKOBSON

For thousands of years philosophers have been pondering the meaning of "meaning." Yet, everyone who knows a language can understand what is said to him or her and can produce strings of words which convey meaning.

Learning a language includes learning the "agreed-upon" meanings of certain strings of sounds and learning how to combine these meaningful units into larger units which also convey meaning. We are not free to change the meanings of these words at will, for if we did we would be unable to communicate with anyone.

Humpty Dumpty, however, refused to be so restricted when he said:

"There's glory for you!"

"I don't know what you mean by 'glory,' " Alice said.

Humpty Dumpty smiled contemptuously. "Of course you don't—till I tell you. I meant 'there's a nice knock-down argument for you!' "

"But 'glory' doesn't mean 'a nice knock-down argument,' " Alice objected.

"When *I* use a word," Humpty Dumpty said, in rather a scornful tone, "it means just what I choose it to mean—neither more nor less."

"The question is," said Alice, "whether you *can* make words mean so many different things."

Alice is quite right. You cannot make words mean what they do not mean. Of course if you wish to redefine the meaning of each word as you use it you are free to do so, but this would be an artificial, clumsy use of language, and most people would not wait around very long to talk to you. A new word may be created, but it enters the language with its sound-meaning relationship already determined.

Fortunately there are few Humpty Dumptys—since all the speakers of a language share the basic vocabulary, the sounds and meanings of words. And all speakers know how to combine the meanings of words to get the meanings of phrases and sentences. We have no difficulties in using language to talk to each other. The study of the linguistic meaning of words, phrases, and sentences is called **semantics**.

The Meaning of Morphemes and Words

"My *name* is Alice . . ."

"It's a stupid name enough!" Humpty Dumpty interrupted impatiently. "What does it mean?"

"*Must* a name mean something?" Alice asked doubtfully.

"Of course it must," Humpty Dumpty said with a short laugh: "*my* name means the shape I am—and a good handsome shape it is, too. With a name like yours, you might be any shape, almost."

LEWIS CARROLL, *Through the Looking-Glass*

Not only do we know what the morphemes of our language are, we also know what they *mean*. Dictionaries are filled with words and their meanings. So is the head of every human being who speaks a language. You are a walking dictionary. You know the meaning of words like *boy, girl, ox, child, house, assassin, frighten, love, idea, democracy, problem*. Your knowledge of their meanings permits you to use them appropriately in sentences and to understand them when heard, even though you probably seldom stop and ask yourself: "What does *boy* mean?"

Most words and morphemes in the language have their own meanings. We shall talk about the meaning of words, even though we already know that words may be composed of several morphemes.

Suppose someone said:

The assassin was stopped before he got to Mr. Thwacklehurst.

If the word *assassin* is in your mental dictionary, you know that it was some *person* who was prevented from *murdering* some *important person* named Thwacklehurst. Your knowledge of the meaning of *assassin* tells you that it was not an animal that tried to kill the man and that Thwacklehurst was not likely to be a little old man who owned a tobacco shop. In other words, your knowledge of the meaning of *assassin* includes knowing that the individual to whom that word refers is *human,* is a *murderer,* and is a killer of *very important people*. These then are some of the semantic properties of the word that speakers of the language will agree to. The meaning of all nouns, verbs, adjectives—the "content words"—at least partially can be defined by such properties. Such knowledge about the meanings of words represents part of your semantic knowledge of the language.

In general, a word will have at least one special semantic "defining" property. "Horseness" is included in the meaning of *horse* as well as the meanings "animal," "four-legged," and so on. The word *mare* has all the semantic properties of *horse* plus the meaning "female." Some semantic properties are common to many words; "female," for example, is not only a part of the meaning of *mare*, but of *bitch, doe, ewe,* and *vixen,* to name some animals, as well as of *actress, girl, maiden, spinster,* and *witch.* The last five words are also "human," along with such others as *child, professor, rock 'n' roll star,* and *woman.* All the examples mentioned so far are "animate," but the meanings of *sapling, rock,* and *sincerity* include the fact that those words refer to objects which are "inanimate." *Sapling,* in addition, possesses the semantic property "young" along with *child, kitten,* and *puppy,* while *sincerity* is further distinguished by being "abstract," as is *courage* and *the continuum hypothesis*.

Verbs have semantic properties too. *Darken, kill,* and *uglify* all have the feature "cause" in their meanings. *Darken* means "cause to become dark," *kill* means "cause to die," and *uglify* means "cause to become ugly." *Darken* and *uglify* also have the feature "inchoative," which means "about to become." Of course these are only a fraction of the verbal semantic properties that speakers of English know.

Although many of the semantic properties of verbs are not found in nouns, we do find that part of the meaning of *bridegroom* is "inchoative" (about to become married). "Inchoative" is present in *apprentice,* because an apprentice is "about to become" a craftsman. On the other hand, the adjectives *pregnant* and *virile* have the noun properties "female" and "male," and the verbs *comprehend, think, remember* are all "abstract."

The semantic properties of words are not entirely independent of one another. Certain pairs of semantic properties are mutually exclusive; logically they cannot both be part of the meaning of one word. "Animate" and "inanimate" are such properties, as are "human" and "abstract." For most words "male" and "female" are also "contradictory" features, but *hermaphrodite* is one word which includes the semantic components "male" and "female."

Some semantic properties are predictable given the presence of others; "human" automatically means "animate," since all things which are human are also animate, but the reverse is not true, since a fly is animate but not human. The verbal semantic property "speedily" (of *flee, sprint*) will always be accompanied by the property "motion."

Everyone who speaks sometimes produces "slips of the tongue," or speech errors. In Chapter 5 on phonology we discussed some errors which reveal the internalized phonological rules of the language. Other errors result in the substitution of a word for the intended word. Consider the following word substitution errors:

INTENDED UTTERANCE	ACTUAL UTTERANCE
blond hair	blond eyes
bridge of the nose	bridge of the neck
when my gums bled	when my tongues bled
young	early
the lady with the dachshund	the lady with the Volkswagen

These errors, and thousands of others which we have collected, reveal that the incorrectly substituted words share some "semantic properties" with the intended words. *Hair* and *eyes, nose* and *neck, gums* and *tongues* are all "body parts" or parts of the head. *Young* and *early* both contain semantic properties related to time. *Dachshund* and *Volkswagen* are both "German" and "small."

Errors in speech thus support what we have been saying about the semantic properties of words. In Chapter 2 we also discussed how word substitutions by aphasics reveal that the substituted words fall into the same "semantic class" or "semantic field."

The meaning of a word, then, is specified in part by a set of semantic properties. Consider, for example, the word *kitten*. Knowing the meaning of this word means knowing that it refers to an animal, a young animal, a young feline animal, and so on. The word does not specify a particular kitten. That is, the meaning of *kitten* does not include the size or color or age of any specific kitten or what its name is or where it lives or who owns it. The meaning signifies what all kittens have in common. It defines "kittenness."

Scientists know that water is composed of hydrogen and oxygen. We know that water is an essential ingredient of lemonade or a bath. But one need not know any of these things to know what the word *water* means, and to be able to use and understand this word in a sentence.

We may know what a word means without knowing anything about the situation in which it is used in an utterance. Some philosophers deny this. Hayakawa believes that "the contexts of an utterance determine its meaning" and that "since no two contexts are ever exactly the same, no two meanings can be exactly the same. . . . To insist dogmatically that we know what a word means in *advance of its utterance* is nonsense."[1]

Nonetheless, we must insist on this "nonsense." It is not important that a word mean *exactly* the same thing each time it is used. What is important is that unless the word has essentially the same meaning from one utterance to another, two people speaking the same language could not understand each other. If we are to understand the nature of language, we must explain the fact that speakers can and do communicate meaningfully with other speakers of their language.

Hayakawa attempts to support his view by the following example. He writes:

> . . . if John says "my typewriter" today, and again "my typewriter" tomorrow, the . . . meaning is different in the two cases, because the type-

[1] S. I. Hayakawa, *Language in Thought and Action*, rev. ed. (New York: Harcourt Brace Jovanovich, 1964).

writer is not exactly the same from one day to the next (nor from one minute to the next): slow processes of wear, change and decay are going on constantly.[2]

But, we would answer, such minute changes can hardly be said to affect the *linguistic* meaning of the *word*.

We have no trouble comprehending the meaning of *typewriter*. We know that what is being talked about is an object readily recognized as a "typewriter," and that the meaning of the *word* does not include the materials of which it is made, how old it is, whether it works well or not, its color, its location, or whether the owner knows how to type. Such information does not constitute the semantic properties of the word.

Linguistic knowledge includes knowing the meaning of words and morphemes. Because you know this you can use these words and combine them with other words and understand them when you hear them. This knowledge is part of the grammar of the language.

Homonyms (Homophones): Same Sounds, Different Meanings

"Mine is a long and a sad tale!" said the Mouse, turning to Alice, and sighing.

"It *is* a long tail, certainly," said Alice, looking down with wonder at the Mouse's tail, "but why do you call it sad?"

LEWIS CARROLL, *Alice's Adventures in Wonderland*

"There's a train at 4:04," said McHennie,
"Four tickets I'll take, have you any?"
Said the man at the door,
"Not four for 4:04
For four for 4:04 are too many."

ANONYMOUS

We have already said that knowing a word means knowing its sounds and meanings. Both aspects are necessary, for the same sounds can sometimes mean different things. When different words are pronounced the same but have different meanings, we call them **homonyms,** or **homophones.** (When the same word has different meanings, we say it is **polysemous.** In this section, we are concerned only with homonyms.) Homonyms may create ambiguity. A word or a sentence is ambiguous if more than one meaning can be assigned to it.

The sentence *She cannot bear children* may be understood to mean "She is unable to give birth to children" or "She cannot tolerate children." The ambiguity is because there are two words *bear* with two different meanings. Sometimes additional context can disambiguate the sentence. Thus, *She cannot bear children if they are noisy* is unambiguous, or practically so. The "give birth" interpretation is much less likely. The other meaning is most apparent in *She cannot bear children because she is ster-*

[2] Ibid.

ile. Both words *bear* as used in the above sentences are verbs. There is another homonym, *bear*, the animal, which is a noun with very different semantic properties. The adjective *bare*, despite its different spelling, is pronounced like the above words and also has a different meaning.

The fact that two words with different meanings may sound the same makes such words good candidates for humor, as well as for confusion.

> "How is bread made?"
> "I know *that*!" Alice cried eagerly. "You take some flour—"
> "Where do you pick the flower?" the White Queen asked. "In a garden, or in the hedges?"
> "Well, it isn't *picked* at all," Alice explained: "it's *ground*—"
> "How many acres of ground?" said the White Queen.

The humor of this passage is based on two sets of homonyms: *flower* and *flour* and the two meanings of *ground*. Alice means *ground* as the past tense of *grind*, while the White Queen is interpreting *ground* to mean "earth."

There are many other examples of sentences which are ambiguous because of the particular semantic properties which belong to some of the words of the sentence. For example,

(1) The girl found a book on Main Street.

is ambiguous, whereas

(2) The girl found a glove on Main Street.
or
(3) The girl found a book on language.
or
(4) The girl found a book in New York.

are not ambiguous. Sentence (1) can mean either:

> "The girl found a book which was lying on Main Street."
> *or*
> "The girl found a book while she was on Main Street."
> *or*
> "The girl found a book whose subject matter concerned Main Street."

The ambiguity is caused by the particular semantic properties of the words *book, on*, and *street*. The meaning of *book* includes something like "contains written information about." *On* is a homonym meaning "on the surface of" or "about" (that is, "on the subject of"). *Street* has "surface on which things may be located" among its semantic properties.

In sentence (2), *glove* does not include the meaning "contains written information about" and therefore *on* can be assigned only the meaning "on the surface of." In sentence (3), *language* does not possess any semantic property that would allow it to be used in a phrase of location, and consequently *on* can be interpreted only as meaning "about." In sentence (4), *in* is not ambiguous in the way *on* is (it lacks the semantic property "about"), so the entire phrase is unambiguous and has to do with where the book was found.

The semantic properties of these various words determine the ambiguity or lack of ambiguity of these sentences. They also reveal why in the sentence *He lectured on semantics, on* must be interpreted to mean "about" or "concerning," since *semantics* cannot be interpreted as a place; but in the sentence *He lectured on Main Street, Main Street* can be interpreted as the topic of his lecture (with *on* meaning "about") or as the place where he lectured.

The semantic properties also explain why *The girl found a glove on Main Street* is a good sentence, but **The girl found a glove on semantics* is not.

Thus we see that *on* can have two meanings in certain phrases, but only one meaning in other phrases. The semantic properties of the noun which follows it, as well as the semantic properties of the other words in the sentence, are the determining factors.

Such examples of homonyms and ambiguous sentences show that there is no one-to-one relation between sounds and meanings, and that one cannot always determine the precise meaning from the sounds alone. This is further evidence that the sound-meaning relationship in language is arbitrary, and that one must learn how to relate sounds and meanings when learning the language.

Knowing a language, however, allows one to assign possible meanings out of context. It is the fact that you know all the different meanings of the same sequence of sounds which creates ambiguities. The existence of homonyms does not mean that words have no meaning as separate entities. Quite the contrary, such words reveal our semantic knowledge.

A delightful form of humor is punning, despite the humorless view that "puns are the lowest form of humor." In a pun, one uses a homonym or near-homonym for humorous purposes. Again, Lewis Carroll's *Alice's Adventures in Wonderland* illustrates this. In reading the passage below, it is important to know that in British English (the English dialect spoken by Lewis Carroll) an *r* which follows a vowel is not pronounced when a consonant follows the *r*. Thus *tortoise*, pronounced [tɔrtəs] in American English, is pronounced [tɔtəs] (just like *taught us*) in British English.

> "When we were little, . . . we went to school in the sea. The master was an old Turtle—we used to call him Tortoise—"
> "Why did you call him Tortoise, if he wasn't one?" Alice asked.
> "We called him Tortoise because he taught us," said the Mock Turtle angrily.

Describing his education, the Mock Turtle explained:

> "I only took the regular course."
> "What was that?" enquired Alice.
> "Reeling and Writhing, of course, to begin with," the Mock Turtle replied; "and then the different branches of Arithmetic—Ambition, Distraction, Uglification, and Derision."

The passage illustrates how a good humorist not only substitutes similar-sounding words with different meanings, but selects words with specific semantic properties to create the humorous situation. *Reeling* for *reading* and *writhing* for *writing*—these are choices that are inspired! If Carroll had been interested merely in substituting words with similar but nonidentical sounds, he could have selected *reaping* or *reeking* for *reading* and *riding* or *rising* for *writing*. Instead, he chose words that are semantically related

to creatures or activities associated with the sea. *Reeling* includes semantic properties associated with fishing, and of course fish and eels *writhe*.

The same use of like semantic properties and sound-associations is seen
in the following:

> "No wise fish would go anywhere without a porpoise" [the Mock Tur-
> tle said].
>
> "Wouldn't it, really?" said Alice, in a tone of great surprise.
>
> "Of course not," said the Mock Turtle. "Why, if a fish came to *me*,
> and told me he was going a journey, I should say 'With what por-
> poise?' "

The substitution of *porpoise* for *purpose* is particularly humorous again
because of the "fishy" context.

Lewis Carroll, of course, had a great talent for *using* language. Thus
he was able to take advantage of specific properties of language to create
his humor. In the above examples he used the relationship between the
sounds and meanings of words. Since we are not all as talented as Carroll,
many of us cannot use language in this way. But our knowledge of language
does permit us to enjoy the humor. Again we see the difference between
language knowledge and language use, between linguistic competence and
linguistic performance. We have the competence to interpret the passages
as humorous because we know the meanings of the words and the sentences. Our knowledge of the meaning of words includes knowing their
specific semantic properties. Our competence enables us to see the humor
in the substitution of *reeling* and *writhing* for *reading* and *writing*. Carroll's competence was the same as that of other speakers of his dialect, but
his performance was a reflection of his genius.

We also noted that perfect homonyms in one dialect can lead to a humorous situation that may be lost on speakers of another dialect, because
for them the homonym doesn't exist. Homonyms, then, further attest to
our knowledge of the semantics of our language.

Synonyms: Different Sounds, Similar Meanings

Does he wear a turban, a fez or a hat?
Does he sleep on a mattresss, a bed or a mat, or a Cot,
The Akond of Swat?
Can he write a letter concisely clear,
Without a speck or a smudge or smear or Blot,
The Akond of Swat?
EDWARD LEAR, "The Akond of Swat"

O precious codex, volume, tome,
  Book, writing, compilation, work
Attend the while I pen a pome,
  A jest, a jape, a quip, a quirk.

For I would pen, engross, indite,
  Transcribe, set forth, compose, address,
Record, submit—yea, even write
  An ode, an elegy to bless—

To bless, set store by, celebrate,
  Approve, esteem, endow with soul,
Commend, acclaim, appreciate,
  Immortalize, laud, praise, extol

Thy merit, goodness, value, worth,
  Expedience, utility—
O manna, honey, salt of earth,
  I sing, I chant, I worship thee!

How could I manage, live, exist,
  Obtain, produce, be real, prevail,
Be present in the flesh, subsist,
  Have place, become, breathe or inhale,

Without thy help, recruit, support,
  Opitulation, furtherance,
Assistance, rescue, aid, resort,
  Favor, sustention and advance?

Alas! alack! and well-a day!
  My case would then be dour and sad,
Likewise distressing, dismal, gray,
  Pathetic, mournful, dreary, bad.

Though I could keep this up all day,
  This lyric, elegiac, song.
Meseems hath come the time to say
  Farewell! adieu! good-by! so long!
FRANKLIN P. ADAMS, "To a Thesaurus"[3]

Not only do languages contain different words which sound the same, they also contain words which sound different but have the same or nearly the same meanings. Such words are called **synonyms.** There are dictionaries of synonyms that contain many hundreds of such words. You find, for example: *apathetic/phlegmatic/passive/sluggish/indifferent; pedigree/ancestry/genealogy/descent/lineage*.

On the other hand, it has been said that there are no perfect synonyms —that is, that no two words ever have *exactly* the same meaning. Still there seems to be very little if any difference between the sentences: *I'll be happy to come* and *I'll be glad to come*, or *He's sitting on the sofa* and *he's sitting on the couch*. Some individuals may always use *sofa* instead of *couch*, but if they know the two words they will understand the sentences with either word and interpret them to mean the same thing. The degree of semantic similarity between words depends to a great extent on the number of semantic properties they share. *Sofa* and *couch* refer to the same type of object and share most, if not all, their semantic properties.

There are words which have many semantic features in common but which are not synonyms or near synonyms. *Man* and *boy* both refer to male humans; the meaning of *boy* includes the additional semantic property of "youth" whereby it differs from the meaning of *man*. Thus the semantic system of English permits you to say *A sofa is a couch* or *A couch*

[3] "To a Thesaurus," from the book *Column Book of F.P.A.* by Franklin P. Adams. Copyright 1928 by Doubleday & Company, Inc. Reprinted by permission of the publisher.

is a sofa but not *A man is a boy* or *A boy is a man* except when you wish to describe the "boylike" qualities of the man or the "manlike" qualities of the boy.

Often a polysemous word will share one of its meanings with another word. Thus *mature* and *ripe* are synonymous when applied to fruit, but only *mature* can apply to animals. *Deep* and *profound* are another such pair. Both apply to thought, but only *deep* applies to water.

Words which appear to be synonymous may differ in appropriateness, which is also part of meaning. *Croak* in one of its senses means "die," as does *pass on*, but your kindly Great Aunt Therza "passes on," although her crotchety neighbor may "croak." A game called "conjugating adjectives" is based in part on appropriateness and other subtle features of meaning. One attempts to think of words with similar meaning but different social values. It goes like this: "I'm thrifty, you're tight, he's stingy. I'm firm, you're rigid, she's obstinate."

Synonyms also serve as a vehicle for humor. One story concerns the "educated" son who returns home after four years at college. His mother asks him the meaning of the word *narrative*. "It means a tale," replies the son. She also asks him the meaning of *extinguish*. "To put out," answers the son. That night, at the son's homecoming party, during a lull in the conversation the mother is heard asking her son to "grab that pesky dog by the narrative and extinguish him." The humor of this story depends on the use of the homonyms *tale/tail* and the synonyms *extinguish/put out* and also on the fact that *put out* is homonymous in that it can mean "place outside" as well as "extinguish."

If we did not know the meanings of words, such stories (or any stories) would be impossible. The ability to interpret the same sounds as different in meaning or different sounds as the same in meaning shows that language is a system which relates sounds and meanings.

Antonyms: Different Sounds, Opposite Meanings

As a rule, man is a fool;
When it's hot, he wants it cool;
When it's cool, he wants it hot;
Always wanting what is not.
ANONYMOUS

It's co-existence
Or no existence.
BERTRAND RUSSELL

The meaning of a word may be partially defined by saying what it is *not*. *Male* means *not female*. *Dead* means *not alive*. Words which are opposite in meaning are often called **antonyms**. Ironically, the basic property of two words which are antonyms is that they share all but one semantic property. The property they do not share is present in one and absent in the other. Thus in order to be opposites, two words must be semantically very similar.

There are several kinds of antonymy. There are **complementary** pairs such as *alive/dead* or *married/single*. They are complementary in that *not alive = dead* and *not dead = alive*. And there are also **gradable** pairs such as *big/small, hot/cold, fast/slow, happy/sad*. With gradable pairs the negative of one word is not synonymous with the other. For example, someone who is *not happy* is not necessarily *sad*. It is also true of gradable antonyms that more of one is less of another. More bigness is less smallness; wider is less narrow, and taller is less short. Another characteristic of many pairs of gradable antonyms is that one is **marked** and the other **unmarked**. The unmarked member is the one used in questions of degree. We ask "How *high* is it?" (not "How low is it?") or "How *tall* is she?" And we answer "One thousand feet high" or "Five feet tall" but never "Five feet short," except humorously. *High* and *tall* are the unmarked members of *high/low*, and *tall/short*. Notice that the meaning of these adjectives, and other similar ones, is relational. The words themselves provide no information about absolute size. Because of our knowledge of the language, and of things in the world, this normally causes no confusion. But it does, like every aspect of language, provide a vehicle for humor. The following passage from *The Phantom Tollbooth* by Norton Juster illustrates this potential for humor:

> Milo and Tock walked up to the door whose brass name plate read simply "THE GIANT," and knocked.
>
> "Good afternoon," said the perfectly ordinary-sized man who answered the door.
>
> "Are you the giant?" asked Tock doubtfully.
>
> "To be sure," he replied proudly. "I'm the smallest giant in the world. . . ."
>
> They walked to the rear of the house, which looked exactly like the front, and knocked at the door, whose name plate read "THE MIDGET."
>
> "How are you?" inquired the man, who looked exactly like the giant.
>
> "Are you the midget?" asked Tock again, with a hint of uncertainty in his voice.
>
> "Unquestionably," he answered. "I'm the tallest midget in the world. . . ."
>
> The side of the house looked very like the front and back, and the door flew open the very instant they knocked.
>
> "How nice of you to come by," exclaimed the man, who could have been the midget's twin brother.
>
> "You must be the fat man," said Tock, learning not to count too much on appearance.
>
> "The thinnest one in the world," he replied brightly. . . .
>
> Just as they suspected, the other side of the house looked the same as the front, the back, and the side, and the door was again answered by a man who looked precisely like the other three. . . .
>
> "Are you the fattest thin man in the world?" asked Tock.
>
> "Do you know one that's fatter?" he asked impatiently.[4]

---

[4] Norton Juster, *The Phantom Tollbooth* (New York: Random House, 1961).

Another kind of "opposite" involves pairs like *give/receive, buy/sell, teacher/pupil*. They are called **relational opposites** and display symmetry in their meaning. If A *gives* X to B, then B *receives* X from A. If A is B's *teacher*, then B is A's *pupil*. Pairs of words ending in *-er* and *-ee* are usually relational opposites. If Mary is Bill's employ*er*, then Bill is Mary's employ*ee*.

Comparative forms of gradable pairs of adjectives often form relational pairs. Thus, if Sally is *taller* than Alfred, then Alfred is *shorter* than Sally. If a Cadillac is *more expensive* than a Ford, then a Ford is *cheaper* than a Cadillac.

If meanings of words were indissoluble wholes, there would be no way to make the interpretations that we do. We know that *big* and *red* are not opposites because they have too few semantic properties in common. They are both adjectives, but *big* possesses a semantic property involving size, whereas *red* involves color. Similarly, *buy/sell* can be relational opposites because both contain the meaning "transfer of property," differing only in one feature, direction of transfer.

In English there are a number of ways to form antonyms. You can, for example, add the prefix *un-* before a word and form its opposite, as in *likely/unlikely, able/unable*. Or you can add *non-*, as in *entity/nonentity, conformist/nonconformist*. Or you can add *in-*, as illustrated by *tolerant/ intolerant, discrete/indiscrete, decent/indecent*. As we noted, relational opposites can be formed by suffixing *-er* and *-ee*.

Sometimes by putting a *not* before an adjective we can create a gradable pair. *Far* and *not far* are an example. They are different from *far/ near*, also a gradable pair, because *not far* is not necessarily near. We also have *near/not near* and our semantic knowledge even tells us that an object that is *not far* is closer than one that is *not near*. Because we know the semantic properties of words, which define a great part of their meanings, we know when two words are antonyms, synonyms, or homonyms, or are totally unrelated in meaning.

Names

What's in a name? That which we call a rose
By any other name would smell as sweet.
WILLIAM SHAKESPEARE, *Romeo and Juliet*, II, ii

Her name was McGill and she called herself Lil
But everyone knew her as Nancy.
JOHN LENNON and PAUL McCARTNEY, "Rocky Raccoon"[5]

"What's in a name?" is a question that has occupied philosophers of language for centuries. Plato was concerned with whether names were "natural," though the question didn't bother Adam when he

---

[5] John Lennon and Paul McCartney, "Rocky Raccoon"; © 1968 by Northern Songs Ltd. Used by permission; all rights reserved.

named the animals; Humpty Dumpty thought his name meant his shape, and in part it does.

Usually, when we think of names we think of names of people or places, which are **proper names.** We do not think of canis domesticus as being named "dog." Still, the old view persists that all words name some object, though that object may be abstract. This view presents difficulties. We are unable to identify the objects named by *sincerity* or *forgetfulness*, not to mention *into, brave,* and *think.* In this book, then, "name" will always mean "*proper* name."

Proper names can refer to objects. The objects may be extant, such as those designated by *Robert Rodman, Lake Michigan,* and *The Empire State Building,* or extinct, such as *Socrates* and *Troy. Sherlock Holmes, Dr. John H. Watson, Oz,* and *Wonderland* are proper names of fictional objects.

Proper names are *definite,* which means they can be used to refer uniquely. If I say *Mary Smith is coming to dinner,* my spouse understands *Mary Smith* to refer to our friend Mary Smith, and not to one of the dozens of Mary Smiths in the phone book. The article *the* is used to make common nouns definite, so when I say *I saw the dog,* I have in mind a particular dog which I assume the listener can identify. The indefinite article *a* usually involves no such assumption and the speaker may not know to which dog I refer when I say *I saw a dog.* In the sentence *I want to marry a red-headed man,* however, the phrase *a red-headed man* may refer to a particular man with red hair. This represents a different use of *a.*

Because they are inherently definite, proper names cannot in general be preceded by *the*: *The John Smith, *The California. There are some exceptions, like the names of rivers (*The Eno River*), the names of ships (*The Queen Mary*), the names of buildings and other structures (*The Empire State Building, The Eiffel Tower*). Note that *the* in some of these cases is part of the proper name; you cannot refer to *Empire State Building without the *the,* nor to *a Queen Mary when referring to the ship.

Proper names cannot generally be pluralized, though they can be plural, like *The Great Lakes* or *The Pleiades.* Sometimes, however, to make necessary distinctions, we may talk about "the two fat Johns" and "the two skinny Johns," given a room full of people named John. Here, in fact, it is allowable to use the definite article *the,* and even to precede the proper name by an adjective, which is not usually permitted.

Giving names to things is an act that often reveals linguistic creativity. One need only look at the names of Kentucky Derby winners (*Canonero II, Secretariat*) to realize this. Although the naming of children is more conventional and the language provides a stock of personal names, many parents coin a name for their child that they hope (usually in vain) to be original. But once a proper name is coined, it cannot be pluralized or preceded by *the* or any adjective (except for cases like those cited above), and it will be used to refer uniquely, for these are among the many rules already in the grammar, and speakers know they apply to all proper names, even brand new ones.

Sense and Reference

You mentioned your name as if I should recognize it, but beyond the obvious facts that you are a bachelor, a solicitor, a Freemason, and an asthmatic, I know nothing whatever about you.
SIR ARTHUR CONAN DOYLE, "The Norwood Builder,"
The Memoirs of Sherlock Holmes

Take care of the sense, and the sounds will take care of themselves.
LEWIS CARROLL, *Alice's Adventures in Wonderland*

We hinted in the last section that the name *Humpty Dumpty* not only referred to a fictional object, but had some further meaning, something like "a good round shape." This raises the interesting question of whether proper names have a meaning over and above the fact of pointing out objects. Certainly, the name *Sue* is associated with females, as evidenced by the humor in Johnny Cash's song "A Boy Named Sue." *The Pacific Ocean* is an ocean, and even such names as *Fido* and *Bossie* have become associated with dogs and cows.

Words other than proper names both have a meaning and can be used to refer to objects. The German philosopher and mathematician Gottlob Frege proposed a distinction between the **reference** of a word, which is the object designated, and the **sense** of a word, which is the additional meaning. Frege reasoned that if meaning were equated with reference, then two different expressions with the same reference could be substituted for one another in a sentence without changing its meaning. As an example, he used expressions like *the evening star* and *the morning star*, the reference of both being the planet Venus. He used the question *Is the evening star the evening star?* to which the answer is obviously "yes." Then, for the second occurrence of *the evening star*, he substituted *the morning star* to produce a new question: *Is the evening star the morning star?* This question is quite different from the first question, and its correct answer follows only from careful astronomical observation. Frege concluded that the meaning of words involves more than just reference. He called that "something extra" *sense*. Hayakawa in his discussion of "typewriter" was referring to its reference rather than its sense.

Phrases, like words, normally both have sense and can be used to refer. Thus the phrase *The man who is my father* refers to a certain individual and has a certain sense which is different from that of *The man who married my mother*, although both expressions usually have the same reference. Phrases may, however, have sense, but no reference. If this were not so we would be unable to understand sentences like these:

(5) The present king of France is bald.

(6) By the year 3000, our descendants will have left Earth.

Speakers of English have no trouble comprehending the meaning of these sentences, even though France now has no king, and our descendants of a millennium hence do not exist.

Idioms

DENNIS THE MENACE

BY HANK KETCHAM

" WELL, THAT'S ANOTHER THING UP WITH
WHICH SHE WON'T PUT ! "

Courtesy Field Newspaper Syndicate

Knowing a language obviously means knowing the morphemes, simple words, compound words, and their meanings. But in addition, there are fixed phrases, consisting of more than one word, which have meanings which cannot be inferred by knowing the meanings of the individual words. Such phrases are called **idioms.** English has many such idiomatic phrases: *sell down the river, haul over the coals, eat one's hat, let one's hair down, put one's foot in one's mouth, throw one's weight around, snap out of it, cut it out, hit it off, take for a ride, wind around one's little finger, bite one's tongue, eat one's words, make a clean breast of, give a piece of one's mind.*

There are a number of interesting things about idioms. They appear to be similar in structure to regular phrases. Thus *She put her foot in her mouth* has the same structure as *She put her bracelet in her drawer.* One can say: *The drawer in which she put her bracelet was hers* or *Her bracelet was put in her drawer.* One would hardly say **The mouth in which she put her foot was hers* or **Her foot was put in her mouth* to mean the same thing as *She put her foot in her mouth*, though such expressions may be used humorously.

Some idioms can be changed internally with no unusual effect. We can say *The FBI kept tabs on Ellsberg*, or *Tabs were kept on Ellsberg by the FBI.* And we can admire *The great heed that was taken to prevent oil spills*, which is a relative clause based on the idiomatic expression [They] *took heed to prevent oil spills.*

We see that idioms, grammatically as well as semantically, may have very special characteristics. They must be entered into one's mental dictionary as single "items," with their meanings specified, and one must learn the special syntactic restrictions on their use in sentences.

As we examine how the semantics of language expresses our thoughts, we see how very complex language is. Yet we use it every day and are seldom aware of all the complexities.

The "Truth" of Sentences

. . . having Occasion to talk of *Lying* and *false Representation,* it was with much Difficulty that he comprehended what I meant. . . . For he argued thus: That the Use of Speech was to make us understand one another and to receive Information of Facts; now if any one *said the Thing which was not,* these Ends were defeated; because I cannot properly be said to understand him. . . . And these were all the Notions he had concerning that Faculty of *Lying,* so perfectly well understood, and so universally practised among human Creatures.
JONATHAN SWIFT, *Gulliver's Travels*

We comprehend sentences because we know the meaning of individual words, *and we know rules for combining their meanings.* Jonathan Swift's Gulliver seems to be unaware of this:

. . . I placed all my words with their interpretations in alphabetical order. And thus in a few days, by the help of a very faithful memory, I got some insight into their language.

If you ever study a foreign language, you'll have to learn both word meanings and how to combine them into sentence meanings. Memorizing the words won't get you very far. In acquiring your native language, of course, you learn these semantic rules unconsciously.

We all know the meaning of *red* and *brick.* The combination *red brick* is simply what "redness" and "brickness" have in common. Add *the* to form *the red brick* and the meaning becomes "a particular instance of redness and brickness, presumably known to speaker and audience." If we had begun with *large* and *brick,* the semantic rule for *large brick* could not have been what "largeness" and "brickness" have in common, for what is large for a brick may be small for a house and gargantuan for a cockroach. Yet we correctly understand *large house* and *large cockroach.* The rule needs to specify that *large brick* means "brickness" plus "largeness insofar as bricks go," just as *large house* means "houseness" plus "largeness insofar as houses go," and so on. Had we begun with *false* and *brick,* the combination *false brick* would involve "a resemblance to brickness that is not true brickness." Thus different semantic rules are needed for different adjective-noun combinations.

In understanding the expression *sees a red brick,* we understand that some object which is a combination of "redness" and "brickness" exists and has been perceived as a visual impression. In *John sees a red brick*, we understand the perceiver to be an individual male human being named John. Had we examined *John seeks a red brick* instead, we could not have concluded that a red brick exists, for one can seek for nonexistent objects. This shows that the semantic rules governing combinations with *see* differ from those of *seek*.

The semantic rules allow us to assign a meaning to any well-formed sentence of our language. For example, one could assign a meaning to the sentence

(7) The Declaration of Independence was signed in 1776.

whether it was shouted from the top of a mountain, read from a slip of paper picked up in a muddy gutter, whispered during a movie, or spoken with a mouth full of bubblegum. One can also understand the meaning of the sentence:

(8) The Declaration of Independence was signed in 1700.

even though it is a false statement. Your ability to recognize the "falsity" of the statement depends upon your understanding its meaning and also on your knowledge of history.

A minority of sentences can be recognized as true by virtue of linguistic knowledge alone. Such sentences are called **analytic**. The following statements are examples of analytic sentences:

(9) Dogs are animals.
   John is as tall as himself.
   Babies are not adults.
   My uncle is male.

Naturally, there are contradictory sentences, which are always false. The negative forms of the preceding sentences are all contradictory, as are:

(10) Adults are children.
    Kings are female.

Part of the meaning of a sentence, then, is knowledge of the conditions under which it can be said to be true. Philosophers talk about the "truth value" of a sentence. In this sense, sentence (7) is true and sentence (8) is false. Sentence (8) is false because the particular event to which it refers occurred at a time other than that stated.

Consider this sentence:

(11) Rufus believes that the Declaration of Independence was signed in 1700.

This sentence is true if some individual named Rufus does indeed believe the statement, and it is false if he does not. Your understanding of the sentence permits you to state under what conditions it is true or false. One can understand the sentence, or any sentence—one can assign a meaning to it—even if one is unable to decide on its "truth value." Its meaning, however, partially depends on knowing what conditions would make it a true statement or a false one.

Knowledge of the external world may help you decide if the sentence is true or false, but in addition you must be able to use your linguistic knowledge to understand its meaning. You may never have heard of the Declaration of Independence and may therefore not know whether such a declaration was signed in 1776, 1700, or 1492. But your knowledge of the language permits you to say that sentence (7) means that some document called *The Declaration of Independence* was signed by someone or other in the year 1776. Notice that your linguistic knowledge, not your knowledge about the particular event referred to, also permits you to say that sentence (12) means the same thing as sentence (7):

(12) It was in the year 1776 that the Declaration of Independence was signed.

and means the same thing as sentence (13):

(13) Some person or persons signed the Declaration of Independence in 1776.

The sentence doesn't tell you who signed the document. That fact is not included in the linguistic meaning of the sentence.

Sentences (7), (12), and (13) illustrate something else about language. Not only may different words have the same meaning, but different sentences may also mean the same thing. Thus

(14) John is easy to please.

means the same thing as

(15) It is easy to please John.

Clearly, if two sentences mean the same thing they will have the same truth value; under identical conditions sentences (14) and (15) will both be true or false, but one cannot be true while the other is false. Similarly,

(16) Hector is my maternal uncle.
(17) Hector is my mother's brother.

are synonymous. We say that sentence (16) is a **paraphrase** of sentence (17). Paraphrase and synonymity are similar concepts relating to sentences and words. We know that sentence (16) is a paraphrase of sentence (17) because we know the meanings of both sentences.

Some sentences are paraphrases of others because the meanings of the words chosen are similar. Other sentences are paraphrases because only the syntactic organization of the sentences differs, as in the following:

(18) It is easy to play sonatas on this violin.
    Sonatas are easy to play on this violin.
    This violin is easy to play sonatas on.

(19) Seymour used a knife to slice the salami.
    It was a knife that Seymour used to slice the salami.
    It was the salami that Seymour used a knife to slice.

These sentences may not be exactly synonymous; there are shades of differences. But they are clearly related and all the sentences of group (18) [and all those of group (19)] have the same truth value.

If a sentence contains an ambiguous word, then it may have as many different meanings as that word. Such **lexical ambiguity** is illustrated in sentence group (20):

(20) Mary *licked* her disease.
The Rabbi *married* my sister.
Do you *smoke* after sex?
Thomas Jefferson ate his cottage cheese with *relish*.

A sentence may also be ambiguous because of its structure. Two examples are given in sentence group (21). (Can you figure out the two meanings each sentence has? **Structural ambiguity** will be more fully discussed in the next chapter.)

(21) They are moving sidewalks.
John loves Richard more than Martha.

Sentences, like words, may also be related as antonyms. The negation of sentences illustrates this:

(22) Hector is my uncle.
(23) Hector is not my uncle.

Because you know the language, you know that if sentence (22) is true, then sentence (23) must be false.

Relational opposites are also found among sentences. They often occur as active-passive pairs. Thus, whenever (24) is true, (25) is true, and vice versa.

(24) Zachary hugged Emily. (Active)
(25) Emily was hugged by Zachary. (Passive)

Your ability to assign meanings to sentences also permits you to make other judgments. For example, if someone were to say to you *Would you like another beer?* the meaning of that sentence implies that you have already had at least one beer. Part of the meaning of the word *another* includes this *implication*. The Hatter in *Alice's Adventures in Wonderland* would not agree with us.

"Take some more tea," the March Hare said to Alice, very earnestly.
"I've had nothing yet," Alice replied in an offended tone, "so I can't take more."
"You mean you can't take *less*," said the Hatter: "It's very easy to take *more* than nothing."

The humor in this passage comes from the fact that knowing the language includes knowing the meaning of the word *more*. *More* does not mean "more than nothing" but "more than something."

Knowing a language includes knowing the implications inherent in the meaning of certain words and certain sentences.

Meaning, Sense, No Sense, Nonsense

Don't tell me of a man's being able to talk sense; everyone can talk sense. Can he talk nonsense?
WILLIAM PITT

If in a conversation someone said to you *My brother is an only child*, you might think either that he was making a joke or that he didn't know the meaning of the words he was using. You would know that the sentence was strange, or **anomalous.** Yet, it is certainly an English sentence. It conforms to all the grammatical rules of the language. It is strange because it represents a contradiction; the meaning of brother includes the fact that the individual referred to is a male human who has at least one sibling. The sentence *That bachelor is pregnant* is anomalous for similar reasons; the word *bachelor* includes the fact that the individual is "male" and males cannot become pregnant, at least not on our planet. Such sentences violate semantic rules. If you did not know the meanings of words you could not make judgments of this kind about sentences.

The semantic properties of words determine what other words they can be combined with. One sentence which has been used by linguists to illustrate this is *Colorless green ideas sleep furiously*.[6] The sentence seems to obey all the syntactic rules of English. The subject is *colorless green ideas* and the predicate is *sleep furiously*. It has the same syntactic structure as the sentence *Dark green leaves rustle furiously*. But there is obviously something wrong *semantically* with the sentence. The meaning of *colorless* includes the semantic property "without color," but it is combined with the adjective *green*, which has the property "green in color." How can something be both "without color" and "green in color" simultaneously? Other such semantic violations also occur in the sentence.

Your knowledge of the semantic properties of words accounts for the strangeness of this sentence and sentences such as *John frightened a tree* and *Honesty plays golf*. Part of the meaning of the word *frighten* is that it can occur only with animate nouns as objects. Since you know the meaning of *tree*, and know that it is not "animate," the sentence is anomalous. Similarly, *Honesty plays golf* is anomalous because *honesty* is neither "animate" nor "human" and therefore cannot be the subject of a predicate like *play golf*.

The linguist Samuel Levin has shown that in poetry we find just such semantic violations forming strange but interesting aesthetic images. He cites Dylan Thomas's phrase *a grief ago* as an example. *Ago* is a word ordinarily used with words specified by some temporal semantic feature: *a week ago, an hour ago, a month ago, a century ago*, but not **a table ago, *a dream ago*, or **a mother ago*. When Thomas used the word *grief* with *ago* he was adding a durational-time feature to *grief* for poetic effect.

In the poetry of E. E. Cummings one finds phrases like *the six subjunctive crumbs twitch, a man   wearing a round jeer for a hat*, and *children building this rainman out of snow*. Though all of these phrases violate or break some semantic rules, one can understand them. In any case, it is the breaking of the rules that actually creates the imagery desired. The fact that

[6] Noam Chomsky, *Syntactic Structures* (The Hague: Mouton, 1957).

you can understand these phrases while at the same time recognizing their anomalous or deviant nature shows your knowledge of the semantic system and semantic properties of the language.

Sentences which are anomalous in this way are often known as "nonsense":

> As I was going up the stair
> I met a man who wasn't there.
> He wasn't there again today—
> I wish to God he'd go away.

Nonsense sentences of verses are not strings of random words put together. The words are combined according to regular rules of syntax. Random strings have no meaning and are also not funny. The ability to recognize "nonsense" depends on knowledge of the semantic system of the language and the meanings of words.

There are other sentences which sound like English sentences but make no sense at all because they include words which have no meaning; they are "uninterpretable." One can only interpret them if one dreams up some meaning for each "no-sense" word. Lewis Carroll's "Jabberwocky" is probably the most famous poem in which most of the content words have no meaning—they do not exist in the lexicon of the grammar. Yet all the sentences "sound" as if they should be or could be English sentences:

> 'Twas brillig, and the slithy toves
>   Did gyre and gimble in the wabe;
> All mimsy were the borogoves,
>   And the mome raths outgrabe.
>
>   . . .
>
> He took his vorpal sword in hand:
>   Long time the manxome foe he sought—
> So rested he by the Tumtum tree,
>   And stood awhile in thought.
>
> And as in uffish thought he stood,
>   The Jabberwock, with eyes of flame,
> Came whiffling through the tulgey wood,
>   And burbled as it came!
>
> One, two! One, two! And through and through
>   The vorpal blade went snicker-snack!
> He left it dead, and with its head
>   He went galumphing back.

You probably do not know what *vorpal* means. Nevertheless, you know that *He took his vorpal sword in hand* means the same thing as *He took his sword, which was vorpal, in hand* and *It was in his hand that he took his vorpal sword*. Knowing the language, and assuming that *vorpal* means the same thing in the three sentences (since the same sounds are used), you can decide that the "truth value" of the three sentences is identical. In other words, you are able to decide that two things mean the same thing even though you don't know for sure what either one means. You do this by assuming that the semantic properties of *vorpal* are the same whenever it is used.

We now see why Alice commented, when she had read "Jabber-wocky":

> "It seems very pretty, but it's *rather* hard to understand!" (You see she didn't like to confess, even to herself, that she couldn't make it out at all.) "Somehow it seems to fill my head with ideas—only I don't exactly know what they are! However, *somebody* killed *something*: that's clear, at any rate—"

The semantic properties of words show up in other ways in sentence construction. For example, if the meaning of a word includes the semantic property "human" in English we can replace it by one sort of pronoun but not another. We have already seen that a "nonhuman" noun cannot be the subject of a predicate like *play golf*. Similarly, this semantic feature determines that we call a boy *he*, and a table *it*.

According to Mark Twain, our maternal ancestor Eve also had such knowledge in her grammar, for she writes in her diary:

> If this reptile is a man, it ain't an *it*, is it? That wouldn't be grammatical, would it? I think it would be *he*. In that case one would parse it thus: nominative *he*; dative, *him*; possessive, *his'n*.

These kinds of restrictions based on semantic properties are found in all languages. In one dialect of the Ghanaian language Twi, different numerals are used with human nouns than with nonhuman nouns. The word *baanu* meaning "two" is used exclusively with human nouns, and the word *abieŋ* meaning "two" is used exclusively with nonhuman nouns. Similarly, the words for "three" are *baasã* with humans and *abiesã* with nonhuman objects. Starred phrases are deviant:

HUMAN NOUNS	NONHUMAN NOUNS
nnipa baanu, "two people"	*ŋkokɔ baanu
*nnipa abieŋ	ŋkokɔ abieŋ, "two chickens"
asɔfoɔ baasã, "three priests"	*nsem baasã
*asɔfoɔ abiesã	nsem abiesã, "three things"

Examples like these from English and Twi show the importance of semantic properties in the formation of sentences. It is not that one cannot understand a sentence like *I stumbled into the table, who fell over.* A Twi speaker would know what is meant by *nnipa abieŋ*, "two people," with the wrong form of "two." The point is that these sentences are deviant. They violate rules based on the semantic properties of words.

The discussion in this chapter so far has attempted to show how much speakers of a language know about the meanings of words and sentences—that is, the semantic system of their language.

Speech Acts, Pragmatics, World Knowledge

THE WIZARD OF ID
BY BRANT PARKER AND JOHNNY HART

By permission of Johnny Hart and Field Enterprises, Inc.

You can do things with speech. You can make promises, lay bets, issue warnings, christen boats, place names in nomination, offer congratulations, swear testimony. By saying *I warn you that there is a sheepdog in the closet*, you not only say something, you *warn* someone. Verbs like *bet, promise, warn,* and so on are **performative verbs**. Using them in a sentence may sometimes be tantamount to performing some non-linguistic act.

There are hundreds of performative verbs in every language. The sentences in group (26) illustrate their usage:

(26) I *bet* you five dollars the Yankees win.
    I *challenge* you to a match.

I *dare* you to step over this line.
I *fine* you $100 for possession of oregano.
I *move* that we adjourn.
I *nominate* Batman for mayor of Gotham City.
I *promise* to improve.
I *resign*!

Notice that in all these sentences the speaker is the subject (that is, they are in "first person") and in uttering the sentence is performing some non-linguistic act, such as daring, nominating, resigning. Also, all these sentences are affirmative, declarative, and in the present tense. All this is typical of **performative sentences.**

Actually, every utterance is some kind of speech act. Even when there is no performative verb, as in *It is raining*, we recognize an implicit performance of *stating*. On the other hand, *Is it raining?* is a performance of *questioning*, just as *Leave!* is a performance of *ordering*. In all these we could use, if we chose, an actual performative verb: *I **state** that it is raining; I **ask** if it is raining; I **order** you to leave*.

Language is full of implicit promises, toasts, warnings, and so on. *I will marry you* is an implicit performance of a promise and, under appropriate circumstances, is as much a promise as *I promise I will marry you*. Plainly, to arise from your seat, glass in hand, and shout *The health of our host* is as genuinely a toast as if you said *I toast the health of our host*.

The study of how we do things with sentences is the study of **speech acts.** In studying speech acts, we are acutely aware of the importance of the context of the utterance. In some circumstances *There is a sheepdog in the closet* is a warning, but the very same sentence may be a promise or even a mere statement of fact, depending on circumstances.

Speech act theory aims to tell us when it is that we ask questions but mean orders, or when we say one thing with special (sarcastic) intonation and mean the opposite. Thus, at a dinner table, the question *Can you pass the salt?* means the order *Pass the salt!* It is not a request for information, and *yes* is an inappropriate response. Still, much humor is achieved by characters who take everything literally:

HAMLET: Whose grave's this, sirrah?
CLOWN (gravedigger): Mine, sir . . .

HAMLET: What man dost thou dig it for?
CLOWN: For no man, sir.
HAMLET: What woman then?
CLOWN: For none neither.
HAMLET: Who is to be buried in't?
CLOWN: One that was a woman, sir; but, rest her soul, she's dead.
HAMLET: How absolute the knave is! We must speak by the card, or equivocation will undo us.[7]

The general study of how context influences the way we interpret sentences is called **pragmatics.** The theory of speech acts is part of pragmatics,

---

[7] *Hamlet*, **V,** **i.**

and pragmatics itself is part of what we have been calling linguistic performance.

We have already noted that we can understand a sentence even if we are unable to tell whether it is true or false. Often we do know the truth value of a sentence, and the knowledge we use to decide is knowledge about the world (assuming of course that the sentence is neither analytic nor contradictory). Knowledge of the world is part of context, and so pragmatics includes how language users apply knowledge of the world to interpret utterances.

When we hear a sentence like *John likes milk*, we have to make a "referential connection" between *John* and some person if we are to completely understand the utterance. This is also true of *she* in *She likes milk*, and of *cats* in *Cats like milk*. In all cases, contextual knowledge is applied to determine reference. We see, then, that the reference of a noun or pronoun, and the truth value of a nonanalytic sentence, are similar in that their correct specification is a pragmatic matter requiring knowledge of the world.

Anomaly, as discussed in the previous section, results partly from world knowledge. The anomalous character of *The worm has bad intentions* arises not because *worm* has the semantic property "lacks intentional ability," but because our knowledge of zoology does not ascribe intentions to worms. Pragmatic considerations also work to make semantically anomalous utterances meaningful. Thus *Golf plays John*, when spoken in the clubhouse just after John has played golf miserably, may be interpretable.

Contrary to what we have claimed, some linguists have said that pragmatic knowledge is as much a part of linguistic competence as grammatical knowledge. Another position is taken by other language scholars, who believe that knowledge of speech acts is part of linguistic performance. Whichever position one adopts, it is clear that linguistic knowledge is so vast and complex that it spills over and affects, and is affected by, other kinds of knowledge.

The Meaning of "Meaning"

> "The name of the song is called 'Haddocks' Eyes.' "
> "Oh, that's the name of the song, is it?" Alice said. . . .
> "No, you don't understand," the Knight said. . . .
> "That's what the name is *called*. The name really is 'The Aged Aged Man.' "
> LEWIS CARROLL, *Through the Looking-Glass*

To define the meaning of a morpheme or a word we find ourselves using other words in the definition. If the meaning of the prefix *in-* is "not," what does *not* mean? If the meaning of *man* is defined by such semantic properties as "male," "human," and so on, what is the meaning of *human* and *male*? It is clear that at some point we have to stop and assume that everyone "knows" the definitions of the describing terms. Those words which are left undefined are the basic **primitive semantic elements**. Anyone who has studied geometry is acquainted with this procedure. One reads a definition: "A line is the shortest distance between two points." What is a point? One assumes the knowledge of a point. "Point" is a primitive concept in geometry, just as "male," "human," "abstract," "morpheme," "phoneme," and so on are primitive terms in linguistics.

Though we are not ordinarily aware of it, language has infected us with a kind of cerebral schizophrenia. We constantly (and effortlessly) deal with the world on two levels: the level of actual objects, thoughts, and perceptions and the level of *names of* objects, thoughts, and perceptions. That is, we perceive reality on the one hand and talk about it on the other. Linguists have a tendency to become three-way schizophrenics. They not only have objects and language, but in addition they must treat language itself as an object. Anthropologists might describe a man by saying he is a bipedal, hairless primate. They are using language to talk about certain objects. Linguists wish to describe the language used to talk about these objects. Thus, they might say that *man*, the word, is a "noun," has three "phonemes," or possesses the semantic feature "human."

A language used for describing a language is called a **metalanguage**. Ordinary English is the metalanguage used by anthropologists or botanists or physicists to describe the objects of interest to them. Linguists also have to use ordinary language as a metalanguage to describe ordinary language.

We offer an elementary illustration of these concepts which we hope will clarify the problem:

OBJECT (Real World)	LANGUAGE (Object for Linguists)	METALANGUAGE
	man is a bipedal hairless primate	*man* is a *noun* *man* is composed of three *phonemes* the meaning of *man* includes the semantic property "human"

The terms *noun, phoneme, male,* and *human* are terms in the linguistic metalanguage, in the theory of language. This book is filled with such terms: *phone, allophone, phoneme, syntax, grammar, morpheme, word, sentence.* . . . Thus, while the word *man* is part of our language, when we say "*man* is a word" we are using language to discuss language, and *word* is part of the metalanguage.

One can see why language has intrigued philosophers from the beginning of history. The complexities discussed only punctuate the miracle that all normal human beings learn a language, use the language to express their thoughts, and understand the meanings of sentences used by others.

SUMMARY

Knowing a language is knowing how to produce and understand sentences with particular meanings. The study of linguistic meaning is called **semantics**. Semantics concerns the study of word and morpheme meanings, as well as the study of rules for combining meanings.

The meanings of morphemes and words are defined in part by their semantic properties or features. When two words have the same sounds but differ semantically (have different meanings), they are **homonyms**, or **homophones** (for example, *bear* can mean either "give birth to" or "tolerate"). The use of homophones in a sentence may lead to **ambiguity**. When a single word has several meanings, that word is **polysemous** (for example, the word *good* has somewhat different meanings in *good child, good knife, good check*). Two words with different sounds but which share all semantic properties are **synonyms** (for example, *couch* and *sofa*); two words which are "opposite" in meaning are **antonyms**. There are antonym pairs which are **complementary** (*alive/dead*); there are **gradable** pairs of antonyms (*hot/cold*); and there are **relational** pairs (*buy/sell, employer/employee*).

Words may be combined to form phrases with meanings assigned to the whole unit; such phrases are **idioms** and their meanings are not the sum of their parts (for example, *put one's foot in one's mouth*).

Proper names are special morphemes used to designate particular objects uniquely; that is, they are **definite**. Proper names are normally not preceded by an article or adjective, and they cannot be pluralized.

Words have **sense** and can be used to **refer**. Larger expressions like phrases and sentences also have sense and reference. Frege showed that meaning is more than reference alone. In fact, some meaningful expressions (for example, *the present king of France*) have sense but no reference.

When you know a language you know many rules for combining meanings of words. We have only studied a few such rules. For example, you know a *good king* is a king, but a *former king* is not a king. When you know the meaning of a sentence you are able to tell under what conditions the sentence is true or false. You can understand the sentence even if it is a false statement; in fact, if you didn't understand it you could not make this judgment. Some sentences are **analytic**; that is, true by virtue of linguistic knowledge alone. *Mothers are female* is an analytic sentence. **Contradictory sentences** are the opposite of analytic sentences and are always false (for example, *My aunt is a man*).

Sentences, like words, may be synonymous; that is, mean the same thing. Such sentences are related to each other as **paraphrases**. Sentences may also be homophonous—have two different meanings (be **ambiguous**) but sound the same. Sentences can also be **antonymous,** or have "opposite" meanings.

Some sentences are strange or **anomalous** in that they deviate from what we expect. *The red-haired girl has blond hair* and *The stone ran* are anomalous. Other sentences are "uninterpretable" because they contain "words" which are "nonexistent" (for example, *An orkish sluck blecked nokishly*). The semantic properties of words play a crucial role in determining whether a sentence is anomalous.

Performative verbs like *bequeath* allow us to do things with sentences. One doesn't even need a performative verb; for example, shouting *Look out!* may have the effect of a warning (*I warn you to look out!*). The study of how we do things with utterances is the study of **speech acts.** Context is needed to determine the nature of the speech act. The general study of how context affects linguistic interpretation is **pragmatics.** Speech act theory is part of pragmatics, which itself is part of linguistic performance.

Linguists have to use language to describe language. The language used for description is called a **metalanguage.** Using language to describe objects in the world, we may talk about a man, child, ostrich, and so on. But when we say *man* is a "word" or a "noun," these descriptive terms are part of the metal-anguage of linguistics.

Everything one knows about linguistic meaning is included in the semantic system of one's grammar.

EXERCISES

1. Although language could not function properly if those who conversed failed to agree on the meanings of the words used, there are many situations where one person does not know all the words used in a sentence. Identify some of these situations and in each case imagine what the person might do to increase understanding. (For example, in a conversation with a linguist, a reference is made to your "organs of articulation," but you aren't really sure what *articulation* means.)

2. For each group of words given below, state what semantic property or properties are shared by the (a) words and the (b) words, and what semantic property or properties distinguish between the classes of (a) words and (b) words.
   Example: a. widow, mother, sister, aunt, seamstress
              b. widower, father, brother, uncle, tailor
   The (a) and (b) words are "human"
   The (a) words are "female" and the (b) words are "male"

   A. a. bachelor, man, son, paperboy, pope, chief
       b. bull, rooster, drake, ram

   B. a. table, stone, pencil, cup, house, ship, car
       b. milk, alcohol, rice, soup, mud

   C. a. book, temple, mountain, road, tractor
       b. idea, love, charity, sincerity, bravery, fear

   D. a. pine, elm, ash, weeping willow, sycamore
       b. rose, dandelion, aster, tulip, daisy

   E. a. book, letter, encyclopedia, novel, notebook, dictionary
       b. typewriter, pencil, ballpoint, crayon, quill, charcoal, chalk

   F. a. walk, run, skip, jump, hop, swim
       b. fly, skate, ski, ride, pedal, canoe

   G. a. ask, tell, say, talk, converse
       b. shout, whisper, mutter, drawl, holler

   H. a. alive, asleep, dead, married, pregnant
       b. tall, smart, interesting, bad, tired

   I. a. alleged, counterfeit, false, putative, accused
       b. red, large, cheerful, pretty, stupid

3. We passed lightly over the distinction between homophony (different words with the same pronunciation) and polysemy (one word with more than one meaning). In practice, it is not always easy to make this distinction. For instance, is a human *face* and the *face* of a clock an instance of homophony or polysemy? Dictionary writers must make thousands of decisions of this kind.

In a dictionary, homophonous words have separate entries, whereas the various meanings of a polysemous word occur in the same entry.[8] Using any up-to-date dictionary, look up ten sets of homophones (some homophones have four or five entries; for example, *peak*). Then look up ten polysemous words with five or more given meanings (for example, *gauge*).

4. Explain the semantic ambiguity of the following sentences by providing two sentences which paraphrase the two meanings. Example: *She can't bear children* can mean either *She can't give birth to children* or *She can't tolerate children*.

   a. He waited at the bank.
   b. Is he really that kind?
   c. The proprietor of the fish store was the sole owner.
   d. The long drill was boring.
   e. When he got the clear title to the land it was a good deed.
   f. It takes a good ruler to make a straight line.

5. We gave a few examples of "conjugating" adjectives. Actually, there are hundreds. Beside the one in the cartoon, here are a few more: I'm intelligent, you're overeducated, he's a smart-ass; I'm generous, you're extravagant, she's prodigal; I'm easy-going, you're lazy, he's slovenly.

DENNIS THE MENACE

BY HANK KETCHAM

"HE CALLS IT MED'TATION, MOM CALLS IT A EXERCISE... BUT I CALL IT GOOFIN' OFF."

Courtesy Field Newspaper Syndicate

Try to think up five more sets.

[8] Often, word etymologies are used as the basis for decision. If two different meanings of a form come from historically different sources, the forms are considered to be homophones and receive separate entries.

6. There are several kinds of antonymy. Indicate which among the following are complementary pairs, which are gradable pairs, and which are relational opposites:

A	B
good	bad
expensive	cheap
parent	offspring
beautiful	ugly
false	true
lessor	lessee
pass	fail
hot	cold
legal	illegal
larger	smaller
poor	rich
fast	slow
asleep	awake
husband	wife
rude	polite

7. Not all scholars agree with the view that proper names can have sense as well as reference. They believe that if a proper name has meaning at all, that meaning is the reference. They argue that the sentence *All Davids are male* is not analytic in the way that the sentence *All dogs are animals* is. Their reason is that a word like *dog* has as part of its sense "is an animal," but the name *David* is male merely by convention. Thus, a girl could be named David, but a dog must be an animal. Therefore, according to them, male is not part of the meaning of *David*. Write a short essay stating your views. (You may want to consider whether a sentence like *Paris is a city* is analytic. What if someone names her baby *Paris*? What if someone names her baby *dog*? A hit song of the 1960s was "Walkin' My Cat Named Dog.")

8. A. Which of the following sentences are analytic, and which are merely synthetically true?

   a. Kings are monarchs.
   b. Kings are rich.
   c. Dogs are four-legged.
   d. Cats are felines.
   e. Jimmy Carter is Jimmy Carter.
   f. Jimmy Carter is the thirty-ninth President of the United States.
   g. Uncles are male.
   h. An uncle has at least one brother or one sister.

   B. Which of the following are contradictory, and which are merely "synthetically" false?

   a. My aunt is a man.
   b. Aunts are always wicked.
   c. The evening star isn't the morning star.

   d. The evening star isn't the evening star.
   e. Babies can lift one ton.
   f. Puppies are human.
   g. My bachelor friends are all married.
   h. My bachelor friends are all lonely.

9. The following sentence is semantically anomalous:

   John is older than his sister's only brother.

   A. Give two further examples of such sentences and explain the anomaly.

   The following sentence is "uninterpretable":

   The sklumping skrittery prog climped through the dectary.

   B. Give two further examples of such uninterpretable sentences.

10. In sports and games many expressions are "performative." By shouting *you're out*, the first-base umpire performs an act. Likewise for *checkmate* in chess. Think up a half-dozen or so similar examples and explicate their use.

11. One suggested criterion of a "performance sentence" is whether you can begin it with *I hereby*. Notice that if you say sentence *a* aloud it sounds like a genuine apology, but to say sentence *b* aloud sounds foolish because you cannot perform an act of knowing:

    a. I hereby apologize to you.
    b. I hereby know you.

    One can test a sentence to see if it is a performance sentence by inserting *hereby* and seeing whether it sounds "right." Using such a test, determine which of the following sentences are performance sentences.

    c. I testify that she saw the accident.
    d. I know that she saw the accident.
    e. I suppose the Yankees will win.
    f. He bet her $2500 that Carter would win.
    g. I dismiss the class.
    h. I teach the class.
    i. We promise to leave early.
    j. I owe the I.R.S. $1,000,000.
    k. I bequeath $1,000,000 to the I.R.S.
    l. I swore I didn't do it.
    m. I swear I didn't do it.

12. Which of the following sentences illustrate language, and which metalanguage?

    a. Yellow is the color of my true love's hair.
    b. *Yellow* is a color word.
    c. *Dog* contains the semantic property "animal."
    d. A dog is an animal.
    e. *Halitosis* is spelled h-a-l-i-t-o-s-i-s.
    f. Halitosis is smelled by everyone.

References

Austin, J. L. *How to Do Things with Words*. Cambridge, Mass.: Harvard University Press, 1962.

Chafe, Wallace. *Meaning and the Structure of Language*. Chicago: University of Chicago Press, 1970.

Davidson, D., and G. Harman, eds. *Semantics of Natural Languages*. Dordrecht, The Netherlands: Reidel, 1972.

Dillon, G. L. *Introduction to Contemporary Linguistic Semantics*. Englewood Cliffs, N.J.: Prentice-Hall, 1977.

Fillmore, Charles, and D. T. Langendoen, eds. *Studies in Linguistic Semantics*. New York: Holt, Rinehart and Winston, 1971.

Fodor, J. D. *Semantics: Theories of Meaning in Generative Grammar*. New York: Thomas Y. Crowell, 1977.

Fodor, J. D., and J. Katz, eds. *The Structure of Language: Readings in the Philosophy of Language*. Englewood Cliffs, N.J.: Prentice-Hall, 1964.

Hayakawa, S. I. *Language in Thought and Action*, 3rd ed. New York: Harcourt Brace Jovanovich, 1974.

Katz, J. *Semantic Theory*. New York: Harper & Row, 1972.

Leech, Geoffrey. *Semantics*. Harmondsworth, Middlesex, England: Penguin, 1974.

Lyons, J. *Semantics*. Cambridge, England: Cambridge University Press, 1977.

Nilsen, Don L. F., and Alleen Pace Nilsen. *Semantic Theory: A Linguistic Perspective*. Rowley, Mass.: Newbury House Publishers, 1975.

Palmer, F. R. *Semantics: A New Outline*. Cambridge, England: Cambridge University Press, 1976.

Rapoport, Anatol. *Semantics*. New York: Thomas Y. Crowell, 1975.

Searle, John R. *Speech Acts: An Essay in the Philosophy of Language*. Cambridge, England: Cambridge University Press, 1969.

Steinberg, D., and L. Jacobovitz, eds. *Semantics: An Interdisciplinary Reader in Philosophy, Linguistics, and Psychology*. Cambridge, England: Cambridge University Press, 1971.

CHAPTER

The Sentence Patterns of Language

The Rules of Syntax

Everyone who is master of the language he speaks . . . may form new . . . phrases, provided they coincide with the genius of the language.
MICHAELIS, *Dissertation* (1769)

In the previous chapters we have discussed how the grammar of a language represents the speaker's linguistic knowledge, including knowledge of *phonetics* (the sounds of the language), *phonology* (the sound system of the language), and *semantics* (the meanings of words and sentences). Knowing a language also means being able to put words together to form sentences which express our thoughts.

The meaning of a sentence is a synthesis of the meanings of the morphemes of which it is composed. But the morphemes cannot occur haphazardly in the sentence. *The dentist hurt my teeth* does not have the same meaning as *My teeth hurt the dentist,* and the string of morphemes *my the hurt dentist teeth* has no meaning at all even though it is made up of meaningful elements. There are rules in one's grammar that determine what morphemes are combined into larger grammatical units to get intended meanings, and how these morphemes are to be combined. These are the **syntactic rules** of the language. They permit us to say what we mean, which, at least according to the March Hare, is what we should do.

"Then you should say what you mean," the March Hare went on.

"I do," Alice hastily replied: "at least—I mean what I say—that's the same thing, you know."

"Not the same thing a bit!" said the Hatter. "You might just as well say that 'I see what I eat' is the same thing as 'I eat what I see'!"

"You might just as well say," added the March Hare, "that 'I like what I get' is the same thing as 'I get what I like'!"

"You might just as well say," added the Dormouse . . . "that 'I breathe when I sleep' is the same thing as 'I sleep when I breathe'!"

"It *is* the same thing with you," said the Hatter.

195

If there were no rules of syntax it wouldn't have mattered whether Alice said "I say what I mean" or "I mean what I say." Part of the meaning of a sentence, then, is determined by the order of the morphemes. The syntactic rules of the grammar specify, among other things, such order.

This is true in all languages. In Thai, for example, *mɛɛw hěn mǎa* means "The cat saw the dog," but *mǎa hěn mɛɛw* means "The dog saw the cat" and **hěn mǎa mɛɛw* is not a sentence in Thai. *Où est la télévision?* ("Where is the television?") is a sentence in French. **Est la où télévision?* ("Is the where television?") is not a sentence in French. *ɛhá yɛ̀ hū* ("This place is spooky") is a sentence in Twi. **yɛ̀ ɛhá hū* ("Is place-here spooky?") is not a sentence in Twi.

Strings of morphemes which conform to the syntactic rules of the language are called the **grammatical sentences** of the language, and strings which do not "obey" these rules are called **ungrammatical.**

You don't have to study "grammar" or linguistics to know which sentences are grammatical. Even a very young child knows intuitively that *The boy kissed the girl* is a "good" sentence in English but that something is wrong with the string **Girl the kissed boy the*.

According to *your* knowledge of English syntax, which of the following sentences would you mark with an asterisk (as ungrammatical)?

  (1) a. Sylvia wanted George to go.
      b. Sylvia wanted George go.
      c. Sylvia heard George to go.
      d. Sylvia hoped George go.
      e. Sylvia heard George go.
      f. Clarence looked up the number.
      g. Clarence looked the number up.
      h. Morris walked up the hill.
      i. Morris walked the hill up.

If the syntactic rules of your grammar are the same as those of our grammar (and we expect that they are), you "starred" as ungrammatical sentences (1b, c, d, i). If we agree on the "grammaticality" of any of these sentences, we must be making these decisions according to some rules which we know. Notice that the syntactic rules which account for our "intuitions" in these cases are not *just* "ordering" rules. They "tell" us, for example, that with the verb *wanted* we must use a *to,* but with *heard* we do not use a *to.* And they permit us to "move" the *up* in sentence (1f) but not in sentence (1h).

These examples show that the syntactic rules permit us to make judgments about the "grammaticality" of sentences. In other words, the sentences of a language are well-formed, grammatical strings, not just any strings of morphemes. And it is the **syntax** of the grammar which accounts for this fact.

The syntactic rules also account for other linguistic judgments that speakers are able to make. Consider the following sentence:

  (2) The Mafia wants protection from attack by the police.

You can't be sure whether the Mafia wants the police to protect them against the attack of some unnamed parties or whether the Mafia wants someone to protect them from the attack of the police. The double meaning (or ambiguity) of the sentence is not due to the occurrence of any homonyms or words with two meanings, as it is in the following sentence:

(3) Katerina gave Petruccio a sock.

In sentence (3), Katerina may have given Petruccio an article of clothing or a punch. *Sock* has two meanings. But in sentence (2), the ambiguity can't be explained in this way; it must be due to the *syntactic structure* of the sentence. Your knowledge of the syntactic rules permit you to reconstruct sentence (2) as meaning either:

(4) a. The Mafia wants the police to protect them from attack.
or
b. The Mafia wants protection from being attacked by the police.

Sometimes the multiple meanings are not immediately apparent. But you can usually figure out which sentences are ambiguous because of your knowledge of the syntactic rules. We feel fairly certain that you can not only tell which of the following sentences are ambiguous but can even give the different meanings of the ones you choose:

(5) a. George wanted the presidency more than Martha.
b. Ahab wanted the whale more than glory.
c. Visiting professors can be boring.
d. Complaining professors can be boring.
e. Batman hit the villain with the gloves.
f. Batman hit the villain with the hooked nose.

If you decided that sentences (5a, c, e) were ambiguous (or if you see the ambiguity now that we have told you), something in your grammar must provide you with a basis for making such judgments. That something is syntax.

The syntactic rules also account for an interesting fact about the following sentences:

(6) a. John is eager to please.
b. John is easy to please.

The two sentences seem to be similar in structure. Yet speakers of English know that in sentence (6a) we are talking about *John pleasing,* whereas in sentence (6b) we are talking about *pleasing John.* The ways the different parts of a sentence are related constitute the **grammatical relations** of the sentence. The grammatical relation between *John* and *please* in (6a) is different than in (6b). Knowing the syntactic rules permits you to interpret the grammatical relations of sentences.

These rules also account for the fact that sentence (7) is a paraphrase of sentence (6b):

(7) It is easy to please John.

but that sentence (6a) does not have a similar paraphrase:

(8) * It is eager to please John.

The examples given so far illustrate in part the role of syntactic rules in a grammar:

1. They account for the "grammaticality" of sentences.
2. They determine the ordering of morphemes.
3. They reveal ambiguities.
4. They tell us when different sentences are paraphrases.
5. They determine the grammatical relations between different parts of a sentence.

We have been discussing the syntactic rules which you (and every speaker of a language) must "know." As we stated in the first chapter, to account for this linguistic knowledge, linguists write descriptive grammars. Insofar as the linguist's grammar accounts for your knowledge, it will be a good description of the language you speak. If you know certain rules, these rules must be stated in a clear way. In the next sections we will attempt to describe the kinds of syntactic rules which are found in all languages. For the most part we will illustrate them by using English examples, but no one should think that we are presenting the grammar of English. Our aim is rather to look at the kinds of regularities that might occur in any language, and to show how they can be explained by syntactic rules.

Constituent Structure

Who climbs the grammar-tree distinctly knows
Where noun and verb and participle grows.
JOHN DRYDEN, "Juvenal's Satire," vi

Your knowledge of syntax tells you the correct order of words in a sentence. But sentences are more than just one word placed after another. The words form groups, and within the groups they form subgroups, and so on. How would you divide the following sentence into two parts in the way "most natural" for you?

(9) The child found the puppy.

We believe that most speakers of English would divide the sentence as in (10):

(10) The child / found the puppy.

Any other division, such as in (11), would "feel" wrong because the words in each part do not seem to belong together in as tight a unit as they do in (10).

(11) The / child found the puppy.
The child found the / puppy.

If this "division" process were continued and we diagrammed all the separate units, (12) would be the result:

(12)

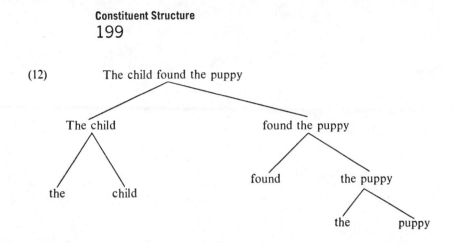

If this analysis agrees with your intuition, then your grammar, like our grammar, specifies that the phrase *found the puppy* would be more "naturally" divided into the two parts *found* and *the puppy* than into *found the* and *puppy*. If this is so, then *the puppy* is a unit of grammar in the sense that *found the* is not.

The groups and subgroups of words that "go together," as in (12), are called the **constituents** of the sentence. Thus *found the puppy* is a constituent, but *found the* is not. Your knowledge of the syntactic rules of English accounts for your intuitions about the **constituent structure** of English sentences.

All sentences in all languages have constituent structure. And all languages have syntactic rules that determine the linear order of words and how the words are grouped to give the constituent structure. Furthermore, your knowledge of constituent structure tells you that certain constituents can be substituted for other constituents without affecting the grammaticality of the sentence (although the meaning may change). In (12) we can substitute the constituents *the puppy* and *the child* for one another to give:

(13) [the puppy] [found [the child]]
"The puppy found the child."
(*Note:* In this example, constituent structure is indicated by means of the brackets instead of the diagram.)

Constituents that can be substituted for one another without loss of grammaticality form a **syntactic category.** The syntactic category that *the child* and *the puppy* belong to is **Noun Phrase (NP).** Noun phrases may be easily identified because they can function as "subject" or "object" in a sentence, and only noun phrases may do so. Noun phrases often, but not always, contain a noun or pronoun. (Infinitives, for example, function as noun phrases, as shown in the famous Alexander Pope quotation: "To err is human; to forgive, divine." In this sentence, *to err* is the subject of the first clause, or sentence.) Part of your syntactic knowledge is knowing the syntactic categories of your language. And you know what a noun phrase is even if you have never heard the term before. You can identify which of the following expressions are noun phrases by substituting each into

"Who sees _____ ?" and "_____ was lost." The ones that "feel right" will be the noun phrases:

(14) a. a bird
b. the red banjo
c. have a disease
d. with a gun
e. the woman who was crying
f. it
g. John
h. run

We assume that you were able to identify (14a, b, e, f, g) as noun phrases.

There are, of course, other syntactic categories. The constituent *found the puppy* is a **Verb Phrase (VP)**. Verb phrases always contain a verb, which may be followed by other constituents, such as a noun phrase. Thus, a syntactic category can include in it other syntactic categories. You can determine which of the following are verb phrases by trying to substitute each one into the slot "The child _____ ."

(15) a. saw a duck
b. a bird
c. slept
d. smart
e. is smart
f. found the cake
g. found the cake in the cupboard

The verb phrases are (15a, c, e, f, g).

Other syntactic categories, with examples, are:

Sentence (S): *The puppy found the child.*
Prepositional Phrase (PP): *in the cupboard, with a gun*
Noun (N): *child, puppy, woman, cake, bird, cupboard*
Verb (V): *find, have, sleep, bite, cry*
Adjective (Adj): *red, smart, lazy, small*
Pronoun (Pro): *it, he, she*
Preposition (P): *at, in, on, to, with*
Article (Art): *the, a*

All languages have syntactic categories, and although different languages may have different syntactic categories, the speakers of any language know the syntactic categories of their language.

We can now be more explicit in representing the constituent structure of *The child found the puppy* by indicating what syntactic category each constituent belongs to. We may also streamline the diagram of (12) by eliminating repetition. This gives us a **constituent structure tree**, or a **phrase-structure tree**.

(16)

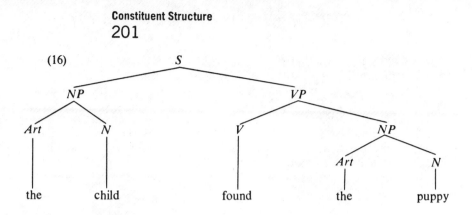

Every sentence of English, and of every other human language, can be represented in a constituent structure tree. Here are several examples that use the syntactic categories mentioned earlier:

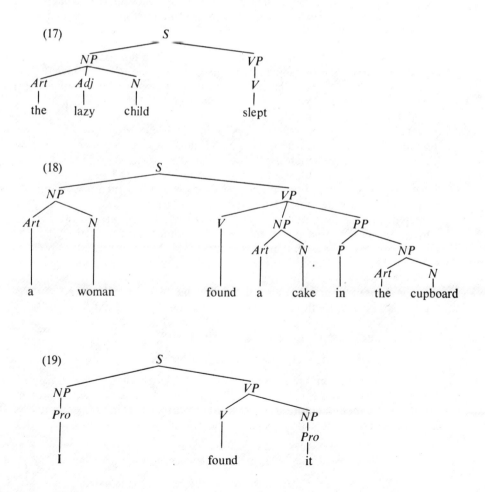

These diagrams reveal that *the child, the puppy, the lazy child, a woman, a cake, the cupboard, I,* and *it* are all noun phrases or NPs; that *found the puppy, slept, found a cake in the cupboard,* and *found it* are verb phrases, or VPs; and so on. Notice that while *the* or *a* are constituents (parts) of noun phrases, since they branch off from that part of the tree which is labeled NP, in themselves they are not NPs. To determine a constituent, one must include all the words and all the smaller constituents under each **node,** or branching point, of the tree.

Phrase-Structure Rules

[The professor had written] all the words of their language in their several moods, tenses and declensions [on tiny blocks of wood, and had] emptied the whole vocabulary into his frame, and made the strictest computation of the general proportion there is in books between the numbers of particles, nouns, and verbs, and other parts of speech.
JONATHAN SWIFT, *Gulliver's Travels*

We have already seen that constituent structures represent regular patterns in a language. In English, an article (Art) followed by a Noun (N) always forms a larger constituent, which we have called noun phrase, or NP. This is one of the syntactic rules of English. It explains the fact that in forming sentences you can form NPs in this way, by combining an article like *the* or *a* with a noun, such as *puppy, girl, boy, hippopotamus,* or *typewriter.* Your knowledge of English also permits you to recognize pronouns (Pro), such as *I, you, it,* and so forth, as another kind of NP.

All of these facts about NPs can be expressed by means of syntactic rules, which are technically called **phrase-structure rules.** Since your knowledge of the language includes your knowledge of permissible constituent structures (phrase structures), such rules must be part of the grammar which constitutes your linguistic competence. The rule in (20) expresses some of the knowledge a speaker of English possesses about noun phrases. In reading these rules, note that what is on the left of the arrow designates the constituent structure being defined. The "→" is often read as "rewrites as," but we will also interpret it by the informal expression "may be." What is on the right of the arrow tells us what "may be," the particular constituent being "defined" or "described."

(20) a. NP → Art N (A noun phrase may be an article followed by a noun.)

If this were the only phrase-structure rule stating what an NP in English "may be," no English sentence could include NPs like *the big dog* or *it.* We have to include more NP phrase-structure rules in the grammar of English to reflect these facts, such as the rules expressed in (20b) and (20c):

(20) b. NP → Art Adj N (A noun phrase may be an article followed by an adjective which is followed by a noun.)

(20) c. NP → Pro (A noun phrase may be a pronoun alone.)

Note that the rule in (20b) will not permit an NP such as *the big white dog* or *a large red brick building*. An interesting fact about NPs which include adjectives is that one cannot determine the limit on the number of adjectives which can occur in an NP. We can express this fact by using a special notation, parentheses with an asterisk, as shown in (20d):

(20) d. NP → Art (Adj)* N   (A noun phrase may be an article followed by zero, one, or more adjectives followed by a noun.)

As we can see, given this rule we do not need the rule in (20a), since the notation (   )*[1] means "zero, one, or more." If we choose to interpret this as "zero" the NP would just be an article followed by a noun, as in *the dog*. If we choose to interpret this rule as selecting one of the constituents included within the parentheses, it would designate an NP, like *the big dog,* and if we selected "more than one" adjective, the NP could be specifying *the big black dog* or *the big black shaggy dog* or *the big black shaggy toothless dog*.

The rules in (20c) and (20d) can be combined by using another notational device; braces can abbreviate two rules, as shown in (21):

(21) NP → $\begin{Bmatrix} \text{Art (Adj)* N} \\ \text{Pro} \end{Bmatrix}$ (A noun phrase may be an article followed by zero, one, or more adjectives, followed by a noun; or it may be a pronoun alone.)

Whenever braces are used in rules in this way, one should interpret the rule as meaning that the constituent on the left of the arrow may be *one* of the constituents enclosed by the braces.

The phrase-structure rule for an NP not only reflects or specifies what an NP is, it also tells what an NP is not. It is not, for instance, a noun followed by an article:

(22) * Boy the loves girl the.

In Danish, however, this would not be true. The article may follow the noun (*bog,* "book"; *bogen,* "the book"). Rule (21) for English also says that adjectives cannot follow nouns in noun phrases:

(23) * We ate the cake delicious

In Spanish or French, however, the opposite is true. Adjectives usually come after nouns in noun phrases:

(24) la casa roja   un gâteau délicieux
      the house red   a cake delicious
      "the red house"   "a delicious cake"

Thus, in these languages part of the phrase-structure rule for the noun phrase would be:

(25) Phrase-structure rule for French and Spanish NPs:
      NP → Art N (Adj)   (A noun phrase may be an article followed by a noun followed optionally by an adjective.)

---

[1] Previously, we used an asterisk before a word, phrase, or sentence to mean "unacceptable" or "ungrammatical." Here the asterisk is being used in a very different way, as a formal device to mean "one or more optional elements."

Because the phrase-structure rule rewriting or specifying the NP is a reflection of linguistic knowledge, it is part of a descriptive grammar of English. All languages have phrase-structure rules, because all sentences in all languages have constituents arranged in hierarchichal structure, and every constituent belongs to some syntactic category. There are, of course, many other phrase-structure rules of English.

In English a verb phrase may consist of:

(1) A verb alone: The boy *slept*.
VP → V
(2) A verb followed by a noun phrase: The child *found the puppy*.
VP → V NP
(3) A verb followed by a noun phrase followed by a prepositional phrase: The woman *put the cake in the cupboard*.
VP → V NP PP
(4) A verb followed by a prepositional phrase: The child *laughed at the puppy*.
VP → V PP

We have presented four separate phrase-structure rules for the VP. In each there is a verb after the arrow, which shows that every VP must have a verb; the verb may *optionally* be followed by an NP, or a PP, or both. If we again use parentheses around a category to mean "optional" (as we did around Adj in the NP rule) we can express Rules **(1)**–**(4)** as a single rule, thus revealing this general fact about VPs:

(26) VP → V (NP) (PP)   (A verb phrase may be a verb, optionally followed by a noun phrase, or a prepositional phrase, or optionally by both a noun phrase and a following prepositional phrase.)

In sentence (18) diagrammed above, and in prepositional phrases like *in the cupboard, on the top shelf, beneath a red blanket,* we can see that every prepositional phrase includes a noun phrase. This can be specified by the rule in (27).

(27) PP → P NP   (A prepositional phrase is a preposition followed by a noun phrase.)

This rule accounts for the fact that *in the cupboard* is a well-formed prepositional phrase of English, but **the cupboard in* is not. In Georgian, a language spoken in the Caucasus Mountains, just the opposite is true: *magidis kveš* "the table under" is well formed, but **kveš magidis* "under the table" is not.

Note how NPs are used in many constituents. When language learners discover what an NP is, they are well on the way to knowing what a PP is, and have also learned something about what a VP is. They also know what the first major constituent of most English declarative sentences is, as shown by the phrase-structure rule in (28):

(28) S → NP VP   (A sentence may be a noun phrase followed by a verb phrase.)

This phrase-structure rule corresponds to what most schoolchildren learn as "Every sentence has a subject and a predicate."[2] And it explains why we recognize that the following are not sentences of English:

(29) The man   (lacks a VP)
     Found it   (lacks an NP)
     Found it the man   (NP and VP in wrong order)

The four phrase-structure rules we have studied so far can be summarized as in (30)—(the one for expanding S will be slightly modified below):

(30) S → NP   VP   (A sentence may be a noun phrase followed by a verb phrase.)

$$NP \rightarrow \left\{ \begin{array}{c} \text{Art (Adj)* N} \\ \text{Pro} \end{array} \right\}$$ (A noun phrase may be an article followed by zero, one, or more adjectives, followed by a noun; or it may be a pronoun alone.)

VP → V (NP) (PP)   (A verb phrase may be a verb, optionally followed by a noun phrase, or a prepositional phrase, or a noun phrase followed by a prepositional phrase.)

PP → P   NP   (A prepositional phrase may be a preposition followed by a noun phrase.)

These rules are valid for English (though not complete), and all speakers "know" these rules, whether they are aware that they know them or not. They weren't ever taught the rules by their mothers, their teachers, or anyone else. Nor did they learn them from a book (illiterate speakers of English know them also). The rules are a part of the syntactic system of the language, and they are "learned" by children when language is acquired.

When we say "learned" by children, we do not mean that these rules are necessarily used by either children or adults to actually form sentences when they speak. They are not rules such as ones like "Before crossing the street look both to the right and left to see if any cars are coming." Rather, these rules express the regularities of the language. Linguists construct these phrase-structure rules to describe what it is that speakers know about these regularities. Understood in this sense, the rules listed above can now be used to construct phrase-structure trees which will reveal the structures of English sentences.

We begin with the rule which has the S on the left side of the arrow and add any rule that can apply, *in any order*. The result will always be a phrase-structure tree that corresponds to a sentence of English, if our rules are correct. Here is one example:

---

[2] Certain "subjectless" sentences will be discussed later. We shall see that what may appear to be a grammatical sentence without a subject actually has an "understood" subject.

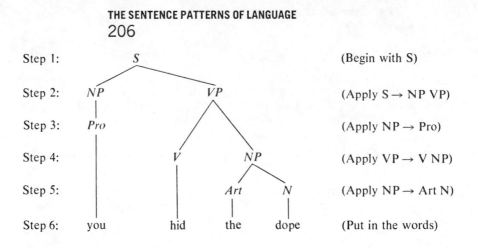

Step 1:	S	(Begin with S)
Step 2:	NP · · · · · · VP	(Apply S → NP VP)
Step 3:	Pro	(Apply NP → Pro)
Step 4:	V · · · NP	(Apply VP → V NP)
Step 5:	Art · · · N	(Apply NP → Art N)
Step 6:	you · · · hid · · · the · · · dope	(Put in the words)

These rules and the phrase-structure trees which can be constructed from them show what speakers know about the structures of the sentences of their language.

Fitting in the Morphemes

We next went to the School of Languages, where three Professors sat in Consultation upon improving that of their own Country.

The first Project was to shorten Discourse by cutting Polysyllables into one, and leaving out Verbs and Participles; because in Reality all things imaginable are but Nouns.

The other was a Scheme for entirely abolishing all Words whatsoever; and this was urged as a great Advantage in Point of Health as well as Brevity. For it is plain, that every Word we speak is in some degree a Diminution of our Lungs by Corrosion. . . .

JONATHAN SWIFT, "A Voyage to Laputa," *Gulliver's Travels*

The learned Professors of Languages in Laputa proposed a scheme for abolishing all words, thinking it would be more convenient if "Men [were] to carry about them, such Things as were necessary to express the particular Business they are to discourse on." We would venture to say that this scheme never came to fruition, even in Laputa.

Our thoughts expressed in sentences are conveyed in part by the particular morphemes or words we combine into the grammatical strings permitted by the syntactic rules. But none of the rules we have given show how the actual words and morphemes get into the phrase-structure trees. The rules given so far only produce trees without words, such as the one shown below:

(31)

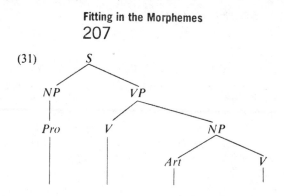

We had to "fudge" at the end of the last section in order to get the words in. To complete this tree, we need to use our knowledge of the syntactic category of individual words. We do have this knowledge, as the following will show:

> (32) Classify the following words into six classes, according to their syntactic category: *child, at, red, decide, puppy, the, smart, woman, agree, she, lazy, see, in, small, cake, a, on, find, it.*

These words fall into six classes:

(33)

N	Adj	V	Pro	P	Art
child	red	decide	she	at	the
puppy	smart	agree	it	in	a
woman	lazy	see		on	
cake	small	find			

One need not know how to label the classes to know that the words under N are words of the same type, those under Adj are words of the same type, and so on. Of course knowing, as you do, the phrase-structure rules of English makes it easy for you to identify the syntactic category of each word correctly. We know that a word is a noun when it can be preceded by an article to form a noun phrase. A word is an adjective if it can follow an article and precede a noun in a noun phrase. A word is a verb if it is the first word of a verb phrase. Note that a word need not be preceded by an article to be a noun; *sincerity* and *golf* are not generally used with articles, and neither are general (or **generic**) plurals, such as *dogs, madmen*, etc. But any word which can be preceded directly by an article must be a noun or adjective. The way words and groups of words function tells us their syntactic categories. We have already seen that we can identify noun phrases and verb phrases by their function and position in a sentence. The syntax of a language is a bit like a jigsaw puzzle. When all the pieces are in the right place, everything fits and makes sense. Your knowledge (usually unconscious knowledge) of the syntactic rules of English allows you to put the pieces of the puzzle in place effortlessly and accurately, without your really having to think about it.

Obviously, when you know a language you know its vocabulary of morphemes and words (which is called the **lexicon**). Each lexical item is specified in the lexicon as to its phonological features and its semantic properties. In addition, each item must also be specified as to its syntactic category: *man*—N, *hot*—Adj. *run*—V, *he*—Pro, and so on (this was discussed in Chapter 6). The syntactic rules of the grammar include **lexical-insertion rules.** Among other things, these rules match the syntactic categories at the bottom of a phrase-structure tree with lexical items of the same category, and then place those words or morphemes under the corresponding node of the tree. Of course the choice of a particular noun, verb, or other part of speech depends on the intended meaning of the sentence.

The lexical-insertion rules have another function. Besides matching lexical items to the correct category in the tree, they also make sure that a lexical item is surrounded by just the right constituents. Some examples will make this clear. The verb *find* must be followed by an NP, its "direct object." **John found* is not a grammatical sentence in English, nor is **John found in the house,* but *John found the girl* is. Part of the specification of a lexical item in the lexicon is the syntactic frame into which that item fits. A **transitive** verb like *find* or *love* or *destroy* will be specified for insertion into a tree only when it would be followed by an NP:

(34)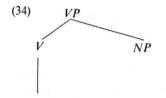

An **intransitive** verb, on the other hand, will be specified for insertion into a tree where there is no NP following, as in (35):

(35)

Die is such a verb. The lexical-insertion rule for *die* corresponds to our intuitive knowledge that *John died* is grammatical, but **John died Mary* is not. These restrictions on the placement of lexical items are called **strict subcategorization.**

You may have noticed one other problem. Although the lexical-insertion rules take care of strict subcategorization, it is still possible for the phrase-structure rules to produce such oddities as:

(36) *The house saw the boy.
　　　 *The rock slept.

According to one theory of grammar, these sentences are syntactically well-formed but semantically deviant. The semantic rules of the language, discussed in the previous chapter, will indicate the strangeness of such sentences. However, since such sentences obey the syntactic rules of the grammar, they can appear in phrase-structure trees on a par with the more normal sentences in (37):

(37) The boy saw the house.
The woman slept.

Some of the excerpts from E. E. Cummings' poetry that we cited in Chapter 7 illustrate that sentences in a language may be syntactically well formed but semantically deviant. The noun phrase *the six subjunctive crumbs* can be diagrammed as:

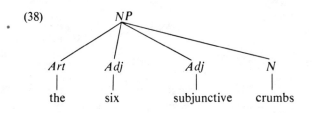

(38)

This is how we would diagram the more sensible NP *the six subjunctive sentences*. But since *subjunctive* normally refers to some syntactic concept, and *crumbs* never do (unless we speak metaphorically of "sentence crumbs"), the result is semantic deviance, or oddness, or anomaly.

Nonsense poetry, such as Carroll's "Jabberwocky," also shows that phrases and sentences can be syntactically well formed, obeying the phrase-structure and lexical-insertion rules, yet semantically uninterpretable, since the "lexical items" selected are possible but nonoccurring forms, having no "agreed-on" meaning. This is further shown by the following poem, "Uffia" by Harriet R. White, which illustrates the humor of clever nonsense:

> When sporgles spanned the floreate mead
>   And cogwogs gleet upon the lea,
>   Uffia gopped to meet her love
> Who smeeged upon the equat sea.

The Infinitude of Language: Recursive Rules

Normal human minds are such that . . . without the help of anybody, they will produce 1000 [sentences] they never heard spoke of . . . inventing and saying such things as they never heard from their masters, nor any mouth.
HUARTE DE SAN JUAN, c. 1530–1592

We observed in Chapter 1 that speakers of any language can produce and understand sentences they have never said or heard before and that the grammar must therefore account for this creative aspect of language. The phrase-structure rules do just this. You may never have heard sentence (39) before reading it now:

(39) The young orangutan strummed the old red banjo.

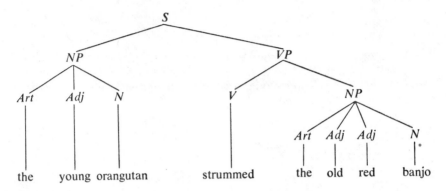

We feel sure you can understand it, however, for you know its structure, you know what the noun phrases refer to, what the adjectives modify, and you know that the verb relates *the young orangutan* to *the old red banjo* through the action of "strumming."

When you consider all the possible NP subjects, adjectives, verbs, and NP objects that can be constructed from the rules in (30) and the huge lexicon every speaker knows, you can begin to appreciate how a few simple rules of grammar permit us to understand a huge number of sentences. And we have only looked at a tiny, oversimplified fraction of the grammar of English.

The rules of the grammar can also account for the fact that speakers can produce single sentences of unlimited length. Notice that we said *can*, not *do*. This was also discussed in Chapter 1, when we pointed out that a person's ability (linguistic competence) is not identical with how that ability is used (linguistic performance). Even a 5-year-old child has the linguistic competence to understand quite long sentences, as is evident from the children's rhyme about the house that Jack built:

> This is the farmer sowing the corn,
> That kept the cock that crowed in the morn,
> That waked the priest all shaven and shorn,
> That married the man all tattered and torn,
> That kissed the maiden all forlorn,
> That milked the cow with the crumpled horn,
> That tossed the dog
> That worried the cat
> That killed the rat
> That ate the malt
> That lay in the house that Jack built.

In fact, you have the linguistic ability to make this sentence, or any sentence, longer. This shows that there is no "longest" sentence in a language. For every sentence of a given length, you can produce a sentence of greater length. You can, for example, add any of the following to the beginning of the rhyme and still end up with a grammatical sentence:

(40) I saw that . . .
   What is the name of the unicorn that noticed that . . .
   Ask someone if . . .
   Do you know whether . . .

So far, the rules of syntax that we have discussed account for such indefinitely long sentences in only a trivial way. We showed that one cannot limit the number of adjectives in principle:

(41) The seedy battered rundown old red wooden shack fell down.

This was accounted for by the (Adj)* in our NP rule. But such a rule could not account for the example above, or many other examples. One could provide another perfectly grammatical (though rather stilted) version of the poem:

(42) This is the farmer sowing the corn,
   and the farmer kept the cock that crowed in the morn,
   and the cock waked the priest all shaven and shorn,
   and the priest married the man all tattered and torn,
   and the man kissed the maiden all forlorn,
   and the maiden milked the cow with the crumpled horn,
   and the cow tossed the dog,
   and the dog worried the cat,
   and the cat killed the rat,
   and the rat ate the malt,
   and the malt lay in the house and Jack built the house.

The ability of any speaker of English to identify this poem as a single sentence must somehow be reflected in the grammar. We can do this by positing another phrase-structure rule:

(43) S → S (and S)*   (A sentence may be any number of sentences, each
                       joined by the conjunction *and*.)

We are again using the abbreviation of parentheses followed by an asterisk to mean that zero, one, or more of whatever is enclosed in the parentheses may occur. In this case, the rule in (43) states that S may rewrite simply as S, or as S *and* S, or as S *and* S *and* S, and so on.

An abbreviated phrase-structure tree for the new version of the poem is given in (44):

(44)

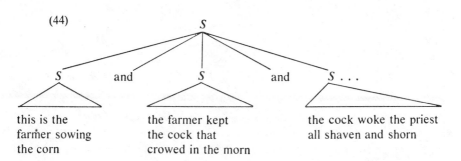

Other rules of syntax reflect the other ways of deriving indefinitely long sentences, such as a rule which would account for the original version of the poem.

Rules such as (43) are called **recursive** rules because a basic element (S in this case) recurs. It is because of such rules that we have the ability to produce an infinite set of sentences with our finite brains and finite set of linguistic rules. Recursive rules occur in all the grammars of all languages because the facts already given are not unique to English. In fact, the rule in (43), or some variant of it, is a "universal" rule occurring in all grammars. Here is an example of such a **conjoined** sentence from Thai:

(45) mǎa   kin   huǎhɔ̌ɔm   láe   mɛɛw   kin   plaa   láe . . .
     the dog ate   onions   and   the cat ate   fish   and . . .

Another recursive rule in English is stated in (46):

(46) NP → NP $\left\{ \begin{matrix} and \\ or \end{matrix} \right\}$(NP)* (A noun phrase may be any number of noun phrases, each joined by either the conjunction *and* or the conjunction *or*.)

This rule accounts for the fact that the phrases in (47) are noun phrases but those in (48) are not:

(47) a. Antony and Cleopatra
     b. The cowboy and the Indian and the soldier
     c. The Democrats or the Republicans or the Whigs
     d. The red flag or the old blue stocking

(48) a. John Mary and
     b. run and play
     c. the or house barn
     d. the girl or dreamed

We have, for example, this structure for (47b):

(49)

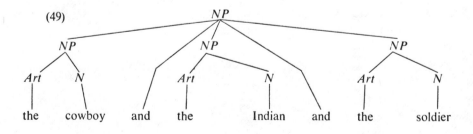

the   cowboy   and   the   Indian   and   the   soldier

The rules of conjunction in (43) and (46) are recursive because noun phrases recur within noun phrases and sentences recur within sentences.

A similar situation occurs when a sentence follows the verb in the verb phrase. Such sentences are called **complements.** In (50) the sentence *you love me* is a complement of *say*:

(50) They say you love me.[3]

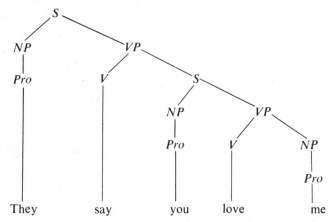

When one sentence is in another sentence, it is **embedded.** We need a rule to permit us to embed sentences within sentences which are embedded in other sentences which are embedded within other sentences . . . as illustrated in (51):

[3] Many linguists would diagram sentences (50) and (51) with each *embedded* S branching from an NP node, as follows:

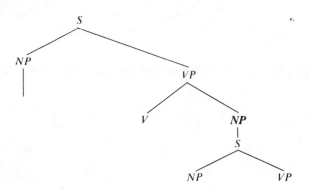

This clearly shows that the embedded sentence is functioning as an NP object. Since we are simply trying to illustrate the notion of "complement," we have chosen not to complicate the phrase-structure tree in this way.

(51)

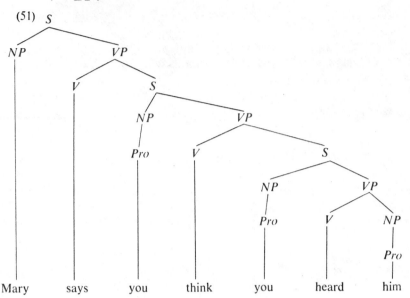

In (51), the S *You heard him* is embedded as the complement in the S *You think you heard him* which itself is embedded as the complement in the S *Mary says you think you heard him*. Clearly, we can keep this up: *I believe Mary says you think you heard him* is a grammatical sentence in English.

To account for the occurrence of sentences like (51), we need to modify the VP rule as in (52):

(52) VP → V S   (A verb phrase may be a verb followed by a sentence.)

When we add this rule to rule (26) already formulated for the VP, using the "braces" notation, we get:

(53) VP → $V \begin{Bmatrix} (NP) & (PP) \\ & S \end{Bmatrix}$ (A verb phrase may be a verb optionally followed by a noun phrase, or a prepositional phrase, or a noun phrase followed by a prepositional phrase; or it may be a verb followed by a sentence.)

Since S also occurs on the left side of rule (28):

(28) S → NP VP

we have a recursive pair of rules in (28) and (53).

There are other ways of embedding Ss. Consider the noun phrase:

(54) The fact that bats suck blood . . .

We know (54) is a noun phrase because it can be the subject of *frighten* in:

                NP   VP

(55) [The fact that bats suck blood] [frightens me.]

or the object of *discover* in :

(56) Zoologists soon discovered [the fact that bats suck blood.]

Noun phrase (54) contains an S because *Bats suck blood* is an S. Thus we have another possibility for recursion, for we know that an S must contain an NP, and an NP may contain an S.

Here are two other sentences in which an NP contains an S:

(57) John made *the suggestion that we skip lunch*.

(58) *The possibility that the moon might float* hasn't been checked.

In (57) the S *We skip lunch* is embedded in the NP *the suggestion that we skip lunch*.[4] Can you identify the embedded sentence in (58)?

We have not exhaustively examined recursion in English, for it is our aim only to give a sampling of the kinds of grammatical knowledge speakers have, and what the rules that account for that knowledge look like.

All languages have recursive rules like the rules in (43) and (46) for conjunction, and all languages have ways of embedding Ss within Ss that allow potentially unlimited numbers of **subordinate clauses**[5] to occur in one sentence.

Here are some examples of subordinate clauses from other languages:

(59) Jean dit que $_S$[Marie boit beaucoup] (French)
    John says that Mary drinks a lot

(60) yaran sun ga sarki lokacin da $_S$[suka shiga birri] (Hausa)
    The children saw the king when they visited the city

(61) kuna pilipili sana $_S$[baba anapopika chakula] (Swahili)
    There's pepper a-plenty (when) papa cooks the food

Transformational Rules

Our life passes in transformation.
RAINER MARIA RILKE, *Duineser Elegien*, vii

THE WIZARD OF ID   **by Brant parker and Johnny hart**

By permission of Johnny Hart and Field Enterprises, Inc.

Phrase-structure rules like those discussed above account for much of the syntactic knowledge that speakers possess about their language, including the linear order of words and morphemes, the constituent structure of sentences, and the creative and open-ended nature of language. Lexical-insertion rules account for the cooccurrence restrictions be-

---

[4] The *that* is a **complementizer**, which indicates that an embedded sentence follows. We will not be concerned about it, however.

[5] Subordinate clauses are embedded Ss other than conjoined Ss.

tween words. Yet syntax is even more complex than this, and our syntactic knowledge which must be accounted for in the description of the language must include additional kinds of rules.

We are ready now for a look at some different kinds of sentences. We continue to illustrate with English, but you should remember that all languages will have a wide variety of sentences.

In English there are a number of **reflexive pronouns**. Traditionally, they are classified according to **person** (first, second, and third), **number** (singular and plural), and **gender** (masculine, feminine, and neuter).

Table 8-1 Reflexive pronouns

	Singular	Plural
First person	myself	ourselves
Second person	yourself	yourselves
Third person		themselves[6]
Masculine	himself[6]	
Feminine	herself	
Neuter	itself	

The distribution of reflexive pronouns is very special. They cannot, for instance, ever function as a subject NP:

(62) *Himself bit John.
(John bit himself)

And in general, anytime a reflexive pronoun appears in a sentence, it must have an **antecedent** elsewhere in the same sentence. An antecedent is an NP containing a noun or pronoun that refers to the same individual as the reflexive pronoun. *John* is the antecedent in *John bit himself*, but:

(63) *The children bought gifts for herself

is ungrammatical because there is no antecedent for *herself*. If we provide *herself* with the antecedent *Mary*, grammaticality is restored:

(64) Mary bought gifts for herself.

We could also change the reflexive pronoun to *themselves*. Then *the children* would be a proper antecedent, and again grammaticality is restored:

(65) The children bought gifts for themselves.

We see from these examples that the antecedent of a reflexive pronoun cannot be just any noun phrase. It must be a noun phrase with the same person, number, and gender. We expect your intuitions will tell you that all of the following are ungrammatical:

(66) a. *You bit herself   (Failure to match person)
    b. *She bit itself   (Failure to match gender
    c. *I bit ourselves   (Failure to match number)

---

[6] In some varieties of English the forms *hisself* and *theirselves* are used.

As usual, we haven't told you anything you don't know about English. We have simply provided some terminology so that your knowledge can be expressed or described. Let us see how a descriptive grammar of English can best account for speakers' knowledge about reflexives. We must make sure that reflexive pronouns occur only as nonsubject NPs with just the "right" antecedents. One possibility would be to observe that reflexive pronouns belong to the category pronoun (Pro). We could suppose that lexical-insertion rules will place reflexive pronouns in a tree under Pro. In some cases this might work. The following tree conforms to the rules of phrase-structure:

(67)

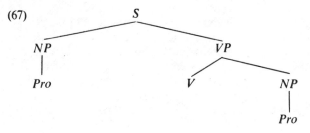

Lexical-insertion rules could, if they were allowed to position reflexive pronouns in a tree, produce the following:

(68)

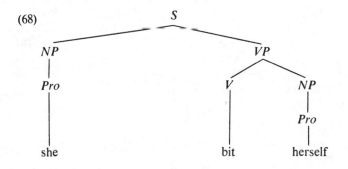

Unfortunately, the same tree may turn out to look like this:

(69)

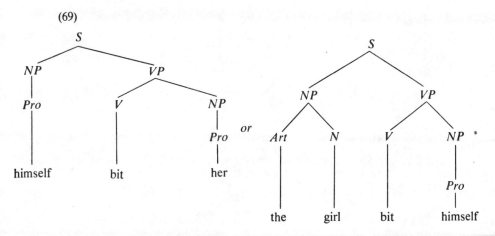

This is because nothing prevents the rules of lexical-insertion from putting any reflexive pronoun under any node Pro. Since *Himself bit her* is ill-formed, something is wrong with the proposed rules to handle reflexive pronouns.

What is wrong is that a reflexive pronoun cannot appear just anywhere in a sentence, as if it were an ordinary pronoun. This situation seems similar to the limitations on the occurrence of verbs in a sentence. We had to formulate the lexical-insertion rules so that, for example, an intransitive verb wouldn't be placed in a tree in which an NP followed the verb. Similar restrictions, however, will not work on reflexive pronouns. The reason is that lexical-insertion rules are sensitive to the syntactic categories of a tree, but they are not sensitive to particular lexical items. The choice of a reflexive pronoun depends on a particular lexical item, namely the noun or pronoun which is in the NP antecedent. The kind of "agreement" that a reflexive pronoun and its antecedent must have is different from the strict subcategorization that governs the lexical-insertion of verbs. Lexical-insertion rules cannot handle this difference, and so we must turn in a different direction if our grammar is to faithfully represent what we unconsciously know.[7]

Suppose then that lexical-insertion rules have nothing to do with reflexive pronouns, and never insert them into trees. The phrase-structure rules will continue to define well-formed phrase-structure trees, and the lexical-insertion rules will match words to the proper category in the tree. When the tree is completely specified, we need a different kind of rule which can "look" at the whole tree. Whenever it "sees" two identical noun phrases in the same sentence that refer to the same individual, it changes the second one to a reflexive pronoun that agrees in person, number, and gender with the first. Thus, the sentence *the girl cheats herself* would first be represented in this tree:

(70)

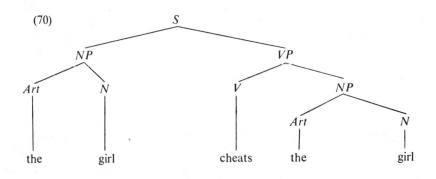

---

[7] Lexical-insertion rules are also insensitive to grammatical relations like "subject" and "direct object," yet we observed that NP subjects may never be reflexive pronouns. Lexical-insertion rules would be unable to accommodate that restriction.

Then the **reflexive rule** would *transform* it to:

(71)

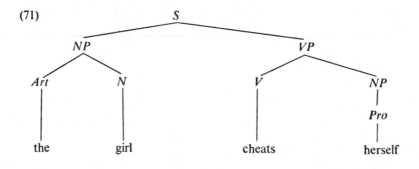

Note that this reflexive rule is very different from the phrase-structure rules which were discussed above. It dcesn't define a category, or state what a particular constituent "may be." Rather, it changes or transforms one phrase-structure tree, which the phrase-structure rules specified by the methods discussed earlier, into a different phrase-structure tree. It changed the NP, which was specified as *Art N* (and as *the girl* after the lexical-insertion rules) into an NP specified as Pro and finally as *herself*. Rules which change, or **transform**, one phrase-structure tree into another phrase-structure tree are called **transformational rules**. The reflexive transformation may be stated as follows:

> (72) *Reflexive transformation:* **Within a sentence, if there are two occurrences of identical noun phrases that refer to the same individual, replace the second with a reflexive pronoun that matches the first in person, number, and gender.**

The reflexive transformation accounts directly for our knowledge that reflexive pronouns are never subjects, and that they have antecedents with which they agree in person, number, and gender.

Here then is a case where a transformational rule is indispensable to a description of English grammar, for it embodies speakers' knowledge that cannot be accounted for by phrase-structure rules.

The reflexive transformation also relates to another interesting fact about English syntax. At one time or another most of us learn that subjectless imperatives like *Eat your veggies!* have a *you* "understood." A good descriptive grammar should reveal why this is true. To do so, another transformation is involved.

Consider the following imperative sentence:

(73) Behave yourself!

It has the tree structure:

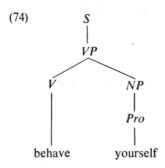

(74)

Despite the fact that (73) is a sentence of English, its tree structure is not produced by our phrase-structure rules, which tell us that an S is an NP followed by a VP. Should we add the rule S → VP to account for (73) and conclude that our intuition that every sentence has an NP subject is wrong?

Before we decide, we should notice something else unexpected about (73). The reflexive pronoun has no antecedent. This imperative sentence diverges from "normal" sentences in two ways, then: It has no subject, and its reflexive pronoun has no antecedent. There is another funny thing about imperative sentences with reflexive pronoun objects. The only reflexive pronouns that can occur in imperative sentences are *yourself* and *yourselves*, as shown in (75):

(75) Watch yourself!
       Watch yourselves!
    *Watch myself!
    *Watch ourselves!
    *Watch himself!
    *Watch herself!
    *Watch itself!
    *Watch themselves!

These special properties of imperative sentences are striking because we find that they are all related. If sentence (73), and all similar imperative sentences, had subjects, then providing that each subject agreed with its reflexive pronoun, it would be a proper antecedent for the reflexive pronoun. Because of the facts revealed in the grammatical and ungrammatical sentences in (75), it must be the case that all imperative sentences have subjects which are either singular or plural second-person pronouns; that is, *you*.

Suppose, then, that there is a phrase-structure tree to represent the sentence *Behave yourself* which looks like (76):

(76)

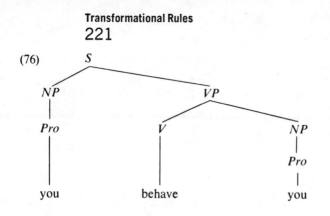

The lexical-insertion rules could not have inserted *yourself* under the second Pro because, as we pointed out above, such rules do not insert reflexive pronouns into trees. The reflexive transformation rule, (72), would apply to the tree in (76) to change it to (77):

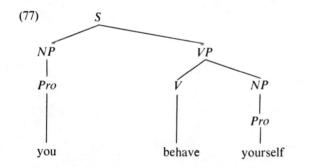

We still have to get rid of the NP subject *you* in (77), since it is absent in (73). Once again, a transformational rule can be stated to *delete* the *you*. Phrase-structure rules which define or specify the structure of constituents cannot delete any part of the phrase-structure rules. But since transformational rules apply to a phrase-structure tree to change or transform it, such rules can delete structure. The **imperative transformation** is a deletion rule and can be stated as (78):

> **(78)** *Imperative transformation:* **In an imperative sentence, delete the second-person subject NP.**

The imperative transformation accounts for our knowledge as speakers of English that there is indeed an "understood *you*" in imperative sentences which appear not to have subjects; we know that such sentences act as if the *you* were really there.

Another aspect of transformational rules is revealed by the reflexive and imperative transformations. They must apply in order. One transformation may apply to the output of a different transformation. One transformation (which we can call a T-rule) applies to a phrase-structure tree and produces a new phrase-structure tree. The next transformation applies to the new phrase-structure tree and once again changes it to produce a new tree, as is illustrated in (79):

(79)

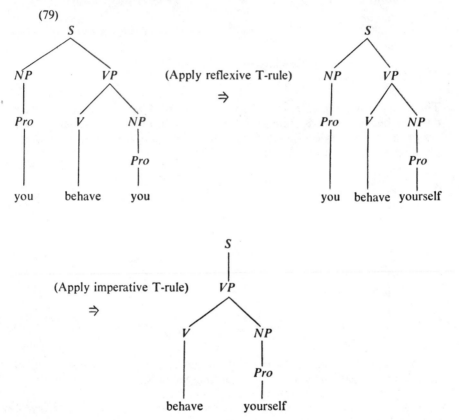

(Apply reflexive T-rule) ⇒

(Apply imperative T-rule) ⇒

The order of application is crucial, for if we apply the imperative transformation first, there will be no antecedent for the reflexive transformation to match the reflexive pronoun with.

There is other evidence of the "underlying" *you* of imperatives. We will look at one case. Consider the following paradigm:

(80)				
I	should keep a cool head on	**my**	shoulders.
You	should keep a cool head on	**your**	shoulders.
He	should keep a cool head on	**his**	shoulders.
She	should keep a cool head on	**her**	shoulders.
We	should keep a cool head on	**our**	shoulders.
You	should keep a cool head on	**your**	shoulders.
They	should keep a cool head on	**their**	shoulders.

The two pronouns in bold type must match in every case.

A sentence such as (81) is very strange, because the pronouns do not match:

(81) *He should keep a cool head on $\left\{\begin{array}{l} \text{my} \\ \text{their} \end{array}\right\}$ shoulders.

If we make an imperative out of (80), we find that the pronoun preceding *shoulders* can only be *your*:

(82) Keep a cool head on $\left\{\begin{array}{l} \text{*my} \\ \text{your} \\ \text{*his} \\ \text{*etc.} \end{array}\right\}$ shoulders.

To be consistent with the matching restriction we saw in (80), there must be a subject pronoun *you* somewhere in (82) for the *your* to match up with. And indeed there is, though the *you* is in the underlying (untransformed) structure, which has this appearance:

(83)

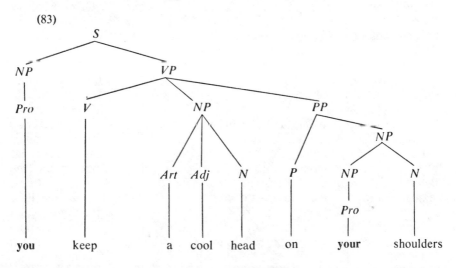

Because there is a *you* in (82), the unacceptable sequences like *Keep a cool head on my shoulders* are never assigned a tree structure, for the condition (which affects underlying structure) that the pronouns match is never met.[8] The imperative transformation applies to the phrase-structure tree in (83) and deletes *you*. The resulting tree corresponds to the acceptable sentence of (82).

All of this may seem a little like "hocus pocus." Still, we have done nothing more than present one means for describing the knowledge of English that we all share. The description is complex because language is complex. Some of the complexities can be characterized by phrase-structure rules, lexical-insertion rules, and transformational rules.

---

[8] Explaining how such "pronoun matching" (actually, "noun phrase matching") is accomplished is beyond the scope of this introductory presentation.

Transformational-Generative Grammars

... the only thing that is important is whether a result can be achieved in a finite number of elementary steps or not.
JOHN VON NEUMANN

As a speaker of English, you can usually tell grammatical from ungrammatical sequences of words, and you are aware of how words and morphemes are organized into sentences. You know, for instance, what a noun phrase is, and you know that if two identical noun phrases are in the same sentence, the second one "shows up" as a reflexive pronoun. You also know that imperative sentences behave as if they had a *you* as the subject, even when *you* fails to appear. All this knowledge must be precisely characterized by the rules of syntax we have been discussing if our descriptive grammar of English is to be adequate.

To check on the rules, we cannot simply compare the sentences of English with the sentences characterized by the rules. The sentences are infinitely numerous, so such a comparison is impossible. Of course, we have to make sure that the rules do indeed specify infinitely many well-formed sentences. We have done that by means of recursive rules. At this point the best we can do is to make sure that every string of words that the rules tell us is grammatical is, in fact, judged by us to be well-formed. And we also hope that a great many sentences that we judge to be well-formed are, or can in principle be, specified by the rules as grammatical.

Any adequate theory of grammar must be able to do all the things we have been discussing. Just as in any science which attempts to characterize the regularities of the subject of concern, there may be alternate models which attempt to reveal these "laws" or "rules." One theory of grammar which has been proposed to account for our linguistic competence is the theory we have been discussing, which includes phrase-structure rules, lexical-insertion rules, and transformational rules. The grammar specified by this theory can be thought of (metaphorically) as a machine which "cranks out," or **generates** (accounts for in an explicit fashion), all the possible sentences of the language. A grammar containing such rules is called a **generative grammar**. When the rules include transformational rules, we have a **transformational-generative grammar**.

The phrase-structure, lexical-insertion, and transformational rules that we are studying make up a transformational-generative grammar that generates sentences in the following fashion: Start with the symbol S and apply the phrase-structure rules by substituting, or **rewriting**, S with the symbols that appear on the right side of the arrow. Rewrite each successive category according to the appropriate phrase-structure rule, stopping only when no more rules apply. The result will be a phrase-structure tree without words.

Now apply the rules of lexical-insertion until every bottommost position in the tree is a word. The phrase-structure tree that results is given a special name: the **deep structure**.[9] It is the first of a sequence of trees that comprise the syntactic description of a sentence. The transformational rules now apply, one after the other in correct order, to produce the re-

---

[9] *Deep structures* are sometimes called *remote structures* or *conceptual structures*.

maining phrase-structure trees in the above-mentioned sequence. The very last one of these trees most nearly corresponds to the actual utterance of the sentence. It is termed the **surface structure**.

We can see how such a "machine" works by recalling the phrase-structure rules of previous sections, and providing a small lexicon. Obviously, neither our lexicon nor our rules are even nearly complete, but we have enough to give you an inkling of what is involved.

(84)   PHRASE-STRUCTURE RULES   LEXICON

    (i) S → NP   VP   Art: *the, a*

    (ii) NP → { Art (Adj)* N / Pro }   Adj: *red, smart, . . .*

                                 N: *child, puppy, book, car . . .*

    (iii) VP → V { (NP) (PP) / S }   P: *at, in, on, to, . . .*

                                 Pro: *I, you, she, they, . . .*

    (iv) PP → P   NP   V:[10] *find(s), sleep(s), laugh(s), see(s), . . .*

(85) Transformational Rules

    (A) Reflexive: Within a sentence, if there are two occurrences of identical noun phrases that refer to the same individual, replace the second with a reflexive pronoun that matches the first in person, number, and gender.

    (B) Imperative: In an imperative sentence, delete the second-person subject NP.

To generate a sentence with these rules, we write the initial symbol S at the top of a tree. We then let the S node "branch" into the category nodes on the right of the arrow of the phrase-structure rule for S:

(86)

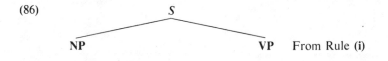

    NP   **VP**   From Rule **(i)**

We repeat this procedure for every category that ever appears in the tree and also occurs on the left side of an arrow, extending the tree downwards:

(87)

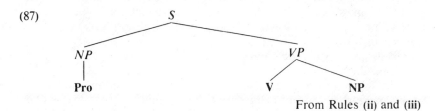

                                            From Rules **(ii)** and **(iii)**

---

[10] The appropriate form of the verb will be added by rules not discussed here. Thus, for example, an inflectional suffix will be added to the verb when the subject NP is third-person singular, as in *She sleeps in the car,* as opposed to *I sleep in the car.*

In (87) we chose to let NP branch into Pro. Of the five ways we could let the VP branch, we chose V NP. We can do nothing more with Pro and V, which are "terminal" symbols. NP, however, appears on the left side of an arrow in (ii). We can expand NP into the "terminal" symbols Art N:

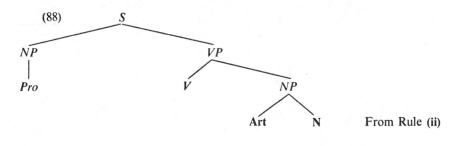

No more phrase-structure rules apply to (88), since none of Pro, V, Art, or N appear on the left of an arrow.

At this point, the lexical-insertion rules take over and provide the tree with actual words. We select a word of the appropriate category from the lexicon and place it in the tree:

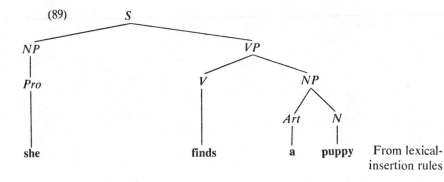

The tree in (89) is the deep structure of *She finds a puppy*. It is also the surface structure, since none of the T-rules apply. You can see that the number and variety of deep structures is virtually limitless, even with the few phrase-structure rules shown. One reason for this is that the rules are recursive. VP occurs on the right of S in (i), and S occurs on the right of VP in (iii).

Rules of morphology and phonology apply to the surface structure to indicate the actual pronunciation of the sentence.

We are not describing how speakers actually produce sentences when they speak. Derivations in a generative grammar such as the one illustrated in (86)–(89) specify, instead, in an explicit fashion, the kinds of structures permitted by the rules of the grammar. Insofar as they agree with the intui-

tions that native speakers have about the constituent structures, the grammaticality, and so forth, they indicate the rules which represent grammatical competence. We have attempted to argue that these rules do indeed
characterize our linguistic knowledge. A generative grammar that uses
these rules can therefore be viewed as a descriptive grammar of the
language.

Perhaps another derivation will help you to gain more confidence in
working with transformational-generative grammars:

(90)

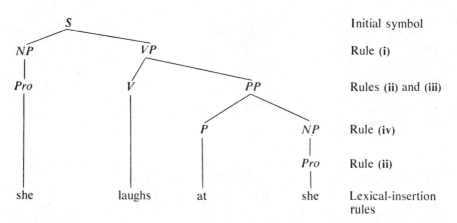

	Initial symbol
	Rule (i)
	Rules (ii) and (iii)
	Rule (iv)
	Rule (ii)
	Lexical-insertion rules

Deep structure of *She laughs at herself.*

⇓ Apply reflexive T-rule

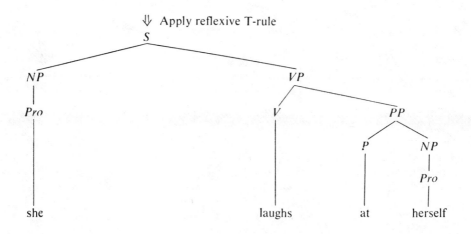

Surface structure of *She laughs at herself* after application of the reflexive
transformational rule.

Ambiguity, Paraphrase, and Grammatical Relations

A smile is the chosen vehicle for all ambiguities.
HERMAN MELVILLE, *Pierre*, iv

In the first section of this chapter we observed that the syntactic rules in a grammar account for grammaticality, determine the ordering of morphemes, reveal ambiguities and paraphrases, and determine the grammatical relations between different parts of a sentence. We have seen how grammaticality is accounted for: the rules generate all, and only, the grammatical sequences. The basic ordering of morphemes is determined by the phrase-structure rules, though certain word-order changes result from transformational rules. (We'll discuss such transformations below.) In this section, we will see how rules can account for ambiguity, paraphrase, and the grammatical relations within a sentence.

(91) Mary and Joe or Bill frightened the dog.

Sentence (91) has the two meanings shown in (92a) and (92b):

(92) a. Mary and Joe frightened the dog or Bill frightened the dog.
b. Mary and Joe frightened the dog or Mary and Bill frightened the dog.

Sentence (91) is syntactically ambiguous. The double meaning is not due to any ambiguous words, but rather to the fact that the words in (91) can appear in two different phrase-structure trees, both of which are permitted by the phrase-structure rules:

(93)

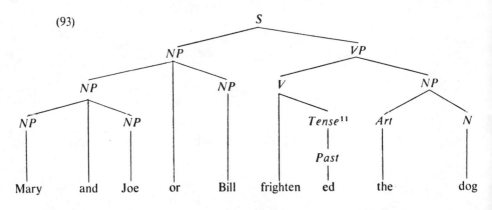

Phrase-structure tree of sentence (91) as paraphrased by sentence (92a).

---

[11] Since we are not trying to present a complete grammar of English, there are many categories, such as *Tense* and so on, which we have not discussed. We hope you will accept these trees merely as illustrative of the concepts we are trying to present.

(94)

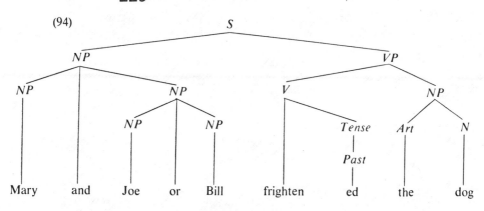

Phrase-structure tree of sentence (91) as paraphrased by sentence (92b).

Sentence (95) is also ambiguous:

(95) They are moving sidewalks.

It could mean either (96a) or (96b):

(96) a. They (those things over there) are sidewalks that move.
b. They (the workmen) are relocating sidewalks.

The meaning of sentence (96a) can be revealed by the tree diagram in (97). (Note that *be* is simply a verb, and *moving* is an adjective.[12])

(97)

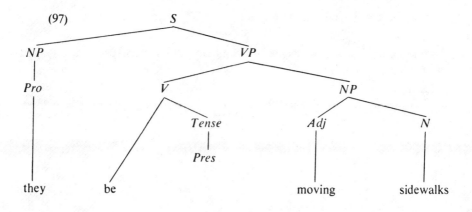

Phrase-structure tree of sentence (95) as paraphrased by sentence (96a).

[12] Plural NPs do not necessarily have an article, a case we have not explicitly discussed. Note that *be* + *Pres* is converted to *are* when the subject is plural.

The meaning of (95) as expressed in (96b) is reflected in (98):

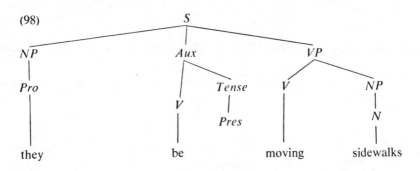

Phrase-structure tree of sentence (95) as paraphrased by sentence (96b).

Note that *be* is an auxiliary verb and that *moving* is the verb form of *move* which occurs with *be*. The differences between (97) and (98) again show that sentences have structure and are not merely morphemes strung together like beads on a string. Speakers must know (in some sense) the structures, because they can interpret sentence (91) as (92a) or (92b), and sentence (95) as (96a) or (96b).

So far the ambiguities we have seen can be accounted for by assigning to each meaning a different *surface structure* phrase-structure tree. Can we account for the two meanings of (99) this way?

    (99) The horse is ready to ride.

The two meanings correspond to (100a) and (100b):

    (100) a. The horse is ready to ride (in his trailer to the track).
            b. The horse is ready (for someone) to ride.

There is only one surface structure that can possibly correspond to (99) in either of its meanings, and that is (101):[13]

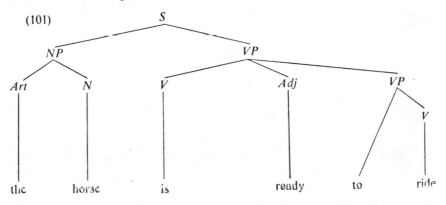

[13] The phrase-structure rules we have seen do not specify this tree. It is vital to remember that the phrase-structure rules generate deep structures; (101) is a surface structure, which, as we shall see, has undergone much deformation by various transformational rules. Also note we are omitting *Tense* in this and subsequent trees.

How, then, can we account for the fact that (99) is syntactically ambiguous? One way is to have the phrase-structure rules assign two different *deep structures* to (99), with each of these corresponding to one of the meanings in (100). Here are the two deep structures. (Don't worry about the fact that you are unfamiliar with some of the rules that specify these trees.)

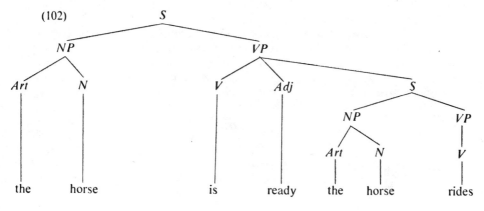

(102)

Deep structure of sentence (99) with the meaning of (100a).

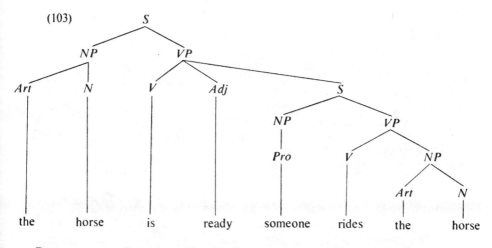

(103)

Deep structure of sentence (99) with the meaning of (100b).

The basic meaning difference between the two readings of (99) is explicitly revealed in the two deep structures. In (102), the fact that it is the horse that will do the riding is expressed in the subordinate clause (the embedded S) by making *horse* the subject of *ride*. In (103) *horse* is the object of *ride* in the embedded S, which corresponds to the fact that someone will ride the horse. Of course in both cases *horse* is the subject of *ready*, which is shown by it being the first NP in both deep structure trees.

We have not discussed the transformational rules that can produce the single surface structure of (101) from the two deep structures in (102) and

(103). We have presented these sentences to show that certain kinds of syntactic ambiguity can be accounted for in a descriptive grammar using T-rules. In the illustrative sentences, we see that the number of different meanings for an ambiguous sentence corresponds to the number of deep structures from which the one surface structure can be derived.

The above example illustrates the fact that in this model of grammar some ambiguities are not explainable in terms of phrase-structure alone, but require transformational rules.

In a way, **paraphrase** is the opposite of ambiguity. With ambiguity, one sentence has two (or more) meanings. With paraphrase, two (or more) sentences have one meaning. With ambiguity, one sentence has two or more deep structures. With paraphrase, then, two or more sentences may have one deep structure.

The pair in (104) are paraphrases:

> (104) a. The detective looks up the address.
>   b. The detective looks the address up.

They have a common deep structure:

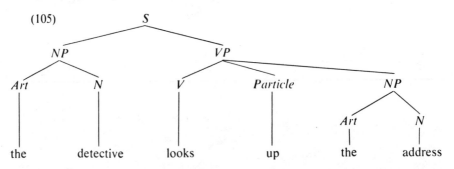

The syntactic category **Particle** appears in (105). Particles look like prepositions, but they are different from prepositions in several ways. For example, particles can occur on both sides of the NP direct object, as we see in (104). Prepositions do not behave this way:

> (106) a. The detective ran up the stairs.
>   b. *The detective ran the stairs up.

Both (104a) and (104b) have the deep structure shown in (105). Since (104b) differs from its deep structure with respect to the position of its particle, we can posit a **particle movement transformation:**

> (107) *Particle movement transformation:* **When a verb is followed by a particle and a noun phrase direct object, the particle may be repositioned to directly follow the direct object.**

The particle movement transformation is an example of an **optional transformational rule.** It may apply to the deep structure (105) or it may not. If it does, the surface structure represented by (104b) results. If it does not, (104a) results. This rule differs then from the reflexive transformation, which is an **obligatory transformational rule**, and which applies in every derivation where the antecedent and the pronoun are identical.

Another optional transformation is the **passive transformation**. It will relate the *b* sentences in (108), which are **passive** sentences, to their *a*-sentence paraphrases, which are **active** sentences:

(108) a. The child broke the Mongolian urn.
      A committee will examine the problem.
    b. The Mongolian urn was broken by the child.
      The problem will be examined by a committee.

We have only given a tiny fraction of the paraphrases of English and of the transformational rules that account for them in the grammar. A more complete study would, for example, give transformational rules that relate all of the sentences in (109) to one another:

(109) a. Mary glipped a snoozle.
    b. It's a snoozle that Mary glipped.
    c. What Mary glipped was a snoozle.
    d. It was Mary who glipped a snoozle.
    e. The one who glipped a snoozle was Mary.
    f. A snoozle was glipped by Mary.
    g. It's a snoozle that was glipped by Mary.
    h. What was glipped by Mary was a snoozle.
    i. It was Mary who a snoozle was glipped by.
    j. The one who a snoozle was glipped by was Mary.

Speakers of English recognize the relatedness of these sentences, even though they do not know what *glip* and *snoozle* mean. They can do so because their linguistic knowledge includes the transformational rules of their language.

The sentences of (109) demonstrate another important point about transformational rules which relates to the notion **grammatical relation**. The grammatical relations of a sentence are the ways each noun phrase in the sentence relates to the verb. They are, in many cases, virtually "who does what to whom." We have referred informally to the grammatical relations **subject of** and **direct object of**. The subject of a sentence is often, but not always, the "doer," or **agent**. The direct object is often the person or thing most directly affected by the verb. In English, the subject usually precedes the verb; the direct object usually follows it.

Linguistic knowledge includes knowledge of the grammatical relations in a sentence. These grammatical relations are shown, not in the surface structure, but in the deep structure. For example, from the deep structure *The child broke the Mongolian urn*, we may apply the passive transformation to derive the surface structure passive sentence *The Mongolian urn was broken by the child*. It shows that *the Mongolian urn* is the subject. But speakers know that it is the child who is the "doer" and the Mongolian urn that is the recipient of the action of breaking. That is, the grammatical relations that you understand are not the ones explicitly represented in the surface structure.

But in deep structure *The child broke the Mongolian urn*, *the child* is explicitly represented as the subject, and *the Mongolian urn* is explicitly represented as the direct object. And this representation does correspond to our knowledge of what the grammatical relations are.

We have made another discovery, too, about transformational rules: *they do not affect the underlying grammatical relations*. Thus, although the passive transformation rearranges structure drastically, it does not change the way the sentence is understood. Hence, you understand active-passive pairs like those in (108) as being paraphrases. Similarly, in (109) you understand that the grammatical relations of *Mary* and *snoozle* to *glip* are the same in every single case.

Such sentences explain why Alice often felt "dreadfully puzzled" in Wonderland. "The Hatter's remark seemed to have no meaning in it, and yet it was certainly English." By choosing "words" that have sound sequences which obey the phonological rules of English and by constructing sentences that have structures which obey the syntactic rules of English, one can, in effect, simulate the language.

In this section we have seen how transformational rules can help account for our knowledge of ambiguity, paraphrase, and grammatical relations. Together with phrase-structure rules and lexical-insertion rules, they provide an account of syntactic knowledge.

SUMMARY

Speakers of a language recognize the grammatical sentences of their language, know how the morphemes in a grammatical sentence must be arranged, and can detect ambiguities. They also know when different sentences are paraphrases, and they correctly perceive the grammatical relations in sentences. All this knowledge is accounted for in the grammar by **syntactic rules**.

Phrase structure rules are one kind of syntactic rule. They specify the acceptable **constituent structures** of sentences, which show that all sentences are made up of various parts (**constituents**), such as noun phrases, verb phrases, nouns, adjectives, verbs, and so on. Constituent structures also exhibit the hierarchical relations among the constituents of a sentence. These relationships are expressed in the **phrase-structure tree**.

Lexical-insertion rules are responsible for placing lexical items in phrase-structure trees. These rules select from the **lexicon** a word or morpheme of the appropriate syntactic category and appropriate meaning and "insert" it under a terminal node of the tree. The lexical-insertion rules also ensure that a lexical item is surrounded by the right constituents. These are the **strict subcategorization** restrictions of the language.

We showed that just a few, simple phrase-structure rules, in conjunction with the lexicon, can specify huge numbers of acceptable phrase-structure trees. We also showed that by using **recursive rules**, or **recursive sets of rules**, we can specify an infinite set of phrase structure trees. In addition, those rules account for the fact that there is no "longest" sentence in any language. Thus, the very important fact that speakers can understand and produce totally new sentences is explained.

Phrase-structure rules are not sufficient to account for all syntactic knowledge. **Transformational rules** are needed, for example, to account for the special distribution of reflexive pronouns. They also account for "understood" missing elements, such as the *you* in (a), or *going to the football game* in the second clause of (b):

    a. Bring the beer!
    b. Dad is going to the football game and Gramps is . . . too.

Transformational rules also account for the fact that speakers understand an ambiguous sentence such as (c) to have two meanings:

    c. The horse is too excited to ride. (Either the horse is riding in a vehicle or someone is riding the horse.)

The phrase-structure, together with the lexical-insertion rules, **generate** the **deep structures** of sentences, in which the **grammatical relations** are explicitly stated. The deep structures are interpreted by semantic rules to give sentence meanings. Deep structures are also changed by transformational rules to give **surface structures**, which provide the necessary information for determining the pronunciation of sentences.

EXERCISES

1. Consider the following sentences:

    a. I hate war.
    b. You know that I hate war.
    c. He knows that you know that I hate war.

    A. Write another sentence which includes sentence *c*.
    B. What does this ability you have demonstrated reveal about the nature of language?
    C. How is this characteristic of human language related to the difference between linguistic competence and performance?

2. In all languages, sentences can occur within sentences. For example, in Exercise 1, sentence *b* contains sentence *a*, and sentence *c* contains sentence *b*; or sentence *a* is *embedded* in sentence *b*, and sentence *b* is embedded in sentence *c*. Sometimes embedded sentences appear slightly changed from their "normal" form, but you should be able to recognize and write down the embedded sentences in the sentences below:

    a. Becky said that Jake would play the piano.
    b. Yesterday I noticed my accountant repairing the toilet and my plumber computing my taxes.
    c. I deplore the fact that bats have wings.
    d. That Guinevere smells bad is known to all my friends.
    e. Who promised the teacher that Max wouldn't be absent?
    f. It's ridiculous that he washes his own face.
    g. The girls pleaded for Charlie to leave them alone.
    h. The person who spilled this soft drink on my new mink coat is banished to Los Angeles.
    i. The idea of Romeo beating his wife is disconcerting.

    j. I gave my hat to the nurse who was helping me with the bedpan.
    k. For your wife to spend all your royalty payments is a shame.
    l. Give this water pipe to the girl whom Ralph Mintz is growling at.
  m. khǎw chŷa   wǎa khruu   maa.
      he   believe   teacher   come
      He believes the teacher is coming.
   n. Je me demande quand il   partira.
      I me ask   when he will leave
      I wonder when he'll leave.

3. Here are several phrase-structure trees with some of the syntactic categories missing. Fill in the blanks:

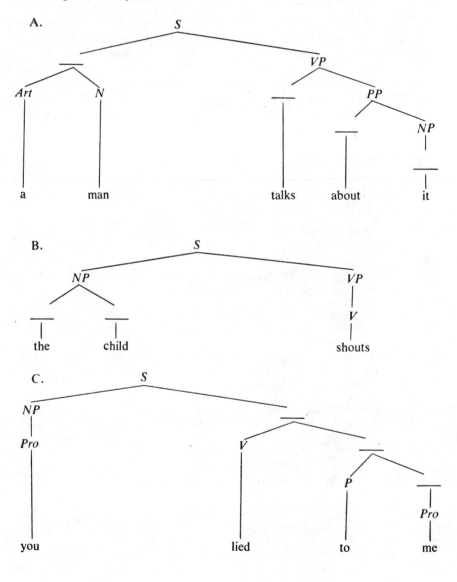

4. Here is a set of made-up phrase-structure rules. The "initial symbol" is still S, and the "terminal symbols" (that is, the ones that don't appear to the left of an arrow) are actual words:

   (i) S → A B C
  (ii) A → the
 (iii) B → children
 (iv) C → ran
  (v) C → C and D
 (vi) D → ran and D
(vii) D → ran

  A. Give three phrase-structure trees that these rules characterize.
  B. How many phrase-structure trees could these rules characterize? How do you know? (Hint: Look for recursive rules.)

5. The VP rule of (26), VP → V (NP) (PP), is actually an abbreviation of four rules:

   (i) VP → V
  (ii) VP → V NP
 (iii) VP → V PP
 (iv) VP → V NP PP

Each of these four rules corresponds to a possible strict subcategorization of a verb class. Thus, intransitive verbs like *die* are strictly subcategorized to enter a verb phrase that has been expanded as in (i). Transitive verbs like *feed* can be inserted only if the VP is expanded as in (ii).

  A. Think of ten verbs strictly subcategorized like *die*; that is, *intransitive* verbs.
  B. Think of ten verbs strictly subcategorized like *feed*.

The verb *put* is unusual in that it is strictly subcategorized to take only NP PP:

*She put
*She put the bone
*She put in the cupboard
 She put the bone in the cupboard.

  C. Can you think of one other verb that is strictly subcategorized just like *put*?

6. We used the expression "keep a cool head on one's shoulders" to show the presence of an underlying *you* in imperative sentences. There are many similar expressions that exhibit the same "matched" pronouns:

$$\text{He craned} \left\{ \begin{array}{l} \text{his} \\ \text{*her} \\ \text{*my} \\ \text{*etc.} \end{array} \right\} \text{neck.}$$

$$\text{I stubbed} \left\{ \begin{array}{l} \text{my} \\ \text{*your} \\ \text{*etc.} \end{array} \right\} \text{toe.}$$

Crane $\begin{Bmatrix} \text{your} \\ *\text{her} \\ *\text{its} \\ *\text{etc.} \end{Bmatrix}$ neck!

Don't stub $\begin{Bmatrix} \text{your} \\ *\text{my} \\ *\text{etc.} \end{Bmatrix}$ toe!

Think of five other expressions that follow a similar pattern.

7. How do the following data show us that imperative sentences have an underlying *you*?

I chose $\begin{Bmatrix} \text{my} \\ *\text{her} \\ *\text{its} \\ *\text{etc.} \end{Bmatrix}$ own seat.

He chose $\begin{Bmatrix} \text{his} \\ *\text{her} \\ *\text{its} \\ *\text{my} \\ *\text{etc.} \end{Bmatrix}$ own seat.

She chose $\begin{Bmatrix} \text{her} \\ *\text{my} \\ *\text{his} \\ *\text{its} \end{Bmatrix}$ own seat.

Choose $\begin{Bmatrix} \text{your} \\ *\text{my} \\ *\text{his} \\ *\text{her} \\ *\text{etc.} \end{Bmatrix}$ own seat!

8. Using the phrase-structure rules and the lexicon given in the chapter in (84), construct deep structures for the following sentences:

   a. The child sees a puppy.
   b. The smart puppy sleeps.
   c. A child laughs at the red book.
   d. Sleep!
   e. She sees herself.

9. To each of the deep structures you gave in Exercise 8, apply the transformational rules of (85) that do apply, and therefore show how the surface structures are derived. [Hint: follow the pattern in (90).]

10. Paraphrase each of the following sentences in two different ways to show that you understand the ambiguity involved:

    a. Smoking grass can be nauseating.
    b. Dick finally decided on the boat.
    c. The professor's appointment was shocking.
    d. Old men and women are hard to live with.
    e. That sheepdog is too hairy to eat.

    f. Could this be the invisible man's hair tonic?
    g. The governor is a dirty street fighter.
    h. I cannot recommend him too highly.
    i. Terry loves his wife and so do I.
    j. They said she would go yesterday.

11. The sentence

    a. John is easy to please.

has a single meaning in which the grammatical relations are parallel to those in the deep structure of *The horse is ready to ride* in (103). The sentence

    b. John is eager to please.

has a single meaning in which the grammatical relations are parallel to (102).

    A. Following the structure of (102) and (103), give deep structures for sentences *a* and *b*.
    B. Following the structure of (101), give surface structures for sentences *a* and *b*.
    C. Explain how the difference in grammatical relations of sentence *a* and sentence *b* is accounted for by the deep structures you constructed in 11A.

12. Consider the following sentences from Thai (the diacritics are tone marks):

a. dèg	maa.		The boy comes.
boy	come		
b. dèg	hěn	mǔu.	The boy sees the pig.
boy	see	pig	
c. mǎa	maa.		The dog comes.
dog	come		
d. mǎa	hěn	mǔu.	The dog sees the pig.
dog	see	pig	
e. mǔu	maa.		The pig comes.
f. dèg	chɔ̂ɔb	mǎa.	The boy likes the dog.
boy	like	dog	
g. mǎa	chɔ̂ɔb	dèg.	The dog likes the boy.
h. *maa	dèg.		
i. *dèg	mǔu	hěn.	
j. *chɔ̂ɔb	mǎa	dèg.	

    A. Write a grammar to generate these sentences using phrase-structure rules and a lexicon.
    B. List three other sentences that your grammar generates. Be sure that your grammar doesn't generate any ungrammatical strings.

Add the following sentences to those listed above:

k. dèg   khon   níi   maa.
   boy *classifier* this come
   This boy comes.

l. dèg   khon   níi   hěn   mǔu   tua   nán.
   boy *classifier* this see   pig *classifier* that
   This boy sees that pig.

m. mǎa tua   nán maa.
   dog *classifier* that come
   That dog comes.

n. mǎa tua   níi hěn mǎa tua   nán.
   dog *classifier* this see dog *classifier* that
   This dog sees that dog.

o. dèg khon   nán chɔ̂ɔb múu tua   níi.
   boy *classifier* that like pig *classifier* this
   That boy likes this pig.

p. *khon níi dèg maa.

q. *mǎa níi tua hěn mǔu tua nán.

r. *dèg níi maa.

C. Extend your grammar to generate sentences *k–o*. (*Classifier* is a syntactic category in Thai. Don't worry about what it means—just make sure your grammar generates it in the right place. You will notice that certain classifiers go with certain nouns. The lexical-insertion rules—which needn't concern you—will take care of this.)

D. List three other sentences that your new grammar generates, being sure that the classifier *tua* goes with the animals, and *khon* with the humans.

E. After writing the grammar for A–D, suppose you discovered *s* and *t,* and you were told they were grammatical. (Actually, they are not.)

s. dèg maa khon   nii.
   boy come *classifier* this
   This boy comes.

t. mǎa maa tua   nán.
   dog come *classifier* that
   That dog comes.

As you can see, sentences *k* and *s,* and *m* and *t,* are syntactic variants. Extend your phrase-structure grammar into a transformational grammar by adding a transformation to account for sentences *s* and *t*. Write out in words what the transformation does.

References

Akmajian, A., and F. Heny. *Introduction to the Principles of Transformational Syntax*. Cambridge, Mass.: M.I.T. Press, 1975.

Bach, E. *Syntactic Theory*. New York: Holt, Rinehart and Winston, 1974.

Chomsky, Noam. *Language and Mind*, rev. ed. New York: Harcourt Brace Jovanovich, 1972.

Chómsky, Noam. *Reflections on Language*. New York: Pantheon, 1976.

Chomsky, Noam. *Syntactic Structures*. The Hague: Mouton, 1957.

Culicover, Peter. *Syntax*. New York: Academic Press, 1976.

Fodor, J., and J. Katz, eds. *The Structure of Language: Readings in the Philosophy of Language*. Englewood Cliffs, N.J.: Prentice-Hall, 1964.

Grinder, J., and S. Elgin. *Guide to Transformational Grammar*. New York: Holt, Rinehart and Winston, 1973.

Jacobs, R., and P. Rosenbaum. *English Transformational Grammar*. Lexington, Mass.: Xerox College Publishing, 1968.

Jacobs, R., and P. Rosenbaum, eds. *Readings in English Transformational Grammar*. Boston: Ginn (Blaisdell), 1970.

Jespersen, O. *Essentials of English Grammar* (reprint). Montgomery, Ala.: University of Alabama Press, 1964.

Keyser, J., and P. M. Postal. *Beginning English Grammar*. New York: Harper & Row, 1976.

Lees, R. "Review of *Syntactic Structures*," *Language* 33 (1957): 375–407. Also available in Bobbs-Merrill reprint series.

Lester, M. *Introductory Transformational Grammar of English*. New York: Holt, Rinehart and Winston, 1971.

Lyons, J. *Introduction to Theoretical Linguistics*. Cambridge, England: Cambridge University Press, 1969.

Postal, P. M. *Constituent Structure: A Study of Contemporary Models of Syntactic Description*. The Hague: Mouton, 1964.

Reibel, D., and Sanford Schane, eds. *Modern Studies in English*. Englewood Cliffs, N.J.: Prentice-Hall, 1969.

Stockwell, R. P. *Foundations of Syntactic Theory*. Englewood Cliffs, N.J.: Prentice-Hall, 1977.

Stockwell, R. P., M. Bean, and D. Elliot. *Workbook for Foundations of Syntactic Theory*. Englewood Cliffs, N.J.: Prentice-Hall, 1977.

9

The Child's Acquisition of Language

From this golden egg a man, Prajapati, was born. . . . A year having passed, he wanted to speak. He said *bhur* and the earth was created. He said *bhuvar* and the space of the air was created. He said *suvar* and the sky was created. That is why a child wants to speak after a year. . . . When Prajapati spoke for the first time, he uttered one or two syllables. That is why a child utters one or two syllables when he speaks for the first time.
Hindu myth

Every aspect of language is enormously complex, as we have already seen in the previous discussions on phonetics, phonology, morphology, syntax, and semantics. Yet, as noted above and as Descartes pointed out: "There are none so depraved and stupid, without even excepting idiots, that they cannot arrange different words together, forming of them a statement by which they make known their thoughts." Perhaps even more remarkable is the fact that children—before the age of 5—learn most of this intricate system which we have been calling the grammar of a language. Before they can add 2 + 2 children are conjoining sentences, asking questions, selecting appropriate pronouns, negating sentences, using the syntactic, phonological, morphological, and semantic rules of the grammar. Yet, children are not taught language as they are taught arithmetic. Children learn many things as they are developing from infancy to maturity, but they learn these things in different ways.

A normal human being can go through life without having learned to read or write. Millions of people in the world today prove this. But these same millions all speak and understand and can discuss complex and abstract ideas as well as literate speakers can. Thus, learning a language and learning to read are somehow different. Similarly, millions of humans grow to maturity without ever having learned algebra or chemistry or how to use a typewriter. They must in some sense be taught these skills or systems, but they do not have to be taught to walk or to talk.

We are far from completely understanding the language acquisition process. We are just beginning to grapple with those aspects of the human neurological and biological makeup which explain the child's ability to acquire language. Certainly it is clear that the child is equipped from birth with the necessary neural prerequisites for language and language use.

Our knowledge of the nature of human language tells us something about what the child does and does not do when learning or acquiring a language. The earlier chapters provide us with some of this information:

1. Children do not learn a language by storing all the words and all the sentences in some giant mental dictionary. The list of words is finite, but no dictionary can hold all the sentences, which are infinite in number.
2. Children learn to construct sentences, most of which they have never produced before.
3. Children learn to understand sentences they have never heard before. They cannot do this by matching the "heard utterance" with some stored sentence.
4. Children must therefore learn "rules" which permit them to use language creatively.
5. No one teaches them these rules. Their parents are no more aware of the phonological, syntactic, and semantic rules than are the children. Children, then, seem to act like very efficient linguists equipped with a perfect theory of language, who use this theory to construct the grammar of the language they hear.

If you can remember your early years, you will not remember anyone telling you to form a sentence by adding a verb phrase to a noun phrase, or the class of sounds which are followed by an [s] to form plurals. In St. Augustine's *Confessions,* written around 400 A.D., he writes of how he learned to speak:

> . . . for I was no longer a speechless infant; but a speaking boy. This I remember; and have since observed how I learned to speak. It was not that my elders taught me words . . . in any set method; but I . . . did myself . . . practice the sounds in my memory. . . . And thus by constantly hearing words, as they occurred in various sentences . . . I thereby gave utterance to my will.

In addition to acquiring the complex rules of the grammar (that is, linguistic competence), children must also learn the complex rules of the appropriate social use of language, what certain scholars have called communicative competence. These include, for example, the greetings which are to be used, the "taboo" words, the polite forms of address, the various styles which are appropriate to different situations, and so forth.

Stages in Language Acquisition

DENNIS THE MENACE
                    BY HANK KETCHAM

"JOEY'S BABY SISTER SAID HER FIRST WORD TODAY,
BUT NOBODY KNOWS WHAT IT MEANS."

Courtesy Field Newspaper Syndicate

Children do not wake up one morning with a fully formed grammar in their heads or with all the "rules" of social and communicative intercourse. The language is acquired by stages, and, it is suggested, each stage more closely approximates the grammar of the adult language. Observations of children in different language areas of the world reveal that the stages are very similar, possibly universal. Some of the stages last for a short time; others remain longer. Some stages may overlap for a short period, though the transition between stages has often been observed to be quite sudden.

The earliest studies of child language acquisition come from diaries kept by parents. More recent studies include the use of tape recordings, videotapes, and planned experiments. Spontaneous utterances of children are recorded and in addition various elicitation techniques have been developed so that the child's production and comprehension can be studied under controlled conditions.

Some linguists divide the stages of language acquisition into prelinguistic and linguistic stages. There continues to be disagreement as to what should be included in these periods. Perhaps some day when we know more about this complex phenomenon we will be able to resolve these questions. But most scholars agree that the earliest cries and whimpers of the newborn, or neonate, cannot be considered early language. Such noises are completely stimulus-controlled; they are the child's involuntary responses to hunger, discomfort, the desire to be cuddled, or the feeling of well-being. A major difference between human language and the communication systems of other species is that human language is creative, as we discussed earlier, in the sense of being free from either external or internal stimuli. The child's first noises are, however, very much stimulus responses.

THE BABBLING STAGE

In the first few months, however, usually around the six-month period, the infant begins to **babble.** The sounds produced in this period (apart from the continuing stimulus-controlled cries and gurgles) seem to include the sounds of human languages. Most linguists believe that in this babbling period infants produce a large variety of sounds, many of which do not occur in the language of the household. Deaf children also babble and it is reported that their babbling up to the age of around six months seems very similar to that of normal children. Nondeaf children born of deaf parents who do not speak also babble. Thus, babbling does not depend on the presence of acoustic, auditory input. There are however at least two different schools of thought concerning babbling. One group believes that babbling is a necessary prerequisite for normal language acquisition. Others, like Eric Lenneberg, consider babbling to be less crucial. Lenneberg reported on a child of 14 months who for medical purposes had been mechanically prevented from making any vocal sounds for six months. Yet, one day after the mechanical restraint was removed, his output was equivalent to what one would expect from a normal 14-month-old child.

One thing is absolutely clear, however. In order for language to finally develop, the child must receive either auditory input (to develop oral language) or sign language input (for a deaf child to acquire sign language). But the role of babbling in the acquisition of oral language is not clearly understood.

One view suggests that it is during this period that children are learning to distinguish between the sounds of their language and the sounds which are not part of the language. During the babbling period children learn to maintain the "right" sounds and suppress the "wrong" ones.

During the babbling stage the pitch, or intonation contours, of infants' utterances begin to resemble the intonation contours of sentences spoken by adults. It has been suggested that the semantically different intonation contours are among the first linguistic contrasts that children perceive and produce.

THE HOLOPHRASTIC STAGE

Sometime after one year (it varies from child to child and has nothing to do with how intelligent the child is), children begin to use the same string of sounds repeatedly to "mean" the same thing. At this point they have learned that sounds are related to meanings and they are producing their first "words." Most children seem to go through the "one word = one sentence" stage. These one-word sentences (if one can call them sentences at all) are called **holophrastic** sentences (from *holo,* "complete" or "undivided," plus *phrase,* "phrase" or "sentence").

Perhaps a picture of one child, J. P., at this stage will illustrate how much the young child has already learned. J. P.'s words as of April 1977 (age 16 months) were as follows:[1]

[ʔaw]	"not," "no," "don't"	[baw] ~ [daw]	"down"
[bʌʔ] ~ [mʌʔ]	"up"	[dæ]	"daddy"
[da]	"dog"	[s:]	"aerosol, etc., spray"
[sæ:] ~ [əsæ:]	"what's that?", "hey, look!"		
[iʔo] ~ [šiʔo]	"Cheerios"	[sʸu:]	"shoe"
[sa]	"sock"	[hay]	"hi"
[ay] ~ [ʌy]	"light"	[sr̩]	"shirt," "sweater"
[ma]	"mommy"		

J. P.'s mother reports that before April he also used the words [bʊ] for "book," [ki] for "kitty," and [tsi] for "tree" but seemed to have "lost" them.

What is more interesting than merely the list of J. P.'s vocabulary is the way he used these words. "Up" originally was restricted to mean "get me up" when he was either on the floor or in his high chair, but later was used to mean "get up!" to his mother as well. His word for "Cheerios" was first used to label or ask for Cheerios only when they were visible; then he began to use it to ask for Cheerios even when he could not see them. J. P. used his word for "sock" when pointing to anyone's socks as well as other undergarments that go on over the feet, which illustrates how a child may extend the meaning of a word from a particular referent to encompass a larger class.

When he first began to use these words, the stimulus had to be present. But by May this was no longer true. "Dog," for example, was first only used when pointing to a real dog but then was used in pointing to pictures of dogs in various books. A new word which entered J. P.'s vocabulary in May was "uh-oh," which he would say after having an accident like spilling juice, or when he deliberately poured his yogurt over the side of his high chair. His use of this word shows his growing use of language for social purposes. At this time he also added two new words meaning "no," [do:] and [no]. He used these frequently when anyone attempted to take something from him which he wanted or tried to make him do something he didn't want to do. He used this negative either imperatively (for example, "Don't do that!") or assertively (for example, "I don't want to do that."). One can see that, as early as this holophrastic stage, words are being used to communicate a variety of ideas, feelings, and social awareness.

According to some child-language researchers, the words in the holophrastic stage serve three major functions; they are either linked with a child's own action or desire for action (as when J. P. would say "up" to express his wish to be picked up), or are used to convey emotion (J. P.'s "no"), or serve a naming function (J. P.'s "Cheerios," "shoes," "dog," and so on).

---

[1] We would like to give special thanks to John Peregrine Munro for providing us with such rich data and for being such a delight in every possible way. Also, thanks are in order to Drs. Pam and Allen Munro, J. P.'s parents, for their painstaking efforts in recording these data.

At this stage the child uses just one word to express concepts or predications which will later be expressed by complex phrases and sentences.

Phonologically, J. P.'s first words are, like the words of most children at this stage of learning English and other languages, generally monosyllabic with a CV (consonant-vowel) form; the vowel part may be diphthongal, depending on the language being acquired. His phonemic or phonetic inventory (at this stage they are equivalent) is much smaller than is found in the adult language. It has been suggested by the linguist Roman Jakobson that children will acquire the sounds found in all languages of the world first, no matter what language they are exposed to, and in later stages will acquire the "more difficult" sounds.[2]

J. P.'s phonological inventory includes the consonants [b, m, d, k], which certainly are frequently occurring sounds in the world's languages.

Many studies have shown that children in the holophrastic stage can perceive or comprehend many more phonological contrasts than they can produce themselves. Thus, even at this stage, it is not possible to determine the extent of the grammar of the child simply by observing or noting speech production.

THE TWO-WORD STAGE

Around the time of their second birthday (but remember, this can be earlier or later, since there is great variability among children), children begin to produce two-word utterances. At first these appear to be strings of two of the child's earlier holophrastic utterances, each word with its own single-pitch contour. J. P. had not reached this stage at the time of writing, but we expect he will soon be saying utterances like "[sa] · [sʸu:]" ("sock

shoe"), which could mean any number of things, such as "There is a sock. There is a shoe." or "I want my sock. I don't want my shoe." Soon after this juxtaposition, J. P., like other children, will begin to form actual two-word sentences, with the relation between the two words showing definite syntactic and semantic relations and the intonation contour of the two words extending over the whole utterance rather than being separated by a pause between the two words. The following "sentences" illustrate the kinds of patterns which are found in children's utterances at this stage.[3]

> allgone sock
> hi Mommy
> byebye boat
> allgone sticky
> more wet
> beepbeep bang
> it ball
> Katherine sock
> dirty sock
> here pretty

[2] Jakobson, R. *Kindersprache, Aphasie, und allgemeine Lautgesetz* (Uppsala, Sweden: Almqvist and Wiksell, 1941); English translation by A. Keiler, *Child Language, Aphasia, and Phonological Universals* (The Hague: Mouton, 1968).

[3] All the examples given in this chapter are taken from utterances produced by children actually observed by the authors or as reported in the literature. The various sources are listed in the reference section at the end of the chapter.

During the two-word utterance stage there are no syntactic or morpho-logical markers; that is, no inflections for number, or person, or tense, and so on. Pronouns are rare, although many children do use "me" to refer to themselves, and some children use other pronouns as well. Bloom has noted that in noun+noun sentences, such as *Mommy sock,* the two words can express a number of different grammatical relations which will later be expressed by other syntactic devices.[4] Bloom's conclusions were reached by observing the situations in which the two-word sentence was uttered. Thus, for example, *Mommy sock* can be used to show a subject+object relation in the situation when the mother is putting the sock on the child, or a possessive relation when the child is pointing to Mommy's sock. Two nouns can also be used to show a subject-locative relation, as in *sweater chair* to mean "the sweater is on the chair," or to show conjunction, to mean "sweater and chair."

TELEGRAPH TO INFINITY

There doesn't seem to be any "three-word" sentence stage. When a child starts stringing more than two words together, the utterances may be two, three, four, or five words or longer. Many linguists working on child language do, however, study the increasing lengths of the utterances which children use. They believe that a comparison across children as to stage of language acquisition can best be made by the **mean length of utterances** (MLU) rather than by chronological age. That is, children who are produc-ing utterances which on the average are 2.3 to 3.5 morphemes seem to have acquired in similar fashion other aspects of the grammar.

But these first utterances of children which are longer than two words have a special characteristic. Usually the small "function" words such as *to, the, can, is,* and so on, are missing; only the words which carry the main message—the "content" words—occur. Children often sound as if they were reading a Western Union message, which is why such utterances are called **telegraphic speech:**

> Cat stand up table
> What that?
> He play little tune
> Andrew want that
> Cathy build house
> No sit there

When the child begins to produce utterances that are longer than two words, these utterances appear to be "sentence-like"; they have hierarchi-cal, constituent structures similar to the syntactic structures found in the sentences produced by the adult grammar:

---

[4] L. M. Bloom, *Language Development: Form and Function in Emerging Grammar* (Cambridge, Mass.: M.I.T. Press, 1970).

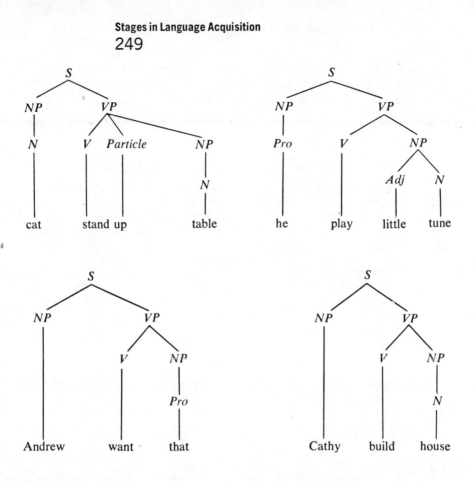

The child's utterances are not simply randomly strung together words but, from a very early stage, reveal his or her grasp of the principles of sentence formation.

When we refer to these simple sentences as telegraphic, clearly this is just a descriptive term, since the child does not deliberately leave out the noncontent words, as does an adult sending a telegram.

As children acquire more and more language, or more closely approximate the adult grammar, they not only begin to use syntactic or grammatical function words but also acquire the inflectional and derivational morphemes of the language. Brown and his associates at Harvard studied the spontaneous utterances of three children—Adam, Sarah, and Eve—over a long period of time, noting the appearance of grammatical morphemes, free and bound.[5] They found that the sequences of acquisition of the morphemes were pretty much the same, and this has been replicated by other researchers working with other children. It seems that *-ing,* the ending which represents the present progressive form of the verb, as in *Me going*

---

[5] R. O. Brown, *A First Language: The Early Stages* (Cambridge, Mass.: Harvard University Press, 1973).

park is the earliest inflectional morpheme acquired. The prepositions *in* and *on* enter the children's speech next, and then the regular plural ending.

Eventually all the other inflections are added, along with the syntactic rules, and finally the child's utterances sound like those spoken by adults.

Theories of Child Language Acquisition

Various theories have been proposed to explain how children manage to acquire the adult language. There are those who think that children merely imitate what they hear. Imitation is involved to some extent, of course, but the sentences produced by children show that children are *not* imitating adult speech. From whom would children hear *Cat stand up table* or any of the sentences like these they produce?

a my pencil
other one pants
two foot
Mommy get it my ladder
what the boy hit?
cowboy did fighting me.

Even when children are deliberately trying to imitate what they hear they are unable to produce sentences which cannot be generated by *their* grammar.

Adult: He's going out	*Child:* He go out
Adult: That's an old-time train	*Child:* Old-time train
Adult: Adam, say what I say:	
Where can I put them?	*Child:* Where I can put them?

Neither can the "imitation" theory account for another important phenomenon. There are children who are unable to speak for neurological or physiological reasons. Yet these children learn the language spoken to them and understand what is said. When they overcome their speech impairment they immediately become able to use the language for speaking.

Another equally untenable theory of language acquisition suggests that children learn to produce "correct" sentences because they are positively reinforced when they say something right and negatively reinforced when they say something wrong. This view assumes that children are being constantly corrected for using "bad grammar" and patted on the head when they use "good grammar." Even if this happened (and it seldom does), how do children learn from such adult responses what it is they are doing right or wrong? This view does not tell us how children construct the correct rules. Whatever "correction" takes place is based more on the content of the message than on its *form*. That is, if a child says "Nobody don't like me," the mother may say "Everybody likes you."

Besides, all attempts to "correct" a child's language are doomed to failure. Children don't know what they are doing wrong and are even unable to make the corrections when they are pointed out to them, as is shown in the following examples:

(1) *Child:*   Nobody don't like me.
    Mother: No, say "Nobody likes me."
    Child: Nobody don't like me.
      (dialogue repeated eight times)
    Mother: Now, listen carefully, say *"Nobody likes me."*
    Child: Oh, nobody don't likes me.

(2) *Child:*   Want other one spoon, Daddy.
    Father: You mean, you want *"the other spoon."*
    Child: Yes, I want other one spoon, please, Daddy.
    Father: Can you say "the other spoon"?
    Child: Other . . . one . . . spoon.
    Father: Say . . . "other."
    Child: Other.
    Father: Spoon.
    Child: Spoon.
    Father: Other . . . spoon.
    Child: Other . . . spoon. Now give me other one spoon?

Such conversations between parents and children do not take place very often. Mothers and fathers (unless they are linguists) are too busy to correct their children's speech. Besides, they are usually delighted that their young children are talking at all and consider every utterance to be a gem. The "mistakes" children make are "cute" and repeated endlessly to anyone who will listen.

The "reinforcement" theory fails along with the "imitation" theory. Neither of these views accounts for the fact that children are constructing their own rules. Different rules govern the construction of sentences as the grammar is learned. Consider, for example, the increasing complexity of one child's negative sentences. At first the child simply added a *no* (or some negative morpheme) at the beginning or at the end of a sentence:

     no heavy
     no singing song
     no want stand head
     no Fraser drink all tea
     no the sun shining.

He didn't hear such sentences. This is a simple way to *transform* a declarative into a negative. At some point he began to insert a *no* or *can't* or *don't* inside the sentence.

     He no bite you
     I no taste them
     That no fish school
     I can't catch you.

The child progressed from simple rules to more complex rules, as is shown below:

Declarative: I want some food.
Negative (i): No want some food.   (*no* added to beginning of sentence)

Negative (ii): I $\begin{Bmatrix} \text{no} \\ \text{don't} \end{Bmatrix}$ want some food.   (negative element inserted; no other change)

Negative (iii): I don't want no food.   (negative element inserted; negation "spread"; i.e. *some* becomes *no*)

Negative (iv): I don't want any food.   (negative element correctly inserted, *some* changed to *any*)

All children do not show the same development as the child described above, but they all show similarly regular changes. One child studied by the linguist Carol Lord first differentiated affirmative from negative sentences by pitch; her negative sentences were all produced with a much higher pitch. When she began to use a negative morpheme, the pitch remained high but then the intonation became normal as the negative syntactic markers "took over."

The same increasing complexity is found in the learning of question constructions. Again, our examples are taken from the study of one child. Other children show some differences, but all show the same regular kind of development. At first, the child forms a question by using a "question intonation" (a rise of pitch at the end of the sentence):

> Fraser water?
> I ride train?
> Sit chair?

At the next stage the child merely "tacks on" a question word in front of the sentence; he doesn't change the word order, or insert *do*.

> What he wants?
> What he can ride in?
> Where I should put it?
> Where Ann pencil?
> Why you smiling?

Such sentences are perfectly regular. They are not "mistakes" in the child's language; they reflect his grammar at a certain stage of development.

The child seems to form the simplest and most general rule he can from the language input he receives, and is so "pleased" with his "theory" that he uses the rule wherever he can. The most obvious example of this "overgeneralization" is shown when children treat irregular verbs and nouns as if they were regular. We have probably all heard children say *bringed, goed, doed, singed,* or *foots, mouses, sheeps, childs.*

These mistakes tell us more about how children learn language than the "correct" forms they use. The child couldn't be imitating; children use such forms in families where the parents would never utter such "bad English." In fact, children may say *brought* instead of *bringed,* or *broke* instead of *breaked,* before they begin to use these incorrect forms. At the earlier stage they never use any regular past-tense forms like *kissed, walked,* or *helped.* Thus, they probably don't know that *brought* is a "past" at all. When they begin to say *played* and *hugged* and *helped* as well as *play, hug,* and *help,* they have "figured out" how to form a past tense—*they have constructed the rule.* At that point they form *all* past tenses by this rule—they overgeneralize—and they no longer say *brought* but *bring* and *bringed.* Notice that the "correct forms" were already learned (reinforced?), but the acquisition of the rule is more important than any previous or "practice" reinforcement. At some time later, children will learn that there are "exceptions" to the rule. Only then will they once more say *brought.* Children seem to look for general patterns, for systematic occurrences.

Such overgeneralizations have also been observed in children's acquisition of the semantic system. They may learn a word such as *papa* or *daddy* which they first use only for their own father. This word may then be extended to apply to all men. As they acquire new words, the "overgeneralized" meaning becomes narrowed down until once more it has a single referent. The linguist Eve Clark has found this to be true of many other words and semantic features. She has observed that children make overgeneralizations which are based on shape, size, sound, taste, and texture. One child's word for "moon" /mo:i/ became the name for cakes, round marks on windows, writing on a window, round shapes in books, tooling on leather book covers, round postmarks, and the letter *O.* Similarly, the word for "watch," *tick tock,* was used for all objects shaped like a watch: clocks, gas meters, a fire hose wound on a spool, a bath scale. The word for *fly* /flai/ was used for other small-sized objects like specks of dirt, dust, all small insects, his own toes, crumbs; and /dani/ was first used for the sound of a bell, and then for a clock, a telephone, a door bell. As more words are added, and semantic features become more specified, the meaning of these words becomes narrowed. But again the child's ability to find general systematic patterns is observed.

The child's ability to generalize patterns and construct rules is also shown in phonological development. In early language children may not distinguish between voiced and voiceless consonants, for example. But when they first begin to contrast one set—that is, when they learn that /p/ and /b/ are distinct phonemes—they also begin to distinguish between /t/ and /d/, /s/ and /z/, and so on.

Such regular stages and patterns support the notion that language acquisition is grammar construction. The Russian linguist Kornei Chukovsky writes: "It seems to me that, beginning with the age of two, every child becomes for a short period of time a linguistic genius. Later, beginning with the age of five or six, this talent begins to fade."[6]

Children have to construct all the phonological, syntactic, and semantic rules of the grammar. This is a difficult task indeed, especially since all

[6] Kornei Chukovsky, *From Two to Five,* trans. and ed. by M. Morton (Berkeley: University of California Press, 1968).

they ever hear are the "surface structures" of sentences. The learning of negative and question rules shows they are forming transformational rules, and at some stage children, like adults, will know that *It is too hot to eat* has at least three meanings.

Children seem to be equipped with special abilities, residing principally in the left side of the brain, to know just what generalizations to look for, to know what they can ignore, to find all the regularities in the language. Chomsky explains this in the following way:

> It seems plain that language acquisition is based on the child's discovery of what from a formal point of view is a deep and abstract theory—a generative grammar of his language. . . . A consideration of the character of the grammar that is acquired, the degenerate quality and narrowly limited extent of the available data, the striking uniformity of the resulting grammars, and their independence of intelligence, motivation, and emotional state, over wide ranges of variation, leave little hope that much of the structure of the language can be learned by an organism initially uninformed as to its general character . . . it may well be that the general features of language structure reflect, not so much the course of one's experience, but rather the general character of one's capacity to acquire knowledge. . . .[7]

The details of the "innate" language-acquisition device are far from understood. As we gain more information about brain functions and the preconditions for language acquisition, we will learn more about the nature of human language.

SUMMARY

When children learn a language, they learn the grammar of that language—the phonological, morphological, syntactic, and semantic rules. No one teaches them these rules; children just "pick them up," and in so efficient a manner as to suggest that their brains are preprogramed for language learning.

A child does not learn the language "all at once." Children's first utterances are one-word "sentences" (**holophrastic** speech). After a few months, two-word sentences appear which are not random combinations of words; the words have definite patterns and express grammatical and semantic relationships. Still later, more complex sentences are used. At first the child's grammar lacks many of the rules of the adult grammar, but eventually the child's grammar mirrors the language used in the community.

A number of theories have been suggested to explain the acquisition process. Neither the **imitation theory,** which claims that children learn their language by imitating adult speech, nor the **reinforcement theory,** which hypothesizes that children are conditioned into speaking correctly by being negatively reinforced for "errors" and positively reinforced for "correct" usage, is supported by observational and experimental studies. Neither can explain how children form the *rules* which they then use to produce new sentences.

[7] Noam Chomsky, *Aspects of the Theory of Syntax* (Cambridge, Mass.: M.I.T. Press, 1965).

Children acquire the rules of the grammar in stages of increasing complexity. They seem to have a propensity for making broad, simple linguistic generalizations and "overgeneralizations." As they are exposed to more data, they narrow down and revise their "rules" until they match those of the adult grammar.

All normal children everywhere learn the language of their society.

EXERCISES

1. In this chapter the way a child learns "negation" of sentences and "question formation" was discussed. Can these be considered examples of a process of overgeneralization in syntax acquisition? If so, for each stage indicate *what* is being overgeneralized.

2. Suppose a friend of yours has a son, Tommy, who is 3 years old. Your friend has been explaining to you that Tommy has a problem in his speech in that he does not form "past tenses" of verbs. That is, Tommy says "Yesterday I go to park" and "Last week I swim in pool." But your friend has a plan: He is going to spend one hour each day with Tommy, having the child imitate the past-tense forms of the verbs, and he will give Tommy a piece of candy for each correct imitation. Explain to your friend (and to us) why his plan won't work.

3. *Baby talk* is a term used to label the word-forms which many adults use when speaking to children. Examples in English are words like *choo-choo* for "train" and *bow-wow* for "dog." Baby talk seems to exist in every language and culture. At least two things seem to be universal about baby talk: The words which have baby-talk forms fall into certain semantic categories (for example, food), and the words are "phonetically simpler" than the adult forms (for example, *tummy* for "stomach"). List all the baby-talk words you can think of in your native language, then (1) separate them into semantic categories, and (2) try to state general rules for the kinds of phonological "reductions" or "simplifications" that occur.

4. Find a 2-year-old child and play with her/him for about thirty minutes. Keep a list of all words which are used inappropriately. Can you describe what the child's meanings for these words probably are?

References

Bellugi-Klima, U. "Linguistic Mechanisms Underlying Child Speech," in E. M. Zale, ed., *Proceedings of the Conference on Language and Language Behavior*. New York: Appleton-Century-Crofts, 1968.

Bloom, L. M. *Language Development: Form and Function in Emerging Grammar*. Cambridge: M.I.T. Press, 1972.

Brown, R. O. *A First Language: The Early Stages*. Cambridge, Mass.: Harvard University Press, 1973.

Brown, R. O., C. B. Cazden, and U. Bellugi. "The Child's Grammar from I to III," in R. O. Brown, ed., *Psycholinguistics*. New York: Free Press, 1970.

Clark, E. "What's in a Word? On the Child's Acquisition of Semantics in His First Language," in T. E. Moore, ed., *Cognitive Development and the Acquisition of Language*. New York: Academic Press, 1973.

Dale, P. S. *Language Development: Structure and Function*. Hinsdale, Ill.: Dryden, 1972.

Ervin, S. M. "Imitation and Structural Change in Children's Language," in E. H. Lenneberg, ed., *New Directions in the Study of Language*. Cambridge, Mass.: M.I.T. Press, 1964.

McNeill, D. *The Acquisition of Language: The Study of Developmental Psycholinguistics*. New York: Harper & Row, 1970.

Menyuk, P. *Sentences Children Use*. Cambridge, Mass.: M.I.T. Press, 1969.

Slobin, Dan I. *Psycholinguistics*. Glenview, Ill.: Scott, Foresman and Company, 1971.

CHAPTER

10

The Diversity of Language

Dialects

I have noticed in traveling about the country a good many differences in the pronunciation of common words. . . . Now what I want to know is whether there is any right or wrong about this matter. . . . If one way is right, why don't we all pronounce that way and compel the other fellow to do the same? If there isn't any right or wrong, why do some persons make so much fuss about it?

Letter quoted in "The Standard American" in
J. V. WILLIAMSON and V. M. BURKE, eds., *A Various Language*

All speakers of English can talk to each other and pretty much understand each other. Yet no two speakers speak exactly alike. Some differences are due to age, sex, state of health, size, personality, emotional state, and personal idiosyncrasies. That each person speaks somewhat differently from all others is shown by our ability to recognize acquaintances by hearing them talk. Thus every speaker of a language has an individual "dialect" (called an *idiolect*); English may then be said to consist of 400,000,000 idiolects.

Even beyond these individual differences, the language of a group of people may show regular variations from that used by other groups. English spoken in different geographical regions and different social groups shows **systematic** differences. Such groups are said to speak different **dialects** of the same language. A language is composed of its dialects in much the same way that a baseball league is composed of its individual teams. No single team is the league; no single dialect is the language.

Dialectal diversity tends to increase proportionately to the degree of communicative isolation between the groups. **Communicative isolation** refers to such a situation as existed between America, Australia, and England in the eighteenth century. There was some contact through commerce and emigration, but an Australian was less likely to talk to an Englishman than to another Australian. Today the isolation is less pronounced because of the mass media and jet airplanes. But even within one country, regionalisms persist. Children learn the language spoken to them and reinforce the unique features characteristic of the dialect used.

The changes which occur in the language spoken in one area are not necessarily spread to another area. The variability of linguistic changes accounts, to a great extent, for the early dialect splits. Within a single group of speakers who are in regular contact with one another, the changes are spread among the group and "relearned" by their children. When some communication barrier separates groups of speakers—be it a physcial barrier like an ocean or a mountain range, or social barriers of a political, racial, class, or religious kind—linguistic changes are not easily spread and dialectal differences are reinforced.

It is not always easy to decide whether the language differences reflect two dialects or two different languages. A rule-of-thumb definition can be used: "When dialects become mutually unintelligible, they are different languages." But to define "mutually intelligible" is itself a difficult task. Danes speaking Danish and Norwegians speaking Norwegian can converse with each other. Yet Danish and Norwegian are considered separate languages because they are spoken in separate countries and because there are regular differences in their grammars. Similarly, Hindi and Urdu are mutually intelligible "languages" spoken in Pakistan and India.

The continuum of intelligibility that exists between dialects makes an objective definition difficult. We shall, however, use the rule-of-thumb definition and refer to dialects of one language as mutually intelligible versions of the same basic grammar, with systematic differences between them.

In the next chapter, when we discuss language change in time and space, we will discuss regional dialects and "accents" in greater detail. In this chapter we will be mainly concerned with other kinds of dialect differences, like those which exist between different social groups, different professions or trades, and even different communicative settings.

The "Standard"

We don't talk fancy grammar and eat anchovy toast. But to live under the kitchen doesn't say we aren't educated.
MARY NORTON, *The Borrowers*

Even though every language is a composite of dialects, many people talk and think about a language as if it were a "well-defined" fixed system with various dialects diverging from this norm. This is analogous to equating the American Baseball League of the 1950s to the New York Yankees. The Yankees enjoyed so much success in that decade that many baseball enthusiasts did just that. Similarly, a particular dialect of a language may enjoy such prestige that it becomes equated with the language itself.

The prestigious dialect is often that used by political leaders and the upper socioeconomic classes; it is the dialect used for literature or printed documents; it is taught in the schools, used by the military, and propagated by the mass media. Once a dialect gets a head start, it often builds up momentum. The more "important" it gets, the more it is used; the more it is used, the more important it becomes. Such a dialect may be that spoken in the political or cultural center of a country and may spread into other regions. The dominance in France of the Parisian dialect, and in England (to a lesser extent) of the London dialect, is attributable to this cause.

Such a dominant dialect is often called the **standard dialect. Standard American English (SAE)** is a dialect of English which many Americans *almost* speak; divergences from this "norm" are labeled "Philadelphia dialect," "Chicago dialect," "Black English," and so on.

SAE is an idealization. Nobody speaks this dialect, and if somebody did, we wouldn't know it because SAE is not defined precisely. Several years ago there actually was an entire conference devoted to one subject: a precise definition of SAE. This convocation of scholars did not succeed in satisfying everyone as to what SAE should be. The best hint we can give you is to listen to national broadcasters (though nowadays some of these people may speak a regional dialect).

When two languages are compared, it is necessary to compare one of the dialects of each language. The "standards" are usually used. When American and British English are compared, SAE and the British spoken by educated British people, called Received Pronunciation (RP),[1] are the dialects used for this purpose. The standard dialect is taught to nonnative speakers and is usually the most widespread; speakers of all dialects usually understand it easily even if they do not use it. Speakers of different dialects use the standard as the written form, since this dialect is the accepted literary language.

In France, a notion of the "standard" as the only correct form of the language is propagated by an official academy of "scholars" who determine what usages constitute the "official French language." This Academy recently enacted a law forbidding the use of "Franglais" words in advertising (words of English origin like *le parking*). The Parisian dialect is considered the "standard" at the expense of the hundreds of local village dialects (called *patois* [patwa] by the Academy). Many of these *patois* are actually separate languages, derived from Latin (as are French, Spanish, and Italian). In the past (and to some extent in the present) a Frenchman or Frenchwoman from the provinces who wished to succeed in French society nearly always had to be bidialectal. In recent years in France the regional "nationalist" movements have placed as a major demand the right to use their own languages in their schools and for official business. In the section of France known as l'Occitanie, the popular singers sing in the regional language, Languedoc, both as a protest against the official "standard language" policy and as part of the cultural revival movement. The most popular of these singers, Marti, has recorded a very popular song concerned with just this question. The final chorus in Languedoc, French, and English reveals this:

[1] Received Pronunciation (commonly called RP) is the British pronunciation that is "received" (accepted as "proper") at the royal court.

LANGUEDOC	FRENCH	ENGLISH
Mas perqué, perqué	Mais pourquoi, pourquoi	But why, why
M'an pas dit à l'escòla	Ne m'a-t-on pas dit à l'école	Did they not speak to me at school
La lenga de mon pais?	La langue de mon pays?	The language of my country?

In the province of Brittany in France there is also a strong movement for the use of Breton in the schools, as opposed to the "standard" Parisian French. The Breton singer Gilles Servat has gained considerable popularity in Brittany and in other sections of France where this Breton movement is supported.

Those who interpret "standard" literally and consider other dialects as inferior are not confined to Paris. Although a standard dialect is in no *linguistic* way "superior," we still find self-appointed guardians of "the purity of our language" in practically all countries, and certainly in the United States. In April 1977 the State Transportation Director of California became incensed because she would receive memos which she believed included "improper" English. She sent a memorandum to all the employees of the Department of Transportation: "I would . . . like to point out two words which are frequently used around here are plural and not singular; those words are 'criteria' and 'data.' " She goes on to say she hopes never again to see these incorrectly used. The problem of course is that this leading California citizen seems unaware that language changes and that change does not mean corruption. For the great majority of American English speakers, *criteria* and *data* are now mass nouns, like *information*. Information can include one fact or many facts, but one would still say "The information is. . . ." For some speakers it is equally correct to say "The criteria is . . ." or "The criteria are. . . ." Those who say "The data are . . ." would or could say "The datum (singular) is. . . ."

The idea that language change equals corruption goes back at least as far as the Greek grammarians at Alexandria, circa 100–200 B.C. They were concerned that the Greek spoken in their time was different from the Greek of Homer, and they believed that the earlier forms were purer. They also tried to "correct" the imperfections but failed as miserably as do any modern counterparts. Similarly, the Moslem Arabic grammarians in the eighth and ninth centuries A.D. working at Basra attempted to purify Arabic in order to restore it to the perfection of the Koran Arabic.

A standard dialect (or prestige dialect) may have social functions—to bind people together or to provide a common written form for multidialectal speakers. It is, however, neither more expressive, more logical, more complex, nor more regular than any other dialect. Any judgments, therefore, as to the superiority or inferiority of a particular dialect are social judgments, not linguistic or scientific ones.

Black English

For some blacks and some whites (notice the infamous all has been omitted) it is not a matter of you say e-ther and we say i-ther, but rather:

. . . You kiss your children, and we give 'em some sugar. . . .

You cook a pan of spinach, and we burn a mess of greens. You wear clothes, and we wear threads. . . . You call the police, and we drop a dime. You say wow! We say ain't that a blip. You care, love and hurt, and we care, love and hurt. The differences are but a shade.

SANDRA HAGGERTY, "On Digging the Difference" (Los Angeles *Times,* April 2, 1973)

LUTHER   **BY BRUMSIC BRANDON, JR.**

© 1972 Los Angeles Times; reprinted with permission

    While the majority of American dialects are free from stigma to a great extent, especially the many regional dialects, one dialect of American English has been a victim of prejudicial ignorance. This is the dialect spoken by a large section of non-middle-class American blacks; it is usually referred to as Black English (BE) or Negro English or Nonstandard Negro English. The distinguishing features of this English dialect persist for social, educational, and economic reasons. The historical discrimination against black Americans has created ghetto living and segregated schools. Where social isolation exists, dialect differences are intensified. In addition, particularly in recent years, many blacks no longer consider their dialect to be inferior and it has become a means of positive black identification.

    Since the onset of the civil-rights movement, Black English has been the focus of national attention. There are those who attempt to equate the use of Black English with inferior "genetic" intelligence and "cultural deprivation," and justify these incorrect notions by stating that BE is a "deficient, illogical, and incomplete" language. Such epithets cannot be applied to any language and are as unscientific in reference to BE as to Russian, Chinese, or Standard American English. The cultural-deprivation myth is as false as the idea that some dialects or languages are inferior. A person may be "deprived" of one cultural background but very rich in another.

    There are people, white and black, who think they can identify an unseen person's race by hearing him talk, believing that different races inherently speak differently. This assumption is equally false; a black child raised in an upper-class British household will speak RP English. A white child raised in an environment where Black English is spoken will speak Black English. Children construct grammars based on the language they hear.

There are, however, systematic differences between BE and SAE, just as there are systematic differences between Australian and American English. Dialect differences may show up in the phonological rules of the grammars. British grammar has a rule which can be stated as: "Delete the /r/ except before a vowel." Black English has the same rule (as do some nonblack Southern dialects). Words like *guard* and *god*, *nor* and *gnaw*, *sore* and *saw*, *poor* and *pa*, *fort* and *fought*, and *court* and *caught* are pronounced identically in BE because of the presence of this phonological rule in the grammar.

Other words that do not rhyme in SAE do rhyme in BE: *yeah* and *fair*, *idea* and *fear*. In BE (and other Southern dialects) the "*r*-deletion" rule has been extended in some cases, so that it is also deleted between vowels. *Carol* is pronounced identically with *Cal*, and *Paris* with *pass*. It is possible, however, that in these words no deletion rule applies but the lexical representations of *Carol* and *Cal*, for example, are identical, without the *r*.

For some speakers of BE, an "*l*-deletion" rule also occurs, creating homophones like *toll* and *toe*, *all* and *awe*, *help* and *hep* [hɛp]. (Again, some of these may not include the *l* as part of their phonological representations.)

A regular phonological rule which exists in BE and not in SAE simplifies consonant clusters, particularly at the end of words and when one of the two consonants is an alveolar (/t/, /d/, /s/, /z/). The application of this rule may delete the past-tense morpheme; *past* and *passed* (*pass +ed*) are both pronounced *pass*. When speakers of this dialect say *I pass the test yesterday*, they are not showing an ignorance of past and present, but are pronouncing the past tense according to the rule present in their grammar:

"passed" /pæs + t/ → apply rule → [pæs]

Because of this consonant rule, *meant* and *mend* are both pronounced the same as *men*. And when combined with the "*l*-deletion" rule, *told*, *toll*, and *toe* have identical pronunciations.

	told	*toll*	*toe*
Phonemic Representation	/told/	/tol/	/to/
Consonant cluster simplification rule	↓ ø	NA	NA
l-deletion rule	ø	ø	NA
Phonetic Representation	[to]	[to]	[to]

There are other systematic differences between the phonology of BE and SAE. BE shares with many regional dialects the lack of any distinction between /ɪ/ and /ɛ/ before nasal consonants, producing identical pronunciations of *pin* and *pen*, *bin* and *Ben*, *tin* and *ten*, and so on. The vowel used in these words is roughly between the [ɪ] of *pit* and the [ɛ] of *pet*.

In BE the phonemic distinction between /ay/ and /aw/ has been lost, both having become /a/. Thus *why* and *wow* are pronounced [wa]. Another change which has occurred has reduced the /ɔy/ (particularly before /l/) to the simple vowel [ɔ] without the glide, so that *boil* and *boy* are pronounced [bɔ]. One other regular feature is the change of a final /θ/ to [f] so that *Ruth* is pronounced [ruf] and *death* [dɛf].

Notice that these are all systematic changes and "rule-governed." The kinds of changes which have occurred are very similar to sound changes which have taken place in languages all over the world, including Standard English. Some dialects of Black English drop final nasal consonants. The preceding vowel, however, retains its nasalization, so the words end in nasalized vowels. (Note the rule in Standard English that nasalizes a vowel before a nasal consonant, discussed in Chapter 5.) This is precisely how French developed nasal vowels. Linguistic change caused final nasal consonants to be dropped, leaving behind a nasal vowel to distinguish the word.

Every dialect of every language has its own lexical items and its own phonological rules. The preponderance of likenesses of Black English to Standard English—the two dialects share most lexical forms and rules—is what makes the differences so conspicuous. If Black English were as incomprehensible as Russian, many Americans would probably have more respect for it.

Syntactic differences, as noted above, also exist between dialects. Recently linguists like William Labov have begun to investigate the syntactic structures of Black English. It is the syntactic differences that have often been used to illustrate the "illogic" of BE, and yet it is just such differences that point up the fact that BE is as syntactically complex and as "logical" as SAE.

Following the lead of early "prescriptive" grammarians, some "scholars" and teachers conclude that it is illogical to say *he don't know nothing* because two negatives make a positive. Since such negative constructions occur in BE, it has been concluded by some "educators" that speakers of BE are deficient because they use language "illogically." Consider the following sentences from BE and SAE:

	SAE	BE
Affirmative:	He knows something.	He know something.[2]
Negative:	He doesn't know anything.	He don't know nothing.
	He knows nothing.	He know nothing.
Affirmative:	He likes somebody.	He like somebody.
Negative:	He doesn't like anybody.	He don't like nobody.
	He likes nobody.	He like nobody.
Affirmative:	He has got some.	He got some.
Negative:	He hasn't got any.	He ain't got none.
	He's got none.	He got none.

[2] As the examples in this list show, Black English also regularizes the present tense verb forms. In SAE the third person singular verb forms are inflected by adding to the verb the particular phonetic form that is the same as the plural ending (for example, [z] as in *loves* or *knows*, [s] as in *kicks*, or [əz] as in *kisses*). The absence of this ending in Black English may be the result of the application of phonological rules such as those discussed above.

In Black English when the verb is negated the indefinites *something*, *somebody*, and *some* become the negative indefinites *nothing, nobody*, and *none*. The rule is simple and elegant and of a type quite common in the world's languages. This was the rule which existed in earlier periods for all dialects of English. In Standard English, if the verb is negated the indefinites become *anything, anybody,* and *any.* If in the negative sentences in SAE the forms *nothing, nobody,* and *none* are used, then the verb is not negated. The speakers of both SAE and BE know how to negate sentences. The rules are essentially the same, but differ in detail. Both dialects are strictly rule-governed, as is every syntactic process of every dialect in the world.

It has also been said that BE is "illogical" because the copula (that is, the verb *to be*) is deleted in sentences such as *He nice.* Consider the following sentences from SAE and BE:

SAE	BE
He is nice/He's nice.	He nice.
They are mine/They're mine.	They mine.
I am going to do it/I'm gonna do it.	I gonna do it.

Note that wherever the standard can use a contraction (he + is → he's), Black English can delete the copula. The following sentences, however, will show that where a contraction *cannot* be used in SAE, the copula *cannot* be deleted in BE:[3]

SAE	BE
*He is as nice as he says he's.	*He as nice as he say he.
*How beautiful you're.	*How beautiful you.
*Here I'm.	*Here I.

These examples further illustrate that syntactic rules may operate slightly differently from one dialect to another, but that the surface forms of the sentences are derived by rule—they are not strings of words randomly put together. It is interesting to note that many languages allow such copula deletion. In Russian the copula is never used in such sentences. In Swahili, *mimi ni mwanafunzi* "I am a student" is grammatical and so is *mimi mwanafunzi* "I a student" with the copula, *ni,* missing.

In BE, the possessive morpheme *-'s* is absent whenever possession is redundantly specified by word order:

SAE	BE
That is John's house.	That John house.
That is your house.	That you house.
That house is John's.	That house John's.
	(but not *That house John.)
That house is yours.	That house yours.
	(but not *That house your.)

---

[3] Sentences taken from W. Labov, "The Logic of Nonstandard English" (Georgetown University, 20th Annual Round Table, No. 22, 1969).

There is nothing "illogical" about the presence of such a rule; when word order suffices to indicate possession, the possessive ending is "superfluous."

Other BE sentences that are formed by syntactic rules different from those in the grammar of SAE are:

> He done told me.
> I been seen it.
> I ain't like it.
> I been washing the car.

These are not "corruptions" of the standard but dialect sentences that appear strange to nonspeakers of the dialect, although not as strange as the following sentence appears to a nonspeaker of French:

> Il me l'a   donné
> he me it has given
> He has given it to me.

There are many more differences between the grammars of BE and SAE than those we have discussed. But the ones we have listed are enough to show the "regularity" of BE and to dispel the notion that there is anything "illogical" or "primitive" about this dialect.

The study of Black English is important for linguists, of course, but it is also important for nonlinguists. When teachers in an American school teach French or German or Russian, we expect them to know both English and the language they are teaching. Yet, in many schools in our country where the students are primarily speakers of Black English, instruction seldom if ever takes place in Black English. There is nothing inherently wrong with attempting to teach the standard dialect in all schools for nonlinguistic reasons, but the standard will be learned much more easily by speakers of other dialects if teachers are aware of the systematic differences and permit children to use their own dialect to express themselves. Certainly, there would be less of a communication breakdown between students who speak Black English (not to mention other speakers of nonstandard dialects) and their teachers if these nonstandard dialects were not considered to be inferior versions of the standard. Children who read *your brother* as *you bruvver* are using their own pronunciation rules. They would be more likely to respond positively to the statement "In the dialect we are using, the "th" sound is not pronounced [v], as it is in yours" than they would be to a teacher who expressed an attitude of contempt toward their grammar. To give another example, when speakers of BE do not add the -'s in possessive phrases like *Mary hat* (instead of *Mary's hat*), an attempt to "correct" them which assumes that they do not understand possession as a *concept* creates serious problems for both the children and their teachers. The children know perfectly well what they mean, but their teachers may not know that they know, and the children do not know why the teachers cannot understand them and keep telling them they are "wrong." Thus, a linguistic study of the systematic differences between dialects may, hopefully, repair some of the damage which has been done in situations like these—whatever the motivations of those involved.

Another important reason for studying these dialects is that such study provides rich data for an understanding of the extent to which dialects differ and leads to a better knowledge of human language. Furthermore, the history of any dialect reveals important information about language change in general.

Take the history of Black English as an example. It is simple enough to date its beginning—the first blacks arrived in Virginia in 1619. There are, however, different theories as to the factors which led to the systematic differences between Black English and other American English dialects.

One view suggests that the origins of Black English can be traced to the fact that the Negro slaves learned English from their white masters as a second language. The difficulties of second-language learning for an adult are all too clear to anyone who has attempted to do this. The basic grammar may be learned, but many surface differences persist. These differences, it is suggested, were reflected in the grammars constructed by the children of the slaves, since they heard English primarily from the slaves. Had they been exposed to the English spoken by the whites as children, their grammars would have been less different from regular Southern speech. The dialect differences persisted and grew because the black in America was isolated by social and racial barriers as important as the geographic barriers which isolated the New Zealander from other English speakers. The proponents of this theory point to the fact that Black English and Standard American are basically identical in their deep structures; that is, they suggest that the phrase-structure rules are the same but transformational rules and phonological rules change sentences to produce surface differences.

A second view suggests that many of the particular features found in Black English are traceable to influences of the African languages spoken by the slaves. During the seventeenth and eighteenth centuries, Africans who spoke different languages were purposefully grouped together by the slave traders to discourage communication between the slaves, the idea being to prevent slave revolts. This theory suggests that in order to communicate with each other the slaves were forced to use the one common language all had access to, namely, English, and used a simplified form—called a *pidgin*—with various features from West African languages. According to this view, the differences between BE and other dialects are due more to "deep" syntactic differences than to surface distinctions.

That Black English is closer to the Southern dialect of English than to other dialects is quite apparent. This fact does not favor either of the opposing views. The theory which suggests that the Negro slaves imitated the English of their white Southern masters explains the similarities in this way. One might also explain the similarities by the fact that for many decades a large number of Southern white children were raised by black women and played with black children. It is not unlikely that many of the distinguishing features of Southern dialects were acquired from Black English in this way. A publication of the American Dialect Society in 1908–1909 makes this point clearly:

For my part, after a somewhat careful study of east Alabama dialect, I am convinced that the speech of the white people, the dialect I have spoken all my life and the one I tried to record here, is more largely colored by the language of the negroes than by any other single influence.[4]

The two-way interchange still goes on. Standard American English is constantly enriched by words, phrases, and usage originating in Black English, and Black English, whatever its origins, is one of the many dialects of English, influenced by the changes which go on in the other dialects.

Lingua Francas

Language is a steed that carries one into a far country.
Arab proverb

Many areas of the world are populated by people speaking divergent languages. In such areas, where groups desire social or commercial communication, one language is often used by common agreement. Such a language is called a **lingua franca.**

In medieval times, a trade language came into use in the Mediterranean ports. It consisted of Italian mixed with French, Spanish, Greek, and Arabic, and was called Lingua Franca, "Frankish language." The term *lingua franca* was generalized to other languages similarly used. Thus, any language can be a lingua franca.

English has been called "the lingua franca of the whole world," French, at one time, was "the lingua franca of diplomacy," and Latin and Greek were the lingua francas of Christianity in the West and East, respectively, for a millennium. Among Jews, Yiddish has long served as a lingua franca.

More frequently, lingua francas serve as "trade languages." East Africa is populated by hundreds of tribes, each speaking its own dialect, but most Africans of this area learn at least some Swahili as a second language, and this lingua franca is used and understood in nearly every marketplace. A similar situation exists in West Africa, where Hausa is the lingua franca.

Hindi and Urdu are the lingua francas of India and Pakistan, respectively. The linguistic situation of this area of the world is so complex that there are often regional lingua francas—usually the popular dialects near commercial centers. The same situation existed in Imperial China. An old Chinese saying which is still quoted today notes that two people separated by a blade of grass cannot understand each other. In modern China, the Chinese language as a whole is often referred to as *Zhongwen*, which technically refers to the written language, while *Zhongguo hua* refers to the spoken language. Ninety-four percent of the people living in the People's Republic of China are said to speak Han languages, which can be divided

[4] L. W. Payne, "A Word-List from East Alabama," *Dialect Notes*, 3:279–328, 343–391.

into eight major dialects (or language groups) which for the most part are mutually unintelligible. Within each group there are hundreds of dialects. In addition to these Han languages there are more than fifty "national minority" languages, including the five principal ones: Mongolian, Uighur, Tibetan, Zhuang, and Korean. The situation is clearly very complex and for this reason an extensive language reform policy was inaugurated in the People's Republic to spread a standard language, called Putonghua, which embodies the pronunciation of the Peking dialect, the grammar of Northern Chinese dialects, and the vocabulary of modern colloquial Chinese. The Linguistics Delegation sponsored by the American Academy of Sciences, which visited the People's Republic in 1974, was very impressed by the program, which aims at making all Chinese conversant in Putonghua, as a second dialect or language. The native languages and dialects are not considered inferior; rather, the approach is to spread the "common speech" (the literal meaning of *putonghua*) so that all may communicate with each other in this lingua franca.[5]

Certain *lingua francas* arise naturally; others are developed due to government policy and intervention. In many places of the world, however, there are still areas where people cannot speak with neighbors just a few miles away.

Pidgins and Creoles

Padi dɛm; kɔntri; una ɔl we de na Rom.
Mɛk una ɔl kak una yes. A kam bɛr Siza,
a nɔ kam prez am.
Dɛn kin mɛmba bad we pɔsin kin du
lɔŋtem afta pɔsin kin dɔn dai;
bɔt plɛnti tɛm di gud we pɔsin du
kin bɛr wit im bon dɛm.
Mɛk i bi so wit Siza.
Julius Caesar III, ii, translated to Krio by Thomas Decker

A lingua franca is typically a language with a broad base of native speakers, likely to be used and learned by persons whose native language is in the same language family. Often in history, however, missionaries and traders from one part of the world have visited and attempted to communicate with peoples residing in another area. In such cases the contact is too specialized, and the cultures too widely separated for the usual kind of lingua franca to arise. Instead, the two (or possibly more) groups use their native languages as a basis for a rudimentary language of few lexical items and "straightforward" grammatical rules. Such a "marginal language" is called a **pidgin.**

The most notable pidgin that exists today is called **Tok Pisin.** It was once called Melanesian Pidgin English. It is widely used in Papua New

[5] For further information, see W. P. Lehmann, ed., *Language and Linguistics in the People's Republic of China* (Austin, Texas: Texas University Press, 1975). One of the authors of this book, V. Fromkin, was a member of this delegation.

Guinea. Like most pidgins, many of its lexical items and much of its structure are based on just one language of the two or more contact languages,
in this case English. Tok Pisin has about 1,500 lexical items, of which
about 80 percent are derived from English.

Although pidgins are in some sense rudimentary, they are not devoid
of grammar. The phonological system is rule-governed, as in any human
language. The inventory of phonemes is generally small, and each phoneme may have many allophonic pronunciations. In Tok Pisin, for example, [č], [š], and [s] are all possible pronunciations of the phoneme /s/; [ma-
sin], [mašin], and [mačin] all mean *machine*. When a New Guinean says
[masin] and an Englishman says [mašin], the difference in Pidgin is nondistinctive and no more serious than the different *p*'s in *gap* [gæp] and [gæpʰ],
that is, they are freely variant.

Although case, tense, mood, and voice are generally absent from pidgins (as from many nonpidgin languages), one cannot speak an English pidgin by merely using English without inflecting verbs or declining pronouns.
Pidgins are not "baby talk" or Hollywood "Injun talk." *Me Tarzan, you
Jane* may be understood, but it is not pidgin as it is used in West Africa.

Pidgins are simple, but are rule-governed. In Tok Pisin, verbs that take
a direct object must have the suffix -*m,* even if the direct object is absent
in surface structure; this is a "rule" of the language:

> Mi driman long kilim wanpela snek.
> I dreamed that I killed a snake.
> Bandarap em i kukim.
> Bandarap cooked (it).

Other rules determine word order, which, as in English, is usually quite
strict in pidgins because of the lack of case endings on nouns.

With their small vocabularies, pidgins are not very good at expressing
fine distinctions of meaning. Many lexical items bear a heavy semantic bur-
den, with context being relied upon to remove ambiguity. Much circumlo-
cution and metaphorical extension is necessary. All of these factors combine to give pidgins a unique flavor. What could be a friendlier definition
of friend than the Australian aborigine's *him brother belong me,* or more
poetic than this description of the sun: *lamp belong Jesus?* A policeman
is *gubmint catchum-fella,* whiskers are *grass belong face,* and when a man
is thirsty *him belly allatime burn.* And who can top this classic announce-
ment by a Chinese servant that his master's prize sow had given birth to
a litter: *Him cow pig have kittens?*

Pidgin has come to have negative connotations, perhaps because the
best-known pidgins are all associated with European colonial empires. The
Encyclopaedia Britannica once described Pidgin English as "an unruly
bastard jargon, filled with nursery imbecilities, vulgarisms and corruptions." It no longer uses such a definition, since in recent times there is
greater recognition of the fact that pidgins reflect human creative linguistic
ability. Tok Pisin has its own writing system, its own literature, and its own
newspapers and radio programs, and it has even been used to address a
United Nations meeting.

Some people would like to eradicate Tok Pisin. A pidgin spoken on

New Zealand by the Maoris was replaced, through massive education, by Standard English, and the use of Chinese Pidgin English was forbidden by the government of China. It, too, has died out. Pidgins have been unjustly maligned; we must realize that they may serve a useful function. The linguist Robert A. Hall points out that a New Guinean can learn Tok Pisin well enough in six months to begin many kinds of semiprofessional training.[6] To learn English for the same purpose might require ten times as long. In an area with well over 500 mutually unintelligible languages, Tok Pisin plays a vital role in unifying similar cultures.

During the seventeenth, eighteenth, and nineteenth centuries many pidgins sprang up along the coasts of China, Africa, and the New World to accommodate the Europeans. Chinook Jargon is a pidginized American Indian language used by various tribes of the Pacific Northwest to carry on trade. The original Lingua Franca was an Italian-based pidgin used in Mediterranean ports, and Malay, the language of Indonesia and Malaysia, has been highly influenced by a Dutch-based pidgin. Some linguists have even suggested that Proto-Germanic was originally a pidgin, arguing that ordinary linguistic change cannot account for certain striking differences between the Germanic tongues and other Indo-European languages. They theorized that in the first millennium B.C. the primitive Germanic tribes that resided along the Baltic Sea traded with the more sophisticated, seagoing cultures. The two peoples communicated by means of a pidgin, which either grossly affected Proto-Germanic, or actually became Proto-Germanic. If this is true, English, German, Dutch, and Yiddish had humble beginnings as a pidgin.

One distinguishing characteristic of pidgin languages is that no one learns them as native speakers. When a pidgin comes to be adopted by a community as its native tongue, and children learn it as a first language, that language is called a **creole**; the pidgin has become **creolized**. Creoles are more fully developed languages than pidgins, generally having more lexical items and a broader array of grammatical distinctions. In time, they become languages as complete in every way as other languages.

Creoles often arose on slave plantations in certain areas where Africans of many different tribes could communicate only via the plantation pidgin. Haitian Creole, based on French, developed in this way, as did the "English" spoken in parts of Jamaica. Gullah is an English-based creole spoken by the descendants of African slaves on the islands off the coast of Georgia and South Carolina. Louisiana Creole, related to Haitian Creole, is spoken by large numbers of blacks and whites in Louisiana. Krio, the language spoken by as many as 200,000 Sierra Leoneans, developed, at least in part, from an English-based pidgin.

The development of pidgins with subsequent creolization may account for both a reduction in the number of the world's languages (for many languages may be replaced by a single Creole, as is happening today on New Guinea) and much of the linguistic diversity—the multiplicity of languages —in the world today.

[6] Robert A. Hall, *Hands Off Pidgin English* (New South Wales: Pacific Publications, 1955).

Styles, Slang, and Jargon

"Let us rap."

Drawing by Donald Reilly; © 1970 The New Yorker Magazine, Inc.

. . . but there was no law yet against prodding some of the
new veshches which they used to put into the old moloko,
so you could peet it with vellocet or synthemesc or
drencrom or one or two other veshches which would give
you a nice quiet horrorshow fifteen minutes admiring Bog
And All His Holy Angels and Saints in your left shoe with
lights bursting all over your mozg. Or you could peet milk
with knives in it, as we used to say, and this would sharpen
you up and make you ready for a bit of dirty twenty-to-one,
and that was what we were peeting this evening I'm
starting off the story with.
ANTHONY BURGESS, *A Clockwork Orange*

You were probably not surprised to learn that your lan-
guage is "spoken differently" in the different parts of the world; dialects
are a common phenomenon. But you may not be aware that you speak two
or more "dialects" of your own language. When you are out with your
friends, you talk one way; when you go on a job interview, you talk differently. These "situation dialects" are called **styles.**

Nearly everybody has at least an informal and a formal style. In an informal style the rules of contraction are used more often, the syntactic rules of negation and agreement may be altered, and many words are used that do not occur in the formal style. Many speakers have the ability to use a number of different styles, ranging between the two extremes of formal and informal. Speakers of minority dialects sometimes display virtuosic ability to slide back and forth along a continuum of styles that may range from the informal patterns learned in a ghetto to "formal standard." When William Labov was studying Black English used by Harlem youths he encountered difficulties because the youths (subconsciously) adopted a different style in the presence of white strangers. It took time and effort to gain their confidence to the point where they would "forget" that their conversations were being recorded and so use their normal style.

Many cultures have rules of social behavior that strictly govern style. In some Indo-European languages there is the distinction between "*you* familiar" and "*you* polite." German *du* and French *tu* are to be used only with "intimates"; *Sie* and *vous* are more formal and used with nonintimates. French even has a verb *tutoyer* which means "to use the 'tu' form," and German uses the verb *duzen* to express the informal, or less-honorific style of speaking.

Other languages have a much more elaborate code of style usage. In Thai one uses *kin* "eat" to his intimates, and very informally; but he uses *thaan* "eat" informally with strangers, and *rábpràthaan* on formal occasions or when conversing with dignitaries or esteemed persons (like one's parents). Thai also has a style for talking about Buddhist monks. The verb "eat" is *chăn* when said of a monk. The ordinary third-person pronoun in Thai is *khăw* "he, she, it, they," but if the person referred to is a monk a Thai must use *thân*. Japanese and Javanese are also languages with elaborate styles that must be adhered to in certain social situations.

One mark of an informal style is the frequent occurrence of **slang.** Almost everyone uses slang on some occasions, but it is not easy to define the word. One linguist has defined slang as "one of those things that everybody can recognize and nobody can define."[7] The use of slang, or colloquial language, introduces many new words into the language, by recombining old words into new meanings. *Spaced out, right on, hangup,* and *rip-off* have all gained a degree of acceptance. More rarely, slang will come up with an entirely new word for the language, such as *barf, flub,* and *pooped.* Slang often consists of using old words with totally new meanings ascribed to them. *Grass* and *pot* have widened their meaning to "marijuana"; *pig* and *fuzz* are derogatory terms for "policeman"; *rap, cool, dig, stoned, bread,* and *split* have all extended their semantic domain. The words we have cited sound "slangy" because they have not gained total acceptability. Words such as *dwindle, freshman, glib,* and *mob* are former slang words that in time overcame their "unsavory" origin. It is not always easy to know where to draw the line between "slang" words and "regular" words. This seems always to have been true. In 1890, John S. Farmer, coeditor with W. E. Henley of *Slang and Its Analogues,* remarked: "The

---

[7] Paul Roberts, *Understanding English* (New York: Harper & Row, 1958), p. 342.

borderland between slang and the 'Queen's English' is an ill-defined territory, the limits of which have never been clearly mapped out."

Hippie and *pot* are no longer recognized as slang by some persons, but are by others. Also, one generation's slang is not another generation's slang. *Fan* (as in "Dodger fan") was once a slang term, short for *fanatic*. *Phone,* too, was once a slangy, clipped version of *telephone,* as *TV* was of *television*. In Shakespeare's time, *fretful* and *dwindle* were slang, and recently *goof, blimp,* and *hot dog* were all hard-core slang.

The use of slang varies from region to region, as one would expect, so slang in New York and slang in Los Angeles are not the same. Interestingly, the word *slang* is slang in British English for "scold."

Slang words and phrases are often "invented" in keeping with new ideas and customs. They may represent "in" attitudes better than the more conservative items of the vocabulary. Their importance is shown by the fact that it was thought necessary to give the returning Vietnam prisoners of war a glossary of eighty-six new slang words and phrases, from *acid* to *zonked*. The words on this list—prepared by the Air Force—had come into use during only five years. Furthermore, by the time this book is published, many of these terms may have passed out of the language, and many new ones will have been added.

A number of slang words have entered English from the "underworld," such as *snow* for "cocaine," *payola, C-note, G-man, to hang paper* ("to write 'bum' checks"), *sawbuck,* and so forth.

Practically every conceivable science, profession, trade, and occupation has its own set of words, some of which are considered to be "slang" and others "technical," depending on the status of the people using these "in" words. Such words are sometimes called **jargon** or **argot**. Linguistic jargon, some of which is used in this book, consists of terms such as *phoneme, morpheme, case, lexicon, rule, style,* and so on. The existence of argots or jargons is illustrated by the story of a seaman witness being cross-examined at a trial, who was asked if he knew the plaintiff. Indicating that he didn't know what *plaintiff* meant brought a chide from the attorney: "You mean you came into this court as a witness and don't know what *plaintiff* means?" Later the sailor was asked where he was standing when the boat lurched. "Abaft the binnacle," was the reply, and to the attorney's questioning stare he responded: "You mean you came into this court and don't know where *abaft the binnacle* is?"

Like every aspect of language, jargon changes. A recent newspaper article on gambling casinos discussed the dying out of gambler's jargon:

> "Tom" and "George" were signals casino employees used to describe a player.
>
> "Here comes George" meant a good tipper or "live one."
>
> "Tom" meant an approaching person was a poor tipper, a "stiff," a wiseguy, or possibly an irate husband.
>
> Now, the old-timers say, when they occasionally use one of the old signals from habit, the less experienced dealers just stare blankly, or reply, "I didn't know his name was Tom."[8]

[8] Los Angeles *Times,* Nov. 19, 1972.

Many jargon terms pass into the standard language. Jargon spreads from a narrow group until it is used and understood by a large segment of the population, similar to slang. Eventually, it may lose its special status as either jargon or slang and gain entrance into the respectable circle of formal usage.

This is true of the now ordinary French word meaning "head," *tête*, which was once a slang word derived from the Latin *testa*, which meant "earthen pot." But some slang words seem to hang on and on in the language, never changing their status from slang to "respectable." Shakespeare used the expression "beat it" to mean "scram" (or more politely, "leave!"), and "beat it" would be considered by most English speakers to still be a slang expression. Similarly, the use of the word *pig* for policeman goes back at least as far as 1785, when Grose called a Bow Street police officer a China Street pig.

Taboo or Not Taboo

Sex is a four-letter word.
Bumper-sticker slogan

An item in the Los Angeles *Times* included the following paragraph (the names have been deleted to protect the guilty):

> "This is not a Sunday school but it is a school of law," the judge said in warning the defendants he would not tolerate the "use of expletives during jury selection." "I'm not going to have my fellow citizens and prospective jurors subjected to filthy language," the judge added.

How can language be filthy? In fact, how can it be clean? The filth or beauty of language must be in the ear of the beholder, or in the collective ear of society.

There can't be anything about a particular string of sounds which makes it intrinsically clean or dirty, ugly or beautiful. If you tell someone that you pricked your finger when sewing, it would not raise an eyebrow, but if you refer to your professor as a prick, the judge quoted above would undoubtedly consider this a "dirty" word.

Certain words in all societies are considered **taboo**—words that are not to be used, or, at least, not to be used in "polite society." The word *taboo* was borrowed from Tongan, a Polynesian language, and in that society it refers to acts which are forbidden or which are to be avoided. When an act is taboo, reference to this act may also become taboo. That is, first you are forbidden from doing something; then you are forbidden from talking about it.

What acts or words are forbidden reflect the particular customs and views of the society. Some words may be used in certain circumstances and not in others. Peter Farb reports that among the Zuñi Indians it is improper to use the work *takka*, meaning "frogs," during a religious ceremony; what must be used instead is a complex compound word which literally translated would be "several-are-sitting-in-a-shallow-basin-where-they-are-in-liquid."[9]

[9] Peter Farb, *Word Play* (New York: Bantam Books, 1975), p. 85.

In certain societies, words which have religious connotations are considered profane if used outside of formal or religious ceremonies. Christians are forbidden to "take the Lord's name in vain" and this has been extended to the use of curses which are believed to have magical powers. Thus *hell* and *damn* are changed to *heck* and *darn,* perhaps with the belief or hope that this will fool the "powers that be." In England the word *bloody* is a taboo word. One version has it that this is because it originally referred to the blood of Christ. In the Oxford English Dictionary it states that it has been in general colloquial use from the Restoration and is "now constantly in the mouths of the lowest classes, but by respectable people considered 'a horrid word' on a par with obscene or profane language, and usually printed in the newspapers . . . 'b - - - - y.' " It further states that its origin is not quite certain. This itself gives us a clue about "dirty" words; people who use these words often do not know why they are taboo, only that they are, and, to some extent, this is why they remain in the language, to give vent to strong emotional feelings.

Words relating to sex, sex organs, and natural bodily functions make up a large part of the set of taboo words of many cultures. Some languages have no native words to mean "sexual intercourse" but do borrow such words from neighboring people. Other languages have many words for this common and universal act, most of which are considered taboo.

What is rather surprising is that two words or expressions can have the identical linguistic meaning and one can be acceptable for use and the other strictly forbidden or the cause of embarrassment or horror. In English, words which we have borrowed from Latin and French seem to carry with them a "scientific" connotation and thus appear to be technical terms and "clean," while good old native Anglo-Saxon words are taboo. This seems to reflect the view that the vocabulary used by the upper classes was clearly superior to that used by the lower classes, a view that was, of course, held and propagated by the upper classes. Peter Farb points out that this distinction must go back at least as far as the Norman conquest in 1066, when "a duchess *perspired* and *expectorated* and *menstruated*— while a kitchen maid *sweated* and *spat* and *bled*."[10]

There doesn't seem to be any good reason why the word *vagina* is "clean" while *cunt* is "dirty"; or why *prick* or *cock* is taboo, but *penis* is acknowledged as referring to part of the male anatomy; or why everyone clearly *defecates,* but only vulgar people *shit.* For many people, of course, even words like *breast, intercourse, testicles,* and so on are avoided as much as are words like *tits, fuck,* and *balls.* But this is because of nonlinguistic attitudes, not because of the words or language.

The existence of taboo words or taboo ideas stimulates the creation of **euphemisms.** A euphemism is a word or phrase which replaces a taboo word, or which is used in the attempt to avoid either fearful or unpleasant subjects. Probably because in so many societies, including our own, death is something feared, there are a number of euphemisms which have been created to deal with this subject. People are less apt to *die* and more apt to *pass on* or *pass away.* And, those who take care of your *loved ones* who have *passed away* are more likely to be *funeral directors* than *morticians* or *undertakers* these days.

---

[10] Ibid., p. 89.

Ogden Nash's poem "Ode to the Four-Letter Words" exhorts against such euphemisms, as the following verse demonstrates:

> When in calling, plain speaking is out;
> When the ladies (God bless 'em) are milling about,
> You may wet, make water, or empty the glass;
> You can powder your nose, or the "johnny" will pass.
> It's a drain for the lily, or man about dog
> When everyone's drunk, it's condensing the fog;
> But sure as the devil, that word with a hiss
> It's only in Shakespeare that characters – – – –.

The linguist Jay Powell has made an interesting study of euphemisms used by Australian speakers of English.[11] The expressions which revolve around the idea "toilet" or the functions connected with it show that there is more than "prudery" involved, as is illustrated by the Australian euphemisms which replace the verb *urinate:*

> drain the dragon
> syphon the python
> water the horse
> squeeze the lemon
> drain the spuds
> see if the horse has kicked off his blanket
> wring the rattlesnake
> shake hands with wife's best friend
> point Percy at the porcelain
> train Terence on the terracotta

Similar "metaphors" exist for *have intercourse:*

> shag
> root
> crack a fat
> dip the wick
> play hospital
> hide the ferret
> play cars and garages
> hide the egg roll (sausage, salami)
> boil bangers
> slip a length
> go off like a beltfed motor
> go like a rat up a rhododendron
> go like a rat up a drainpipe
> have gin on the rocks
> have a northwest cocktail

These euphemisms, as well as the differences between the accepted Latinate "genteel" terms and the "dirty" Anglo-Saxon terms show that a word or phrase not only has a linguistic **denotative** meaning, but also has what some linguists call a **connotative** meaning, an implication represent-

[11] Paper delivered at the Western Conference of Linguistics, University of Oregon, 1972.

ing a feeling, an emotion, or a value judgment. In learning a language, children learn which words are "taboo," and these taboo words differ from one child to another, depending on the value system accepted in that family or group in which the child grows up.

Thus, while we maintain that words or phrases or language cannot be bad or dirty in themselves, they can be used to express particular values of the speaker. The taboo words reflect society's values, or the opinions of parts of society.

The use of epithets for people of different religions, nationalities, or color tell us something about the users of these words. The word *boy* is not a taboo word when used generally, but when a 20-year-old white man calls a 40-year-old black man "boy," the word takes on an additional meaning; it reflects the racist attitude of the speaker. So also words like *kike, wop, nigger,* and so forth express racist and chauvinist views of society. If racial and national and religious bigotry and oppression did not exist, then in time these words would either die out or lose their racist connotations.

Language and Sexism

doc·tor, *n.* . . . . a man of great learning.
The American College Dictionary, 1947

A businessman is aggressive, a businesswoman is pushy. A businessman is good on details, she's picky. . . . He follows through, she doesn't know when to quit. He stands firm, she's hard. . . . His judgments are her prejudices. He is a man of the world, she's been around. . . . He isn't afraid to say what is on his mind; she's mouthy. He exercises authority diligently; she's power mad. He's close-mouthed; she's secretive. He climbed the ladder of success; she slept her way to the top.
From "How to Tell a Businessman from a Businesswoman," Graduate School of Management, UCLA, *The Balloon,* vol XXII, no. 6

In the discussion of obscenities, blasphemies, taboo words, and euphemisms, we have seen that language use, and the words which are introduced into a language, reflect the views and values of society. We also suggested that a language or words of a language cannot be either good or bad but can only be viewed as such by the people who use it. One word may have positive connotations, while another word with the identical linguistic meaning may have negative connotations. Thus we find the same individual referred to as a terrorist by one group and as a freedom fighter by another. A woman may be referred to as a castrating female (or ballsy women's libber) or as a courageous feminist advocate.

. The question as to whether the language we use affects the culture and views of society is still being debated. But there is pretty much a unanimous opinion that the language we use is affected by the views and values of society. This is very apparent when we look at how the sexism in society is reflected in our language. Language cannot be sexist in itself, just as it can't be "dirty," but it can reflect sexist attitudes just as it can reflect attitudes as to what is or is not considered "taboo."

The fact that on hearing someone say *My cousin is a professor* (or *a doctor*, or *a lawyer*, or *a CPA*, or *the Chancellor of the University*, or *the President of the country*, or *the delegate to the U.N.*) most people would conclude that the cousin was a man has nothing to do with the English language but a great deal to do with the fact that, historically, women have not been prominent in these professions. Similarly, if you heard someone say *My cousin is a nurse* (*elementary school teacher*, *model*, *whore*, *prostitute*), you would no doubt conclude that the cousin was a woman. The linguist Sol Saporta pointed out that it is less easy to understand why the sentence *My neighbor is a blond* brings the response that the speaker is referring to a woman.[12] This could be due to the fact that the physical characteristics of women in our society assume greater importance than those of men because women are constantly exploited as sex objects. This is further borne out by studies analyzing the language used by men in reference to women which often has derogatory or sexual connotations. Such terms go very far back into history and sometimes enter the language with no pejorative implications but gradually gain them. Thus, from Old English *huswif* "housewife" the word *hussy* was derived. Muriel Schulz points out, for example, that "In their original employment, a *laundress* made beds, a *needlewoman* came to sew, a *spinster* tended the spinning wheel, and a *nurse* cared for the sick. But all apparently acquired secondary duties in some households, because all became euphemisms for a mistress or a prostitute at some time during their existence."[13]

Words for women—all with abusive or sexual overtones—abound: *dish, tomato, piece, piece of ass, chick, piece of tail, bunny, pussy, pussycat, bitch, doll, slut, cow*, to name just a few. Many fewer such pejorative terms exist for men.

One striking fact about the asymmetry between male and female terms in many languages is that when there are male/female pairs it is the male form which for the most part is *unmarked* and the female term which is created by adding a bound morpheme or by compounding. We have many such examples in English:

MALE	FEMALE
prince	princess
count	countess
host	hostess
heir	heiress
hero	heroine
Paul	Pauline

One talks of a *male nurse* because it is expected that a nurse will be female, and for parallel reasons we have the compounds *lady doctor, career woman*, and *woman athlete*.

[12] Sol Saporta, "Language in a Sexist Society." Paper delivered at a meeting of the Modern Language Association, New York, December 1974.

[13] Muriel R. Schulz, "The Semantic Derogation of Woman," in B. Thorne and N. Henley, eds., *Language and Sex* (Rowley, Mass.: Newbury House Publishers, 1975), pp. 66–67.

The unmarked, or male, nouns also serve as the general terms, as do the male pronouns. The *brotherhood of man* includes women, but *sisterhood* does not include men. At the University of California at Santa Cruz not only are there *chairpersons* of departments but a *freshperson* class as well as sophomore, junior, and senior classes.

Such changes in the language are taking place and reflect the growing consciousness of sexism in society. Changes in the language follow changes in society; hopefully, they may also affect male attitudes toward women. But the language is not responsible for the sexism; it merely reflects it.

It is, however, unfortunate that the asymmetries mentioned above do exist. The fact that the woman adopts the man's name in marriage can be traced back to early (and to a great extent, current) legal practices. Thus we often refer to someone as Mrs. Jack Fromkin but seldom refer to a man as Mr. Joanne Rodman. We talk of Professor and Mrs. John Smith but seldom, if ever, of Mr. and Dr. Mary Jones. Furthermore, it is insulting to be called a *spinster* and even more so an *old maid* but certainly not to be called a *bachelor*. There is nothing inherently pejorative about the word *spinster*. The connotations reflect the different views society has about an unmarried woman as opposed to an unmarried man. It isn't the language which is sexist; it is society.

There has been an increasing number of researchers who have been investigating language and sex and language and sexism. One area of research has concerned the differences between male and female speech styles. There is nothing inherently wrong in the development of differing styles, which may include intonation, phonology, syntax, and lexicon. What we have been stressing throughout this chapter is that the language is neither good nor bad but its use may be for good or bad. If one views women as inferior, then special speech characteristics will be viewed as inferior. When everyone in society is indeed created equal, and treated as such, there will be little concern for the sexual asymmetries which exist in language.

Language Games

All-may as-way urned-tay o-tay ollity-jay and-may ames-gay.
JOHN MILTON, *Paradise Lost* (in Pig Latin, Dialect 1)

Once you know a language you can use it to speak to others, to write, to read, to make speeches, to think, to tell secrets. Our creative use of language is also revealed by "distorting" language in *regular* ways to create "secret" languages. In all languages, children (and adults) play language games. To the uninitiated, the language is transformed into gibberish, but for the players the distortion hardly interferes with communication and adds special amusement.

Pig Latin is the most common language game of English. Children teach it to one another by some such instructions as: "Take the first sound of each word and put it at the end, and then add *a* [e]." Even Pig Latin has a number of dialects. In one version, if two or more consonants precede the first vowel, the whole "cluster" goes to the end: *strike* [strayk] becomes *ike-stray* [aykstre]. In another, only the first phoneme is moved: *strike* becomes *trike-say* [traykse]. The invention of such "rules" shows that speakers of the language clearly can segment a word into its individual segmental parts, even breaking up consonant clusters, revealing their linguistic competence.

There are at least three Pig Latin dialects, with different rules applying when a word begins with a vowel:

> Dialect 1: Insert an *m* between the end of the word and the *a* sound: *at* becomes *at-may; eat* becomes *eat-may.*
> Dialect 2: Insert an *h: at* becomes *at-hay; eat* becomes *eat-hay.*
> Dialect 3: Insert nothing; just add the *a: at* becomes *at-ay; eat* becomes *eat-ay.*

Speakers of Pig Latin have no problem in "breaking up" words with more than one syllable because they know the language. More than phonology is involved. *Detective* becomes *etective-day,* but football becomes *oot-fay all-bay.* Even though *football* is one word, its compound composition is known by English speakers.

Thousands of such language games exist. In "G gibberish" or "L gibberish" a *g* or *l* suffix is added to each word:

> How do you do → Howg dog youg dog
> → Howl dol youl dol

Sometimes a syllable is inserted after each syllable:

> Better late than never → Bet-eez ter-eez late-eez than-eez nev-eez er-eez

In other languages, prefixes are added:

> English: You can talk skimono jive → sk-you sk-can sk-talk sk-skimono sk-jive
> Russian: Ja idu v kino → Kata-ja kata-i kata-du kata-və kata-ki kata-no

There are rhyming games, as in this French example:

> Crois-tu qu'il m'aime → Croisvois tuvu qu'ilvil m'aimevaime

There are reversals of phonemes, transpositions of phonemes, insertions of syllables, and various combinations of all of these "rules.

One of the most fascinating language games is used by the Walbiri, who are natives of central Australia. The adults use a secret language that may be described as "upside-down talk." Unlike games such as Pig Latin which distort the phonology, upside-down talk distorts meaning. In this language, all nouns, verbs, pronouns, and adjectives are replaced by their semantic opposites. The phonology and syntax remain otherwise unaffected. The sentence *These things are small* means *That one is big; Another is standing on the sky* would mean *I am sitting on the ground;* and *They are just beginning* means *We have come to the end.*

The study of such "secret languages" has provided evidence for linguists wishing to understand the grammars of different languages and language in general. We find support for the assumption that words are stored in abstract phonological representations, that distinct semantic features are specified, that rules exist. The players of these language games reveal over and over that all language is rule-governed.

Research on regional dialects, social dialects, dialect changes, and language games is of linguistic and social interest. The more we look at the fascinating diversity, the more we find that humans everywhere communicate in basically the same way.

Artificial Languages

La inteligenta persono lernas la interlingvon Esperanton rapide kaj facile. (Esperanto for: "The intelligent person learns the international language Esperanto rapidly and easily.")

Since the scattering at Babel, many people have hoped for a return to the blissful state when everyone would speak a universal language. Lingua francas are a step in that direction, but none has gone far enough. Since the seventeenth century, scholars have been inventing artificial languages with the hope that they would achieve universal acceptance and that universal language would bring universal peace. With stubborn regularity the world has rejected every attempt. Perhaps the world has seen too many civil wars to accept this idea.

The obituary column of artificial languages indicates the constant attempts and regular failures: Bopal, Kosmos, Novial, Parla, Spokil, Universala, and Volapük are but a few of the deceased hundreds. Most artificial languages never get beyond their inventors, because they are abstruse and difficult and uninteresting to learn.

One artificial language has enjoyed some success. **Esperanto** was invented by the Polish scholar Zamenhof, who wrote under the pseudonym of Dr. Esperanto ("one who hopes"). He gave his "language" the advantages of extreme grammatical regularity, ease of pronunciation, and a vocabulary which was based mainly on Latin-Romance, Germanic, and Greek. Esperanto is spoken, it is claimed, by several million speakers throughout the world, including some who learned it as one of their native languages. There is a literature written in it, a number of institutions teach it, and it is officially recognized by some international organizations.

Esperantists claim that their language can be learned easily by any intelligent person. But despite the claims of its proponents, it is not maximally simple. There is an obligatory accusative case (*Ni lernas Esperanton* "We're learning Esperanto"), and adjectives and nouns must agree in number (*inteligenta persono* "intelligent person," but *inteligentaj personoj* "intelligent persons"). Speakers of Chinese or Malaysian (and even English) would find this very different from the rules of their grammars. Esperanto is regular insofar as all nouns end in -*o*, with plural -*oj*; all adjectives end in -*a*, with plural -*aj*; the present tense of all verbs ends in -*as*, the future in -*os*, and the past in -*is*; and the definite article is always *la*. But to speakers of Thai, a language that does not have a definite article at all, Esperanto is far from "simple," and speakers of the many languages that indicate tenses without verb endings (as English indicates the future tense with *shall* or *will*) will find that aspect of Esperanto difficult to learn.

A modification of Esperanto, called **Ido** ("offspring" in Esperanto), has further simplified the language by eliminating the accusative case and abolishing adjective and noun agreement, but the basic problem remains. Esperanto is essentially a Romance-based pidgin with Greek and Germanic influence, albeit a highly developed one with an immense vocabulary. It therefore remains "foreign" to speakers of most languages; a Russian or a Hungarian or a Nigerian or a Hindu would find Esperanto as unfamiliar as French or Spanish.

Still, Esperanto is easier to learn than the languages it is derived from, as pidgins usually are, and because of that it has the potential of playing an important role as a second language in unifying linguistically diverse but culturally or economically related peoples.

The problems besetting the world community are basically nonlinguistic, despite the linguistic problems that do exist. Language problems may intensify social and economic problems, but they do not generally cause wars, unemployment, poverty, pollution, disease.

SUMMARY

Every person has his or her own **idiolect** reflecting the particular idiosyncratic features of his or her language. Besides the individual linguistic differences, the language used by groups of speakers may show systematic differences, which are called **dialects.** Dialects develop and are reinforced because languages change, and the changes which occur in one group or area may differ from those which occur in another. Regional dialects and social dialects develop for this reason.

Dialect differences include pronunciation differences (often called "accents"), vocabulary distinctions, and syntactic rule differences. The grammar differences between dialects are not as great as the parts which are shared, thus permitting speakers of different dialects to communicate with each other.

In most countries one dialect assumes the role of being the **standard.** While this particular dialect is not linguistically superior, it may be considered by some to be the only "correct" form of the language. Such a view has unfortunately led to the idea that some nonstandard dialects are "deficient," as is erroneously suggested regarding Black English, the dialect used by large numbers of black Americans. A study of Black English shows it to be as logical, complete, rule-governed, and expressive as any other dialect.

In areas where many languages are spoken, the people often use one language as a **lingua franca** to communicate with each other. In other cases, the languages spoken by two or more groups may be simplified lexically, phonologically, and syntactically to become a **pidgin.** When a pidgin becomes the language learned natively, it is **creolized.** Such **creole languages** exist in many parts of the world.

Besides regional and social dialects, speakers may use different **styles** of their dialect depending on the particular context. **Slang** may not be used in formal papers or situations, but is widely used in speech; **argot** and **jargon** are words used to describe the special terms of a professional or trade group.

In all societies certain acts or behaviors are frowned on, forbidden, or considered **taboo.** The words or expressions referring to these taboo acts are then also avoided, or considered "dirty." Language itself cannot be clean or dirty; the views toward parts of the language reflect the views of society toward the acts or behaviors referred to by the language. Taboo words and acts give rise to **euphemisms,** which are words or phrases which replace the expressions to be avoided. Thus, *powder room* is a euphemism for *toilet.*

Just as the use of some words may reflect society's views toward sex or natural bodily functions, so also some words may reflect racist, chauvinist, and sexist attitudes in society. The language itself is not racist or sexist but reflects these views of various sectors of a society.

The development of jargons and slang attests to the creative linguistic ability of humans. Similarly, the language games played by children and the "secret languages" which are constructed in most cultures further reveal that all languages have built-in mechanisms for expansion.

The communication barriers which exist because of the thousands of languages used in the world have led to the invention of artificial languages which, the inventors hope, could be used universally. All such attempts have failed. Most such languages, including the most widely known, Esperanto, are not "universal" in any sense but are pidgins based on a small number of languages from one language family, and may still be difficult to learn.

EXERCISES

1. On page 268 we cited part of a speech by Mark Antony from Shakespeare's *Julius Caesar,* as translated into Sierra Leone Krio by Thomas Decker. We repeat it here. See how much of it you can understand. Then see if you can find this particular passage in the play. What are some of the ways in which Krio resembles English? List some of the obvious differences between Krio and English as exemplified in this passage:

   Padi dɛm; kɔntri; una ɔl we de na Rom.
   Mɛk una ɔl kak una yes. A kam bɛr Siza,
   a nɔ kam prez am.
   Dɛn kin mɛmba bad we pɔsin kin du
   lɔŋtɛm afta pɔsin kin dɔn dai;
   bɔt plɛnti tɛm di gud we pɔsin du
   kin bɛr wit im bon dɛm.
   Mɛk i bi so wit Siza.

2. In the period from 1890 to 1904, the book *Slang and Its Analogues* by J. S. Farmer and W. E. Henley was published in seven volumes. The following entries are included in this dictionary. For each item: (1) state whether the word or phrase still exists; (2) if not, state what the modern slang term would be; (3) if the word remains but its meaning has changed, provide the modern meaning.

   all out—entirely, completely, as in "All out the best." (The expression goes back to as early as 1300.)

to have apartments to let–to be an idiot; one who is empty-headed.

been there–as in "Oh, yes, I've been there." Applied to a man who is shrewd and who has had many experiences.

belly-button–the navel.

berkeleys–a woman's breasts.

bitch–the most offensive appellation that can be given to a woman, even more provoking than that of whore.

once in a blue moon–extremely seldom.

boss–a master; one who directs.

bread–employment. (1785—"out of bread" = "out of work.")

claim–to steal.

cut dirt–to escape.

dog cheap–of little worth. (Used in 1616 by Dekker: "Three things there are Dog-cheap, learning, poorman's sweat, and oathes.")

funeral–as in "It's not my funeral." "It's no business of mine."

to get over–to seduce, to fascinate.

grub–food.

groovy–settled in habit; limited in mind.

head–toilet (nautical use only).

hook–to marry.

hump–to spoil.

hush money–money paid for silence; blackmail.

itch–to be sexually excited.

jam–a sweetheart or a mistress.

to lift a leg on–to have sexual intercourse.

leg bags–stockings.

looby–a fool

to lie low–to keep quiet; to bide one's time.

malady of France–syphilis (used by Shakespeare in 1599).

nix–nothing.

noddle–the head.

old–money. (1900—"Perhaps it's somebody you owe a bit of the old to, Jack.")

to pill–to talk platitudes.

pipe layer–a political intriguer; a schemer.

poky–cramped, stuffy, stupid.

pot–a quart; a large sum; a prize; a urinal; to excel.

puny–a freshman.

puss-gentleman–an effeminate.

3. Suppose someone said, "I don't got nothin' " and you heard someone reply, "That's an illogical statement, since two negatives make a positive." How would you argue with the "corrector"?

4. Suppose someone asked you to help compile items for a new dictionary of slang. List ten "slang" words that you use regularly and provide a dictionary definition for each.

5. Below are given some words used in British English for which different words are usually used in American English. See if you can find the American equivalents.

a. clothes peg	k. biscuits
b. braces	l. queue
c. lift	m. torch
d. pram	n. underground
e. waistcoat	o. high street
f. shop assistant	p. crisps
g. sweets	q. chips (fish and chips)
h. boot (of car)	r. lorry
i. bobby	s. holiday
j. spanner	t. tin

6. Compile a list of argot (or jargon) terms from some profession or trade (for example, *lawyer, musician, doctor, longshoreman,* and so forth). Give a definition for each term in "nonjargon" terms.

7. Below are listed some sentences representing different English language games. Write each sentence in its undistorted form; state the language-game "rule."

   a. Io tooko myo dogo outo too theo countryo.
   b. this-ly is-ly a-ly more-ly com-ly-pli-ly-cate-ly-ed-ly game-ly.
   c. Mary-shmary can-shman talk-shmalk in-shmin rhyme-shmyme.
   d. betpetterper latepate thanpan nevpeverper.
   e. kool ta eth namow.
   f. thop-e fop-oot bop-all stop-a dop-i opum blop-ew dap-own.
      [ðapə fapʊt bapɔl stape dapi apəm blapu dapawn]

8. Invent a secret language; state the rule(s) which must be used and give five examples.

9. "Translate" the first paragraph of any well-known document or speech—such as the Declaration of Independence, the Gettysburg Address, or the Preamble to the Constitution—into informal, colloquial language.

References

Burling, Robbins. *Man's Many Voices.* New York: Holt, Rinehart and Winston, 1970.

Dillard, J. L. *Black English: Its History and Usage in the United States.* New York: Random House, 1972.

Hymes, Dell, ed. *Language in Culture and Society.* New York: Harper & Row, 1964.

Hymes, Dell, ed. *Pidginization and Creolization of Languages.* Cambridge, England: Cambridge University Press, 1971.

Kirshenblatt-Gimblett, Barbara, ed. *Speech Play.* Philadelphia: University of Pennsylvania Press, 1976.

Labov, W. "The Logic of Nonstandard English." Georgetown University 20th Annual Round Table, Monograph Series on Languages and Linguistics, No. 22, 1969.

Labov, W. "The Study of Nonstandard English." National Council of Teachers of English, Champaign, Ill., 1970.

Lehmann, W. P., ed. *Language and Linguistics in the People's Republic of China*. Austin, Texas: Texas University Press, 1975.

Partridge, Eric. *A Dictionary of Slang and Unconventional English*, 7th ed. New York: Macmillan, 1970.

Thorne, Barrie, and Nancy Henley, eds. *Language and Sex: Difference and Dominance*. Rowley, Mass.: Newbury House Publishers, 1975.

Williamson, Juanita V., and Virginia M. Burke. *A Various Language: Perspectives on American Dialects*. New York: Holt, Rinehart and Winston, 1971.

11

The Syllables of Time: Language Change

> The language of this country being always upon the flux, the Struldbruggs of one age do not understand those of another, neither are they able after two hundred years to hold any conversation (farther than by a few general words) with their neighbors the mortals, and thus they lie under the disadvantage of living like foreigners in their own country.
> JONATHAN SWIFT, *Gulliver's Travels*

All languages change with time. It is fortunate for us that though languages change, they do so rather slowly compared to the human life span. It would be inconvenient to have to relearn our native language every twenty years. In the field of astronomy we find a similar situation. Because of the movement of individual stars, the stellar configurations we call constellations are continuously changing their shape. Fifty thousand years from now we would find it difficult to recognize Orion or the Big Dipper. But from year to year the changes are not noticeable. Linguistic change is also slow, in human, if not astronomical, terms. If we were to turn on a radio and miraculously receive a broadcast in our "native language" from the year 3000, we would probably think we had tuned in some foreign-language station. Yet from year to year, even from birth to grave, we hardly notice any change in our language at all.

Where languages have written records it is possible to see the actual changes that have taken place. We know quite a bit about the history of the English language, because about a thousand years of English is preserved in writing. Old English, spoken in England around the end of the first millennium, is scarcely recognizable as English. (Of course our linguistic ancestors didn't call their language Old English!) A speaker of modern English would find the language unintelligible. There are college courses in which Old English is studied in much the same way as any foreign language like French or Swahili.

The following example from *Caedmon's Hymn* of Old English spoken and written in the period between A.D. 658 and 680 will reveal why it must be studied as a "foreign" language:

Nū sculon herian   heofon-rīces Weard,
Now we must praise   heaven-kingdom's Guardian

Meotodes meahte   and his mōd-ġeþanc
the Creator's might   and his mind-plans,

weorc Wuldor-Fæder,   swā hē wundra ġehwæs,
the work of the Glory-Father, when he of wonders of every one

ēċe Dryhten   ōr astealde
eternal Lord,   the beginning established.

The tenth-century epic *Beowulf*, written in Old English, further exemplifies the need for a translation, as students of English literature well know (the letter þ is pronounced like the *th* in *think*):

Wolde guman findan þone þe him on sweofote sare geteode.
He wanted to find the man who harmed him while he slept.

Almost 400 years later, Chaucer wrote *The Canterbury Tales*. The language used by Chaucer, now called Middle English, was spoken from around 1100 to 1500; as one might expect, it is more easily understood by present-day readers, as is seen by looking at the opening of the *Tales*:

Whan that Aprille with his shoures soote
The droghte of March hath perced to the roote . . .

When April with its sweet showers
The drought of March has pierced to the root . . .

Two hundred years after Chaucer, in a language that can be considered an earlier dialect of Modern English, Shakespeare's Hamlet says:

A man may fish with the worm that hath eat of a king, and eat of the fish that hath fed of this worm.

Shakespeare wrote in the sixteenth century. A passage from *Everyman*, written about 1485, further illustrates why it is claimed that Modern English was already spoken by 1500:

The Summoning of Everyman called it is,
That of our lives and ending shows
How transitory we be all day.
The matter is wonder precious,
But the intent of it is more gracious
And sweet to hear away.

The division of English into Old English (449–1100 A.D.), Middle English (1100–1500), and Modern English (1500–present) is somewhat arbitrary, being marked by the dates of events in English history which profoundly influenced the English language. Thus the history of English and the changes that occurred in the language reflect, to some extent, nonlinguistic history.

An examination of the changes that have occurred during the 1500 years since the "birth" of English shows that the sound system has changed, the syntactic rules have changed, and the semantic system has changed. Since speakers' knowledge of their language is represented by their grammar, the changes that occur in a language are changes in the grammar; all parts of the grammar may change. Although we have discussed linguistic change only in relation to English, the histories of other languages show that similar changes occur in all languages.

Regularity of Sound Change

That's not a regular rule: you invented it just now.
LEWIS CARROLL, *Alice's Adventures in Wonderland*

New York City offers a variety of surprises to its visitors, not the least of which is linguistic. You will not be on the streets of Manhattan for long before you hear a reference to "thoid" avenue, or discover that our little winged friends are called "boids" by many natives.

What you are hearing is a dialect difference, sometimes called an "accent." Remarkably enough, those New Yorkers who speak this dialect pronounce *all* words like *third, bird, first, heard,* and so forth as "thoid," "boid," "foist," "hoid." This is an example of a **regular sound correspondence**. Wherever a Californian, say, pronounces [ər] at the beginning or in the middle of a word, speakers of this New York dialect pronounce [ɔy] ("oi").[1] To a great extent, it is such differences in pronunciation that define different dialects. In a dialect other than our own, many hundreds of words may be pronounced differently, but because the differences are due to a small number of regular sound correspondences, we are able to figure out what is said.

It is safe to assume that the different pronunciations of *third, bird,* and so on did not always exist in English. One of the questions we will investigate in this chapter is how such dialectal differences arose, and why the sound differences are generally regular, and not confined to just a few words.

First, though, we take a look at a similar situation in the history of the English language. In Chaucer's time, 600 years ago, the small rodent we call a mouse [maws] was called a *mūs* [mu:s], and this mūs may have lived in someone's *hūs* [hu:s], which is the way *house* [haws] was pronounced. In general, where we now pronounce [aw], speakers of Chaucer's time pronounced [u:]. This correspondence, like the one between [ər] and [ɔy], is quite regular. For example, *out* [awt] was pronounced *ūt* [u:t] and *south*

---

[1] Some speakers of this dialect use the diphthong [ʌy] or [əy].

[sawθ], *sūð* [su:ð]. Many other such regular correspondences can be found, relating older and newer forms of English. In general, all languages exhibit similar correspondences in their history.

The same situation can be observed when we compare different languages. If you ever studied a Romance language such as French or Spanish, you may have noticed that where an English word begins with *f*, the corresponding word in a Romance language often has a *p*. Thus *father*, French *père*, Spanish *padre*; or English *fish*, French *poisson*, Spanish *pescado*. This *f-p* correspondence is another example of a regular sound correspondence.[2]

Many languages exhibit such correspondences. For instance, the American Indian languages Cree and Ojibwa show a *t-n* correspondence: Cree *atim*, Ojibwa *anim*, "dog"; Cree *nītim*, Ojibwa *nīnim*, "my sister-in-law."

We have already seen evidence that languages change in time. In fact, the regular sound correspondences we observe between older and modern forms of a language are due to changes in the language's phonological system that affect certain sounds, or classes of sounds, rather than individual words. English underwent the sound shift [u:] becomes [aw] centuries ago. The regularity we observe is precisely because it is the *sound* that undergoes the change, not the lexical item.

The process of sound shift can account for dialect differences to a great extent. At an earlier stage of English a sound change of [ər] to [ɔy] took place among certain speakers. The change did not spread, perhaps because these speakers were isolated in some ways, or perhaps because the pronunciation of [ɔy] became a "regionalism" that others did not imitate. Whatever the case, we are quite sure that many dialect differences in pronunciation result from a sound shift whose spread is limited.

It is important to be aware that regional dialect differences in pronunciation arise from the perfectly natural linguistic phenomenon of sound change. Many of the world's modern languages were at first regional dialects that had the good fortune to become widely spoken and to survive as separate languages. Thus we should remember that there is nothing "degenerate" or "illiterate" about regional pronunciations. They are simply a result of natural sound change which failed to spread beyond certain limits. Language change is inevitable, and while it may be desirable to maintain a certain literary standard that spans a number of different dialects, it is absurd to label all change, and all regional variations, as a sign of the corruption of the tongue.

When one dialect undergoes many sound shifts that other dialects of the language do not, that dialect may no longer be intelligible to speakers of the other dialects. At that point, often after many centuries, that dialect is considered a separate language. Thus dialects of a language may in time develop into separate languages. These languages are said to be **genetically related** because they developed from the same ("parent") language. (See the next chapter for some language "families.") All genetically related languages were dialects of the same language at an earlier stage.

---

[2] The individual histories of English and the Romance languages have somewhat obscured the regularity of this correspondence, but even so it is quite striking.

Regular sound correspondences between languages indicate that the languages are genetically related. To see why this is so, consider the diagram in Figure 11-1:

Earlier   Language L containing a sound A breaks into two groups

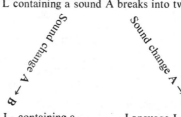

Later   Language L₁ containing a   Language L₂ containing a
            sound B wherever L had   sound C wherever L had
            the sound A   the sound A

Regular sound correspondence
B ⟷ C

Figure 11-1   Genetic sound correspondences.

Speakers of language L, for whatever reasons, split into two groups. One group undergoes a sound shift A → B. The other group undergoes a sound shift A → C. When the sound shifts are complete, the two languages display the sound correspondence B ⟷ C, which can only be explained by positing for each the same parent language, having some sound A wherever L₁ has B and L₂ has C. For the same reason, if we compare L₁ with its older form L, we discover the regular correspondence B ⟷ A.

It is this kind of situation that resulted in the *f-p* correspondence, mentioned above, that is found between English and the Romance languages. Speakers of Indo-European, the language that, ultimately, both English and French descended from, once broke up into smaller groups. One of those groups underwent a sound shift of *p* → *f*. Their descendants eventually spoke "Germanic" languages (for example, English and German). The other Indo-Europeans, in particular the ones whose descendants spoke Romance languages, did not experience the change. Today we see the result of this ancient sound change in the *f-p* sound correspondence.

Thus, we see that one way in which languages change in time is in the phonological system. These changes show up as regular sound correspondences between older and more modern forms of a language, as dialect differences, and as differences between languages that are related genetically by virtue of descent from a common ancestor.

Phonological Change

Etymologists . . . for whom vowels did not matter and who cared not a jot for consonants.
VOLTAIRE

In Chapters 1 and 5 we discussed the kinds of knowledge one has about the phonological system. This includes knowledge of the phonological units in the language, the phonetic pronunciation of morphemes, and the phonological rules. Any of these aspects of the phonology is subject to change.

INVENTORY OF SOUNDS

If you know modern English you know that /x/, the velar fricative, is not part of the English sound system. One of the changes that occurred in the history of our language was the loss of this particular sound. *Night* was once pronounced [nɪxt], *drought* was pronounced [druxt], and *saw* was pronounced [saux]. A phonological change—the loss of /x/—took place sometime between the times of Chaucer and Shakespeare. All the words which were once pronounced with a /x/ no longer include this sound. In some cases the /x/ became /f/, as in *rough* and *tough*. In other cases it disappeared leaving no trace, as in *night* and *light*. In other cases the /x/ became a /k/, as in *elk* (Old English *eolh* [ɛlx]). In some cases it was "vocalized"—that is, it became a vowel, as in *hollow* (Old English *holh* [holx]) or *sorrow* (Old English [sorx]). There are British dialects, such as Scottish, that have kept the /x/ sound in some of these words.

This example shows that the **inventory** of sounds can be changed. English *lost* a phoneme. The inventory can also change by the *addition* of new phonemes to the language. Old English did not have the phoneme /ž/. When words like *azure, measure,* and *rouge* were borrowed from French, this sound was added to the inventory of phonological units.

A phonetically predictable sound may also become distinctive or contrastive and be elevated in status to an independent phonological unit—that is, a phoneme. In Old English, for example, the phoneme /f/ was pronounced as [f] in initial and final position of words, but as [v] between two vowels. Just as [p] and [pʰ] are variants of the same /p/ phoneme in modern English, [f] and [v] were variants of the phoneme /f/ in Old English. Later, when English borrowed words from French with an initial [v], such as *veal*, the [v] was pronounced, perhaps because English already had a pho netic [v]. *Veal* now contrasted with *feel*; the voicing of the labiodental consonant in initial position became distinctive, and [v] became a separate phoneme /v/.

These examples show that phonemes may be lost (for example, /x/), or added (for example, /ž/), or may "split" to become two phonemes (for example, /f/ became /f/ and /v/).

Such changes occur in all languages. For example, in Latin the phoneme /k/ had allophones [č] and [k]. By the time Italian had developed from Latin, both *č* and *k* had achieved phonemic status /č/ and /k/, as exhibited in modern Italian *ciarpa* [čarpa] "scarf" and *carpa* [karpa] "carp." An older stage of Russian had the phoneme /æ/, but in modern Russian [æ] is merely an allophone of /a/ and so has lost its phonemic status.

PHONOLOGICAL RULES

We know that the phonological system includes more than the set of sounds in the language; it also includes the rules which show the different pronunciations of the same morpheme when these morphemes occur in different contexts. These rules "tell" us to pronounce the /t/ which occurs at the end of *democrat* as a [t] but to pronounce it as an [s] in *democracy*.

In the course of linguistic change, such rules can be made more general. At one time, for example, the nouns *house* and *bath* were differentiated from the verbs *house* and *bathe* by the fact that the verbs ended with a short vowel sound (still reflected in the spelling). Furthermore, there was a rule in English (mentioned above in relation to [f] and [v]) which said: "When a voiceless consonant occurs between two vowels, make that consonant voiced." Thus the /s/ in the verb *house* was pronounced [z] and the /θ/ in the verb *bathe* was pronounced [ð]. Then a rule was added to the grammar of English which first "weakened" and then "deleted" unstressed short vowels in certain contexts. The final vowel sound was thus deleted from the verb *house* (that is, we do not pronounce it [hawzə] but [hawz]) and also from *bathe*. The deletion of the vowels also resulted in the new phonemes /z/ and /ð/, which prior to this change were simply the phonetic realizations of the phonemes /s/ and /θ/ between vowels.

Eventually, the "intervocalic-voicing" rule was "dropped" from the grammar of English, showing that the set of phonological rules can change by loss of a rule.

Five hundred years ago, Fante, a language of Ghana, did not have the sounds [ts] or [dz]. The addition of a phonological rule to the language "created" these sounds; this rule said: "pronounce a /d/ as [dz] and a /t/ as [ts] when these phonemes occur before /i/." The addition of this rule to the grammar of Fante did not create new phonemes; [dz] and [ts] are predictable phonetic realizations of the underlying phonemes /d/ and /t/. The grammar, however, was changed—a new rule was added.

At the time of the English colonization of America, the colonial settlers, like their countrymen who remained in England, pronounced the *r* wherever it was spelled: *farm, mother,* and *margin* were pronounced [farm], [mʌðər], and [marǰən]. Between 1607 and 1900 a phonological rule was added to the grammar of British English. The same rule was added to the grammars of the English spoken by the American settlers in Boston, perhaps largely because of the close commercial contact which was maintained between the British and Boston merchants, but it was not added to the grammars of many other Americans. This rule said: "Pronounce an *r* only when the *r* occurs before a vowel."

Thus by 1900, British and Bostonian speakers pronounced *farm* [fam], *mother* [mʌðə], and *margin* [maǰən]: this pronunciation is part of what we call a "Boston accent," or Boston dialect. All English speakers continued to pronounce the *r* in words like *Mary* and *breakfast*. This additional rule did not change the phonological representation of any words. When *four* [fɔ], for example, is followed by a word which begins with a vowel, the /r/ shows up, as in *four acts* [fɔrækts]. Thus the word must be phonemically /fɔr/. The new phonological rule in the grammars of speakers of this "r-less" dialect "deletes" the *r* only when it does not precede a vowel.

The addition of phonological rules can affect the pronunciation of words, resulting in dialect differences, and may cause changes in the phonological inventory as well.

All phonological changes like those cited above took place gradually over the course of many generations of speakers. Those speakers didn't plan the changes, any more than we are presently planning on what changes will take place in English by the year 2300. They would have been aware of the changes only through dialect differences. "Progressive" dialects would have shown the changes sooner than "conservative" dialects, though no one could predict whether the changes would sweep the entire language.

THE GREAT VOWEL SHIFT

The most dramatic change that English underwent involved the vowels. The Great Vowel Shift started right around the death of Chaucer in 1400 and was still taking place when Shakespeare died in 1616. The seven long, or tense, vowels of Middle English underwent the following change:

MIDDLE ENG.		MODERN ENG.	MIDDLE ENG.		MODERN ENG.	
[i:]	→	[ay]	[mi:s]	→	[mays]	*mice*
[u:]	→	[aw]	[mu:s]	→	[maws]	*mouse*
[e:]	→	[i:]	[ge:s]	→	[gi:s]	*geese*
[o:]	→	[u:]	[go:s]	→	[gu:s]	*goose*
[ɛ:]	→	[e:]	[brɛ:ken]	→	[bre:k]	*break*
[ɔ:]	→	[o:]	[brɔ:ken]	→	[bro:k]	*broke*
[a:]	→	[e:]	[na:mə]	→	[ne:m]	*name*

By diagraming the Great Vowel Shift on a vowel chart, we can see that each long vowel underwent an increase in tongue height, with the highest vowels [i:] and [u:] "falling off" to become the diphthongs [ay] and [aw]. In addition, [a] was "fronted."

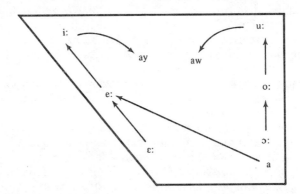

Figure 11-2 The Great Vowel Shift.

These changes are among the most dramatic examples of regular sound shift. The pronunciation of many thousands of words changed. Today, some reflection of this vowel shift is seen in the alternating forms of morphemes in English: *please, pleasant; serene, serenity; sane, sanity; crime, criminal; sign, signal;* and so on.

Reconstructing "Dead" Languages

. . . Philologists who chase
A panting syllable through time and space,
Start it at home, and hunt it in the dark,
To Gaul, to Greece, and into Noah's Ark.
COWPER, *Retirement*

That branch of linguistics which deals with how languages change, what kinds of changes occur, and why they occurred is called **historical and comparative linguistics**. It is *historical* because it deals with the history of particular languages; it is *comparative* because it deals with relations between languages.

The main linguistic work in the nineteenth century was historical-comparative research. In that century, Darwin's theory of evolution had a profound influence on all areas of science, linguistics included, which led to theories of language and language development that were analogous to biological theories. Language was considered to have a "life cycle" and to develop according to evolutionary laws. In addition, it was believed that language, like the human animal, has a "genealogical tree"—that is, that each language can be traced back to a common ancestor. This theory of biological naturalism is known by the name of the *Stammbaum* ("family tree") theory. In the next chapter, we will discuss the Indo-European family tree of languages.

The nineteenth-century historical and comparative linguists based their theories on the observations that there is a resemblance between certain languages, and that the differences among languages showing such resemblance are *systematic*: in particular, that there are regular sound correspondences. They also assumed that languages displaying systematic differences, no matter how slight in resemblance, had descended from a common source language—that is, were genetically related.

The chief goal of the nineteenth-century historical-comparativists was to develop and elucidate the genetic relationships which exist among the world's languages. They aimed to establish the major language families of the world and to define principles for the classification of languages. Their work grew out of earlier research.

In 1786 Sir William Jones (a British scholar who found it best to reside in India because of his sympathy for the rebellious American colonists) delivered a paper in which he observed that Sanskrit bore to Greek and Latin "a stronger affinity . . . than could possibly have been produced by accident." Jones suggested that these three languages had "sprung from a common source" and that probably Germanic and Celtic had the same origin. The classical philologists of the time attempted to disprove the idea that there was any genetic relationship between Sanskrit, Latin, and Greek, since if such a relationship existed it would make their views on language and language development obsolete. A Scottish philosopher, Dugall Stewart, for example, put forth the hypothesis that Sanskrit and Sanskrit literature were inventions of Brahmans, who used Greek and Latin as models to deceive Europeans. This "scholar" wrote on this complex question without knowing a single Sanskrit character, whereas Jones was an eminent Sanskritist.

The work of Jones was supported by many scholars. About thirty years after Jones delivered his important paper, the German linguist Franz Bopp pointed up the relationship between Sanskrit, Latin, Greek, Persian, and Germanic. At the same time, a young Danish scholar named Rasmus Rask corroborated these results, and brought Lithuanian and Armenian into the relationship as well. Rask was the first scholar to describe formally the regularity of certain phonological differences between related languages.

Rask's investigation of these regularities was followed up by the German linguist Jakob Grimm (of fairy-tale fame), who published a four-volume treatise (1819–1822) which specified the regular sound correspondences between Sanskrit, Greek, Latin, and the Germanic languages. It was not only the similarities that intrigued Grimm and the other linguists, but the systematic nature of the differences. Where Latin has a [p], English often has a [f]; where Latin has a [t], English often has a [θ]; where Latin has a [k], English often has a [h].

Grimm pointed out that certain phonological changes must have occurred early in the history of the Germanic languages, which did not take place in Sanskrit, Greek, or Latin. Because the changes were so strikingly regular, they became known as "Grimm's law," which is illustrated in Figure 11-3.

Earlier stage:[3]	bh	dh	gh	b	d	g	p	t	k
	↓	↓	↓	↓	↓	↓	↓	↓	↓
Later stage:	b	d	g	p	t	k	f	θ	x (or h)

Figure 11-3 Grimm's Law (an early Germanic sound shift).

By observing **cognates**, which are words in related languages that developed from the same word (and hence often, but not always, have the same meaning), we can observe sound correspondences and from them deduce sound changes. Thus, from the cognates shown in Figure 11-4 of Sanskrit, Latin, and English (representing Germanic), we observe the regular correspondence *p-p-f* that indicates that the languages are genetically related. We posit Indo-European *p[4] as the reflex of the *p-p-f* correspondence:

INDO-EUROPEAN	SANSKRIT		LATIN		ENGLISH	
*p	p	pitar-	p	pater	f	father
		pad-		pēs		foot
		No cognate		piscis		fish
		pasu		pecu		fee

Figure 11-4 Cognates of Indo-European *p.

A more complete chart of correspondences is given in Figure 11-5. Here we give but a single representative example of each regular cor-

---

[3] This "earlier stage" is the original parent of Sanskrit, Greek, the Romance and Germanic languages, and other languages—namely, Indo-European. The symbols *bh, dh,* and *gh* are "breathy voiced" stop phonemes, often called "voiced aspirates."

[4] The asterisk before a letter indicates a "reconstructed" sound. It does not mean an unacceptable form, nor does it have anything to do with one or more optional elements. It is unfortunate that the asterisk has so many different uses; we apologize.

INDO-EUROPEAN	SANSKRIT		LATIN		ENGLISH	
*p	p	pitar-	p	pater	f	father
*t	t	trayas	t	trēs	θ	three
*k	ś	śun-[5]	k	canis	h	hound
*b	b	No cognate	b	labium	p	lip
*d	d	dva-	d	duo	t	two
*g	j	ajras	g	ager	k	acre
*bh	bh	bhrātar-	f	frāter	b	brother
*dh	dh	dhā	f	fē-ci	d	do
*gh	h	vah-	h	veh-ō	g	wagon

Figure 11-5   Some Indo-European sound correspondences.

respondence. You should bear in mind that in most cases there are *many cognate sets* exhibiting the same correspondence. These cognate sets lead us to reconstruct the Indo-European sound shown in the first column.

We can see that Sanskrit underwent the fewest consonant sound changes in its history, while Latin underwent somewhat more, and Germanic (under Grimm's law) underwent almost a complete restructuring. Nonetheless, the fact that it was the phonemes and phonological rules which changed and not individual words has resulted in the remarkably regular correspondences that allow us to reconstruct much of the sound system of Indo-European.

Exceptions can be found to these regular correspondences, and Grimm was aware of this. He stated: "The sound shift is a general tendency; it is not followed in every case." Karl Verner in 1875 was able to explain some of the exceptions to Grimm's law; "Verner's law" explained why Indo-European **p, t,** and **k** failed to correspond to **f, θ,** and **x,** in some cases: *when the preceding vowel was unaccented, f, θ, and x underwent a further change to b, d, and g.*

A group of young linguists who became known as the Neo-Grammarians went beyond the idea that such sound shifts represented only a tendency, and claimed that sound laws have no exception. They viewed linguistics as a natural science, and therefore believed that laws of sound change were unexceptionable natural laws. The laws which they put forth often had exceptions, however, and could not always be rescued as dramatically as Grimm's law had been rescued by Verner's law. But the work of these linguists provided important data and insights into the changes which occurred and, in some cases, into why such changes do occur. And the assumption that sound change is exceptionless is an important concept in modern historical linguistics.

When the differences among two or more languages are systematic and regular, as exemplified by regular sound correspondences, then, as we have noted, we have reason to believe the languages are related. We often find languages that we feel sure are related, but whose "parent" has long since disappeared. This is certainly the case for the languages studied by Bopp, Rask, Grimm, and those scholars who followed them. It is nonetheless possible that by comparing the "daughter" languages we may deduce many facts about the parent language. The method of **reconstruction** of a

[5] ś is a sibilant different from *s*.

parent language from a comparison of its daughters is called the **Comparative Method**.

A brief example will illustrate how the Comparative Method works. Consider these words in four Romance languages.[6]

FRENCH	ITALIAN	SPANISH	PORTUGUESE	
cher	caro	caro	caro	"dear"
champ	campo	campo	campo	"field"
chandelle	candela	candela	candeia	"candle"

In French we find $š$ where we find k in the three other languages. This regular sound correspondence, $š\text{-}k\text{-}k\text{-}k$, along with other facts, supports the view that French, Italian, Spanish, and Portuguese descended from a common language. The Comparative Method leads us to reconstruct a k in "dear," "field," and "candle" of the parent language. More important, it tells us the k underwent a change to $š$ in French, which did not occur in Italian, Spanish, and Portuguese. Those languages retained the original k of the parent language, Latin.

To use the Comparative Method, analysts identify regular sound correspondences (not always easy to do) in what they take to be "daughter" languages, and for each correspondence, they reconstruct a sound of the parent language. In this way the entire sound system of the parent may be reconstructed. The various phonological changes that occurred in the development of each "daughter" language as it descended and changed from the parent are then identified. Sometimes the sound that analysts choose in their reconstruction of the parent language will be the sound that appears most frequently in the correspondence. This was illustrated above with the four Romance languages.

It is not unusual for other considerations to outweigh the "majority rules" principle. The likelihood of certain phonological changes to occur may persuade the analyst to reconstruct a "minority" sound, or even a sound that doesn't occur at all in the correspondence. For instance, consider data in these four Austronesian languages:[7]

MAORI	HAWAIIAN	SAMOAN	FIJIAN	
hono	hono	fono	vono	"stay, sit"

These data typify *many* instances of the sound correspondence $h\text{-}h\text{-}f\text{-}v$. Based on it, we might be tempted by the Comparative Method to reconstruct h in the parent language. But from other data on historical change, and from phonetic research, we know that h seldom becomes f or v. Generally, the reverse is the case; thus, linguists reconstruct an f in the parent, and posit the sound change "f becomes h" in Maori and Hawaiian, and "f becomes v" in Fijian.

It is by means of the Comparative Method that nineteenth-century linguists, beginning with August Schleicher in 1861, were able to initiate the

---

[6] Data from Winfred P. Lehmann, *Historical Linguistics*, 2nd ed. (New York: Holt, Rinehart and Winston, 1973). *Note:* ch = [š]; c = [k].

[7] Data from Anthony Arlotto, *Introduction to Historical Linguistics* (Boston: Houghton Mifflin, 1972).

reconstruction of the long-lost parent language so aptly conceived by Jones, Bopp, Rask, and Grimm. This language, which we believe flourished about 6000 years ago, we have been calling **Indo-European**.

A single language, through the mechanism of linguistic change, spawned languages now spoken by over half the world's population, represented on every continent.

Historical Evidence

You know my method. It is founded upon the observance of trifles.
SIR ARTHUR CONAN DOYLE, "The Boscombe Valley Mystery"

One might wonder how we know about all these phonological changes. How do we know how Shakespeare or Chaucer or the writer of *Beowulf* pronounced their versions of English? Obviously, we have no phonograph records or tape recordings that would give us direct knowledge of the pronunciation used.

We mentioned that for many languages there are historical records which go back more than a thousand years. These records are studied to find out how languages were pronounced long ago. The spelling in early manuscripts tells us a great deal about the sound systems of older forms of modern languages. If certain words are always spelled one way, and other words another way, it is logical to conclude that the two groups of words were pronounced differently, even if the precise pronunciation is not known. For example, if you didn't know English, but you consistently found that the word which meant "deep hole" was written as *pit*, and the word for a domesticated animal was written as *pet*, it would be safe to assume that these two words were pronounced differently. Once a number of orthographic contrasts are identified, good guesses can be made as to actual pronunciation. These guesses are greatly assisted by certain common words which show up in all stages of the language, allowing their pronunciation to be traced from the present, step by step, into the past.

Another clue to earlier pronunciation is provided by non-English words used in the manuscripts of English. Suppose a French word which scholars know contains the vowel [o:] is borrowed into English. The way the borrowed word is spelled reveals a particular spelling-sound correspondence. A number of spelling symbols were related to certain sounds in this way.

Other documents can be examined for evidence. Private letters are a great source of data. Linguists care little for the gossip they contain but cherish the linguistic information provided. Linguists prefer letters written by "naive" spellers, since they will misspell words according to the way they pronounce them. For instance, at one point in English history all words spelled with *er* in their stems were pronounced as if they were spelled with *ar*. Naive spellings show this to be the case. Some poor letter writer kept writing *clark* for *clerk*, which did his reputation as a scholar little good, though it helped linguists to discover the older pronunciation.

Clues are also provided by the writings of scholars interested in the correct spelling and correct pronunciation of the language of their period. Between 1550 and 1750, there existed a group of people in England known as **orthoepists**, who desired to preserve the purity of English. They busied themselves telling people what they should say, and in so doing they told us how the people of their time actually pronounced words. Suppose an orthoepist lived today who wished all speakers in America to pronounce words "correctly." He might write in his manual: "All those who pronounce *Cuba* with a final *r* are wrong! *Cuba* should not be pronounced as if it were spelled *Cuber*." In the future, scholars would know that there were speakers of English who did pronounce the word in this way.

Probably some of the best clues to earlier pronunciation are provided by puns and rhymes in literature. Two words rhyme if the vowels and final consonants of these words are the same. When a poet rhymes the verb *found* with the noun *wound*, it strongly suggests that the vowels of these two words were identical:

> BENVOLIO: . . . 'tis in vain to seek him here that means to not be found.
> ROMEO: He jests at scars that never felt a wound.

Shakespeare's rhymes are very helpful in reconstructing the sound system of Elizabethan English:

> Where's the place? Upon the heath
> There to meet with Macbeth

In the speech of Shakespeare's Elizabethan audience, *heath* [hɛ:θ] rhymed with *Macbeth* [məkbɛθ]. The pronunciation of *heath* has changed as a result of changes in the sound system of English.

Dialect differences may provide clues as to what earlier stages of a language were like. There are many dialects of English spoken around the world, including a fair number in the United States. By comparing the pronunciation of various words in several dialects, we can "reconstruct" earlier forms and see what changes took place in the inventory of sounds and in the phonological rules. When we study different dialects it becomes apparent that all language change is not "hidden." We can actually observe some changes in progress.

For example, since some speakers of English pronounce *Mary, merry,* and *marry* with three different vowels (that is, [meri], [mɛri], and [mæri], respectively), we suspect that at one time all speakers of English did so. (The different spellings are also a clue.) For some dialects, however, only one of these sounds can occur before /r/, namely the sound [ɛ], so we can "see" a change taking place. When language historians hundreds of years from now are trying to reconstruct the various dialects of English, they will be helped by this "drinking song" sung by students of the University of California:

> They had to carry Harry to the ferry
> And the ferry carried Harry to the shore
> And the reason that they had to carry Harry to the ferry
> Was cause Harry couldn't carry any more.

This song was written by someone who rhymed *Harry, carry,* and *ferry.* It doesn't sound quite as good to those who do not rhyme *Harry* and *ferry.*

One can see such changes taking place. The linguist William Labov has studied "language change in progress" in New York City, and is now studying contemporary linguistic change in the Philadelphia community.

The historical-comparativists working on Indo-European languages, and other languages with written records, had a difficult job, but not nearly so difficult as those scholars who are attempting to discover genetic relationships among languages with no written history. Linguists have, however, been able to establish language families and reconstruct the histories of such individual languages. They first study the grammars of the languages and dialects spoken today and compare the sound systems, the vocabularies, and the syntax, seeing what correspondences exist. By this method, Major John W. Powell, Franz Boas, Edward Sapir, Mary Haas, and others have worked out the complex relationships of American Indian languages. Other linguists have worked with African languages and have established a number of major and minor language families in Africa, each containing many subgroups. It has also been established that over a thousand different languages are spoken in Africa.

Morphological and Syntactic Change

Of all the words of witch's doom
There's none so bad as which and whom.
The man who kills both which and whom
Will be enshrined in our Who's Whom.
FLETCHER KNEBEL

Changes in the phonological component of the grammar are by far the most studied type of language change. This is due to the relative ease with which phonological changes can be recognized, and the success of the Comparative Method in reconstructing extinct members of the Indo-European family. More recently, there has been an increasing interest in change other than phonological. Morphological and syntactic changes in the grammar also take place. Rules of morphology and syntax may be lost, added, or changed. We can observe some of these changes by comparing older and newer forms of the language, or by looking at different dialects.

For example, an advertising slogan once caused a great deal of furor among language "purists" in America. They insisted that "Winston tastes good like a cigarette should" is "bad" English, because they said that there is a "rule" in our grammar stating that *like* can only be followed by a "noun phrase" and cannot be used as a "conjunction" to introduce an embedded sentence. According to them, the slogan should read "Winston tastes good *as* a cigarette should." But the grammar of many speakers of English has changed, so that *like* is now a conjunction, and for them the Winston jingle is a perfectly grammatical sentence.

For a number of centuries, English speakers had no more trouble deciding when to use *who* and *whom* than they had deciding when to use *he* or *him*. The rule which once governed the occurrence of *who* and *whom* is slowly fading out of the language. Some speakers say *I don't know who to give it to*; others still use *whom*. Some speakers are not quite sure which pronoun to use. We are able to witness this change in progress.

Many such changes have occurred in the history of English (and the histories of all languages). An examination of Chaucer's English (end of the fourteenth century) and even Shakespeare's English (beginning of the seventeenth century) makes us aware of some of these changes.

We look again at the opening line of *The Canterbury Tales*:

> Whan that Aprille with *his* shoures *soote* . . .

Literally:

> When that April with his showers sweet . . .

In modern English, the form of the possessive pronoun is *its*. *His* would only be used with an "animate masculine" noun: the rule deriving possessive forms has been changed.

The syntactic rules relating to the English negative construction underwent a number of changes from Old English to the present. In Modern English, negation is expressed by adding *not* or *do not*. One may also express negation by adding words like *never*[8] or *no*:

> I am going → I am not going.
> I went → I did not go.
> I go to school → I never go to school.
> I want meat → I don't want any meat; I want no meat.

In Old English the main negation element was *ne*. It usually occurred before the "helping verb" or **auxiliary** (or before the main verb if there was no auxiliary), as illustrated by these examples from Old English manuscripts:

1. þæt he *na*   siþþan geboren *ne* wurde
   that he never after   born   not would-be
   that he should never be born after that

2. ac hie *ne* dorston þær on cuman
   but they not dared   there on come
   but they dared not land there[9]

Notice in example 1 that not only is the word order different from that in Modern English, but that there are two negatives: *na* (a contraction of *ne* + *a*; "not" + "ever" = "never") and *ne*. This use of a "double negative" which occurred in Old English is considered by some grammarians to be "substandard" and "ungrammatical" today. Whether it is grammatical depends upon the rules of one's own grammar; it was grammatical in Old English, as it is in certain English dialects of modern times.

In addition to the contraction of *ne* + *a* → *na*, other negative contractions occurred in Old English; *ne* could be attached to *habb*- "have," *wes*-

---

[8] From a contraction of *not ever*.

[9] From E. C. Traugott, *The History of English Syntax* (New York: Holt, Rinehart and Winston, 1972). *Note:* þ, or "thorn," was pronounced [θ].

"be," *wit-* "know," and *will-* "will" to form *nabb-, nes-, nyt-,* and *nyll-,* respectively.

We also have "contraction" rules which change *do + not* or *did + not* into *don't* and *didn't*; other contraction rules are similar to those found in Old English: *not + ever → never; will + not → won't; can + not → can't;* and so on. Notice that in our contractions the phonetic form of the negation element in *won't, can't, haven't, isn't,* and *wasn't* always comes at the end of the word. This is because in modern English the grammatical word order puts the *not* after the auxiliary. In Old English the negative element shows up at the beginning, since it typically preceded the auxiliary. The rules of word order have changed.

As late as the fifteenth and sixteenth centuries, one could merely add *not* at the end of an affirmative sentence to negate it. One finds such sentences in the writings of Malory at the end of the fifteenth century:

> He saw you not.

Similarly, such sentences are found in Shakespeare:

> I love thee not, therefore pursue me not.

In modern English, *not* must precede the main verb of the clause, and a *do,* marked for the proper tense, must be inserted, in colloquial use:

> He saw you → he did not see you.
> I love you, therefore pursue me → I do not love you, therefore don't pursue me.

Another change which has occurred in English since Malory's time affected the rules of "comparative" and "superlative" constructions. Today we form the comparative by adding *-er* to the adjective or by inserting *more* before it; the superlative is formed by adding *-est* or by inserting *most*. In Malory one finds many examples of double comparatives and superlatives which are now ungrammatical: *more gladder, more lower, moost royallest, moost shamefullest*. These would be "starred" forms today.

When we study a language whose only source is written records, such as Elizabethan English, we see only sentences that are grammatical unless the author is *deliberately* using ungrammatical sentences. There being no native speakers of Elizabethan English around for us to query, we can only infer what sentences were ungrammatical. Such inference leads us to believe that expressions like *the Queen of England's crown* were ungrammatical in former versions of English. The occurrence of *The Wife's Tale of Bath* (rather than *The Wife of Bath's Tale*) in *The Canterbury Tales* supports this inference. Modern English, on the other hand, allows some rather complex constructions that involve the possessive marker. It is not uncommon to hear an English speaker use possessive constructions such as *The girl whose sister I'm dating's roommate is really pretty,* or *The man from Boston's hat fell off*. Older versions of English would have to resort to an *of* construction to express the same thought (*The hat of the man from Boston fell off*). It is clear that a syntactic change took place that accounts for the extended use of the possessive morpheme *'s*.

To appreciate fully the extent to which the morphological component of a grammar may change, we can look beyond English, or even the family of Germanic languages, and consider other Indo-European languages. These changes in many cases resulted in changes in the syntax. In Classical Latin, as well as in Russian, Lithuanian, and other languages, one finds an extensive system of *case endings* on nouns. Whenever speakers of Latin used a noun, they had to add the correct case suffix to the noun stem, according to the function of the noun in the sentence (all of which a native speaker would do without thinking, of course). Latin had six cases. Below are the different forms (the declension) for the noun *lupus*, "wolf":

CASE	NOUN STEM		CASE ENDING		
nominative	lup	+	us	lupus	The *wolf* runs.
genitive	lup	+	ī	lupī	A sheep in *wolf's* clothing.
dative	lup	+	ō	lupō	Give food *to the wolf*.
accusative	lup	+	um	lupum	I love the *wolf*.
ablative	lup	+	ō	lupō	Run *from a wolf*.
vocative	lup	+	e	lupe	*Wolf*, come here!

In *Alice's Adventures in Wonderland*, Lewis Carroll has Alice give us a brief lesson in grammatical case. Alice, greatly shrunken, is swimming around in a pool of her own tears with a mouse, whom she wishes to befriend:

> "Would it be of any use, now," thought Alice, "to speak to this mouse? Everything is so out-of-the-way down here, that I should think very likely it can talk: at any rate, there's no harm in trying." So she began: "O Mouse, do you know the way out of this pool? I am very tired of swimming about here, O Mouse!" (Alice thought this must be the right way of speaking to a mouse: she had never done such a thing before, but she remembered having seen in her brother's Latin Grammar, "A mouse —of a mouse—to a mouse—a mouse—O mouse!")

Alice gives us an English "translation" of the nominative, genitive, dative, accusative, and vocative cases (she omits the ablative).

Such an extensive case system (of which we have seen only part) was present in Latin, Ancient Greek, and Sanskrit. It was also present in Indo-European, the ancestor of all these languages. Modern languages such as Lithuanian and Russian retain much of the Indo-European case system, but these languages are in the minority. In most modern Indo-European languages, changes have all but obliterated the case system. English still retains the genitive case, calling it possessive (in *a sheep in wolf's clothing*, the noun *wolf* is in the genitive case). Pronouns retain a few more traces: *he* is nominative, *him* is accusative and dative (note the *m* in the Latin accusative), and *his* is genitive.

English has replaced its depleted case system with an equally expressive system of prepositions, and stricter constraints on word order. For example, in Latin *lupus dat dōnum virō* means "the wolf gives a gift to the man." The dative ending ō on *virō* "man" indicates the dative case, or the receiver. In English this same meaning is conveyed either by the preposition *to*, and the word order **accusative object-*to*-dative object**, or by the word order **dative object-accusative object** without the preposition: *The wolf gives the man a gift.* And in English, word order is stricter than in Latin, for in Latin *lupus dōnum virō dat*, literally "the wolf a gift to the man gives," is a grammatical sentence, which it obviously is not in English.

Old English also had a rich case-ending system, as illustrated by the following:

1. CASE	MODERN ENGLISH	OE SINGULAR	OE PLURAL
nominative	stone/stones	stān	stānas
genitive	stone's/stones'	stānes	stāna
dative	stone/stones	stāne	stānum
accusative	stone/stones	stān	stānas

2. CASE	MODERN ENGLISH	OE SINGULAR	OE DUAL	OE PLURAL
nominative	I/we two/we	ic [ɪč]	wit [wɪt]	wē [we:]
genitive	my-mine/our-ours	min [mɪn]	uncer [unker]	ūre/ūser
dative	me/us	mē [me:]	unc [unk]	ūs [u:s]
accusative	me/us	mec [meč]	uncit [unkit]	ūsic [u:sɪč]

In these examples, *stone* represents the principal "strong" masculine noun declension. There were "weak" declensions also. The interesting thing is that the plural of this "strong" declension in the nominative and accusative cases became generalized to all the English regular nouns, another example of historical change.

We have mentioned a phonological rule which weakened certain short unstressed vowels. When the vowel was dropped in the plural form of "stones" [stɔ:nəs] (the stem vowel had changed by this time), it became [stɔwnz], and when the "weak" syllables representing case endings in the forms of the singular, genitive plural, and dative plural were dropped, English lost much of its case system.

With the loss of these case endings, new syntactic rules regulating word order entered the language, possibly so that excessive ambiguity would not result. In Old English, word order was not as crucial, because the language was so highly inflected. The doer of the action (that is, the subject) and the object of the action were revealed unambiguously by various case endings. This does not mean that there was no preferred word order, but even if the normal order was violated, the sentence meaning was perfectly clear. Thus, the following sentences all meant "The man slew the king":

Se man sloh þone kyning.
þone kyning sloh se man.
Se man þone kyning sloh.
þone kyning se man sloh.
Sloh se man þone kyning.
Sloh þone kyning se man.

Se was a definite article used only with the subject noun, and *þone* was the definite article used only with the object noun.

Notice how only the first literal (word-for-word) translation of these Old English sentences would mean what the original meant:

> The man slew the king.
> The king slew the man.
> *The man the king slew.
> *The king the man slew.
> *Slew the man the king.
> *Slew the king the man.

Furthermore, the last four examples would not be grammatical in Modern English as whole sentences—the syntactic rules which determine proper word order are violated.

Thus we see that the syntactic parts of grammars undergo change just as do the phonological components.

Lexical Change

Curl'd minion, dancer, coiner of sweet words.
MATTHEW ARNOLD, "Sohrab and Rustum"

As noted in the previous chapters, knowing a language means knowing what words and morphemes are in the language, and that means knowing what they "mean." These basic units of meaning constitute the vocabulary, or **lexicon,** which is part of the grammar. Changes in the lexicon can include the addition of new words, changes in the meanings of words, or the loss of words.

When speakers start to use a new word—that is, when a word is **added** to the lexicon—the change may be quite obvious and relatively abrupt. When speakers fail to use a word—that is, when a word is **lost** from the lexicon—the process takes place gradually over the course of several generations.

There are a number of ways in which new words can enter the language. In Chapter 6 we discussed *compounding*, the recombining of old words to form new ones, with new meanings. Thousands of common English words entered the language via this process, as the earlier examples showed. A few others may be cited: *afternoon, bigmouth, chickenhearted, do in, egghead, force feed, g-string, icecap, jetset, longshoreman, moreover, nursemaid, offshore, pothole, railroad, sailboat, takeover, undergo, water cooler, x-axis, zoo-ecology*.

We also saw that new words may be formed by derivational processes, as in *uglification*. Other methods for enlarging the vocabulary include word coinage, blends, back-formations, and borrowing.

WORD COINAGE

A new word can be coined—created outright to fit some purpose. Madison Avenue has added many new words to English in this way, showing the truth of the old proverb "Necessity is the mother of invention." *Kodak, nylon, Orlon,* and *Dacron* were names made up for certain consumer items. Specific brand names such as *Xerox, Kleenex, Jell-o, Frigidaire, Brillo,* and *Vaseline* are now often used as the general name for many brands of the actual product. Notice that some of these words were created from existing words: *Kleenex* from the word *clean*, *Jell-o* from *gel, Frigidaire* from *frigid* plus *air*.

ACRONYMS

Drawing by D. Fradon; © 1974 The New Yorker Magazine, Inc.

Acronyms are words derived from the initials of several words. Such words are pronounced as the spelling indicates: NASA as [næsə], UNESCO as [yunɛsko], and CARE as [ker]. *Radar,* from "**r**adio **d**etecting **an**d **r**anging," *laser,* from "**l**ight **a**mplification by **s**timulated **e**mission of **r**adiation," and *scuba* from "**s**elf-**c**ontained **u**nderwater **b**reathing **a**pparatus," show the creative efforts of word coiners, as does *snafu,* which is rendered in polite circles as "situation normal, all fouled up."

BLENDS

Blends are compounds that are "less than" compounds. *Smog,* from *smoke + fog; motel,* from *motor + hotel; urinalysis* from *urine + analysis* are examples of blends that have attained full lexical status in English. *Broasted,* from *broiled + roasted,* is a blend that has limited acceptance in the language, as does Lewis Carroll's *chortle,* from *chuckle + snort.* Carroll is famous for both the coining and the blending of words. In *Through the Looking-Glass* he described the "meanings" of the made-up words he used in "Jabberwocky" as follows:

... "Brillig" means four o'clock in the afternoon—the time when you begin *broiling* things for dinner. ... "Slithy" means "lithe and slimy." ... You see it's like a portmanteau—there are two meanings packed up into one word. ... "Toves" are something like badgers—they're something like lizards—and they're something like corkscrews ... also they make their nests under sun-dials—also they live on cheese. ... To "gyre" is to go round and round like a gyroscope. To "gimble" is to make holes like a gimlet. And "the wabe" is the grass-plot round a sun-dial. ... It's called "wabe" ... because it goes a long way before it and a long way behind it. ... "Mimsy" is "flimsy and miserable" (there's another portmanteau for you).

Carroll's "portmanteaus" are what we have called blends, and such words can become part of the regular lexicon.

THE WIZARD OF ID   **by Brant parker and Johnny hart**

By permission of Johnny Hart and Field Enterprises, Inc.

BACK-FORMATIONS

New words may be formed from already existing words by "subtracting" an affix thought to be part of the old word. Thus *peddle* was derived from *peddler* on the mistaken assumption that the *er* was the "agentive" suffix. Such words are called **back-formations.** The verbs *hawk, stoke, swindle,* and *edit* all came into the language as back-formations—of *hawker, stoker, swindler,* and *editor. Pea* was derived from a singular word, *pease*, by speakers regarding *pease* as a plural. Language purists sometimes rail against back-formations and cite *enthuse* (from *enthusiasm*) and *ept* (from *inept*) as examples of language corruption. Nonetheless, many accepted words have entered the language this way.

EXTENDING WORD FORMATION RULES

New words may also be formed from already existing words which appear to be analyzable—that is, composed of more than one morpheme.

The word *bikini*, for example, is from the Bikini atoll of the Marshall Islands. Since the first syllable *bi-* in other cases, like *bi-polar,* means "two," some clever person called a topless bathing suit a *monokini.* Historically, a number of new words entered the English lexicon in this way. Based on analogy with such pairs as *act/action, exempt/exemption, revise/revision,* new words *resurrect, preempt, televise* were formed from the older words *resurrection, preemption,* and *television.*

ABBREVIATIONS

Abbreviations of longer words or phrases also may become "lexicalized": *nark* for *narcotics agent; tec* (or *dick*) for *detective; telly,* the British word for *television; prof* for *professor; teach* for *teacher;* and *doc* for *doctor* are just a few examples of such "short forms" which are now used as whole words. Some other examples are *ad, bike, math, gas, gym, phone, bus, van.* This process is sometimes called **clipping.**

BORROWINGS

We define borrowing as the "process by which one language or dialect takes and incorporates some linguistic element from another."[10] Borrowing is an important source of language change, and loans from other languages are an important source of new words. Most languages are borrowers, and the lexicon of any language can be divided into native and nonnative words (often called **loan words**). A **native word** is one whose history (or **etymology**) can be traced back to the earliest-known stages of the language.

A language may borrow a word *directly* or *indirectly.* A *direct* borrowing means that the borrowed item is a native word in the language it is borrowed from. The native Middle French word *festa* (Modern French *fête*; the Old French was *feste,* from Latin *festa*) was directly borrowed by Middle English, and has become Modern English *feast.* On the other hand, the word *algebra* was borrowed from Spanish, which in turn had borrowed it from Arabic. English borrowed *algebra* indirectly from Arabic, with Spanish as an intermediary.

Some languages are heavy borrowers; Albanian has borrowed so heavily that few native words are retained. On the other hand, many American Indian languages have borrowed but lightly from their neighbors.

English has borrowed extensively. Of the 20,000 or so words in common use, about three-fifths are borrowed. However, the figure is misleading. Of the 500 most frequently used words, only two-sevenths are borrowed, and since these "common" words are used over and over again in sentences, the actual frequency of appearance of native words is much higher than the statistics on borrowing would lead one to believe. "Little" words such as *and, be, have, it, of, the, to, will, you, on, that,* and *is* are all native to English, and constitute about one-fourth of the words regularly used. Thus it is not unreasonable to suppose that more than four-fifths of the words commonly used in speaking English are native to the language.

One can almost trace the history of the English-speaking peoples by studying the kinds of loan words in the language and when they entered the language. Up until the Norman Conquest in 1066, England was inhabited chiefly by the Angles, the Saxons, and the Jutes, peoples of Germanic origin who came to England in the fifth century A.D. and remained to eventually become the English. (The word *England* is derived from *Angles.*) Originally, they spoke Germanic dialects, from which Old English

[10] Arlotto, op. cit., p. 184. Note that the "borrowee" does not give up the borrowed element.

developed directly, and these contained a number of Latin borrowings, but were otherwise undiluted by foreign elements. These Germanic tribes, who had displaced by force the earlier Celtic inhabitants of the islands, adopted a few Celtic place names, which were borrowings in Old English alongside the Latin, but the Celts were so thoroughly vanquished that their language had little effect on the language of the invaders.

For three centuries after the Norman Conquest, French was the language used for all affairs of state and for most commercial, social, and cultural matters. The West Saxon literary language was abandoned, but regional varieties of English did continue to be used in the homes of the people, and in their churches when they worshipped, and even in the market places of their small villages. During these three centuries, vast numbers of French words entered English, of which these are but a few: *government, crown, prince, state, parliament, nation, jury, judge, crime, sue, attorney, property, miracle, charity, court, lechery, virgin, saint, pray, mercy, religion, value, royal, money, society.*

Until the Norman invasion, when an Englishman slaughtered an ox for food, he ate *ox*. If it was a pig, he ate *pig*. If it was a sheep he ate *sheep*. But "ox" served at the Norman tables was *beef* (*boeuf*), "pig" was *pork* (*porc*), and "sheep" was *mutton* (*mouton*). The French language also gave English the food-preparing words *boil, broil, fry, stew,* and *roast*.

Many languages supplied words for English to borrow and assimilate. Between 1500 and 1700, the time of the Renaissance in England, there was much study of the Greek and Roman classics, and "learned" words from these sources entered our lexicon. In 1476 the printing press was introduced to England by William Caxton, and by 1640, 55,000 books had been printed in English. The authors of these books made free use of many Greek and Latin words, and some people grasped hungrily at this source of erudition. As a result, many words of Ancient Greek and Latin came into the language.

From Greek came *drama, comedy, tragedy, scene, botany, physics, zoology, atomic,* and many other words. Greek roots have also provided English with a means for coining new words. *Thermos* "hot" plus *metron* "measure" give us *thermometer*. From *akros* "topmost" and *phobia* "fear" we get *acrophobia*, "abnormal dread of heights." An ingenious American cartoonist, Robert Osborn, has "invented" some phobias, each of which he gives an appropriate name:

logizomechanophobia	"fear of reckoning machines" from Greek *logizomai* "to reckon or compute" + *mekhane* "device" + *phobia*
ellipsosyllabophobia	"fear of words with a missing syllable" from Greek *elleipsis* "a falling short" + *syllabē* "syllable" + *phobia*
pornophobia	"fear of prostitutes" from Greek *porne* "harlot" + *phobia*[11]

[11] From *An Osborn Festival of Phobias*. Copyright © 1971 by Robert Osborn. Text Copyright © 1971 by Eve Wengler. Reprinted by permission of Liveright Publishers, New York.

Here is a sampling of words borrowed by English from Latin: *bonus, alumnus, quorum, exit, scientific, orthography, describe, advantage, rape, violent*.

Latin, like Greek, has also provided prefixes and suffixes that are used productively with both native and nonnative roots. The prefix *ex-* comes from Latin: *ex-husband, ex-boss, ex-wife, ex-sister-in-law, exhibit, extend, export, exhale, exterminate, exclude, exalt*. The suffix *-able/-ible* is also Latin, borrowed via French, and can be attached to almost any English verb: *writable, readable, answerable, movable, kissable, intelligible, trainable, laughable, typewritable, operable, questionable*.

During the ninth and tenth centuries, the Scandinavian raiders who first raided and then settled on the British Isles left their traces in the English language. In fact, the pronouns *they, their,* and *them* were borrowed from the Scandinavians. This is the only time that English ever borrowed pronouns. Many English words beginning with [sk] are of Scandinavian origin: *scatter, scare, scrape, skirt, skin, sky*.

Ass, bin, flannel, clan, slogan, and *whiskey* are all words of Celtic origin, borrowed at various times from Welsh, Scots-Gaelic, or Irish.

From Dutch we borrowed such words as *buoy, freight, leak, pump, yacht*.

From German, *quartz, cobalt,* and—as we might guess—*sauerkraut* and *beer*.

From Italian, many musical terms, including words describing opera houses, have been borrowed: *opera, piano, virtuoso, balcony,* and *mezzanine*.

Words having to do with mathematics and chemistry were borrowed from Arabic, for early Arab scholarship in these fields was quite advanced. *Alcohol, algebra, cipher,* and *zero* are a representative sample. Often Arabic borrowing finds its way to English through Spanish, the original borrower. Such indirect borrowing is common, and sometimes it is difficult to trace the history of a borrowed word accurately. This is especially true in the case of French and Latin. English has borrowed extensively from both, and since French descended from Latin, confusion may arise as to the actual source. Borrowing both from a language and its ancestor leads to the kind of unusual situation that we find in the etymology of *animal*, which as a noun is borrowed from Latin, but as an adjective (for example, *animal magnetism*) is borrowed from French.

Spanish has loaned us *barbecue, cockroach, guitar,* and *ranch,* as well as *California,* literally "hot furnace."

With the settlement of the "New World," the English-speaking Americans borrowed from Indian languages as well as from Spanish. American Indian languages provided us with *pony, hickory,* and *squash,* to mention a few, and nearly half the state names of the United States are Indian.

Hundreds of "place names" in America are of non-English origin. One certainly can't call Indian names "foreign," except in the sense that they were foreign to English.

American Indian place names: *Connecticut, Potomac, Ohio, Mississippi, Erie, Huron, Michigan, Alleghenies, Appalachians, Ozarks, Massa-*

chusetts, Kentucky, Wisconsin, Oregon, Texas, Chattanooga, Chicago, Milwaukee, Omaha, Passaic, Hackensack.

Spanish place names: *Rio Grande, Colorado, Sierra Nevada, Santa Fe, Los Angeles, San Francisco, Santa Barbara, San Jose, Santa Cruz.*

Dutch place names: *Brooklyn* and, would you believe, *Harlem.*

The influence of Yiddish on English is interesting when one realizes that Yiddish words are used by many non-Jews, as well as non-Yiddish-speaking Jews in America. There was even a bumper sticker quite popular (at least in Los Angeles) reading "Marcel Proust is a yenta." *Yenta* is a Yiddish word meaning "gossipy woman" or "shrew." *Lox* "smoked salmon," *bagel* "a hard roll resembling a doughnut," and *matzo* "unleavened cracker" belong to American English, as well as a number of Yiddish expressions introduced via comedians: *schmaltz, schlemiel, schmoe, kibbitz.*

Other languages also borrow words, and many of them have borrowed extensively from English. Twi speakers drank palm wine before the white man arrived in Africa. Now they also drink [bia] "beer," [hwiski] "whis-key," and [gɔrdɔn ǰin] "Gordon's gin."

The Japanese are playing *besibaru* "baseball," and getting quite good at it, too. Japanese has also borrowed copiously from English technical vocabulary.

Italian is studded with "strange" words like *snack, poster,* and *puzzle* (pronounced "pootsle"), and Italian girls use *blushes* and are warned by their mothers against *petting.*

Young Russians, intently aware of western culture, have incorporated into the Russian language words like *jazz, rock,* and the *twist,* which they dance in their *blue jeans* to *rock music.* At the time of Watergate, *Pravda,* the official Communist Party newspaper, used the word *impeechmente* in-stead of the previously used Russian word *ustraneniye,* which is defined as "removal." The borrowing of non-Russian words is not, however, a new one. Fedorenko, the former Soviet delegate to the United Nations, was quoted in the Los Angeles *Times* (August 7, 1974) as saying "Usage of a foreign word when there is an adequate Russian term is insulting to common sense and taste." In support of his view, he refers to Lenin, whom he quotes as saying, "We are spoiling the Russian language using foreign words without necessity. In addition, we use them wrongly." We are not sure whether Lenin was more concerned about the use or the misuse of foreign words in Russian.

Hebrew, used primarily as a religious language for centuries, seems to have lost a number of the obscenities it once had, and so today Israeli citizens have been forced to borrow some of their "four-letter words" from Arabic, which like most spoken languages possesses a wealth of them. One Arabic obscenity used in Hebrew is *kuss ummak,* meaning "your mother's cunt."

French, a language from which English has borrowed heavily, now bor-rows from English. *Le weekend, le picnique, le bar, le club, le hit parade, les hot dogs,* or *le after shave* may not, however, be as freely used as they were before 1977. A new law went into effect on January 4, 1977, prohibit-ing the use of any foreign expression where an equivalent French term exists; and if a French term does not exist, then advertisers are forced to provide an explanation in French. This law applies to all advertisements and documents relating to the sale of goods in France, and lawbreakers will be fined. This attempt to purge borrowed words from the "pure" French language will undoubtedly fail, as all other such efforts have failed in the past, since language and the users are the final arbiters.

Colombia also has declared a war on non-Spanish words, and along with the French purists who shout "down with Franglais" (in French, of course) there are Italian purists who are upset with the "Italish" (English/Italian) besmirching the language of Dante.

All that this proves is that borrowing is a very common form of lexical change.

LOSS OF WORDS

So far in this section we have discussed how words are *added* to a language. It is also true that words can be *lost* from a language, though a word's departure is never as striking as a new word's arrival. When a new word comes into vogue, its very presence draws attention. But a word is lost by the act of inattention—nobody thinks of it; nobody uses it; and it fades out of the language.

English has lost many words, which a reading of any of Shakespeare's works will quickly make obvious. Here are a few taken from *Romeo and Juliet: beseem* "to be suitable," *mammet* "a doll or puppet," *wot* "to know," *gyve* "a fetter," *fain* "gladly" or "rather," *wherefore* "why."

Semantic Change

His talk was like a stream which runs
with rapid change from rocks to roses.
It slipped from politics to puns;
It passed from Mahomet to Moses.
WINTHROP MACKWORTH PRAED, *The Vicar*

We have seen that a language may gain or lose lexical items. It is also common for lexical items to shift in meaning, providing yet another way in which languages change. There are three ways in which a lexical item may change semantically. Its meaning may become broader; its meaning may become narrower; its meaning may shift.

BROADENING

When the meaning of a word becomes broader, that word means everything it used to mean, and then some. The Middle English word *dogge* meant a specific breed of dog, much like the word *dachshund* in Modern English. The meaning of *dogge* was **broadened** to encompass all members of the species "canis familiaris." The word *holiday* originally meant "holy day," a day of religious significance. Today, of course, the word signifies any day on which we don't have to work. *Butcher* once meant "slaughterer of goats" (and earlier "of bucks"), but its modern usage is more general. Similarly, *picture* used to mean "painted representation," but today you can take a picture with a camera. A *companion* used to mean a person with whom you shared bread, but today it's a person who accompanies you. *Quarantine* once had the restricted meaning "forty days' isolation," and *bird* once meant "young bird." The invention of steam-powered boats gave the verb *sail* an opportunity to extend its dominion to boats without sails, just as the verb *drive* widened in meaning to encompass self-propelled vehicles.

NARROWING

In the King James version of the Bible (1611), God says of the herbs and trees, "to you they shall be for meat" (Genesis 1:29). To a speaker of seventeenth-century English, *meat* meant "food," and *flesh* meant "meat." Since that time, semantic change has **narrowed** the meaning of meat to what it is in Modern English. The word *deer* once meant "beast" or "animal," as its German cognate *Tier* still does. The meaning of *deer* has been narrowed to a particular kind of animal. Similarly, the word *hound* used to be the general term for "dog," like the German *Hund*. Today *hound* means a special kind of dog. Before the Norman Conquest, as we have pointed out before, the words *ox, pig, calf,* and *sheep* meant both the animal and the meat of that animal. The Normans brought with them the words *beef, pork, veal,* and *mutton,* which were borrowed into English, thus narrowing the meaning of *ox, pig, calf,* and *sheep*. The Old English word that occurs as modern *starve* once meant "to die." Its meaning has narrowed to become "to die of hunger." *Token* used to have the broad meaning "sign," but long ago was specialized to mean a physical object that is a sign, such as a *love token. Liquor* was once synonymous with *liquid, reek* used to mean "smoke," and *girl* once meant "young person of either sex."

MEANING SHIFTS

The third kind of semantic change that a lexical item may undergo is a shift in meaning. The word *bead* originally meant "prayer." During the Middle Ages the custom arose of repeating one's prayers (that is, *beads*) over and over and counting them by means of little wooden balls on a rosary. The meaning of *bead* shifted from "prayer" to the visible manifestation of a prayer. The word *knight* once meant "youth" but was elevated in meaning in time for the age of chivalry. *Lust* used to mean simply "pleasure," with no negative or sexual overtones. *Lewd* was merely "ignorant," and *immoral* meant "not customary." *Silly* used to mean "happy" in Old English. By the Middle English period it had come to mean "naive," and only in Modern English does it mean "foolish." The overworked Modern English word *nice* meant "ignorant" a thousand years ago. When Juliet tells Romeo, "I am too *fond*," she is not claiming she likes Romeo too much. She means "I am too *foolish*."

Regional Dialects and Accents

The educated Southerner has no use for an *r* except at the beginning of a word.
MARK TWAIN, *Life on the Mississippi*

Semantic shifts, like most other changes in the grammar, do not take place all of a sudden within the speech community. Rather, they take place gradually, often originating in one region and slowly spreading to others, and often taking place throughout the lives of several generations of speakers.

As we discussed above, when a change occurs in one region and fails to spread to other regions of the speech community, a **dialect difference** arises. When enough such differences give the language spoken in a particular region (for example, the city of Boston) its own "flavor," we identify that version of the language as a **regional dialect**. Most Americans have had some exposure to regional dialects in the United States. The phonological or phonetic distinctions are often referred to as different "accents." A person is said to have a Boston accent, a Brooklyn accent, a Southern accent, a Midwestern drawl, and so on. Diversity of pronunciation is what accounts for such "accents."

A tongue-in-cheek *Language Guide to Brooklyn* illustrates the kinds of pronunciation differences that exist:

> earl: a lubricant
> oil: an English nobleman
> tree: the numeral that precedes four
> doze: the ones yonder
> fodder: male parent

A similar glossary was published to "translate" a Southern dialect:

> sex: one less than seven, two less than than eh-et, three less than noine, foe less than tin.

American regional dialects remain a constant source of humor. A sports writer, Jim Murray, discussing the Southern regional dialect in a column entitled "Berlitz of the South," begins: "When the North conquered the South in the late unpleasantness between the two, it tore down the rebel flag, broke up the Confederacy, sent the carpetbaggers in, but it never could do much about the language."[12] He then provides "a few common translations you may want to have" if you are ever in the South, including:

> watt: primary color, as in "the flag is raid, watt, and blue"
> height: where you don't like someone
> pa: something good to eat
> bike: what you do with a pa
> mine: principal or chief
> mane: Homo sapiens, your best friend is your mine mane
> rod: what you do in auto

[12] Los Angeles *Times*, April 5, 1973.

These regional dialects tell us a great deal about how languages change. Their origins can be traced to the history of the people who first settled America. American English, in all its varieties, derived principally from the English spoken in southern England in the seventeenth and eighteenth centuries.

An example of how regional dialects developed may be illustrated by examining changes in the pronunciation of words with an *r*.

The English colonists who first settled this country pronounced an *r* wherever it was spelled. In the seventeenth century, Londoners and Jamestowners pronounced *farm* as [farm] and *father* as {faðər]. By 1800 the citizens of London no longer pronounced *r* in places where it was formerly pronounced; an *r* was now pronounced only when it occurred before vowels. *Farm* had become [fa:m] and *father* [fa:ðə] and *far* [fa:]. In New England and along the Southern Atlantic Seaboard, close commercial (and linguistic) ties with England were maintained. In these areas, American English reflected the same "*r*-dropping" that occurred in England, but in other regions the change did not enter the language, which is why most Americans today pronounce *r* before consonants as did our English ancestors two hundred years ago.

By the time of the American Revolution, there were three major dialect areas in America: the Northern dialect spoken in New England and around the Hudson River; the midland dialect spoken in Pennsylvania; and the Southern dialect. These dialects differed from each other in systematic ways and from the English spoken in England. Some of the changes that occurred in British English spread to America; others did not. Pioneers from all three dialect areas spread westward. The intermingling of their dialects "leveled" or "submerged" many of their dialectal differences, which is why language used in large sections of the Midwest and the West is very similar. Many of the features which characterized seventeenth-century British persisted in the States long after these were changed in England, as is shown in Table 11-1.

Other regional changes took place in the United States, further separating American regional "accents." In the Southern dialect, for example, when the *r* was dropped it was replaced by a "schwa-like" glide: *farm* is pronounced as two syllables [faəm], as are *four* [foə] and *poor* [poə]. This led Jim Murray to end his column cited above with the admonition: "Also remember, there is no such thing as a one-syllable word." This, of course, is not so, as his own examples show, but it is true that many words which are monosyllabic in Standard American are disyllabic in the Southern dialect: the word *right*, pronounced as [rayt] in the Midwest, New England, and the Middle Atlantic states and in British English is pronounced [raət] in many parts of the South.

Regional dialects also may differ in the words people use for the same object. Hans Kurath, an eminent American dialectologist, opens his paper "What Do You Call It?" by asking: "Do you call it a *pail* or a *bucket*? Do you draw water from a *faucet* or from a *spigot*? Do you pull down the *blinds*, the *shades*, or the *curtains* when it gets dark? Do you *wheel* the baby, or do you *ride* it or *roll* it? In a *baby carriage*, a *buggy*, a *coach*, or a

Table 11-1 Comparison between seventeenth- and nineteenth-century London English

Seventeenth-century London	Nineteenth-century London
1. r was pronounced wherever it was spelled: *farm* [farm], *father* [faðər], *farther* [farðər] (Standard American English of today retains this pronunciation)	1. r was only pronounced when it occurred before a vowel: *farm* [fa:m], *father* [fa:ðə], *farther* [fa:ðə] (In New England and the South, a similar change occurred)
2. The vowel in words like *half, last, path,* and *laugh* was [æ] (This is the vowel still used in these words in Standard American)	2. The vowel [æ] in these words changed to the back vowel [a:] (A similar change occurred in New England: *laugh:* British [la:f], New England [laf]
3. The vowel in *due, duty, true* was a diphthong: *due* [dyu]	3. The diphthong was maintained except after r (The [yu] was also maintained in New England and the South; in Standard American the [yu] became [u] after an alveolar: *due* [du])
4. The *h* in *which, when, what, where* signified a voiceless w /ʍ/; *which* contrasted with *witch* (The contrast was maintained in areas of the Midwest and West)	4. The voiceless /ʍ/ was lost; all *wh* words were pronounced with a voiced /w/; *which* and *witch* became homophones (This change spread to many regions of America)
5. Words like *laboratory, dictionary, cemetery* were given both primary and secondary stress: *laboratory* [lǽbərətɔ̀ri] (American dialects preserved this stress pattern)	5. Secondary stress was lost in such words with subsequent syllable loss, and stress shifted to the second syllable: *laboratory* [ləbɔ́rətri]

cab?"[13] One takes a *lift* to the *first floor* (our *second floor*) in England, but an *elevator* in America; one gets five gallons of *petrol* (not *gas*) in London; in Britain a *public school* is "private" (you have to pay) and if a student showed up there wearing *pants* ("underpants") instead of *trousers* he would be sent home to get dressed. If you ask for a *tonic* in Boston you will get a drink called a *soda* or *soda-pop* in Los Angeles, and a *freeway* in Los Angeles is a *thruway* in New York, a *parkway* in New Jersey, a *motorway* in England, and an *expressway* or *turnpike* in other dialect areas.

Kurath produced **dialect maps**. These were maps on which dialect differences were geographically plotted. For instance, he might use black dots to mark every village whose speakers retained the voiceless *w* pronunciation of *wheelbarrow*, and a white dot where voiced *w* was pronounced. Often in such cases, the black dots fall together, as do the white

[13] Hans Kurath, "What Do You Call It?" in Juanita V. Williamson and Virginia M. Burke, eds., *A Various Language: Perspective on American Dialects* (New York: Holt, Rinehart and Winston, 1971).

dots. These define dialect areas. When a line can be drawn on the map between the areas, it is called an **isogloss.** When you "cross" an isogloss, you are passing from one dialect area to another. Sometimes several isoglosses will coincide, usually at a political boundary, or at a natural boundary such as a river or mountain range. Linguists call these a **bundle of isoglosses,** and the regional dialects thereby defined are particularly distinctive.

Systematic syntactic differences also distinguish dialects. In most American dialects sentences may be conjoined as follows:

John will eat and Mary will eat → John and Mary will eat.

But in the Ozark dialect this transformation is also possible:

John will eat and Mary will eat → John will eat and Mary.

In some American dialects the past tense of *see* is *seen*, as in *I seen it*; for other dialects this would be a starred (ungrammatical) sentence. American speakers use *gotten* in a sentence such as *He should have gotten to school on time*; in British English, only the form *got* occurs. In a number of American dialects the pronoun *I* occurs when *me* would be used in British English and in other American dialects.

Am.	between you and I	*Br.* between you and me
Am.	Won't he permit you and I to swim?	*Br.* Won't he permit you and me to swim?

In British English a syntactic transformation permits the deletion of the pronoun in the sentence *I could have done it* to form *I could have done,* which is not permitted in the American grammar.

With all such differences we still are able to understand the speakers of another dialect. Even though dialects differ as to pronunciation, vocabulary, and syntactic rules, these are minor differences when compared with the totality of the grammar. The largest part of the vocabulary, the sound-meaning relations of words, and the syntactic rules are shared, which is why the dialects are mutually intelligible.

Why Do Languages Change?

Stability in language is synonymous with rigor mortis.
ERNEST WEEKLEY

No one knows exactly how or why languages change. Certainly linguistic changes do not happen suddenly. It is not the case that all speakers of English awoke one morning and decided to use the word *beef* for "ox meat." Nor is it true that all the children of one particular generation grew up to adopt this new word usage. Changes are more gradual, particularly changes in the phonological and syntactic system.

Of course certain changes may occur instantaneously for any one speaker. For example, when a speaker acquires a new word, he doesn't "gradually" acquire it. Even when a new rule is incorporated into his grammar, the rule is either in or not in his grammar. It may at first be an optional rule; he may use it only some of the time, its use perhaps being determined by social context. What is gradual is the spread of certain changes over the entire speech community.

A basic cause of change can be attributed to the way children acquire the language. No one teaches the child the rules of the grammar; each child constructs his or her grammar on his or her own, generalizing rules from the linguistic input he or she receives. As was discussed in Chapter 9, observations of the language used by children show stages in the development of their grammars. The early simple grammars become more and more complex until they approximate the grammars used by adults. The child's grammar is never exactly like the adults'. He or she receives input from many dialects used around him or her, many individual styles, and so on. The features of these grammars may then merge. Certain rules may be simplified or overgeneralized.

The older generation may be using "variable" rules. For example, at certain times they may say "It's I" and at other times "It's me." The less formal style is usually used with children. The next generation may use only the "me" form of the pronoun in this construction. In such cases, the grammar will have changed.

The reasons for some changes are relatively easy to understand. Before the advent of television there was no such word as *television* in the language. It soon became a common lexical item. We have already seen how words may be coined or borrowed, and their entry into the language is not mysterious. Other changes are more difficult to explain. For example, no one knows why vowels shifted in English.

We have also discussed how external borrowing—loans from other languages—can affect the phonological system of a language as well as the lexicon. Thus, when English borrowed French words containing /ž/ and /v/, they were eventually added to the inventory of English phonemes. Metaphorically, we can say that English borrowed /ž/ and /v/ from French.

We have some plausible explanations for some of the phonological changes in languages. Some of these changes are due to physiological mechanisms. Some sounds and combinations of sounds are "easier to pronounce" than others. For example, it is universally the case that vowels are nasalized before nasal consonants. This is because it is difficult to time the lowering of the velum to produce the nasal sound so that it coincides exactly with the production of the consonant. In anticipation of the nasal consonant, then, the velum is lowered during the vowel and the result is a nasalized vowel. As stated in Chapter 4, the effect of one sound on another is called **assimilation;** the vowel **assimilates** to the nasality of the nasal consonant. Once the vowel is nasalized, the contrast that the nasal consonant provided can be equally well provided by the nasalized vowel alone, and the redundant consonant may be deleted. The contrast between oral and nasal vowels which exists in many languages of the world today results from just such a historical sound change.

In French, at one time, *bol* "basin," *botte* "high boot," *bog* "a card game," *bock* "Bock beer," and *bon* "good" were [bɔl], [bɔt], [bɔg], [bɔk], and [bɔ̃n], respectively. Notice that in *bon* there was a final nasal consonant which *conditioned* the nasalization of the preceding vowel. Today, *bon* is pronounced [bɔ̃]; the nasal vowel effectively maintains the contrast with the other words.

Another example from English illustrates how such assimilative processes can change a language. In English when we say *key*, the /k/ is articulated forward in the mouth in anticipation of the high front "palatal" vowel /i/. But when we say the /k/ in *cot*, the [k] is backed in anticipation of the low back vowel [a]. The /k/ in *key* is thus "palatalized." In Old English there were a number of words which began with a palatalized /k^y/. When these were followed by /i/ they developed into our modern palatal affricate /č/, as is illustrated by the following:

OLD ENGLISH [k^y]		MODERN ENGLISH [č]
ciese	→	cheese
cinn	→	chin
cild	→	child

The same process that produced the /č/ in English—the palatalization of the /k/—is also found in many other languages. In Twi, for example, the word meaning "to hate" was once pronounced [ki]. The [k] became [k^y] and then finally a [č], so that today it is pronounced [či].

Such assimilative processes at work in languages gave rise to a "theory of least effort" to explain linguistic change. According to this theory, sound changes are primarily due to linguistic "laziness"; we exert as little effort as possible in speaking. We might call this the "mumbling tendency." We tend to assimilate one sound to another, to drop out unstressed syllables, and so on.

Linguistic history reveals that many exceptional morphemes lost their special status because of a different kind of "laziness." This kind of change has been called **internal borrowing**—that is, we "borrow" from one part of the grammar and apply the rule generally. It is also called **analogic change.** One could say that it is by analogy to *foe/foes* and *dog/dogs* that speakers started saying *cows* as the plural of *cow* instead of the earlier plural *kine*. By analogy to *reap/reaped, seem/seemed*, and *ignite/ignited*, children and adults are presently saying *I sweeped the floor, I dreamed that I went to the Presidential Ball in my Maidenform Bra, She lighted the bonfire*, instead of using *swept, dreamt*, and *lit*.

The same kind of analogic change is exemplified by our "regularization" of exceptional plural forms. We borrowed words like *datum/data, agendum/agenda, curriculum/curricula, memorandum/memoranda, medium/media, criterion/criteria, bandit/banditti, virtuoso/virtuosi*, to name just a few. The irregular plurals of these nouns have been replaced by regular plurals among many speakers: *agendas, curriculums, memorandums, criterias, virtuosos*. Notice that in some cases the borrowed original plural forms were considered to be the singular (as in *agenda* and *criteria*) and that the new plural is therefore a "plural-plural." Also, many speakers now regard *data* and *media* as nouns that do not have plural forms, like *information*.

The "theory of least effort" does seem to account for some linguistic changes, but it cannot account for others. Simplification of grammars occurs, but so does elaboration or complication.

Simplification often reduces redundancies, but some redundancy is required to make language efficient. When case endings are lost, confusion can result unless the grammar compensates for the loss; stricter word-order constraints are thus placed on the grammar. While one sees a tendency toward greater simplification, one also finds a countertendency, the desire to be intelligible.

We find many factors which contribute to linguistic change—simplification of grammars, elaboration (to maintain intelligibility), borrowing, lexical additions. Basically, however, it must be remembered that it is the children learning the language who finally incorporate the ongoing changes or create new changes in the grammar of the language. The exact reasons for linguistic change are still elusive. Perhaps language changes for the same reason all things change: that it is the nature of things to change. As Heraclitus pointed out, thousands of years ago, "All is flux, nothing stays still. Nothing endures but change."

Linguistic Paleontology

History is too serious to be left to historians.
IAIN MACLEOD, in the *Observer* (July 16, 1961)

A fascinating application of historical linguistics is deducing information about the culture and location of an ancient civilization for which we have no written history, using as data its partially reconstructed language. Such studies are known as **linguistic paleontology**, and have been carried out extensively on Indo-European.

We have no direct written knowledge of the Indo-European peoples. They are prehistoric. Yet with Holmesian ingenuity and tenacity, linguists have deduced quite a few things about the ancestors of many of us. For instance, in reconstructing Proto-Indo-European, we find a word for "daughter-in-law," but no word for "son-in-law." This leads us to believe that when a couple "married," they lived in the man's family. This in turn indicates that these people did not form matriarchal families.

We find that the Indo-Europeans had terms for "cow," "sheep," "goat," "pig," "dog," "wolf," "duck," "bee," "oak," "beech," "willow," and "grain." But the lack of terms for vegetables or for special kinds of grain indicates a people that relied heavily on animal sources for food.

The words for "beech," "oak," "salmon," and "wolf," which are known to have existed in Proto-Indo-European, have been used in an attempt to pinpoint the geographical location of the Indo-European speech community. The lack of terms for trees of the Mediterranean or Asiatic areas, such as the olive, cypress, and palm, coupled with the presence of terms for beech and oak trees, which are indigenous to eastern and central Europe, suggests an Indo-European homeland near those places, though this homeland might well have extended as far east as the Volga River. This hypothesis is supported by the presence of terms for "wolf" and "salmon," creatures of that geographic area, and the lack of terms for animals indigenous to Asia. Archeological discoveries in Rumania and the Ukraine support this hypothesis.

Knowing that Proto-Indo-European had no terms for silver, gold, and iron, we can deduce, though not without some doubts, that they were pre-iron-age peoples, placing them in time before 4000 B.C.

For language families without any written history, the attempt to reconstruct an earlier language from several modern languages shown to be related may be the only way of gaining any information about the history of the speakers of those languages. This method has proved to be modestly effective in the case of American Indian languages, although detailed knowledge is still lacking. But we do get a rough picture of where the various American Indian people were at what point in time. Knowing that two languages are closely related, but widely separated geographically, tells us that one or the other group of speakers migrated (or that they both migrated in opposite directions). By linguistic means it is sometimes possible to determine approximately when the languages separated, and therefore when the peoples themselves separated.

By this means, scholars have now concluded that the ancestors of the African Bantu people began their migration about 2,300 years ago, spreading from a small region in Africa throughout much of the continent. Archeologists and linguists have worked together to trace the migration of these people. The historical search started in the nineteenth century, when European explorers found that many of their porters, cooks, and escorts were able to speak a language that was understood in wide areas of Africa. While there were many differences among the languages the explorers encountered, there were also many similarities, and it appeared that all these languages were related. This family of languages was named Bantu by the nineteenth-century German scholar Wilhelm H. I. Bleek, when he found that *mu-ntu* meant "man" and *ba-ntu* meant "men" in many of these languages. It is now generally believed that more than 130 million Africans speak languages derived from a common Bantu ancestor. Through archeological evidence and linguistic evidence the history of these people has been traced. Professor Christopher Ehret of the University of California at Los Angeles has conducted intensive research on the non-Bantu words which have entered the Bantu languages, words which illustrate the sequence of events in the migration of the Bantu people.

Linguistic paleontology thus shows that the study of linguistic change brings with it auxiliary rewards of knowledge in other fields.

A study of linguistic change could have been the inspiration for Shelley, who pointed out in his poem "Mutability" that:

> Man's yesterday may ne'er be like his morrow:
> Nought may endure but Mutability.

SUMMARY

In this chapter we discussed the fact that all languages change through time. Evidence of linguistic change is found in the history of individual languages, and in the **regular correspondences** that exist between different languages and dialects. **Genetically related** languages "descend" from a common "parent" through linguistic change. An early stage in the history of related languages is that they are dialects of the parent language.

All parts of the grammar may change. That is, **phonological, syntactic, lexical,** and **semantic** changes occur. The particular types of changes were discussed: phonemes, phonological and syntactic rules, and words may be added, lost, or altered. The meanings of words also change.

No one knows all the causes for linguistic change. Basically, change comes about through children's restructuring of the grammar. Grammars are both simplified and elaborated; the elaborations may arise to counter the simplifications which could lead to unclarity and ambiguity.

It was shown that some sound changes result from physiological, **assimilative** processes. Others, like the Great Vowel Shift, are more difficult to explain. Grammatical changes may be explained, in part, as **analogic** changes. External borrowing from other languages also affects the grammar of a language.

The study of linguistic change is called **historical and comparative linguistics.** Linguists of the eighteenth and nineteenth centuries studied the internal changes which occurred in a language. They also compared languages, reconstructed earlier forms of particular language families, and classified languages according to their "family trees."

Historical-comparative linguists use many methods and a wide variety of data. Old written records are studied. Differences between related dialects and languages provide important clues to earlier stages. A particularly effective technique for reconstructing "dead" languages is the **Comparative Method.** By comparing the various "daughter" languages (or "daughter" dialects, as the case may be) it is possible to partially reconstruct the linguistic history of a people.

When language change occurs in one region of a language community but not another, **regional dialects** arise. All American regional dialects derive from the seventeenth-century English used by the early settlers. Some of the changes that took place in British English were spread to the American areas which maintained close contact with England, whereas in other areas the earlier forms were preserved.

Finally, we saw that knowledge of the linguistic prehistory of peoples may provide clues to knowledge in other areas of prehistory.

EXERCISES

1. Many changes in the phonological system have occurred in English since 449 A.D. Below are some Old English words (given in their spelling and phonetic forms), and the same words as we pronounce them today. They are typical of regular sound changes that took place in English. What sound changes have occurred in each case?

   Example: OE: hlūd [xlu:d] → Mod. Eng.: loud
           Change: (1) the [x] was lost; (2) the long vowel [u:] became [aw].

OE			MOD E
a. crabbe	[krabə]	→	crab
b. fisc	[fɪsk]	→	fish
c. fūl	[fu:l]	→	foul
d. gāt	[ga:t]	→	goat
e. lǣfan	[læ:van]	→	leave
f. tēþ	[te:θ]	→	teeth

2. The Great Vowel Shift in English left its traces in modern English in such pairs as:

   a. ser*e*ne/ser*e*nity ([i]/[ɛ])
   b. div*i*ne/div*i*nity ([ay]/[ɪ])
   c. s*a*ne/s*a*nity ([e]/[æ])

   List as many pairs as you can which relate [i] and [ɛ] as in example *a*, [ay] and [ɪ] as in example *b*, and [e] and [æ] as in example *c*.

3. At one time in English, the final *g* of the following words was pronounced: *sing, long, bring*. Did a change take place in the phonemic inventory? the phonetic inventory? the phonological rules? Why?

4. Below are given some sentences taken from Old English, Middle English, and early Modern English texts, illustrating some changes which have occurred in the syntactic rules of English grammar. (Note: In the sentences, the earlier spelling forms and words have been changed to conform to modern English. That is, the OE sentence *His suna twegen mon brohte to bæm cyninge* would be written as *His sons two one brought to that king*, which in Modern English would be *His two sons were brought to the king*.) Underline the parts of each sentence which differ from Modern English. Rewrite the sentence in Modern English. State, if you can, what changes must have occurred. Example:

   It *not* belongs to you.
   —SHAKESPEARE, *Henry IV*

   Mod. Eng.: *It does not belong to you.*
   Change: It was once possible to negate a sentence by merely adding the negative morpheme *not* before the verb. Today, one must insert a *do* (in its proper morphological form) in addition to the *not*.

   a. It nothing pleased his master.
   b. He hath said that he would lift them whom that him please.
   c. I have a brother is condemned to die.
   d. I bade them take away you.
   e. I wish you was still more a Tartar.
   f. Christ slept and his apostles.
   g. Me was told.

5. A. The vocabulary of English consists of "native" words and also thousands of borrowed words. Look up the following words in a dictionary which provides the etymologies (history) of words. In each case speculate as to how the particular word came to be borrowed from the particular language.

a. size	h. robot	o. skunk	v. pagoda
b. royal	i. check	p. catfish	w. khaki
c. aquatic	j. banana	q. hoodlum	x. shampoo
c. heavenly	k. keel	r. filibuster	y. kangaroo
e. skill	l. fact	s. astronaut	z. bulldoze
f. ranch	m. potato	t. emerald	
g. blouse	n. muskrat	u. sugar	

   B. The *Encyclopaedia Britannica Yearbook* has usually published a new-word list, which is, in the *Britannica*'s editors' view, a list of those words which had entered the language during the year. Though there was no new-word list in 1977, in 1976 a number of entries were noted, among them *galacto-chemistry, hoolifans* (to describe rowdy fans at a sports event), and *chairperson*. Would you expect a yearbook to publish a "lost-word list," recording the words dropped from the language during the year? Defend your answer.

6. The following are some different pronunciations of the same utterances. How do these illustrate some possible causes for language change? What happens in each case?

   a. lots of money   lota money
   b. I've got to   I gotta
   c. John and Mary   John an Mary
   d. why don't you?   whyncha?
   e. do you want to eat?   wanna eat?
   f. how would you?   howdja [hawǰə]
   g. how do you do   [hadu]
   h. did you eat?   [ǰit]

7. Below is a passage from Shakespeare's *Hamlet,* Act IV, scene iii:

   HAMLET: A man may fish with the worm that hath eat of a king, and eat of
           the fish that hath fed of that worm.
   KING: What dost thou mean by this?   3
   HAMLET: Nothing but to show you how a king may go a progress through the
           guts of a beggar.
   KING: Where is Polonius?   6
   HAMLET: In heaven. Send thither to see. If your messenger find him not there,
           seek him i' the other place yourself. But indeed, if you find him not
           within this month, you shall nose him as you go up the stairs into 9
           the lobby.

   Study these lines and identify every difference in expression between Elizabethan and Modern English that is evident. (For example, in line 3, *thou* is now *you*.)

8. Each pair of words below is pronounced as shown phonetically in at least one American dialect. State whether you pronounce them in this way. If not, state how your pronunciations would differ.

   a. "horse"   [hɔrs]   "hoarse"   [hors]
   b. "morning"   [mɔrnɪŋ]   "mourning"   [mornɪŋ]
   c. "for"   [fɔr]   "four"   [for]
   d. "ice"   [ʌys]   "eyes"   [ayz]
   e. "knife"   [nʌyf]   "knives"   [nayvz]
   f. "mute"   [myut]   "nude"   [nyud]
   g. "pin"   [pɪn]   "pen"   [pɛn]
   h. "hog"   [hɔg]   "hot"   [hat]
   i. "marry"   [mæri]   "merry"   [mɛri]
   j. "cot"   [kat]   "caught"   [kɔt]
   k. "father"   [faðə]   "farther"   [faðə]
   l. (to) "lease" [lis]   (to) "grease"   [griz]
   m. "what"   [ʍat]   "watt"   [wat]
   n. "ant"   [ænt]   "aunt"   [ant]
   o. "creek"   [krik]   "sick"   [sɪk]

9. Here is a table showing, in phonemic form, the Latin ancestors of ten words in modern French:

LATIN	FRENCH	
kor	kør	"heart"
kantāre	šãte	"to sing"
klārus	kler	"clear"
kervus	sɛrf	"hart" (deer)
karbō	šarbɔ̃	"coal"
kwandō	kã	"when"
kentum	sã	"hundred"
kawsa	šoz	"thing"
kinis	sãdrə	"ashes"
kawda ⎫ koda ⎭	kø	"tail"

Are the following statements true or false?

a. The modern French word for "thing" shows that a [k] which occurred before the vowel [o] in Latin became an [š] in French.

b. The French word for "tail" probably derived from the Latin word [koda] rather than from [kawda].

c. One historical change illustrated by these data is that [s] became an allophone of the phoneme /k/ in French.

d. If there was a Latin word *kertus*, the modern French word would probably be *sert*. (Consider only the initial consonant.)

10. Consider these data from two American Indian langauges:

YERINGTON PAVIOTSO = YP	NORTHFORK MONACHI = NM	GLOSS
mupi	mupi	"nose"
tama	tawa	"tooth"
piwɨ	piwɨ	"heart"
sawaʔpono	sawaʔpono	"a feminine name"
nɨmɨ	nɨwɨ	"liver"
tamano	tawano	"springtime"
pahwa	pahwa	"aunt"
kuma	kuwa	"husband"
wowaʔa	wowaʔa	"Indians living to the west"
mɨhɨ	mɨhɨ	"porcupine"
noto	noto	"throat"
tapa	tape	"sun"
ʔatapɨ	ʔatapɨ	"jaw"
papiʔi	papiʔi	"older brother"
patɨ	petɨ	"daughter"
nana	nana	"man"
ʔatɨ	ʔetɨ	"bow," "gun"

A. Identify each sound correspondence. (Hint: There are ten different correspondences of consonants and six different correspondences of vowels.)

B. a. For each correspondence you identified in A not containing an *m* or *w*, reconstruct a proto-sound. (For example, for *h-h*, **h; o-o, *o*.)

   b. If the proto-sound underwent a change, indicate what the change is and in which language it took place.

C. a. Whenever a *w* appears in YP, what appears in the corresponding position in NM?

   b. Whenever an *m* occurs in YP, what two sounds may correspond to it in NM?

   c. On the basis of the position of *m* in YP words, can you predict which sound it will correspond to in NM words? How?

D. a. For the three correspondences you discovered in A involving *m* and *w*, should you reconstruct two or three proto-sounds?

   b. If you chose three proto-sounds in D(a), what are they and what did they become in the two "daughter" languages, YP and NM?

   c. If you chose two proto-sounds in D(a), what are they and what did they become in the "daughter" languages? What further statement do you need to make about the sound changes? (Hint: One proto-sound will become two different pairs, depending on its phonetic environment. This is an example of a **conditioned** sound change.)

E. Based on the above, reconstruct all the words given in the common ancestor from which both YP and NM descended. (For example, "porcupine" is reconstructed as **mihi*.)

References

Anttila, Raimo. *An Introduction to Historical and Comparative Linguistics*. New York: Macmillan, 1972.

Arlotto, Anthony. *Introduction to Historical Linguistics*. Boston: Houghton Mifflin, 1972.

Baugh, A. C. *A History of the English Language*, 2nd ed. New York: Appleton-Century-Crofts, 1957.

Bloomfield, L. *Language*. New York: Holt, Rinehart and Winston, 1933.

Bloomfield, L., and H. Hoijer. *Language History* (from *Language*). New York: Holt, Rinehart and Winston, 1965.

Bloomfield, M. W., and Leonard Newmark. *A Linguistic Introduction to the History of English*. New York: Knopf, 1963.

Cowan, William. *Workbook in Comparative Reconstruction*. New York: Holt, Rinehart and Winston, 1971.

Hoenigswald, Henry M. *Language Change and Linguistic Reconstruction*. Chicago: University of Chicago Press, 1960.

Jespersen, Otto. *Growth and Structure of the English Language*, 9th ed. New York: Doubleday, 1955.

Jespersen, Otto. *Language, Its Nature, Development, and Origin*. London: Allen & Unwin, 1922; New York: Norton, 1964.

King, Robert D. *Historical Linguistics and Generative Grammar*. Englewood Cliffs, N.J.: Prentice-Hall, 1969.

Kurath, H., et al. *Handbook of the Linguistic Geography of New England*. Providence, R.I.: Brown University Press, 1939.

Lass, Roger, ed. *Approaches to English Historical Linguistics: An Anthology* New York: Holt, Rinehart and Winston, 1969.

Lehmann, W. P. *Historical Linguistics: An Introduction*, 2nd ed. New York: Holt, Rinehart and Winston, 1973.

McKnight, George H. *The Evolution of the English Language*. New York: Dover, 1968.

Pedersen, H. *The Discovery of Language*. Bloomington, Ind.: University of Indiana Press, 1962.

Pyles, Thomas. *The Origins and Development of the English Language*. New York: Harcourt, Brace & World, 1964.

Robertson, Stuart, and Frederick G. Cassidy. *The Development of Modern English*. Englewood Cliffs, N.J.: Prentice-Hall, 1969.

Sturtevant, E. H. *Linguistic Change*. Chicago: University of Chicago Press, 1917.

Traugott, Elizabeth Closs. *A History of English Syntax*. New York: Holt, Rinehart and Winston, 1972.

CHAPTER

The Tower of Babel: Languages of the World

Let us go down, and there confound their language, that they may not understand one another's speech.
THE BOOK OF GENESIS

How many people of the world can be brought together so that no one person understands the language spoken by any other person? Considering that there are billions of people in the world, the number of mutually unintelligible languages is rather small—"only" about 3,000, according to one suggestion, and as many as 8,000, according to another. Table 12-1 at the end of this chapter lists some of these languages. Despite the seemingly large number of languages spoken in the world today, one-half of the world's population (2,100,000,000 people) speak but fifteen languages. As the figures in the table show, if you spoke Chinese,[1] English, Hindi, and Russian, you could speak with more than one billion people.

While there are about 300,000,000 native speakers of English, uncounted millions of individuals speak English, with varying degrees of fluency, as an alternate language. In addition, about 60 percent of the world's radio stations broadcast in English and more than half the periodicals of the world are published in English. This dominance of course reflects political and social factors, not linguistic ones.

But even if you knew English, Chinese, Russian, and Hindi, you would be unable to talk to monolingual speakers of Arabic, Xhosa, Persian, Tamil, Navajo, and the several thousand other languages.

If we consider the superficial differences among these individual languages, the situation appears to be chaotic indeed. This has led some people to conclude that languages can differ in infinite or innumerable ways.

---

[1] Actually you would have to know the eight major "dialects" of Chinese, each of which is for the most part unintelligible to speakers of any of the others. The eight share a common written language (see Chapter 13), however, and knowledge of the writing system allows one to communicate in writing with any literate Chinese.

If this were the case, then the attempt to understand the nature of human language would be doomed to failure, since one human language could differ from another to as great an extent as one human language could differ from, say, the "language" of the bees. Fortunately, this does not seem to be the case. The more we learn about the grammars of these languages, the more we see how basically similar they are. By understanding the similarities, and the limitations on the ways languages may differ, we begin to understand the nature of human language in general.

Language Universals

In a grammar there are parts which pertain to all languages; these components form what is called the general grammar. . . . In addition to these general (universal) parts, there are those which belong only to one particular language; and these constitute the particular grammars of each language.
DU MARSAIS, c. 1750

Throughout the ages, philosophers and linguists have been divided on the question of whether there are universal properties which hold for all human languages and are unique to them. Most modern linguists are on the side of the "universalists," since common, universal properties are found in the grammars of all languages. Such properties may be said to constitute a "universal" grammar of human language.

About 1630, the German philosopher Alsted first used the term *general grammar* as distinct from *special grammar*. He believed that the function of a *general grammar* was to reveal those features "which relate to the method and etiology of grammatical concepts. They are common to all languages." Pointing out that "general grammar is the pattern 'norma'· of every particular grammar whatsoever," he implored "eminent linguists to employ their insight in this matter."[2]

Three and a half centuries before Alsted, the scholar Robert Kilwardby held that linguists should be concerned with discovering the nature of language in general. So concerned was Kilwardby with universal grammar that he excluded considerations of the characteristics of particular languages, which he believed to be as "irrelevant to a science of grammar as the material of the measuring rod or the physical characteristics of objects were to geometry."[3] In a sense, Kilwardby was too much of a universalist, for the particular properties of individual languages are relevant to the discovery of language universals, and are, in addition, of interest for their own sake.

The emphasis these scholars placed on the universal properties of language may lead someone attempting to study Latin, Greek, French, or Swahili as a second language to assert, in frustration, that those ancient scholars were so hidden in their ivory towers that they confused reality

---

[2] V. Salmon, review of *Cartesian Linguistics* by N. Chomsky, *Journal of Linguistics* 5: 165–187.

[3] V. Salmon, op. cit.

with idle speculation. Yet, if we summarize some of what has already been discussed in previous chapters, we may better understand the universalist's position. The following list of "linguistic universals" is far from complete; literally hundreds of entries could be added:

1. Wherever man exists, language exists.
2. There are no primitive languages—all languages are equally complex and equally capable of expressing any idea in the universe. The vocabulary of any language can be expanded to include new words for new concepts.
3. All languages change through time.
4. All normal human languages utilize sounds to express meaning, and the relationships between sounds and meanings are for the most part arbitrary.[4]
5. All normal human languages utilize a finite set of discrete sounds which are combined to form "meaningful" elements (morphemes), which themselves are combined to form "whole thoughts" (sentences).
6. All grammars contain phonological and syntactic rules of a similar kind.
7. Similar grammatical categories (for example, noun, verb) are found in all languages.
8. There are universal semantic concepts found in every language in the world. Every language has a way of referring to past time, the ability to negate, the ability to form questions, and so on.
9. Speakers of all human languages are capable of producing and comprehending an infinite set of sentences.
10. Any normal child, born anywhere in the world, of any racial, geographical, social, or economic heritage, is capable of learning any language to which he or she is exposed. The differences we find among languages cannot be due to biological reasons.

It seems that Alsted and Du Marsais (and we could add many other "universalists" from all ages) were not spinning idle thoughts. We all speak "human language."

In addition to the foregoing **absolute universals,** languages have **universal tendencies,** which are properties shared by the overwhelming majority of languages, but which admit exception. The number of universal tendencies that have been discovered is quite large. Here are a few:

1. Languages tend to have at least one nasal phoneme, and when they have only one, it tends to be /n/. When there are two, the second one is usually /m/.
2. If a language has fricatives (most do), it will have /s/.
3. A stop in the labial region tends to be bilabial; a fricative in the labial region tends to be labiodental.

[4] Sign languages of the deaf, of course, do not use sounds. They are discussed in a later section.

4. In most languages, the "subject" of the sentence precedes the "object."
5. Languages tend to incorporate the following semantic distinctions into certain words of the language: dry/wet (for example, *dirt/mud*), young/old, alive/dead, long/short, male/female, light/dark, and so on.

Language Without Sounds

People talking without speaking,
People hearing without listening. . . .
PAUL SIMON, "The Sounds of Silence"[5]

© 1977 United Feature Syndicate, Inc.

There are human languages that do not utilize sounds to express meanings. The various sign languages of the deaf, in which hand and body gesticulations carry meaning, are fully developed languages. Their "speakers" are capable of creating unlimited numbers of new sentences that express delicate shades of meaning, just like the speakers of spoken languages do.

About one in a thousand babies is born deaf, or with a severe hearing deficiency. One major effect of such a tragedy is the difficulty the deaf have in learning a spoken language. It is extremely difficult to learn to speak naturally for those unable to hear language. Normal speech also depends to a great extent on constant auditory feedback. Hence a deaf child will not learn to speak without extensive training in special schools or programs designed especially for the deaf.

Although deaf persons can be taught to speak a language intelligibly, they can never understand speech as well as a hearing person. Seventy-five percent of the words spoken cannot be read on the lips with any degree of accuracy.

If, however, human language is universal in the sense that all members

---

[5] Paul Simon, "The Sounds of Silence"; © 1964 by Paul Simon. Used by permission of the publisher.

of the human species have the ability to learn a language, it is not surprising that nonspoken languages developed as a substitute for spoken languages among the nonhearing part of humanity. Deaf children learn sign language, if that is the language used around them, in much the same way as normal, hearing children learn spoken language. No one teaches them the language; they construct the grammars of the particular sign language used which they receive as input. When deaf children are born to hearing parents, they must be exposed to speakers of a sign language in order to learn it. Often, hearing members of the family will learn sign language in order to be able to communicate with a deaf family member.

The major language used by the deaf in the United States is **American Sign Language** (or AMESLAN or ASL). AMESLAN is an independent, fully developed language which historically is an outgrowth of the sign language used in France and brought to the United States by the great deaf educator Gallaudet. It has its own morphology, syntax, and semantics, and its formal units corresponding to the phonology of spoken language have been called **cheremes** by some scholars of sign language.

The signs of the language which correspond to morphemes or words of spoken language can be described by a number of different feature sets, including the hand configuration, the motion of the hand(s) toward or away from the body, the part of the body toward which the motion is directed, and so forth. For example, the sign that means "arm" is described as a flat hand, moving to touch the upper arm. Thus it has three features: flat hand, motion toward, upper arm. Stokoe calls these features *cheremes* and lists a set of 55 out of which the signs of any particular sign language are composed.[6] Just as spoken language has sequences of sounds which are not permitted in the language, so sign languages have combinations of features not permitted. These differ from one sign language to another, just as the constraints on sounds and sound sequences differ from one spoken language to another. A permissible sign in a Chinese sign language may not be a permissible sign in AMESLAN, and vice versa.

The study of the syntax of AMESLAN reveals similarly that there are syntactic rules in the language which parallel those found in spoken languages.

The other sign language used in the United States is called **Signed English**. Essentially, it consists in the replacement of each spoken English word (and morpheme) by a sign. Thus, the syntax and semantics of Signed English are approximately the same as that of ordinary English.

One mechanism employed by speakers of a sign language to add new proper nouns, or an extensive technical vocabulary, is the system of **finger spelling**. A manual alphabet consisting of various finger configurations, hand positions, and movements gives visible symbols for the alphabet and ampersand.

An accomplished signer can "speak" at a normal rate, even when there is a lot of finger spelling. Public television stations sometimes have programs which are interpreted in sign for the deaf in a corner of the TV

[6] W. C. Stokoe, et al. *A Dictionary of American Sign Language on Linguistic Principles* (Washington, D.C.: Gallaudet College Press, 1965).

screen. If you've ever seen such a program, you were probably amazed at how well the interpreter kept pace with the spoken sentences.

Language arts are not lost to the deaf. Poetry is composed in sign language, and stage plays such as Sheridan's *The Critic* have been translated into sign language and acted by the National Theatre of the Deaf (NTD). Sign language is so highly thought of by anthropologist Margaret Mead that, in an article discussing the possibilities of a universal *second* language, she suggests using some of the basic ideas that sign languages incorporate.

Recently, many teachers of the deaf have been advocating a philosophy of **total communication.** Deaf children are taught one or more sign languages, and are encouraged to learn to speak, speech read, read and write, and use amplification (for example, hearing aids) in order to exploit every means of communication. When you realize the enormous effort that a deaf person expends to achieve what most of us are granted—knowledge of a human language—you suddenly appreciate both the courage of the deaf and the wondrousness of language.

How Languages Differ

He that understands grammar in one language,
understands it in another as far as the essential properties
of Grammar are concerned. The fact that he can't speak,
nor comprehend, another language is due to the diversity
of words and their various forms, but these are *the
accidental properties of grammar.*
ROGER BACON (1214–1294)

The "accidental properties" of which Bacon spoke make it impossible for a French speaker and an Arabic speaker to converse and understand each other. What are these "properties" which differentiate between languages?

The **phonological systems** of languages differ. Different languages have different inventories of sounds, though all languages will have some of the same sounds; in fact, certain sounds are found in every language. All languages have vowels and consonants, and the consonants always include stops and continuants, while the vowels always include a high front vowel.

Consider, for example, English and Twi, two widely different languages from two distinct language families. They both contain the consonants [p], [t], [k], [b], [d], [g], [m], [n], [ŋ], [f], [s], [h], [r], [w], [y], [č], and [ǰ] and the vowels [i], [ɪ], [e], [ɛ], [u], [ʊ], [o], [ɔ], and [a]. There are sounds in English not found in Twi, such as [z], [v], [θ], [ð], and [l], and there are sound in Twi not found in English, such as [čʷ] (which is like the *ch* sound in *church* but with your lips rounded) or [ǰʷ] (like the *j* sound in *judge* with the lips rounded).

Languages may also differ as to the particular **phonological rules** in their grammars, although the rules often refer to the same classes of sounds. In English there is a rule that aspirates voiceless stops if they are word-initial. In Thai there is a rule that states: "Voiceless stops are 'unreleased' (unexploded) in word-final position." The following rule is found in English and in many other languages: "When two similar consonants come together, simplify them into one consonant." Thus, when we combine *big* /bɪg/ with *girl* /gərl/ we may delete one *g:*

/bɪg gərl/ → [bɪgərl].

This rule is not found in all languages (that is, it is a universal tendency), but the rule in English which states that a vowel is nasalized before a syllable-final nasal consonant is probably an absolute universal rule. In English, from /bæn/ *ban* we get the phonetic [bæ̃n]; in Twi from /kum/ "kill" we get the phonetic [kũm]. This phonological rule seems to be conditioned by general physiological constraints.

The **syntactic rules** of languages may also differ. The basic phrase-structure rules, which produce the "deep structures" of sentences, are more similar across languages than the transformational rules, which alter word order, add elements, delete elements, and so on. We find in all languages that sentences contain a noun-phrase subject (S), a verb or predicate (V), and possibly a noun-phrase object (O). In some languages the basic or "preferred" order of these elements is subject-verb-object (SVO). Many familiar languages, such as French, Spanish, and English, are examples. Other languages, such as Japanese and Korean, have the preferred order subject-object-verb (SOV). Others, such as classical Hebrew and Welsh, are VSO languages; and, rarely, one finds a language like Malagasy (spoken on Madagascar), which is VOS, or Dyirbal, an Australian language, which is OSV. No language has been discovered which has the preferred word order OVS.

The transformational rules, however, may cause the production of a nonpreferred order, as in the "cleft" sentence *It's a wombat that Willy whipped.* In general, transformations may produce any word order, so these rules vary more from language to language than the phrase-structure rules.

Languages may also differ syntactically in the way questions are formed. Many languages (including English) may form a simple "yes-no" question merely by changing the pitch contour of the sentence. A declarative sentence is spoken with a falling pitch at the end:

You are going.

The question is spoken with a rising pitch at the end:

You are going?

This intonational distinction seems to be very common. That is, in languages which can use pitch alone to distinguish statements from questions, one often finds the rising pitch at the end of the question. If one uses a change in word order in English, however, it is the word order which marks the "interrogative," and the pitch may fall, as in the neutral or declarative sentence:

Are you going?

Other languages use other means to form yes-no questions. Thai, for example, adds an interrogative particle to the end of a sentence that would otherwise be a declarative statement:

khăw cà maa "he'll come" → khăw cà maa măj "will he come?"

Măj [măy] is virtually a phonetic question mark. Twi behaves like Thai, but Zapotec, an Indian language of Mexico, adds a particle at the beginning of the interrogative sentence, or one at the beginning and one at the end, much like the question mark of Spanish orthography.

In English, as in most Indo-European languages, a common way of forming a yes-no question is to change word order:

> He is mad.   → Is he mad?
> John is mad.   → Is John mad?

In French one finds a similar "transformation." The same sentences in French are:

> Il est fou.   → Est-il fou?
> Jean est fou.   → Jean est-il fou?

In all these languages there must be a special transformational rule specifying just what must be done to form yes-no questions. The specifics of the individual rules differ. Notice that in French, word order is changed as in English when the subject is a pronoun; but when the subject is not a pronoun the rule does not change the position of the subject, but inserts a pronoun after the verb.

Despite the differences in specific rules, all languages have a rule for yes-no question formation. This *type* of rule, then, is "universal."

There are many other syntactic differences which are found. Language is so complex that this should not be surprising. There are languages where the auxiliary (such as the English words *will, may,* and so on) precedes the verb, and other languages where the auxiliary follows the verb (for example, Japanese). There are languages where noun modifiers (adjectives) normally precede the noun in a noun phrase:

> English: the *red* book
> Russian: *interesnaya* gazeta ("interesting newspaper")

There are languages where the modifier usually follows the noun:

> French: le livre rouge ("the book red")
> Igbo: éféré úkwú ("plate large")

There appear to be systematic relations between syntactic differences. Joseph Greenberg has proposed (as a starter) forty-five universals which relate to syntax and word formation. One of his universals is: "In languages with dominant order SOV an inflected auxiliary always follows the main verb."[7] So even certain differences between languages are "regular."

The relations between particular strings of sounds and particular meanings *(lexical differences)* are the most obvious differences between languages, as is illustrated by the following translations of *water: wasser* (German), *agua* (Spanish), *uisce* (Irish), *maji* (Swahili), *ǹsú* (Twi), *pani* (Hındı), *voda* (Russian), *šuudek* (Pıma), *čaƛak* (Nootka), *nåam* (Thai), *shuĭ* (Mandarin Chinese), *oyu* (Japanese).

---

[7] Joseph Greenberg, *Universals of Language* (Cambridge, Mass.: M.I.T. Press, 1963).

We have seen that languages may differ phonologically, syntactically, and lexically. The differences one finds in the grammars of languages of the world play an important role when we try to define "human language." A theory of language must be able to account for just those differences that actually exist, as well as for all the universal properties which are found.

Types of Languages

All the Oriental nations jam tongue and words together in the throat, like the Hebrews and Syrians. All the Mediterranean peoples push their enunciation forward to the palate, like the Greeks and the Asians. All the Occidentals break their words on the teeth, like the Italians and Spaniards. . . .
ISADORE OF SEVILLE, 7th century A.D.

In order to determine the similarities and differences which exist between languages, it is helpful to put some order into the apparent chaos. Many different classification schemes have been devised.

One system classifies languages according to various properties they possess. In such a "typological" classification, August Schleicher, an outstanding linguist of the nineteenth century, set up a tripartite division of language classification: **isolating, agglutinating,** and **inflecting.** The classification he proposed is certainly not absolute. Rather, languages may perhaps be classified according to what degree they are isolating, agglutinating, or inflectional.

In **isolating** languages, one morpheme equals one word. Highly isolating languages, typified by Chinese, are characterized by a lack of derivational and inflectional processes. Derivational and inflectional affixes are virtually nonexistent in Chinese. Verbs are never inflected for person, number, or tense, or nouns for number, and prefixes or suffixes are rarely found. English is partially isolating. It has thousands of morphemes that occur as one word: *the, can, red, ball,* and so on. The expression of future tense by means of the uninflected morpheme *will* is typical of an isolating language.

In **agglutinating** languages, various morphemes are combined to form a single word; each element maintains a distinct and fixed meaning. In such languages, prefixes, suffixes, and even "infixes" are used over and over again to build new words. They usually keep their same phonological shape, except for changes resulting from the regular phonological rules of the language.

English, according to this definition, is somewhat agglutinating. The suffix *-ness,* for example, can be attached to most adjectives to form nouns: *good/goodness, red/redness, tired/tiredness.* The prefix *in-* is another example; it produces negative adjectives: *incomplete, intolerant, indecisive, inescapable, indispensable.* Of course, as we have already pointed out, the phonological rules of English change the phonetic shape of /in-/ according to the sound that follows.

Turkish and Swahili are agglutinating languages; Swahili mostly by prefixing, Turkish mostly by suffixing. In Turkish, the word for "tooth" is *diš* and the word for "house" is *ev*. The following examples illustrate the "agglutinating" character of the language.

diš "tooth"	dišim "my tooth"	dišimde "in my tooth"
ev "house"	evim "my house"	evimde "in my house"

The suffixes *-im* and *-de* can be attached to most noun stems and carry the meaning of "my" and "in the" respectively. In Turkish several suffixes may be attached to a stem, resulting in a complex polymorphemic word (which may be a whole sentence). Thus:

kɨr+ɨl+ma+dɨ+lar+mɨ (kɨrɨlmadɨlarmɨ)
Were they not broken?

In this case,

kɨr = "break"
ɨl   = passive voice
ma = negative
dɨ   = past tense
lar = plural
mɨ = interrogative

The stem "break" has been modified by the addition of five distinct morphemes to give the meaning shown above. To accomplish the same effect in English we must do the following:

Concept: *break*
Passive voice: *to be broken*
Negative: *to not be broken*
Past tense: (it) *was not broken*
Plural: (they) *were not broken*
Question: *were* (they) *not broken?*

It is clear that English is not an "agglutinating" language to the degree that Turkish is, although from the examples above it appears to have some agglutinating characteristics.

Swahili would also be classified as "agglutinating" by the definition given, but it is a "prefixing" rather than a "suffixing" language, as the following examples illustrate:

ni + na + penda	"I" + present tense + "love" ("I love")
ni + na + sema	"I" + present tense + "speak" ("I speak")
ni + li + penda	"I" + past tense + "love" ("I loved")

An examination of the languages of the world shows that there are many languages which use only suffixes as their "additive" elements, but very few which use only prefixes. Swahili uses mostly prefixes but uses some suffixes, too. Thai, often considered an isolating language, does use prefixes when it uses any affixes at all, but this is truly exceptional.

The third type of language in this classificatory scheme is **inflectional**. In such languages, a word or morpheme undergoes a change in form when its grammatical function in the sentence is changed. Morphemes are added to lexical stems, but these added elements fuse with the stem and have no independence.

Modern English is somewhat inflectional. Some adjectives and their corresponding nouns reveal this "fusion": *deep/depth, long/length, wide/width*.

At one time, as was discussed in Chapter 11, Old English was highly inflectional. Many inflectional endings were lost and English became more "isolating"; the syntactic information provided by these endings was then supplied by other syntactic means (for example, more use of prepositions and stricter word order). The remnants of English inflection are exemplified by the different forms of the second-person pronoun:

you: when it occurs as the subject or object NP of a sentence.

your: when it occurs as the possessive pronominal adjective (*Your* book was stolen.).

yours: when it occurs as a possessive pronoun (The book is *yours*.).

The different forms for the first-person-singular pronoun demonstrate how difficult it would be to separate out the individual syntactic and semantic features that are fused into one morpheme. This is also revealed in English by the inflectional ending *-s* added to the present-tense form of the verb after a third person singular subject (pronounced differently, of course, according to the last sound in the verb stem):

I hit	you hit	he/she/it hit+s	we hit	they hit
I love	you love	he/she/it love+s	we love	they love
I catch	you catch	he/she/it catch+es	we catch	they catch

This inflectional ending—one of the few remaining in English—combines the meaning "third person," "present tense," and "singular" in an indissoluble form.

On the other hand, the *-d* attached to the verb to form the past tense means only "past tense." Neither the singular or plural distinction nor the "person" is specified in the *-d* suffix. This is, then, an "agglutinative" suffix.

Latin and Greek are highly inflected languages. In Latin the verb stem is inflected for person, number, and tense:

amo	first person, singular, present tense	"I love"
amas	second person, singular, present tense	"you love"
amat	third person, singular, present tense	"he/she loves"
amamus	first person, plural, present tense	"we love"
amatis	second person, plural, present tense	"you love"
amant	third person, plural, present tense	"they love"

Notice that the *-o* in *amo* represents "first person" + "singular" + "present." One cannot separate out these elements as independent units.

Schleicher proposed that these three types represent different stages in the evolution of languages. Like many other nineteenth-century linguists, he was strongly influenced by Darwin. He believed that each language has a "life cycle" and like plants and animals is subject to "natural" evolution —that is, a language is born, lives, gives birth to a new language (a daughter) which in turn replaces it, and the daughter in time will also be replaced by its progeny. Schleicher also assumed that the inflectional stage represents the highest level of a language; when a language reaches this stage it has nowhere to go but down. This idea was compatible with the classicist notion that Greek and Latin represented the highest, most beautiful forms of language.

Schleicher also supported his view by analogies with nature. According to him, each stage corresponds with one of the basic forms of the world. Languages in the isolating stage correspond to the crystals found in nature; the agglutinating stage he related to plants; and the inflectional stage he correlated with animal life.

The last scholar to pay serious attention to this kind of development was Otto Jespersen, but he suggested that the development was just the opposite from that put forth by Schleicher. According to Jespersen, who wrote early in this century, the highest stage a language could reach was the isolating stage.

Linguists have discovered that no language is purely one type or another, nor does one type represent a higher stage than another type. Also, despite their differences, languages of the three "types" have much in common. They all have similar syntactic categories, and although transformational rules "look" different in languages of one type or another, they often perform the same function. Thus, possession may be expressed on the surface by an inflectional form (for example, *the book's cover*) or by an isolating form (*the cover of the book*), but the basic relationship remains the same.

Why Languages Differ and Yet Remain the Same

Get used to thinking that there is nothing Nature loves so well as to change existing forms and to make new ones like them.
MARCUS AURELIUS, *Meditations*

The ways in which languages change account to a great extent for the kinds of differences one finds in the world's languages. Even when languages are in one language family, different changes occur in each.

We can illustrate how many of the world's languages arose by a rather oversimplified hypothetical situation. Consider a community of people speaking one language. If they all stay in the same place, communicate with one another, send their children to the same schools, go to the same movies, and watch the same television shows, the changes that occur will be reflected in the whole community. No one will notice them.

But suppose from among this one language community, a group of people decide that the hunting or the farming or the climate is better over the mountains, and so set off to settle new regions. Suppose, further, that they settle very far from the first group and have no way of communicating.

Group A, the people that "stay put," and Group B, the travelers, start out speaking the same language, L. Once they are separated, some changes occur in L spoken by Group A, and other changes occur in language L spoken by Group B. After some time, say 100 years, Group A will speak L_1 and Group B will speak L_2. At this point they will probably still understand each other. They will thus be speaking two dialects of L. But in 500 years the changes may be so great that the two dialects are no longer mutually understandable. Thus, two languages have arisen from one parent language.

This hypothetical case reflects what happened over the thousands of years of human wandering around the earth. In earlier periods of history when a group took off for a new place, regular contact with the motherland (and the mother tongue) was broken, and the language was free to change independently in both groups.

German, for example, changed in different ways than did its sister, English. German retained more "inflectional" processes than English, and German syntax differs from English syntax with regard to the position of the verb and auxiliary verbs, which often come at the end of the sentence. This particular characteristic of German inspired Mark Twain to say:

> Whenever the literary German dives into a sentence, that is the last you are going to see of him till he emerges on the other side of the Atlantic with his verb in his mouth.[8]

Languages differ in their particular elements and rules because elements and rules change, are added, or are dropped from grammars. Meanings change and all aspects of the sound system also change. But the changes which occur are all within the limits which constrain human languages and their grammars. No language will ever be without vowels, nor will the syntactic rules of a language ever change to allow it to become an object-verb-subject (OVS) language.

We have seen that the "preferred" order of the subject, verb, and object may differ from one language to another. We have also seen that transformational rules may switch the order of elements:

> Unicorns are stunning → Are unicorns stunning?
> My sheepdog loves to eat popcorn → It's popcorn my sheepdog
> loves to eat.
> Spiro sent a letter to the president → Spiro sent the president a letter.

But we never find in any language of the world a rule which says "Reverse the order of all the words in the sentence" or "Reverse the sounds of an adjective to get its opposite." Such rules are not possible rules. An adequate theory of language must not allow such rules, as it is the nature of human language not to have them.

Similarly, we find in many languages a type of rule that permits the deletion of certain elements. Thus, syntactic rules of English permit the following:

> I know that he is coming late → I know ø he is coming late.
> Joanne is lazier than I am → Joanne is lazier than I ø
> or
> Joanne is lazier than me.

---

[8] Mark Twain, *A Connecticut Yankee at King Arthur's Court.*

But we never find in any language a rule that says "Delete every other word of a sentence" or "Delete all final words." Again we see that there are universal constraints on what can occur. If there were no holds barred where language diversity is concerned, there would not be such universal restrictions.

Knowing that universal constraints on rules exist in all languages may help when one is trying to learn a foreign language. An English speaker studying French for the first time may have to learn that the NP expansion rule in French is: NP → Art + N + Adj, whereas the English rule he already knows says NP → Art + Adj + N, but he already intuitively know what an NP is, what an article is, and how nouns differ from adjectives.

This is the meaning of Bacon's statement that "a person knowing grammar in one language knows the grammar of all languages, except for accidental differences."

The Genetic Classification of Languages

The Sanskrit language, whatever be its antiquity, is of a wonderful structure, more perfect than the Greek, more copious than the Latin, and more exquisitely refined than either, yet bearing to both of them a stronger affinity, both in the roots of verbs and in the forms of grammar, than could possibly be produced by accident; so strong, indeed, that no philologer could examine all three, without believing that they have sprung from some common source, which, perhaps, no longer exists . . .
SIR WILLIAM JONES, 1786

Languages, like humans, are created equal. But it seems that, also like humans, some languages are "more equal" than others. French speakers can learn Spanish more easily than they can learn Russian, although that wouldn't be true of Bulgarian speakers. This is because French and Spanish are both descendants of Latin, just as Russian and Bulgarian are descendants of Slavic. It is not surprising that languages in the same family resemble each other more than languages descending from a different branch of the genealogical tree.

The languages of the world belong to families and bear offspring. Chapter 11 discussed how different languages are "born" from one language, and how historical and comparative linguists classify languages into families and reconstruct earlier forms of the ancestral language. When we examine the languages of the world, we perceive similarities and differences among them that provide further evidence for the "genetic" relatedness we know exists.

Counting to five in English, German, and Pima (a southwestern American Indian language) shows similarities between English and German not shared by Pima:

ENGLISH	GERMAN	PIMA
one	eins	hermako
two	zwei	gohk
three	drei	waik
four	vier .	giik
five	fünf	hetasp

This similarity between English and German is pervasive. Sometimes it is extremely obvious (*man/Mann*), other times a little less obvious (*child/Kind*).

Because German and English are human languages, we expect to find certain similarities between them. But there are more similarities than in other languages. It is not the case that they are related because they are highly similar, however. Rather, they are highly similar because they are related. They are related because at one time in history they were the same language, namely the language spoken by the German tribes, some of which settled in Britain in the fifth century. Languages which are related were, at some point in the past, one language.

Fifth-century Germanic is the parent of Modern English and Modern German, which are its daughters; English and German are sisters. Sisterhood is the fundamental genealogical relationship between languages. Similarly, Latin has mothered the Romance languages; French, Spanish, Portuguese, Italian, and Romanian are daughters of Latin and sisters to one another.

Where there are mothers and sisters, there must be *cousins*. At one time, well over 2000 years ago, an early form of the Germanic, from which English ultimately descended, and an early form of Latin were sisters. The respective offspring are cousins. The five Romance languages listed above are cousins to English. The numbers from one to three in the three languages reveal this relationship:

SPANISH	FRENCH	ENGLISH
uno	un	one
dos	deux	two
tres	trois	three

Norwegian, Yiddish, Danish, Icelandic, and Dutch are all close relatives of English. They, like English, are Germanic. Greek is a somewhat more distant cousin. The Celtic language gave birth to Irish, Scots Gaelic, Welsh, and Breton, all cousins of English. Breton is spoken by the people living in the northwest coastal regions of France called Brittany. It was brought there by Celts fleeing from Britain in the seventh century and has been preserved as the language of some Celtic descendants in Brittany ever since. Russian is also a distant cousin, as are its sisters, Bulgarian, Serbo-Croatian, Polish, Czech, and Slovak. The Baltic language Lithuanian is related to English, as is its sister language, Latvian. A neighboring language, Estonian, however, is not a relative. Sanskrit, as pointed out by Sir William Jones, as far removed from the European languages as it appears to be, is a distant cousin of these languages, as are its daughters, Hindi,

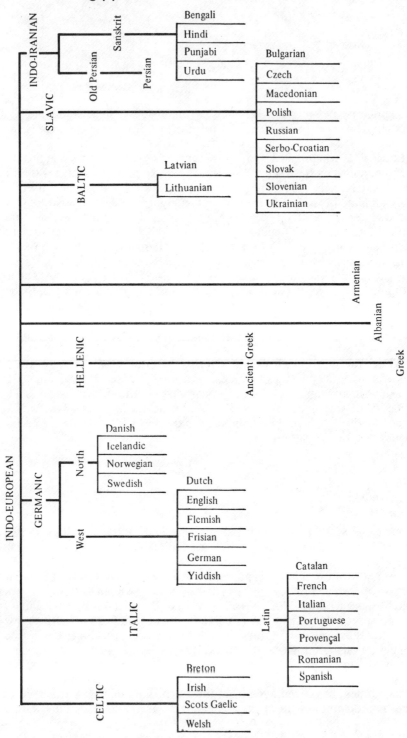

Figure 12-1 The Indo-European family of languages.

spoken in India, and Bengali, spoken primarily in Bangladesh. Even Modern Persian, the language of Iran in the Middle East, is a distant cousin of English.

All the languages mentioned in the last paragraph, except for Estonian, are related, more or less distantly. As such they must have evolved from a single ancient language, spoken at one time in the distant past—approximately 6000 years ago. It is called Indo-European by linguists. No one knows what name, if any, its speakers used for it.

Figure 12-1, an abbreviated "family tree" of the Indo-European family of languages, gives a genealogical and historical classification of the languages shown. All the languages of the world may be similarly classified. This diagram of the Indo-European family is actually somewhat oversimplified. For one thing, the "dead-ends"—languages that evolved and died, leaving no offspring—are not included. A language dies when no children learn it. This may come about in two ways: either all the speakers of the language are annihilated by some tragic event, perhaps a volcanic eruption or a war, or, more commonly, the speakers of the language are absorbed by another culture that speaks a different language. The children, at first bilingual, grow up using the language of the dominant culture. Their children, or their children's children, fail to learn the old language, and so it dies. This is what has become of many American Indian languages. Cornish, a Celtic language akin to Breton, met a similar fate in England in the seventeenth century. In fact, all the Celtic languages left in the world today, Irish, Scots Gaelic, Welsh, and Breton, are relentlessly being squeezed out of existence by English and French, which are dominant where these languages are spoken. Today, however, there are "revival" movements among these people to "resurrect" their old languages. In Brittany, for example, many of the popular singers use only Breton.

The family tree also fails to show a number of intermediate stages that must have existed in the evolution of modern languages. Languages do not evolve abruptly. It is difficult to determine precisely when a "new" language appears. There is evidence that Germanic had at first three daughters. From the northernmost daughter, the Scandinavian languages evolved; English, German, and Dutch evolved from the westernmost daughter.

Finally, the diagram fails to show a number of Indo-European languages because of lack of space. We tried to choose those languages that would be most interesting to readers with an American or European background. For a comprehensive Indo-European family tree, a more specialized reference should be consulted.

Obviously, most of the world's languages do not belong to the Indo-European family. Linguists have also attempted to classify the non-Indo-European languages according to their genetic relationships. The task is to identify the languages which constitute a family, and the relationships which exist among those languages.

The results of this research are often surprising; faraway Bengali is an Indo-European language, whereas Hungarian, surrounded on all sides by Indo-European languages, is not.

For linguists interested in the nature of human language, the number of languages in the many different language families provides necessary data. Although these data are diverse in many ways, they are also remarkably similar in many ways. We find that the languages of the "wretched Greenlanders," the Maoris of New Zealand, the Hottentots of Africa, and the people of North America have similar sounds, similar phonological and syntactic rules, and similar semantic systems. There is evidence, then, that we need a theory of language which aims at universality as well as specificity.

In Mark Twain's *Huckleberry Finn,* the slave Jim showed himself to have a real understanding of universal grammar. (In the following passage it should be noted that Twain was attempting to capture the vernacular used by the slaves at that time. That he was in no way making fun of such a dialect is evident from the passage itself and, of course, from his strong antislavery position.)

"Why, Huck, doan' de French people talk de same way we does?"

"No, Jim, you couldn't understand a word they said—not a single word—"

"Well, now, I be ding-busted! How do dat come?"

"I don't know, but it's so. I got some of their jabber out of a book. S'pose a man was to come to you and say Polly-voo-franzy. What would you think?"

"I wouldn't think nuffin, I'd take en bust him over de head—dat is, if he warn't white." . . .

"Shucks, it ain't calling you anything. It's only saying, do you know how to talk French?"

"Well, den, why couldn't he say it?"

"Why he *is* a-saying it. That's a Frenchman's *way* of saying it."

"Well, it's a blame ridicklous way, en I doan' want to hear no mo' bout it. Dey ain't no sense in it."

"Looky here, Jim, does a cat talk like we do?"

"No, a cat don't."

"Well, does a cow?"

"No, a cow don't nuther."

"Does a cat talk like a cow, or a cow talk like a cat?"

"No, dey don't."

"It's natural and right for 'em to talk different from each other, ain't it?"

"Course."

"And ain't it natural and right for a cat and a cow to talk different from us?"

"Why mos sholy it is."

"Well, then, why ain't it natural and right for a Frenchman to talk different from us? You answer me that."

"Is a cat a man, Huck?"

"No."

"Well, den, dey ain't no sense in a cat talkin' like a man. Is a cow a man? er is a cow a cat?"

"No, she ain't either of them."

"Well, den, she ain't got no business to talk like either one er the yuther of 'em. Is a Frenchman a man?"

"Yes."

"Well, den. Dad blame it, why doan he *talk* like a man? You answer me *dat.*"

What Jim did not know was that he and a Frenchman did both talk like men—and to a great extent spoke the same language, human language—except for the "accidental differences."

Table 12-1 Some languages of the world*

Language subfamily	Language	Principal geographic areas where spoken	Number of speakers (rank in parentheses)	
		INDO-EUROPEAN FAMILY (see Figure 12-1)		
Germanic	Danish	Denmark		5,000,000
	Dutch	Netherlands, Indonesia		13,000,000
	English	North America, Great Britain, Australia, New Zealand	(2)	300,000,000
	Frisian	Northern Holland		400,000
	Flemish	Belgium		5,000,000
	German	Germany, Austria, Switzerland	(7)	100,000,000
	Icelandic	Iceland		200,000
	Norwegian	Norway		4,300,000
	Swedish	Sweden		8,000,000
	Yiddish	(diffuse)		4,000,000
Latin	Catalan	Andorra, Spain		5,000,000
	French	France, Belgium, Switzerland, Canada	(11)	75,000,000
	Italian	Italy, Switzerland	(12)	60,000,000
	Portuguese	Portugal, Brazil	(7)	100,000,000
	Provençal	Southern France		9,000,000
	Spanish	Spain, Latin America	(3)	200,000,000
Celtic	Breton	Brittany (France)		1,000,000
	Irish	Ireland		500,000
	Scots Gaelic	Scotland		500,000
	Welsh	Wales		750,000
Hellenic	Greek	Greece, Cyprus		10,000,000
Baltic	Latvian	Latvia (USSR)		2,000,000
	Lithuanian	Lithuania (USSR)		3,000,000
Slavic	Bulgarian	Bulgaria		8,000,000
	Czech	Czechoslovakia		10,000,000
	Macedonian	Southern Yugoslavia		1,000,000
	Polish	Poland	(22)	35,000,000
	Russian	USSR	(3)	200,000,000
	Serbo-Croatian	Yugoslavia		15,000,000
	Slovak	Czechoslovakia		4,000,000
	Slovenian	Yugoslavia		1,500,000
	Ukrainian	Southwest USSR	(20)	40,000,000

* Much of this data is from Ruhlen (1976). The number of speakers is the number of native speakers. Languages such as Dutch/Flemish or Norwegian/Danish, which are close enough to be considered dialects, are nonetheless listed as separate languages out of political considerations. Similarly for Hindi/Urdu and Malay/Indonesian.

Table 12-1   Some languages of the world—*continued*

Language subfamily	Language	Principal geographic areas where spoken	Number of speakers (rank in parentheses)	
		INDO-EUROPEAN FAMILY (see Figure 12-1)		
Indo-Iranian	Bengali	Bangladesh, India	(6)	110,000,000
	Hindi	Northern India	(5)	180,000,000
	Marathi	Western India	(17)	45,000,000
	Persian	Iran		25,000,000
	Punjabi	Northern India	(13)	50,000,000
	Urdu	Pakistan	(20)	40,000,000
Armenian	Armenian	Southwest USSR		4,000,000
Albanian	Albanian	Albania		4,000,000

OTHER THAN INDO-EUROPEAN

Language family	Language	Principal geographic areas where spoken	Number of speakers (rank in parentheses)	
Afro-Asiatic	Amharic	Ethiopia		8,000,000
(includes	Arabic	North Africa, Middle East	(7)	100,000,000
Semitic	Berber	Morocco		6,000,000
languages)	Galla	Somaliland, Ethiopia		7,000,000
	Hausa	Northern Nigeria		20,000,000
	Hebrew	Israel		3,000,000
	Somali	Somalia		2,000,000
Altaic	Japanese	Japan	(7)	100,000,000
	Korean	Korea	(23)	34,000,000
	Mongolian	Mongolia		1,600,000
	Turkish	Turkey		24,000,000
Austro-Asiatic	Cambodian	Cambodia		6,000,000
	Vietnamese	Vietnam	(26)	28,000,000
Austro-Tai	Batak	Sumatra		2,000,000
	Chamorro	Mariana Islands (Guam)		50,000
	Fijian	Fiji Islands		200,000
	Hawaiian	Hawaii		250
	Indonesian	Indonesia	(13)	50,000,000
	Javanese	Java	(17)	45,000,000
	Lao	Laos		10,000,000
	Malagasy	Madagascar		6,500,000
	Malay	Malaysia, Singapore		10,000,000
	Maori	New Zealand		100,000
	Samoan	Samoa		130,000
	Tagalog	Philippines		10,000,000
	Tahitian	Tahiti		66,000
	Thai	Thailand	(24)	30,000,000
Caucasian	Avar	Southwest USSR		270,000
	Georgian	Southwest USSR		2,700,000

OTHER THAN INDO-EUROPEAN—*continued*

Language family	Language	Principal geographic areas where spoken		Number of speakers (rank in parentheses)
Dravidian	Kannada	Southwest India		22,000,000
	Malayalam	Southwest India		22,000,000
	Tamil	Southeast India, Sri Lanka	(17)	45,000,000
	Telugu	Southeast India	(13)	50,000,000
Niger-Kordofanian†	Efik	Southeast Nigeria		2,000,000
	Ewe	Ghana		1,700,000
	Fulani	Northeast Nigeria		8,000,000
	Igbo	Southeast Nigeria		6,000,000
	Luganda	Uganda		1,500,000
	Nupe	Nigeria		325,000
	Shona	Rhodesia		118,000
	Swahili	East Africa		15,000,000
	Twi	Ghana, Ivory Coast		2,000,000
	Yoruba	Nigeria		12,000,000
	Zulu	South Africa		2,000,000
Sino-Tibetan	Burmese	Burma		16,000,000
	Cantonese	South China (Canton)		27,000,000
	Hakka	Southeast China	(23)	30,000,000
	Mandarin	North China	(1)	387,000,000
	Taiwanese	Formosa		15,000,000
	Tibetan	Tibet		4,000,000
	Wu	East central China	(16)	46,000,000
Uralic‡	Estonian	Estonia (USSR)		1,000,000
	Finnish	Finland		5,000,000
	Hungarian	Hungary		12,000,000
	Lapp	Northern parts of Norway, Finland, Sweden, USSR		30,000

Amerindian Subfamily	Language	Principal geographic areas where spoken	Number of speakers
Algonquian	Arapaho	Wyoming	2,000
	Blackfoot	Montana	5,000
	Cheyenne	Montana	3,000
	Cree	Ontario (Canada)	62,000
	Menomini	Wisconsin	300
	Ojibwa	Ontario	40,000
Athapaskan	Apache	Oklahoma	10
	Chipewyan	Alberta (Canada)	5,000
	Navajo	Arizona	120,000
	Sarsi	Alberta	50

† All languages given belong to the subfamily of Niger-Congo. Of these Swahili, Luganda, Shona, and Zulu are Bantu languages.

‡ All languages given belong to the subfamily Finno-Ugric. The other Uralic subfamily is Samoyed.

Table 12-1   Some languages of the world—*continued*

Amerindian Subfamily	*Language*	*Principal geographic areas where spoken*	*Number of speakers*
Iroquoian	Cherokee	Oklahoma, North Carolina	10,000
	Mohawk	Northern New York	1,000
Mayan	Maya	Guatemala	300,000
Quechumaran	Quechua (Incan)	Bolivia, Peru	6,000,000
Uto-Aztecan	Hopi	Northwest Arizona	4,800
	Nahuatl (Aztec)	Southern Mexico	1,000,000
	Pima	Southern Arizona	18,000
Yuman	Diegueño	Southern California	185
	Mohave	Western Arizona	850

NOTE: Obviously, we have omitted thousands of languages. These are given merely to provide some examples of some of the languages in some of the language families and subfamilies.

SUMMARY

There are more than three thousand languages spoken in the world. Despite the differences among these languages, they are surprisingly similar. There are **absolute universals,** which all languages have, and **universal tendencies,** which most languages have.

Languages may differ in their phonetic inventory, in their phonological rules, in their syntactic rules, and in their lexicons. The large number of sounds utilized by the world's languages can be specified by a relatively small set of universal phonetic features. Syntactically, certain restrictions constrain the rules of grammars. Since any idea or concept which can be expressed in one language can also be expressed in any other language, we know that the semantic systems of languages are similar.

Languages may be classified by **type** or by **genetic** relationships. Typological classification has traditionally been based on word formation: **isolating languages** are those in which one morpheme equals one word; **agglutinative languages** are those in which words are composed of independent, "immutable" strings of morphemes; **inflectional languages** are those in which the strings of morphemes are fused with each other and with the lexical stem.

Languages are classified genealogically according to their "life history." The ancestors of the language are specified, including the source or "mother" language. Sisters and cousins, which all sprang up at different points in time from the original source language, are also noted in a "family tree" similar to Figure 12-1. Different language types may be found in a single language family.

In spite of the differences between languages, which we are acutely aware of when we try to learn a foreign language, there are a vast number of ways in which languages are alike. That is, there are language universals as well as language differences.

Human language need not have sounds. AMESLAN, a sign language of the deaf, utilizes visual units of hand and body gesticulations as the building blocks of meaning-bearing signs. Nevertheless, all sign languages have rules of morphology, syntax, and semantics comparable to those of spoken languages.

EXERCISES

1. Here is a list of possible language universals. Which are universal tendencies? Which of them do you think are truly universal? Which are not? Give your reasons in each case.

   a. All languages have kinship terms (that is, words that refer to parents, siblings, inlaws, etc.).
   b. All languages have three nasal phonemes.
   c. All languages have idioms.
   d. All languages have a "morphological plural" (a way of changing the form of a noun to indicate that it is plural).
   e. All languages have pronouns.
   f. All languages have phonological rules that delete unstressed vowels.
   g. All languages have glides in their phonemic inventory.
   h. All languages have a phonological rule that aspirates voiceless stops in word-initial position.
   i. All languages have a "morphological past tense" (a way of changing the form of the verb to indicate that it is in the past tense).
   j. All languages have rules that determine what sounds can occur next to each other.
   k. All languages have fricatives.
   l. All languages have words for "water," "man," and "sun."

2. Which of the three (or four) languages in column B is most closely related to the language in column A?

A	B
a. Bulgarian	Lithuanian
	Russian
	Greek
b. Dutch	Bulgarian
	English
	Indonesian
c. English	Navajo
	Flemish
	Persian

   d. Persian   Serbo-Croatian
                      Arabic
                      Bengali

   e. Russian   Slovenian
                      English
                      Latvian
                      Finnish

   f. Hungarian Russian
                      Finnish
                      Twi

   g. Welsh   French
                      Breton
                      Estonian

   h. Spanish   English
                      Arabic
                      Romanian

3. Here is how to count to five in a dozen languages. Six of these languages are Indo-European and six are not. Identify which is which.[9]

LG. 1	LG. 2	LG. 3	LG. 4	LG. 5	LG. 6
1 en	jedyn	i	eka	ichi	echad
2 twene	dwaj	liang	dvau	ni	shnayim
3 thria	tři	san	trayas	san	shlosha
4 fiuwar	štyri	ssu	catur	shi	arba?a
5 fif	pjeć	wu	pañca	go	chamishsha

LG. 7	LG. 8	LG. 9	LG. 10	LG. 11	LG. 12
1 mot	ün	hana	yaw	uno	nigen
2 hai	duos	tul	daw	dos	khoyar
3 ba	trais	set	dree	tres	ghorban
4 bon	quatter	net	tsaloor	cuatro	durben
5 nam	tschinch	tasŏt	pindze	cinco	tabon

4. Here are some data from five languages. Identify which languages are isolating, which agglutinating, and which inflectional.

   a. Miwok (American Indian language of California)[10]

yilim	I am biting	?inim	I am coming
yilis	you are biting	?inis	you are coming
yili	he is biting	?ini	he is coming
yilimas	we are biting	?inimas	we are coming
yilitos	you (pl.) are biting	?initos	you (pl.) are coming
yilip	they are biting	?inip	they are coming

   [9] Data from John Algeo and Thomas Pyles, *Problems in the Origins and Development of the English Language* (New York: Harcourt Brace Jovanovich, 1966), pp. 90–91.
   [10] Data from Henry Allen Gleason, Jr., *Workbook in Descriptive Linguistics* (New York: Holt, Rinehart and Winston, 1955), p. 45.

b. Serbo-Croatian[11]

	read	drink	smoke
I	ja čitam	ja pijem	ja pušim
you (sg.)	ti čitaš	ti piješ	ti pušiš
he	on čita	on pije	on puši
we	mi čitamo	mi pijemo	mi pušimo
you (pl.)	vi čitate	vi pijete	vi pušite
they	oni čitaju	oni piju	oni puše

c. Thai

	eat	(be) eating	will eat
I	chăn kin	chăn kamlang kin	chăn cà kin
you	khun kin	khun kamlang kin	khun cà kin
he	khăw kin	khăw kamlang kin	khăw cà kin
we	raw kin	raw kamlang kin	raw cà kin

d. Efik (Nigeria)[12]

ńsìn	I am laying	m̀bè	I am passing
ésìn	he is laying	ébè	he is passing
ésìn	they are laying	éhè	they are passing
ńyésín	I will lay	ńyébě	I will pass
éyésín	he will lay	éyébě	he will pass
éyésín	they will lay	éyébě	they will pass
ŋkésín	I laid	ŋkébě	I passed
ékésìn	he laid	ékébě	he passed
ékésìn	they laid	ékébě	they passed

e. Spanish

yo cazo	I hunt	yo cacé	I hunted
tú cazas	You (fam.) hunt	tú cazaste	you (fam.) hunted
el caza	he hunts	el cazó	he hunted
nosotros cazamos	we hunt	nosotros cazamos	we hunted
vosotros cazáis	you (pl.) hunt	vosotros cazasteis	you (pl.) hunted
ellos cazan	they hunt	ellos cazaron	they hunted

5. English forms the regular past tense by adding the morpheme /d/ (which may undergo certain phonological changes, as we saw in Chapters 4 and 5). Is this way of forming past tense an isolating, agglutinating, or inflectional tendency? What about the formation of plurals by adding /z/? And what about the third-person singular agreement morpheme that suffixes to the verb (for example, John knows), which also has the phonological shape /z/?

6. State at least three differences between English and the following languages, using just the sentence(s) given. Ignore lexical differences—that is, the different vocabulary. Example:

---

[11] Data from R. Langacker, *Fundamentals of Linguistic Analysis* (New York: Harcourt Brace Jovanovich, 1972), p. 68.

[12] Data from Gleason, op. cit., p. 37.

Thai:

dèg khon	nĭi	kamlang	kin
boy *classifier*	this	*progressive aspect*	eat

This boy is eating.

măa tua	nán	kin	khâaw
dog *classifier*	that	eat	rice

That dog ate the rice.

Three differences are: (1) Thai has "classifiers." They have no English equivalent. (2) The demonstratives "this" and "that" follow the noun in Thai, but precede the noun in English. (3) The "progressive" is expressed by a separate word in Thai. The verb doesn't change form. In English, the progressive is indicated by the presence of the verb *to be* and the adding of -*ing* to the verb.

a. French

cet	homme	intelligent	arrivera
this	man	intelligent	will arrive

This intelligent man will arrive.

ces	hommes	intelligents	arriveront
these	men	intelligent	will arrive

These intelligent men will arrive.

b. Japanese

watasi	ga	sakana	o	tabete	iru
I	*subject marker*	fish	*object marker*	eat (*ing*)	am

I am eating fish.

c. Swahili

mtoto	alivunja	kikombe				
m-	toto	a-	li-	vunja	ki-	kombe
class marker	child	he	*past*	break	*class marker*	cup

The child broke the cup.

watoto	wanavunja	vikombe				
wa-	toto	wa-	na-	vunja	vi-	kombe
	child	they	*present*	break		cup

The children break the cups.

d. Korean

kɨ	sonyɔn-nɨn	wɨyu-lɨl	masi-ass-ta				
kɨ	sonyɔn-	nɨn	wɨyu-	lɨl	masi-	ass-	ta
the	boy	*subject marker*	milk	*object marker*	drink	*past*	*assertion*

The boy drank milk.

kɨ-nɨn	muɔs-lɨl	mɔk-ass-nya				
kɨ-	nɨn	muɔs-	lɨl	mɔk-	ass-	nya
he	*subject marker*	what	*object marker*	eat	*past*	*question*

What did he eat?

7. We have stated that more than 3,000 languages exist in the world today. State one reason why this number might grow larger and one reason why it might grow smaller. Do you think the number of languages will increase or decrease in the next 100 years? Why?

References

Boas, Franz. *Handbook of American Indian Languages*. Washington, D.C.: Smithsonian Institution, Bureau of American Ethnology, Bulletin 40, 1911. Introduction, with foreword by C. I. J. M. Stuart, reprinted, Washington, D.C.: Georgetown University Press, 1964.

Chomsky, N. *Cartesian Linguistics*. New York: Harper & Row, 1966.

Greenberg, J. *Studies on African Linguistic Classification*. New Haven: Yale University Press, 1955.

Greenberg, J. *Universals of Language*. Cambridge, Mass.: M.I.T. Press, 1963.

Greenberg, J., ed. *Universals of Language*. Cambridge, Mass.: M.I.T. Press, 1966.

Jespersen, O. H. *Language: Its Nature, Development and Origin*. London: Allen and Unwin, 1922.

Meillet, A., and Marcel Cohen. *Les langues du Monde,* new ed., 2 vols. Paris: Champion, 1952.

Muller, S. H. *The World's Living Languages*. New York: Unger, 1964.

Pedersen, H. *The Discovery of Language*. Bloomington, Ind.: University of Indiana Press, 1962.

Ruhlen, Merritt. *A Guide to the Languages of the World*. Language Universals Project, Stanford University, 1976.

Sapir, E. *Language*. New York: Harcourt Brace Jovanovich, 1921.

Stokoe, W. C., D. C. Casterline, and C. G. Croneberg. *A Dictionary of American Sign Language on Linguistic Principles*. Washington, D.C.: Gallaudet College Press, 1965.

Stokoe, W. C. *Semiotics and Human Sign Languages*. The Hague: Mouton, 1970.

CHAPTER

The ABCs of Language: Writing

The Moving Finger writes; and, having writ,
Moves on: nor all thy Piety nor Wit
  Shall lure it back to cancel half a Line,
Nor all thy Tears wash out a Word of it.
OMAR KHAYYAM, *Rubáiyát*

The development of writing was one of the great human inventions. Writing allows us to transcend time and space. It is the wheel of our words, the time machine of our thoughts.

For many of us it is hard to imagine language without writing; the spoken word seems intricately tied to the written word. But children speak before they learn to write. And millions of people in the world speak languages with no written form. Among these people oral literature abounds, and crucial knowledge is memorized and passed between generations. But human memory is short-lived, and the brain's storage capacity is finite. Writing overcame such problems and allowed communication across the miles and through the years.

"The palest ink is better than the sharpest memory," according to an ancient Chinese proverb. The reason for this was stated by the Roman poet Horace: "Once a word has been allowed to escape, it cannot be recalled." Writing permits a society to permanently record its poetry, its history, and its technology.

It might be argued that today we have electronic means of recording sound and cameras to produce films and television, and thus writing is becoming obsolete. If writing became extinct, there would be no knowledge of electronics for TV technicians to study; there would be, in fact, little technology in years to come. There would be no film or TV scripts, no literature, no books, no mail, no newspapers, no science. There would be some advantages: no bad novels, junk mail, poison-pen letters, or "unreadable" income-tax forms, but the losses would far outweigh the gains. The historian Arnold Toynbee has summed up the importance of writing:

356

Man has lived the greater part of his existence on earth, which today is estimated as having lasted between 600,000 and 1 million years, as a "savage." It was only in the comparatively recent blossoming of civilizations in the last six thousand years that the various procedures of dictating and preserving graphic annotations were invented—the art which made man for the first time aware of the "philosophical contemporaneity" of all human evolutions. Thanks to writing, he realized that there was nothing new under the sun, but that he could also descend into the depths of "unhappy, far-off things," and exploit the treasures which countless generations had amassed, guarded and preserved down the ages to grasp at last . . . "the splendors and miseries of man."[1]

The History of Writing

One picture is worth a thousand words.
CHINESE PROVERB

There are almost as many legends and stories on the invention of writing as there are on the origin of language. Legend has it that Cadmus, Prince of Phoenicia and founder of the city of Thebes, invented the alphabet and brought it with him to Greece. (He later was banished to Illyria and changed into a snake.) In one Chinese fable the four-eyed dragon-god T'sang Chien invented writing, but in another, writing first appeared to humans in the form of markings on a turtle shell. In an Icelandic saga, Odin was the inventor of the runic script. In other myths, the Babylonian god Nebo and the Egyptian god Thoth gave humans writing as well as speech. The Talmudic scholar Rabbi Akiba believed that the alphabet existed before humans were created, and according to Islamic teaching, the alphabet was created by Allah himself, who presented it to man but not to the angels.

While these are delightful stories, it is evident that before a single word was ever written, uncountable billions were spoken; it is highly unlikely that a particularly gifted ancestor awoke one morning and decided "today I'll invent a writing system." Momentous inventions are rarely conceived in a moment.

PICTOGRAMS AND IDEOGRAMS

It is widely believed that the early drawings made by ancient humans were the seeds out of which writing developed. Cave drawings such as those found in the Altamira cave in northern Spain, drawn by humans living over 20,000 years ago, can be "read" today. They are literal portrayals of aspects of life at that time. We have no way of knowing why they were produced; they may well be esthetic expressions rather than communication messages. Later drawings, however, are clearly "picture writing," or **pictograms.** Unlike modern writing systems, each picture or pictogram is a direct image of the object it represents. There is a **nonarbitrary** relation-

[1] Arnold J. Toynbee, *An Historian's Approach to Religion* (New York: Oxford University Press, 1956).

By permission of Johnny Hart and Field Enterprises, Inc.

ship between the form and meaning of the symbol. Comic strips, minus captions, are pictographic—literal representations of the ideas to be communicated. This early form of "writing" did not have any direct relation to the language spoken, since the pictures represented objects in the world, rather than the linguistic names given to these objects; they did not represent the sounds of spoken language. Pictographic "writing" has been found among people throughout the world, ancient and modern; among African tribes, American Indians, Alaskan Eskimos, the Incas of Peru, the Yukagirians of Siberia, the people of Oceania. Pictograms are used today, in international road-signs, and signs on public toilets showing which are for men and which for women. The advantage of such symbols is that, since they do not depend on the sounds of any language, they can be understood by anyone. The signs used by the National Park Service exemplify this. One does not need to know any English to understand them. Some of the concepts conveyed in these signs are relatively complicated, in fact; see, for example, the symbol for "environmental study area" in Figure 13-1.

Figure 13-1 Six of seventy-seven symbols developed by the National Park Service for use as signs to indicate activities and facilities in parks and recreation areas. These are: environmental study area; grocery store; men's restroom; women's restroom; fishing; amphitheater. Certain symbols are available with a "prohibiting slash"—a diagonal red bar across the symbol that means the activity is forbidden. (National Park Service, U.S. Department of the Interior)

In the course of time the pictogram's meaning was extended, in that the picture represented not only the original object but attributes of that object, or concepts associated with it. Thus, a picture of the sun could represent "warmth," "heat," "light," "daytime," and so on. It is easy to understand how this came about. Try to imagine a drawing to represent "heat" or "daytime." Pictograms thus began to represent *ideas* rather than objects, and such pictograms are called **ideograms** ("idea pictures" or "idea writing").

Later, the pictograms or ideograms became stylized, probably because of the ambiguities which could result from "poor artists" or "abstractionists" of the time. The simplifying conventions which developed so distorted the literal representations that it was no longer easy to interpret these new symbols without learning the system.

By this period in time, the form and the meaning of a pictogram were fixed in an *arbitrary* relationship. The pictograms were now *linguistic* symbols; since their forms departed drastically from the objects they represented, they became instead symbols for the sounds of these objects—that is, for the words of the language. This stage represents a revolutionary step in the development of writing systems.

A **word-writing system** of this kind relates the symbol to the sounds of a word, but the symbol still stands for the concept rather than representing the sounds directly. Such identical symbols could be used to represent the words in any language, no matter how they were pronounced. The possible advantages of such a "universal" writing system motivated a Dutch journalist, Karel Johnson, and a German professor, André Eckardt, soon after World War II, to develop a pictographic system called Picto. In Picto, the phrase *I have a house in town* (or *Ich habe ein Haus in der Stadt* or *J'ai une maison en ville*) would look like this:

I	have	house	in	town
Ich	haben	Haus	in	Stadt
je	avoir	maison	en	ville

Unfortunately, such a system is only effective when concrete ideas are communicated. Suppose one tried to translate into Picto the following sentence from Kierkegaard's *Fear and Trembling:*

> If there were no eternal consciousness in a man, if at the foundation of all there lay only a wildly seething power which writhing with obscure passions produced everything that is great and everything that is insignificant, if a bottomless void never satiated lay hidden beneath all—what then would life be but despair?

The difficulty is apparent.

Had pictographic writing been adequate to the task, there would have been no reason for it to have developed into the modern writing systems.

CUNEIFORM WRITING

Much of our information on the development described above stems from the records left by the Sumerians, an ancient people of unknown origin who built a civilization in southern Mesopotamia over five thousand years ago. Their writing system is the oldest one known. It appears that they were a commercially oriented people, and as their business deals became increasingly complex the need for permanent records arose. An elaborate pictography was developed along with a system of "tallies." Some examples are shown here:

star, sky, God	hand	corn	5 oxen[2]	13 fish

Over the centuries their pictography was simplified and conventionalized. The characters or symbols were produced by using a wedge-shaped stylus which was pressed into soft clay tablets, made from the clay found on the land between the Tigris and Euphrates rivers. This form of writing

---

[2] The pictograph for "ox" evolved, much later, into our letter *A*.

is called **cuneiform**—literally "wedge-shaped" (from Latin *cuneus*). Here is an illustration of how Sumerian pictograms evolved to cuneiform:

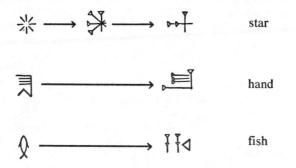

star

hand

fish

Notice that the cuneiform "words" do little to remind one of the meaning represented. As cuneiform evolved, its users began to think of the symbols more in terms of the *name* of the thing represented than the actual thing itself. Ultimately cuneiform script came to represent words of the language, and the Sumerians were in possession of a true word-writing system.

THE REBUS PRINCIPLE

When a graphic sign no longer has any visual relationship to the word it represents, it becomes a symbol for the sounds which represent the word. A single sign can then be used to represent all words with the same sounds—the homophones of the language. If, for example, the symbol ☉ stood for *sun* in English, it could then be used in a sentence like *My* ☉ *is a doctor.* If the symbol ◠ stood for *purse,* it could be combined with ☉ to form *person:* ◠☉. Using symbols which originally represented one-syllable words to represent individual syllables in many-syllable words is writing words according to the **rebus principle**.

A rebus is a representation of words or syllables by pictures of objects whose names *sound like* the intended syllables. Thus ◉ might represent *eye* or the pronoun *I*. The sounds of the two monosyllabic words are identical, even though the meanings are not. In the same way, 🐝🍃 could represent *belief* (*be* + *lief* = *bee* + *leaf* = /bi/ + /lif/), and 🐝🍃🍃 could be the verb form, *believes*.

This is not a very efficient system, since the words of many languages do not lend themselves to subdivision into sequences of sounds which represent independent meaning. It would be difficult, for example, to represent the word *English* (/iŋ/ + /glɪš/) in English according to the rebus principle. *Eng* by itself does not "mean" anything, nor does *glish*. The rebus system, however, led to a syllabic writing system which had many advantages over word-writing.

SYLLABIC WRITING SYSTEMS

The cuneiform writing system was borrowed by a number of peoples, most notably by the Assyrians (or Babylonians) when they conquered the Sumerians, and later by the Persians. In adopting cuneiform to their own languages, the borrowers used them to represent the *sounds* of the *syllables* in their words. In this way cuneiform evolved into a **syllabic writing system.**

Each syllable in the language is represented by its own symbol in a syllabic writing system. Words are written by juxtaposing the symbols of their individual syllables. Cuneiform writing was never purely syllabic; that is, there was always a large residue of symbols which stood for whole words. The Assyrians retained a large number of word symbols, even though every word in their language could be written out syllabically if it were desired. Thus one could write  mātu "country" as:

ma   +   a   +   tu

The Persians (ca. 600–400 B.C.) devised a greatly simplified syllabic alphabet for their language. They had little recourse to word symbols. By the reign of Darius I (522–468 B.C.) the writing system was in wide use. Here are a few characters of the syllabary:

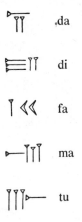

da

di

fa

ma

tu

FROM HIEROGLYPHS TO THE ALPHABET

At the time that Sumerian pictography was flourishing (around 4000 B.C.), a similar system was being used by the Egyptians, later called by the Greeks **hieroglyphics** (*hiero* "sacred," *glyphikos* "carvings"). That the early "sacred carvings" were originally pictography is shown by the following hieroglyphics:

"eye"	"giraffe"	"to rule"[3]	"fresh" or "cool"[4]

Like the Sumerian pictograms, the hieroglyphs began to represent the sounds of the words they symbolized. This **phonetization** of the pictography made hieroglyphics a word-writing system, which paralleled the Sumerian cuneiform development. Possibly influenced by the Sumerians, the Egyptian system also became a word-syllabic writing.

In this advanced "syllabic" stage, hieroglyphics were borrowed by many people, including the Phoenicians, a Semitic people who lived on the eastern shores of the Mediterranean. By 1500 B.C. a system involving twenty-two syllables, the West Semitic Syllabary, was in use. In this system a single symbol represents both a consonant and a following vowel (CV).

This was the system first borrowed by the Greeks in the tenth century B.C. The syllabic system proved to be very inefficient, especially for a language like Greek with a complex syllable structure. In the Semitic languages there are many monosyllabic words, and in polysyllabic words the syllables are simple and regular.

Even in a language with a "simple" and regular syllable structure the number of syllables which would have to be used is enormous. Suppose, for example, a language sound system includes twenty consonants and five vowels. Suppose further that the typical syllable was composed of a consonant plus a vowel plus a consonant: C + V + C. This would permit 2000 separate syllables: 20C × 5V × 20C.

Consider now a language like English. While there are constraints on which consonants can cluster, we still get syllables like:

I	[ay]	V	*an*	[æn]	VC
key	[ki]	CV	*ant*	[ænt]	VCC
ski	[ski]	CCV	*ants*	[ænts]	VCCC
spree	[spri]	CCCV	*pant*	[pænt]	CVCC
seek	[sik]	CVC	*pants*	[pænts]	CVCCC
speak	[spik]	CCVC	*splints*	[splɪnts]	CCCVCCC
scram	[skræm]	CCCVC	*stamp*	[stæmp]	CCVCC
striped	[straypt]	CCCVCC			

When you think of all the vowels and all the consonants that can occur in syllable structures of this kind it is evident that the number of syllables needed would be enormous. This kind of problem motivated the Greeks to use the symbols of the Phoenician writing system, but to represent the individual sounds—consonants and vowels. The Phoenicians had taken

---

[3] The symbol is the Pharaoh's staff.
[4] Water trickling out of a vase

the first step by letting certain symbols stand for consonants alone. The language spoken by the Phoenicians, however, had more consonants than Greek, so when the Greeks borrowed the system they had symbols left over. These they allowed to represent vowel sounds, and thus they invented the **alphabetic writing system.** (The word *alphabet* is derived from *alpha* and *beta,* the first two letters of the Greek alphabet.)

Alphabetic systems are those in which each symbol represents one phoneme. It is clear that such systems are primarily *phonemic* rather than *phonetic,* as is illustrated by the fact that the *l* in both *feel* and *leaf* in the English alphabet system is represented by one rather than two "letters" even though the sounds are phonetically distinct.

There are arguments as to whether this event—the development of an alphabetic writing system—occurred more than once in history. Most scholars believe that all alphabetic systems in use today derive from the Greek system. This alphabet became known to the pre-Latin people of Italy, the Etruscans, who in turn passed it on to the Romans. The Roman Empire spread it throughout the world. Later, Christian missionaries used alphabetic systems to develop writing systems for many preliterate people. (Parts of the Bible have been translated into more than 1600 languages.)

It is a surprising fact that the alphabet, as we know it, did not have many beginnings. According to one linguist, the alphabet was not invented, it was *discovered.*[5] If language did not include discrete individual sounds, one could not have invented alphabetic letters to represent such sounds. When humans started to use one symbol for one phoneme they had merely brought their intuitive knowledge of the language sound system to consciousness; they discovered what they already knew. Furthermore, children (and adults) can learn an alphabetic system only if each separate sound has some psychological reality. Since this is true of all languages, however, it is strange that this "discovery" was not made by many people in many parts of the world.

Modern Types of Writing Systems

... but their manner of writing is very peculiar, being neither from the left to the right, like the Europeans; nor from the right to the left, like the Arabians; nor from up to down, like the Chinese; nor from down to up, like the Cascagians, but aslant from one corner of the paper to the other, like ladies in England.
JONATHAN SWIFT, *Gulliver's Travels*

We have already discussed the three types of writing systems used in the world: *word-writing, syllable-writing,* and *alphabetic writing.*

In a word-writing system the written symbol represents a whole word. The awkwardness of such a system is obvious. For example, the editors of *Webster's Third New International Dictionary* claim more than 450,000

[5] Dr. Sven Ohman, Professor of Phonetics, University of Uppsala, Sweden; paper presented at the International Speech Symposium, Kyoto, Japan, 1969.

entries. When we consider that all these are written using only twenty-six alphabetic symbols, a dot, a hyphen, an apostrophe, and a space, it is understandable why, historically, word-writing has given way to alphabetic systems in most places in the world.

The major exception is the writing system used in China. This system has an uninterrupted history that reaches back more than 3500 years. For the most part it is a word-writing system, each character representing an individual word or morpheme. A morpheme-writing system would be a more appropriate name, since most words are monomorphemic. Longer words may be formed by combining two morphemes, as shown by the word meaning "business" *măimai,* which was formed by combining the words meaning "buy" and "sell."

Chinese writing utilizes a system of **characters,** each of which represents the "meaning" of a word, rather than its sounds. Chinese dictionaries and rhyme books contain tens of thousands of these characters, but to read a newspaper one need know "only" about five thousand. It is not easy to become a scholar in China! In 1956, the difficulties prompted the government of the People's Republic of China to simplify the characters. They also adopted a spelling system using the Roman alphabet, to be used along with the regular ancient system. It is doubtful whether it will replace the traditional writing, which is an integral part of Chinese culture. In China, writing is an art— calligraphy—and thousands of years of poetry and literature and history are preserved in the old system.

There is an additional reason for keeping the traditional system. Chinese is composed of a number of dialects and languages which are all mutually unintelligible in spoken form. But each dialect uses the one writing system; through writing all the Chinese can communicate. A common sight in a city like Hong Kong is for two Chinese to be talking and at the same time furiously drawing characters in the air with a forefinger to overcome their dialectal differences.

The use of written Chinese characters in this way is parallel to the use of Arabic numerals, which mean the same in all European countries. Though the word for "eight" is very different in English, Greek, and Finnish, by writing *8* you can be understood. Similarly, the word for "rice" is different in many Chinese dialects, but the written character is the same. If the writing system in China were ever to become alphabetic, each dialect would be as different in writing as in speaking, and communication would break down completely between the dialect groups.

Every writing system has some traces of word-writing. In addition to numerals in which a single symbol represents a whole word, other symbols, such as $, %, &, ¢, H_2O, +, −, =, are used.

Syllabic writing systems are more efficient than word-writing systems. They are certainly less taxing on our memory. But as discussed above, they still present serious difficulties for recording the sentences of a language.

Japanese is the only major language in the world that uses a syllabic alphabet. They borrowed and modfied fifty Chinese characters to stand for each of the fifty syllables that Japanese words are composed of. This system is not purely syllabic, there being a number of word signs borrowed from Chinese, and many words are represented by a mixture of a word sign and a syllable sign. In theory, all of Japanese could be written in the fifty-character syllabary, but the large number of homophones (*ka* has over two hundred meanings, each indicated by a separate character) provides incentive for retaining the dual word/syllabic system.

In 1821, Sequoyah, often called the "Cherokee Cadmus," invented a syllabic writing system for his native language. Sequoyah's script proved very useful to the Cherokee people for a number of years, and was justifiably a point of great pride for them. The syllabary contains eighty-five symbols, many of them derived from Latin characters, and efficiently transcribes spoken Cherokee. A few symbols are shown here;

J gu

ſ hu

ഛ we

W ta

H mi

English occasionally uses syllabic symbols. In words such as *OK* and *bar-b-q*, the single letters represent syllables (*b* for [bə], *q* for [kyu]).

Alphabetic writing systems are one of the major achievements of civilization. They are easy to learn and convenient to use, and are maximally efficient for transcribing any human language.

The term **sound-writing** is sometimes used in place of alphabetic writing, but this does not truly represent the principle involved in the use of alphabets. One-sound-one-letter would be inefficient, since we do not need to represent the [pʰ] in *pit* and the [p] in *spit* by two different letters. It would also be confusing, because the nonphonemic differences between sounds are seldom perceptible to speakers. Except for the phonetic alphabets whose function is to record the sounds of all languages for descriptive purposes, most, if not all, alphabets have been devised on the **phonemic principle.**

In the twelfth century, an Icelandic scholar developed an orthography derived from the Latin alphabet for the writing of the Icelandic language of his day. Other scholars in this period were also interested in orthographic reform, including the German, Notker, and the Englishman, Orm. But the Icelander, who came to be known as "The First Grammarian" (because his anonymous paper was the first entry in a collection of grammatical essays), was the only one of the time who left a record of his principles. The orthography which he developed was clearly based on the phonemic principle. He used minimal pairs to show the distinctive contrasts; he did not suggest different symbols for voiced and unvoiced [θ] and [ð], nor for [f] or [v], nor for velar [k] and palatal [č], since these pairs, according to him, represented allophones of the phonemes /θ/, /f/, and /k/, respectively. He, of course, did not use these modern technical terms, but the letters of his alphabet represent the distinctive phonemes of Icelandic of that century.

King Seijong of Korea (1417–1450) realized that the same held true for Korean when he designed a phonemic alphabet. The king was an avid reader (so avid that his eyes suffered greatly), and he realized that the more than 30,000 Chinese characters that were being used to write the Korean language discouraged literacy among the people.

The alphabet was not reinvented by Seijong. Indian scholars had visited Korea, and the erudite monarch undoubtedly knew of the Hindu grammarians. Still, his alphabet, called *hankul,* was conceived with remarkable insight. Originally hankul had eleven vowels and seventeen consonants (it is down to fourteen consonants and ten vowels at present). The characters representing consonants were drawn according to the place and manner of articulation. For example, ∧ is meant to represent the teeth, and it is a part of each consonant character in which the tongue is placed behind the teeth (that is, alveolar or alveopalatal sounds). Thus ∧ alone stands for /s/ ([s] or [š]). Cross it to get ∧ and you have the character for [ts] (the initial sound of German *Zeit*) and [tš] (= [č]). A bar above the character means aspiration, so ∧̄ stands for [tsʰ] and [tšʰ] (= [čʰ]). Hundreds of years later, Francis Lodwick, Cave Beck, and Henry Sweet used a similar principle to design their phonetic alphabets.

King Seijong's vowels were conceived somewhat more philosophically. "King Seijong made the eleven vowels represent heaven, earth and man. . . ."[6] Each vowel character was constructed by using one or more of three "atomic" characters: · | and —; for example, | was /i/, ⫟ was /u/ and | · was /a/. Although Korean has the sounds [l] and [r], only a single "letter" was used by Seijong because these sounds are in "complementary distribution" in Korean—allophonic variants of the same phoneme. The same is true for the sounds [s] and [š]. Seijong knew that a narrow phonetic alphabet would be unintuitive to a Korean speaker.

Seijong's contribution to the Korean people has been recorded in a delightful legend. It is said that after he designed the alphabet he was afraid it would not be accepted, and so he concocted a scheme to convince the people that it was a gift from heaven. To do this he wrote each one of his new letters in honey on individual leaves which had fallen from a tree in the palace garden. When the king walked with his soothsayer in the garden the next day, the insects had eaten the honey and the leaf fiber underneath, just as he had hoped, and the leaves were etched with the alphabetic letters. The soothsayer and the Korean people were convinced that these represented a message from the gods. It is essentially this alphabet which is used in Korea today.

Many languages have their own alphabet, and each has developed certain conventions for converting strings of alphabetic characters into sequences of sound (that is, reading), and converting sequences of sounds into strings of alphabetic characters (that is, writing). As we have illustrated with English, Icelandic, and Korean, the rules governing the sound system of the language play an important role in the relation between sound and character.

[6] *King Seijong the Great,* prepared by the King Seijong Memorial Society of the Republic of Korea.

Most European alphabets make use of Latin (Roman) characters, minor adjustments being made to accommodate individual characteristics of a particular language. For instance, Spanish uses /ñ/ (an /n/ with a "tilde") to represent the palatilized nasal of *señor,* and German has added an "umlaut" for certain of its vowel sounds that didn't exist in Latin (for example, *über.*) Such "extra" marks are called **diacritics.** Often languages resort to using two letters together to represent a single sound for which there is no corresponding single letter. English includes **digraphs** such as *sh* [š], *ch* [č], *ng* [ŋ], and so on.

Some languages that have more recently acquired a writing system use some of the IPA phonetic symbols in their alphabet. Twi, for example uses ŋ, ɔ, and ɛ.

Besides the European languages, such languages as Turkish, Indonesian, Swahili, and Vietnamese have adopted the Latin alphabet.

The **Cyrillic** alphabet, named for St. Cyril, who brought Christianity to the Slavs, is used by many Slavic languages, including Russian. It is derived directly from the Greek alphabet without Latin mediation.

The contemporary Semitic alphabets, and those used for Persian and Urdu writing, are derived from the West Semitic Syllabary.

Figure 13-2 shows a greatly abbreviated "family tree" of alphabetic writing systems.

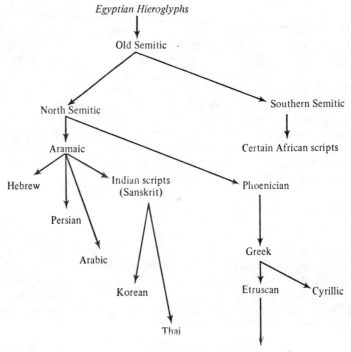

Figure 13-2 Family tree of alphabetic writing systems. (Adapted from Ernst Doblhofer, *Voices in Stone,* Viking, 1961)

Writing and Speech

. . . Ther is so great diversite
In English, and in wryting of oure tonge,
So prey I god that non myswrite thee . . .
GEOFFREY CHAUCER

The development of writing freed man from his earthbound status and took him to the stars, but it is language that makes man what he is. The primacy of the spoken language over the written is revealed in the short history of writing in the preceding pages. To understand language one cannot depend on its written form. A linguist would no more investigate a language via its orthography than a doctor would examine a patient via a photograph. Writing is of interest to the linguist, but only as an indirect means of learning about a language.

The written language reflects, to a certain extent, the elements and rules which together constitute the grammar of the language. The system of phonemes is represented by the letters of the alphabet, although not necessarily in a direct way. Were there no discrete sound units in language, there could be no alphabetic writing. The independence of words in a language is revealed by the spaces in the written string. But in languages where words are composed of more than one morpheme, the writing does not show the individual morphemes, even though speakers know what these are. The sentences of a language are represented in the written form by capitals and periods. Other punctuation, such as question marks, italics, commas, exclamation marks, is used to reveal syntactic structure.

The possible ambiguity in the meanings of some sentences can be prevented by the use of commas:

1. The Greeks, who were philosophers, loved to talk a lot.
2. The Greeks who were philosophers loved to talk a lot.

The difference in meaning between the two sentences is specified by the use of commas in the first and not in the second. Sentence 1, with the commas, clearly means:

1′. The Greeks were philosophers and they loved to talk a lot.

The meaning of the second sentence, without the commas, can be paraphrased as:

2′. Among the Greeks it was the philosophers who loved to talk a lot.

Similarly, by using an exclamation point or a question mark, the intention of the writer can be revealed.

3. The children are going to bed at eight o'clock. *(simple statement)*
4. The children are going to bed at eight o'clock! *(an order)*
5. The children are going to bed at eight o'clock? *(a query)*

These punctuation marks reflect the pauses and the intonations which would be used in the spoken language.

In sentence 6 the *he* can refer to either John or someone else, but in sentence 7 the pronoun must refer to someone other than John:

6. John said he's going.
7. John said, "He's going."

The apostrophe used in contractions and possessives also provides syntactic information:

8. My cousin's friends *(one cousin)*
9. My cousins' friends *(two or more cousins)*

Writing, then, does reflect the spoken language, but it does so imperfectly. Ordinary punctuation marks may be unable to distinguish between two possible meanings:

10. John whispered the message to Bill and then he whispered it to Mary.

In the normal written version of sentence 10, *he* can refer to either John or Bill. In the spoken sentence, if *he* receives extra stress (called **contrastive stress**), it must refer to Bill; if *he* receives normal stress, it refers to John. In speaking one can usually emphasize any word in a sentence by using contrastive stress. One sometimes attempts to show this in writing by using all capital letters or underlining the emphasized word:

11. <u>John</u> kissed Bill's wife.   (Bill didn't)
12. John <u>kissed</u> Bill's wife.   (rather than hitting her)
13. John kissed <u>Bill's</u> wife.   (not Dick's or his own)
14. John kissed Bill's <u>wife</u>.   (not Bill's mother)

While such "visual" devices can help in English, it is not clear that this can be done in a language such as Chinese.

The written language is also more conservative than the spoken language. When we write something—particularly in formal writing—we are more apt to obey the "prescriptive rules" taught in school, or use a more formal style, than we are to use the rules of our "everyday" grammar. "Dangling participles" (for example, *While studying in the library, the fire alarm rang*) and "sentences ending with a preposition" (for example, *I know what to end a sentence with*) abound in spoken language, but may be "corrected" by copy editors, diligent English teachers, and careful writers. A linguist wishing to describe the language that people regularly use therefore cannot depend on written records alone.

Spelling

"Do you spell it with a 'v' or a 'w'?" inquired the judge.
"That depends upon the taste and fancy of the speller,
my Lord," replied Sam.
CHARLES DICKENS, *The Pickwick Papers*

If writing represented the spoken language perfectly, spelling reformers would never have arisen. In Chapter 4 we discussed some of the problems in the English orthographic (spelling) system. These problems prompted George Bernard Shaw to write:

. . . it was as a reading and writing animal that Man achieved his human eminence above those who are called beasts. Well, it is I and my like who have to do the writing. I have done it professionally for the last sixty years as well as it can be done with a hopelessly inadequate alphabet devised centuries before the English language existed to record another and very different language. Even this alphabet is reduced to absurdity by a foolish orthography based on the notion that the business of spelling is to represent the origin and history of a word instead of its sound and meaning. Thus an intelligent child who is bidden to spell debt, and very properly spells it d-e-t, is caned for not spelling it with a b because Julius Caesar spelt the Latin word for it with a b.[7]

The irregularities between **graphemes** (letters) and phonemes have been cited as one reason "why Johnny can't read." Different spellings for the same sound, the same spellings for different sounds, "silent letters," and "missing letters"—all provide fuel for the flames of spelling-reform movements. This was illustrated earlier, but merits further examples:

SAME SOUND, DIFFERENT SPELLING	DIFFERENT SOUND, SAME SPELLING		SILENT LETTERS	MISSING LETTERS
/ay/	thought	[θ]	listen	use /yuz/
	though	[ð]	debt	fuse /fyuz/
aye	Thomas	[t]	gnosis	
buy			know	
by	ate	[e]	psychology	
die	at	[æ]	right	
hi	father	[a]	though	
Thai	many	[ɛ]	arctic	
			balm	
			honest	
			sword	
			bomb	
			clue	

Chapters 4 and 11 discuss some of the reasons for the nonphonemic aspects of our spelling system. "Spelling is the written trace of a word. Pronunciation is its linguistic form."[8] The spelling of most of the words in English today is based on the Late Middle English pronunciation (that used by Chaucer) and on the early forms of Modern English (used by Shakespeare). As was noted, the many changes which have occurred in the sound system of English, like the Great Vowel Shift, were not always reflected in changes in the spelling of the words which were affected.

When the printing press was introduced in the fifteenth century, not only were archaic pronunciations "frozen" but the spelling did not always represent even those pronunciations, since many of the early printers were Dutch and were unsure of English pronunciation.

During the Renaissance, in the fifteenth and sixteenth centuries, many scholars who revered Classical Greek and Latin became "spelling reform-

[7] George Bernard Shaw, Preface to R. A. Wilson, *The Miraculous Birth of Language* (New York: Philosophical Library, 1948).

[8] D. Bolinger, *Aspects of Language* (New York: Harcourt Brace Jovanovich 1968).

ers." Unlike the later reformers who wished to change the spelling to conform with pronunciation, these scholars changed the spelling of English words to conform to their etymologies—the "original" Latin, or Greek, or French spellings. Where Latin had a *b*, they added a *b* even if it was not pronounced; and where the original spelling had a *c* or *p* or *h*, these letters were added, as is shown by these few examples:

MIDDLE ENGLISH SPELLING		"REFORMED" SPELLING
indite	→	indict
dette	→	debt
receit	→	receipt
oure	→	hour

These, then, are the reasons why modern English orthography does not represent, in all cases, what we know about the phonology of the language. In at least one respect this is a good thing. It allows us to read and understand what people wrote hundreds of years ago without the need for translations. If there were a one-to-one correspondence between our spelling and the sounds of our language, we would have difficulty reading even the Constitution or the Declaration of Independence. Constant spellings help our ever-dynamic language to span gaps of time.

Today's language is no more static than was yesterday's; it would be impossible to maintain a perfect correspondence between pronunciation and spelling. This is not to say that certain reforms would not be helpful. Some "respelling" is already taking place; advertisers often spell *though* as *tho*, *through* as *thru*, and *night* as *nite*. For a period of time the Chicago *Tribune* used such spellings, but in 1975 they gave this up. Spelling habits are hard to change.

In the case of homophones, it is very helpful at times to have different spellings for the same sounds, as in the following:

The book was red.   The book was read.

Lewis Carroll once more makes the point with his own inimitable humor:

"And how many hours a day did you do lessons?" said Alice.
"Ten hours the first day," said the Mock Turtle, "nine the next, and so on."
"What a curious plan!" exclaimed Alice.
"That's the reason they're called *lessons*," the Gryphon remarked, "because they *lessen* from day to day."

There are also reasons for using the same spelling for different pronunciations. In Chapter 5 it was shown that a morpheme may be pronounced differently when it occurs in different contexts, and that in most cases the pronunciation is "regular"; that is, it is determined by rules which apply throughout the language. The identical spelling reflects the fact that the different pronunciations represent the same morpheme.

Similarly, the phonetic realizations of the vowels in the following forms are "regular":

ay/ɪ	i/ɛ	e/æ
divine/divinity	serene/serenity	sane/sanity
sublime/sublimate	obscene/obscenity	profane/profanity
sign/signature	hygiene/hygienic	humane/humanity

The spelling of such pairs thus reflects our knowledge of the sound pattern of the language and the semantic relations between the words.

It is doubtful that anyone would suggest that the plural morpheme should be spelled *s* in *cats* and *z* in *dogs*. The sound of the morpheme is determined by rules, and this is just as true in other cases like those given above.

There are also different spellings which represent the different pronunciations of a morpheme when confusion would arise from using the same spelling. For example, there is a rule in English phonology which changes a /t/ to an /s/ in certain cases: *democrat* → *democracy*. The different spellings are due in part to the fact that this rule does not apply to all morphemes, as was shown by some of the words listed above, such as *sanity*. There are many regular phoneme-to-grapheme rules which determine when a morpheme is to be spelled identically and when it is changed. Notice, also, that a *c* always represents the /s/ sound when it is followed by a *y* or *i* or *e*, as in *cynic* and *citizen* and *censure*. Since it is always pronounced [k] when it is the final letter in a word or when it is followed by any other vowel (*coat, cat, cut,* and so on), no confusion results.

Such rules of orthography can be taught to children learning to read, which would lessen the difficulties they have with the spelling system.

There is another important reason why spelling should not always be tied to the phonetic pronunciation of words. Professor David Abercrombie of the University of Edinburgh tells a story about a conversation between an American and an Englishman. The American asks the Englishman what his job is and the Englishman replies: "I'm a clerk." The astonished American shakes his head and asks "You mean you go 'tick-tock, tick-tock'?"

The common spelling *clerk* is pronounced [klərk] by Americans and [kla:k] by the British. A popular song of the 1930s illustrates the difference between American English and what was thought to be British English (there were Americans who thought it was "upper-class" to use British pronunciations):

> You say tomato, and I say tomato,
> [təmeto] [təmato]
> You say potato, and I say potato,
> [pəteto] [pətato]
> Tomato, tomato, potato, potato, let's call the whole thing off.[9]
> [təmeto] [təmato] [pəteto] [pətato]

Other English dialects also have divergent pronunciations. Cockneys drop their "haitches" and Bostonians and Southerners drop their "r's"; *neither* is pronounced [niðər] and [niðə] by Americans, [nayðə] by the Brit-

---

[9] Copyright © 1937 by Gershwin Publishing Corporation. Copyright renewed. Reprinted by permission of Chappell & Co., Inc.

ish, and [neðər] by the Irish; some Scots pronounce *night* as [nɪxt]; one hears "Chicago" and "Chicawgo," "hog" and "hawg," "bird" and "boyd"; *four* is pronounced [fɔ:] by the British, [fɔr] in the Midwest, and [foə] in the South; *orange* is pronounced in at least two ways in the United States: [arənǰ] and [ɔrənǰ].

While dialectal pronunciations differ, the common spellings represent the fact that we can all understand each other. It is necessary for the written language to transcend local dialects. With a uniform spelling system, a native of Atlanta and a native of Glasgow can communicate through writing. If each dialect were spelled according to its own pronunciation, written communication among the English-speaking peoples of the world would suffer more than the spoken communication does today.

An Irish friend of ours has suggested that since the Irish originally taught the English to write (between 600 and 700 A.D.), spelling reforms ought to be made in Ireland. Then, says our friend, the Irish will simply teach the English to write once again. We have no idea what he has in mind for North America, should such a spelling reform movement win out.

Spelling Pronunciations

For pronuncation, the best general rule is to consider those as the most elegant speakers who deviate least from written words.
SAMUEL JOHNSON, 1755

Despite the primacy of the spoken over the written language, the written word is often regarded with excessive reverence. Undoubtedly the stability, permanency, and graphic nature of writing cause some people to favor it over ephemeral and elusive speech. Humpty Dumpty expressed a rather typical attitude: "I'd rather see that done on paper," he announced.

Writing has, however, affected speech only marginally, and most notably in the phenomenon of **spelling pronunciation.** Since the sixteenth century, we find that spelling has influenced standard pronunciation to some extent. The most important of such changes stem from the eighteenth century under the influence and "decrees" of the dictionary-makers and the schoolteachers. The struggle between those who demanded that words be pronounced according to the spelling and those who demanded that words be spelled according to their pronunciation generated great heat in that century. The "preferred" pronunciations were given in the many dictionaries printed in the eighteenth century, and the "supreme authority" of the dictionaries influenced pronunciation in this way.

Spelling also has influenced pronunciation in words that are infrequently used in normal daily speech. Many words which were spelled with an initial *h* were not pronounced with any /h/ sound as late as the eighteenth century. Thus, at that time no /h/ was pronounced in *honest, hour, habit, heretic, hotel, hospital, herb*. Frequently used words like *honest* and *hour* continued to be pronounced without the /h/, despite the spelling. But all those other words were given a "spelling pronunciation." Since people did not hear them very often, when they saw them written they concluded that they must begin with an /h/.

Similarly, many words now spelled with a *th* were once pronounced /t/ as in *Thomas;* later most of these words underwent a change in pronunciation from /t/ to /θ/, as in *anthem, author, theater.* It is interesting that "nicknames" often reflect the earlier pronunciations: "Ka*te*" for "Ca*the*-rine," "Be*tty*" for "Elizabe*th*," "Ar*t*" for "Ar*th*ur." The words *often* and *soften,* which are usually pronounced without a /t/ sound, are pronounced with the /t/ by some people because of the spelling. At one time, however, the /t/ was never pronounced in *often* and *soften.*

The clear influence of spelling on pronunciation is observable in the way place-names are pronounced. *Berkeley* is pronounced [bərkli] in California, although it stems from the British [baːkli]; *Worcester* [wʊstər] or [wʊstə] in Massachusetts is often pronounced [wərčɛstər] in other parts of the country.

While the written language thus has some influence on the spoken, it never changes the basic system—the grammar—of the language. The writing system, conversely, reflects, in a more or less direct way, the grammar that every speaker knows.

Graffiti

Banish the use of the four-letter words
Whose meaning is never obscure;
The Anglos, the Saxons, those bawdy old birds
Were vulgar, obscene, and impure.
But cherish the use of the weasling phrase
That never quite says what it means;
You'd better be known for your hypocrite ways
Than vulgar, impure, and obscene.
OGDEN NASH, "Ode to the Four-Letter Words"

Graffiti means different things to different people. To a lexicographer, it is the plural of *graffito;* to a philologist it is an Italian borrowing that means "scribbling" or "scratching"; to the timid, it is something shocking, and to the insolent a chance to shock; to the radical it is "mass propaganda"; to the city of Philadelphia it is a million dollars a year spent in a losing battle to scrape paint off the walls of its subway platforms; to most of us it is what we see, and perhaps what we scrawl, on the walls of public places, such as toilets.

Graffito was adopted by archeologists as a general term for the casual writings, rude drawings, and markings found on ancient buildings and monuments. It contrasted with the term *inscription,* which was reserved for more deliberate, more conventional writing or drawing. The word has undergone semantic shifting, and for many younger people it now has only a vulgar or obscene connotation, though this was not always so, nor is it so for all speakers.

The graffiti which covered the buildings in Paris during the student demonstrations of May 1968 were far from obscene. They were the written testimonials to the emotional feelings of the students. The painted words of the youth were later whitewashed out, but photographs of the graffiti record a historical moment. LA SOCIÉTÉ EST UNE FLEUR CARNIVORE" ("Society is a carnivorous flower") one sign proclaimed; another, "PRENDS MES DÉSIRS POUR LA RÉALITÉ CAR JE CROIS EN LA RÉALITÉ DE MES DÉSIRS" ("Accept my desires as real, for I believe in the reality of my desires"). By such graffiti the thoughts of the young people of the time are revealed.

Graffiti have been found in great abundance on monuments of ancient Egypt, usually scratched into the stone or plaster. The subjects of these scribblings include rude caricatures, obscenities, election addresses, and lines of poetry. The present-day urban crisis over graffiti has had its counterparts in history. Archeologists have found ancient Roman ruins with inscriptions begging passersby not to scribble on the walls, and in Thera, Greece, rock inscriptions have been found "consisting of . . . the perverse scribblings of street urchins"[10] which date back to the seventh century B.C.

Such graffiti are important historical clues. While "Kilroy was here" (a common "scribble" of a few years ago) may confuse future historians as to who the famous "Kilroy" was, the graffiti proclaiming "Yankee go home" will tell them that the American presence was not always welcomed in other countries.

Linguists do not consider graffiti a nuisance by any means—at least not old graffiti. Graffiti can furnish useful information about the spoken language of a particular period and place, and in the case of graffiti left by foreign "tourists," about the language of another place in the same period. They also provide information about the kind of writing system the "man in the street" was using, and hence provide valuable clues in the saga of evolving writing systems.

SUMMARY

Writing is one of the basic tools of civilization. Without it, the world as we know it could not exist.

The first writing was "picture writing," which used **pictograms** to represent objects directly. Pictograms became stylized and people came to associate them with the *word sounds* that represented the object in their language. The Sumerians first developed a pictographic writing system to keep track of commercial transactions. It was later expanded for other uses and eventually evolved into the highly stylized **cuneiform** writing. Cuneiform was borrowed by several nations and was adapted for use in a syllabic writing system by application of the **rebus principle,** which used the symbol of one word to represent any word or syllable with the same sounds.

The Egyptians also developed a pictographic system that became known as **hieroglyphics.** This system was borrowed by many peoples including the Phoenicians, who improved on it, using it as a **syllabary.** In a syllabic writing

[10] F. N. H. Pederson, *The Discovery of Language: Linguistic Science in the Nineteenth Century,* trans. by John Webster Spargo (Bloomington: Indiana University Press, 1962).

system one symbol is used for each syllable. The Greeks borrowed this Phoenician system and in adapting it to their own language used the symbols to represent individual sound segments, thus inventing the first **alphabet.**

There are three types of writing systems still being used in the world: **word writing,** where every symbol or character represents a word or morpheme (as in Chinese); **syllable-writing,** where each symbol represents a syllable (as in Japanese); and **alphabetic writing,** where each symbol represents (for the most part) one phoneme (as in English).

Many of the world's languages do not have a written form, but this does not mean the languages are any less developed. We learn to speak before we learn to write, and historically tens of thousands of years went by during which language was spoken before there was any writing.

The writing system may have some small effect on the spoken language. Languages change in time, but writing systems tend to be more conservative. When the spoken and written forms of the language become divergent, some words may be pronounced as they are spelled, sometimes due to the efforts of "pronunciation reformers."

There are advantages to a conservative spelling system. A common spelling permits speakers whose dialects have diverged to communicate through writing, as is best exemplified in China, where the "dialects" are mutually unintelligible. We are also able to read and understand the language as it was written centuries ago. In addition, besides some gross lack of correspondences between sound and spelling, the spelling often reflects speakers' morphological and phonological knowledge.

EXERCISES

1. A. "Write" the following words and phrases using pictograms which you invent:

   a. eye   e. tree   i. ugly
   b. a boy   f. forest   j. run
   c. two boys   g. war   k. Scotch tape
   d. library   h. honesty   l. smoke

   B. Which words are most difficult to symbolize in this way? Why?

   C. How does the following sentence reveal the problems in pictographic writing? "A grammar represents the unconscious, internalized linguistic compentence of a native speaker."

2. A *rebus* is a written representation of words or syllables using pictures of objects whose names resemble the sounds of the intended words or syllables. For example, might be the symbol for "eye" or "I" or the first syllable in "idea."

   A. Using the rebus principle, "write" the following

   a. tearing   b. icicle   c. bareback   d. cookies

   B. Why would such a system be a difficult system in which to represent all words in English? Illustrate with an example.

3. A. Construct non-Roman alphabetic letters to replace the letters used to represent the following sounds in English:

t r s k w č i æ f ŋ

B. Use these symbols plus the regular alphabet symbols for the other sounds to write the following words in your "new orthography."

a. character   e. cheat
b. guest   f. rang
c. cough   g. psychotic
d. photo   h. tree

4. Suppose the English writing system were a *syllabic* system instead of an *alphabetic* system. Use capital letters to symbolize the necessary syllabic units for the words listed below and list your "syllabary." Example, given the words *mate, inmate, intake*, and *elfin*, one might use: A = mate, B = in, C = take, and D = elf. In addition, write the words using your syllabary. Example: *inmate:* BA, *elfin:* DB; *intake:* BC; *mate:* A. (Do not use any more syllable symbols than you absolutely need.)

a. childishness   d. lifelessness   g. witness   j. witless
b. childlike   e. likely   h. lethal   k. lesson
c. Jesuit   f. zoo   i. jealous

5. In the following pairs of English words the boldfaced portions are pronounced the same but spelled differently. Can you think of any reason why the spelling should remain distinct? (Hint: *reel* and *real* are pronounced the same, but *reality* shows the presence of a phonemic /æ/ in *real*.)

a. I am   iamb
b. goose   produce
c. fashion   complication
d. Newton   organ
e. no   know
f. hymn   him

6. In the following pairs of words the boldfaced portions in the second column are pronounced differently from those in the first column. Try to state some reasons why the spelling of the words in column B should not be changed.

A	B
a. mingle	long
b. line	children
c. sonar	resound
d. cent	mystic
e. crumble	bomb
f. cats	dogs
g. stagnant	design
h. serene	obscenity

7. Each of the following sentences is ambiguous (can have more than one meaning) in the written form. How can these sentences be made unambiguous when they are spoken?

   a. John punched Bill and then he kicked him.
   b. What are we having for dinner, Mother?
   c. She's a German language teacher.
   d. They formed a student grievance committee.
   e. Charles kissed his wife and George kissed his wife, too.

8. In the written form, the following sentences are not ambiguous, but they would be if spoken. State the devices used in writing which make the meanings explicit.

   a. They're my brothers' keepers.
   b. He said, "He will take the garbage out."
   c. The red book was read.
   d. The flower was on the table.

9. If you were given the task of making changes in the present spelling system of English, what are some of the changes you would propose? Are there any "silent" letters that should be dropped from the orthography? Should some sounds always have the same letters to represent them? Should some letters with different sounds be given additional symbols? Justify your proposals.

10. Discuss the statement quoted in the chapter that "alphabetic writing was not invented, it was discovered." That is, how does the existence of alphabets reflect a linguistic universal?

References

Diringer, D. *The Alphabet*. New York: Philosophical Library, 1948.

Diringer, D. *Writing*. New York: Praeger, 1962.

Doblhofer, E. *Voices in Stone: The Decipherment of Ancient Scripts and Writings*. New York: The Viking Press, 1961.

Gelb, I. J. *A Study of Writing*. Chicago: University of Chicago Press, 1952.

Pyles, Thomas. *Words and Ways of American English*. New York: Random House, 1952.

Robertson, S., and F. G. Cassidy. *The Development of Modern English*. Englewood Cliffs, N.J.: Prentice-Hall, 1954, pp. 353–374 (on spelling and spelling reform).

Schane, Sanford A. "The Phoneme Revisited," *Language*, 47 (1971): 503–521.

Wang, William S-Y. "The Chinese Language," *Scientific American*, vol. 228, no. 2 (Feb. 1973): 50–63.

Index